You and Your Aging Parent

You and Your Aging Parent

The Modern Family's Guide to Emotional, Physical, and Financial Problems

BARBARA SILVERSTONE
AND HELEN KANDEL HYMAN

PANTHEON BOOKS

New York

Grateful acknowledgment is made to the following for permission to reprint previously published material:

The National Council on the Aging, Inc.: Excerpts from *The Myth and Reality of Aging in America,* a study for The National Council on the Aging, Inc. Copyright © 1975 by Louis Harris and Associates, Inc.

New Directions Publishing Corp. and J. M. Dent & Sons Ltd.: Three lines from the poem "Do not go gentle into that good night," from *The Poems of Dylan Thomas.* Copyright © 1952 by Dylan Thomas. Reprinted by permission of the publishers and the Trustees for the Copyrights of the late Dylan Thomas.

The New York Times: Excerpts from the following articles, Copyright © 1975 by The New York Times Company: Article by Will Durant, November 6, 1975, "Interview with Laurence Olivier," December 10, 1975, and "Ma'am, the Door Is Being Jimmied," by William J. Dean, November 8, 1975. Reprinted by permission.

Library of Congress Cataloging in Publication Data

Silverstone, Barbara, 1931-
    You and Your Aging Parent.

    Bibliography: pp. 322–36
    Includes index.
    1. Aged—United States—Family relationship.
2. Parent and child. 3. Conflict of generations.
4. Family—United States. 5. Old age assistance—
United States. 6. Aged—Psychology. I. Hyman, Helen.
II. Title.
HV1461.S54 1976   362.6'0973   76-9608
ISBN 0-394-73406-8

Designed by Irva Mandelbaum

Manufactured in the United States of America

987654

For Our Own Children
Karen and Julie—Lisa, David, and Alex

ACKNOWLEDGMENTS

Our appreciation goes in three directions: to the families of the elderly, whose expressed needs impelled us to undertake this book; to our professional colleagues, whose invaluable advice enriched the substance of the text; and to our own families, whose enthusiasm and endurance were so essential to us.

We are indebted to the Friends and Relatives of the Jewish Home and Hospital for Aged, whose members, particularly Mrs. Eleanor Ferber, planted the first idea for the book. This organization itself grew out of the needs of the families of residents to share their common concerns, to exchange their own doubts and conflicts, and to make themselves felt as a meaningful, concerned consumer group.

Special thanks go to Charlotte Kirschner, M.S.S.W., whose extensive and meticulous research into programs and services, described in both the text and the appendixes, was invaluable. Her special sensitivity to the problems and feelings of individual older people and their families helped in many ways to shape our presentation.

We thank Manuel Rodstein, M.D., Chief of Medical Services of the Jewish Home and Hospital for the Aged, whose careful review of the medical material of the book enabled us to profit from his many years of experience and leadership in geriatric medicine.

Our gratitude also goes to Dr. Ruth Weber, Professor of Social Work of the University of Georgia, who reviewed the manuscript, adding to it valuable suggestions gained from her years of work with older people and their families in various areas of the United States.

For providing detailed information and guidance in the preparation of the sections on government-programs, we are grateful to Theodore De Santis and Eleonor Morris, Department of Health, Education, and Welfare, Region II.

To our husbands, psychoanalyst Stanley Silverstone and sociologist Herbert Hyman, we say thank you for all your invaluable professional advice as well as for your personal support.

Thanks also to Judith Draper, whose efficient typing of our manuscript made life much easier for both of us.

CONTENTS

Acknowledgments   vii

1. Introduction   3

Part I: TAKING STOCK

2. Facing Up to Feelings   15

Feelings Which Spark an Emotional Tug of War   16
  Love, Compassion, Respect, Tenderness, Sadness   18
  Indifference   19
  Love May Not Be Enough   20
  Fear and Anxiety   20
  Anger, Hostility, Contempt   21
  Sexuality, Jealousy, and Competitiveness   22
  Shame   23
  Special Reactions to Aging   24
    Can You Accept Your Parents' Old Age?   24
    Do You Like Your Aging Parents?   25
    Can You Accept a Different Role?   26
    Can You Accept Your Own Aging?   26
    Are You Overburdened?   28
  And Finally—Guilt!   29
    Personal Guilt   30
    The Guilt We All Share   31

What Untouchable, Unresolved Feelings Can Produce   33
  Withdrawal   34
  Oversolicitousness and Domination   34

Faultfinding   35
Denial   35
Outmoded Role-Playing   36
Protracted Adolescent Rebellion and Blind Overinvolvement   37
Scapegoating   38

3. The Family Merry-Go-Round   40

Family Harmony or Family Discord   41

Is Your Sibling Rivalry Still Showing?   43
No One Can Ever Forget "The Favorite"   44

Who's in Charge?   45

"The Caretaker" May Be Chosen   46
"The Caretaker" May Volunteer   48
The Pseudo "Caretaker"   48
"The Caretaker" as Martyr   49
Friend or Enemy?   50
"The Caretaker" Under Fire   51

A Permanent Split or a Closer Bond?   52

Money—The Root of Many Evils   53

What About Your Own Family?   55

Husbands, Wives, and In-laws   55
How Do Your Children Feel?   56

The Games Old People Play   58

Manipulation   58
Denial of Infirmities   59
Exaggeration of Infirmities   59
Self-belittlement   60
Money   60

Family Paralysis   60

Can Old Patterns Be Reversed?   61

4. What Have They Got to Lose?   64

Misconceptions and Misinformation   65
It's a High-Risk Period   67

The Loss of Physical Health   69

The Irreversible Changes   69
There Are Compensations and Sometimes Improvements   72
Some Physical Problems Are Treatable   73
Why Some Function Better than Others   74

Loss of Social Contacts   75

Changes in Human Relationships   76
Changes in Environment   77

Loss of Familiar Roles   78

Loss of Financial Security   79

Loss of Independence and Power   82

Loss of Mental Stability   85

    What Are the Psychological Problems?   86
    "Normal" Reactions to Loss   87
    Extreme Reactions   92
        Depression   93
        Hypochondriasis   93
        Psychotic Reactions   94
        Chronic Organic Brain Disorders   94
    Indirect Psychological Problems   95

5. Marriage, Widowhood, Remarriage, and Sex   97

Marital Adjustment in the Retirement Years   98

In Sickness and in Health—For Richer, for Poorer   101

The Final Years   102

Discord in the "Golden Years"   103

Widowhood   106

    Disruption Is to Be Expected   107
    When Mourning Goes Out of Bounds   109
    The Death of a Parent: The Effect on You   109
    What You Can Do to Help   111

Remarriage   113

Sex After Sixty-five—Myth Versus Reality   115

    The Elderly May Be Misinformed, Too   118
    What Will the Children Say?   119

6. Facing the Final Crisis   121

The Conspiracy of Silence   123

Some People Need to Talk About Death   125

Breaking the Silence   127

Telling the Truth to the Dying   128

Should Life Be Prolonged?   130

A Time for Emotional Daring   133

Part 2: TAKING ACTION

7. Helping—When They Can Manage Independently   137

"I'm Okay"—Those Who Can Manage and Know It   139

The Pseudo-Helpless—Those Who Can Manage but Think
    They Can't   141

    When to Say No   143
    "I Can't Say No"   144

Prepare for the Day When They Can't Manage   145

    Health Care Planning   147
    Social Preparedness   151
    Should They Live with You?   152
    Financial Preparedness   154
        Social Security   155
        Pensions   157
        Supplemental Security Income (SSI)   158
        Indirect Noncash Supplements   160
        Who Pays the Medical Bills?   161
            Medicare   162
            Private Health Insurance   163
            Medicaid   165
        What Can You Do?   166
    What About Your Own Preparedness?   167
    Preparedness Versus Interference   168

8. Helping When They Cannot Manage—Community
    Solutions   169

    Putting All the Pieces Together: The Assessment   171

    The Physical Pieces   172
    The Psychological Pieces   173
    The Functioning Pieces   174
    The Social Pieces   174
    The Financial Pieces   175
    Who Puts All the Pieces Together?   176

    What Kind of Care?   178

    "Off-and-On" Care   178
    Protective or Supportive Care   179
    Long-Term Intensive Care   180
    Helping the Mentally Impaired   182
    What Does Mother Have to Say?   184
    You May Not Be Quite as Important as You Think   185

    What Does the Community Have to Offer?   186

    Information and Referral Services   187
    At-Home Services   187
        Visiting Nurse Services   188
        Homemaker—Home Health Aide Services   188
        Meals on Wheels   190
        Telephone Reassurance Programs   190
        Escort and Transportation Services   191

Chore Services   191
Friendly Visiting   192
Sitting Services   192
Out-of-Home Services   192
Congregate Meals   193
Senior Centers   193
Transportation Services   193
Day Hospitals and Day Care Centers   194
Legal Services   195
Special Housing with Special Care   195
When You Are Far Away   196

Legal Steps for Managing Your Parents' Financial
Affairs   197

The Painful Process of Incompetency Proceedings   198
Protective Services   199

What If They Won't Be Helped—by You or Anyone Else?
199

A Realistic Afterthought   200

9. Helping When They Cannot Manage—the Nursing
Home Solution   202

The Breath of Scandal   204

A Planned Option or a Forced Decision?   205

Step One: Understanding How Money Determines Your
Options   207

Relative Responsibility   208

Step Two: Understanding the Kinds of Care Available   209

The Skilled Nursing Facility   209
Intermediate Care Facilities   209
Homes with Both Levels of Care   210

Step Three: Evaluating Quality   210

A Journey into the Unknown   210
You Can Learn a Lot from Your Reception   212
What Do Other People Have to Say?   212
What to Look For When You Visit   213
Medical, Nursing, and Therapeutic Services   214
Medical Service   214
Nursing Service   214
Specialized Therapeutic Services   214
What About the Mentally Impaired Resident?   215
Is It All Shadow or Substance?   215
Hotel Services: How Good Is the Housekeeping?   216
The Climate: A Home-like or Sterile and Repressive
Atmosphere?   216

Personal Preferences May Dictate Choices   218
When There Is No Choice   218

Making the Final Decision   219

A Time of Crisis for Everyone   219
The Family Conference   220
Honesty   220

Becoming a Nursing Home Resident   222

When Moving Day Comes—Admission and Early
  Adjustment   222
Doing Their Own Thing   223
Once They Are in Residence   224
  There May Be Reversals   224
  Everyone Makes Mistakes   225
  What If They Don't Adjust?   226
  The Role of the Staff   226
  Family and Staff Interaction   227
  The Role of the Family   228
    Meeting the Need for Affection   228
    The Visit Home   229
    Keeping the Elderly in Touch with Their
      Communities   230
    Meeting Idiosyncratic Needs   231
  The Demanding Resident   232
  The Demanding Family   232
  Help for the Troubled Family and Resident   233
  When Things Go Wrong   233
    The Forced Transfer   234
    Don't Be Afraid   235
  A Reasonable Goal   235

10. Taking a Stand   237

Attention, Legislators, Insurance Underwriters,
  Employers!   240

Attention, Planners, Builders, Architects!   241

Attention, Physicians, Psychiatrists, Nurses, Social
  Workers!   242

Join the Action   243

New Images for Old   245

Appendixes

A. Where to Find Help   248
  1. State Offices on the Aging   248
  2. Information and Referral Services   254

B. Selected Services and Programs for the Elderly and Their Families   265

    1. Homemaker–Home Health Aide Services   265
    2. Family Service Agencies   272
    3. Work and Volunteer Opportunities for the Elderly   304

C. Checklists for Evaluating Services   306

    1. Nursing Homes   306
    2. Homemaker–Home Health Aide Services   310

D. Directories to Consult   311

E. Common Diseases and Symptoms of the Elderly   315

    1. Diseases   315
    2. Symptoms and Complaints   319

F. Suggested Readings   322

Index   327

About the Authors   336

You and Your Aging Parent

1.

Introduction

❖ WE ALWAYS HAD THANKSGIVING DINNER at my parents' house: my brother and his family, my husband and my children. Year after year it was always the same—the polished silver, the good china, the wonderful cooking smells. But last year something was different. My father's hands shook so he could barely carve the turkey. My mother looked frail, almost shrunken, at the other end of the table. Suddenly, for the first time, it hit me! My parents were getting old.

Mary Lewis was forty-five years old. Her father was eighty-two and her mother eighty. She knew their ages well. Hadn't she always celebrated their birthdays with them? But she'd never admitted that they were getting older with each celebration. It came to her as a shock.

❖ IT WAS MY MOTHER'S funeral, but I couldn't think about her at all. I kept watching my crippled father and thinking about him. What would happen to him now? Who would take care of him? Where would he live? How would we all manage?

Barry Richards was thirty-eight and his wife was pregnant again. Their apartment was barely big enough for another child and they couldn't afford to move yet. There was no way Barry's father could live with them. But he certainly couldn't live alone. Where would he go now?

❖ I CALLED MY MOTHER last night and I let the phone ring and ring, but she didn't answer. The same old panic started. Was she sick? Had she fallen and broken something? Was she unconscious? Maybe a heart attack? A stroke? I told myself she was probably out at the store—but I couldn't be sure. I'm never sure. I live five hundred miles away and I go through this every time she doesn't answer her phone. Why does she make it so hard for me?

Frances Black's mother insisted on staying on in her old house long after her husband's death even though the neighborhood had changed and was no longer pleasant or even safe. She stubbornly refused repeated invitations to move in with Frances and her family or to move closer to them. So Frances worried constantly, phoned several times a week, and prayed each time that the phone would be answered. She continually felt guilty and inadequate. But that was nothing new—she'd felt that way most of her life. Somehow, Jerry, her younger brother, had always seemed to do everything right. He still did—even though Frances was the one who phoned regularly.

Mary, Barry, and Frances are three separate people, living in different parts of the country, with different lifestyles, different careers, different incomes. They have never met, nor are they likely to. But if they were to meet they would find they have one thing in common. They all belong to a special generation caught in the middle—men and women pulled in three directions, trying to rear their children, live their own lives, and help their aging parents, all at the same time.

This painful three-way pull is not experienced by everyone in the middle generation. Some people have no reason to feel conflicting loyalties if their parents remain active and self-sufficient into the seventies, eighties, and nineties. Many of the elderly take old age surprisingly easily. Far from needing help from younger relatives, vigorous old men and women are often the ones who do the helping, encouraging their children and grandchildren to turn to *them* in times of trouble.

Despite the popular image, to be old is not necessarily synonymous with being weak or helpless or finished. Old age can be a time of enjoyment, contentment, productivity—even creativity. Because of prevailing prejudices, younger generations are rarely aware that all kinds of people—writers, artists, politicians, musicians, philosophers, scientists, businessmen, craftsmen—often keep right on working for decades after their sixty-fifth birthdays, sometimes making major contributions in their seventies and eighties. The young tend to assume that life must be dreadful for the old, but the old themselves, who are experiencing old age firsthand, take a far less negative view of their own lives.

A survey commissioned by the National Council on Aging and conducted by survey expert Louis Harris in 1974 dramatizes the gap between the feelings of the old and the younger generations. The sample of respondents sixty-five and older were asked about their own lives; the sample of respondents eighteen to sixty-four were asked their beliefs about the lives of old people. A few of the findings selected from the Harris tables are enough to illustrate how false are the prevailing assumptions:

	Percent of aged reporting they themselves have a "very serious" problem of:	Percent of those under 65 believing most people over 65 have a "very serious" problem of:
Not enough friends	5	28
Not having enough to do	6	37
Not feeling needed	7	54
Loneliness	12	60
Not having enough money to live on	15	62
Poor health	21	51

These figures can be deceptive. While life may seem easier for most older people than is generally assumed, there are substantial numbers for whom life is tragically difficult. The 12 percent who feel lonely represent only a small minority of the total, but in a country with more than 20 million people over sixty-five, that small percentage translates into almost 3 million lonely old people. The 21 percent who rate their problem of poor health as "very serious" translates into over 4 million ailing old people—one out of every five! Nor does it help much to read the statistics and find out that other people's parents are getting along pretty well if our own parents are getting along pretty badly. If we care about them at all, we usually want to do something to help them to get along better, and most of us don't know what to do.

Americans as individuals tend to think ahead. We spend time and energy planning for future events: vacations, new cars, our children's education, life insurance, long-term career goals. Some of us give more than passing thought to our own old age. But few of us have even vague plans about what we may need to do for our parents if the day ever comes when they cannot manage alone.

The statistics show us that the odds are in our favor—the day may never come. Many of us escape the problem completely. In the back of our minds we may think, "Why plan for something that may never happen—if we're lucky?" Our parents may not live to be old; they may never need help; or, if they do, they may turn to someone else in the family—not us. A brother or a sister may offer to take in both of them, or whichever one is left alone, widowed or divorced. We can sidestep away. But there is always the possibility that the very problem we have refused to think about will one day descend on us, disturbing our lives, our emotions, and our finances.

Even the most careful planner is taking a gamble. Plans we make may be systematically foiled by the very unpredictable nature of the aging process. No one can sit back complacently in middle age and proclaim, "It's all set, I'm ready to take over when my parents need me," because except in certain special situations it is impossible to predict in advance what these parents will need and when.

❖ CLARE FOWLER THOUGHT she was facing the future honestly and intelligently. She had begun thinking about it after her fiftieth birthday when the younger of her two children got married. She knew that women usually outlive men in the United States—she had read the statistics, and in addition she was twelve years younger than her husband, who was already in his sixties. It seemed likely that she would be widowed at some point in the future; naturally, she hoped it would be the far future. Mr. Fowler was willing to discuss the likelihood with her and they went over the financial picture. They both agreed that Mrs. Fowler should try to live an independent life and under no circumstances should live with either of their children. They even discussed some of their ideas with the children themselves, who—like most children—were not too eager to listen.

But things didn't go according to plan. Mrs. Fowler died suddenly of a stroke at the age of fifty-six and her sixty-eight-year-old husband who had never for a moment contemplated his own widowhood was left so emotionally helpless that he seemed incapable of living alone. To pull himself together he made his home "temporarily" with his son and daughter-in-law and their children. There he stayed for the next seventeen years until he died at the age of eighty-five.

Just as the future is unpredictable, the aging process itself does not follow any uniform calendar. Parents of young children know what comes next in early childhood development. Within a reasonable period we know when our children will walk and talk, when their first teeth will come, when they'll be likely to start kindergarten or high school. We can anticipate some of the emotional stages: the negativism at two and a half, the rebellion in adolescence.

The stages of growing old have no such predictable pattern. We can't look at our sixty-year-old parents and announce, "Okay, five years to go until you're over the hill." One man's father may be beginning to decline at sixty-five, it's true. But the next man's father may still be capably running his own life at eighty-five—and still trying to dominate his son's, too, for that matter. We need only to look at the Churchills, the Segovias, the Chaplins, the Casalses, the Picassos—with the Sam Ervins not so far behind. One young woman of twenty-five whom we met recently is currently concerned, not about her mother or her grandmother, but about her great-grandmother. This nonagenarian adamantly lives alone in a somewhat isolated house, stoking her own coal furnace, warming water on her stove, and letting her well-heeled descendants agonize over her welfare—but from a distance.

In addition to the irregular and unpredictable calendar of physical aging, emotional and personality problems intervene and confuse the picture. Failing eyesight or severe arthritis may be overcome by sheer will power and personal vitality by one elderly individual who continues to live and function independently and even productively. By contrast a contemporary, similarly afflicted, may retire quickly into invalidism and total dependency.

The later stages of life, until recently, have never received much attention either from professional experts or from the public at large. Society's interest has been focused mainly on the earlier ones: infancy, youth, middle age. But old age is finally gaining some of the limelight and attracting long-overdue public attention. New scientific terms, coined in this century from the Greek *geron,* "old man," are now heard frequently: *geriatrics, gerontology, geropsychiatry.* Additional evidence of increasing interest in the whole subject of aging is the publication in 1975 of a book by an eminent veterinarian, Dr. George Whitney, *The Health and Happiness of Your Old Dog.*

The mounting concern about life in the later decades is well deserved. The elderly segment of the population has been steadily growing during the past century, increasing faster than any other age group. The average lifespan, which was eighteen in the days of ancient Greece, thirty-three in the year 1600, forty-two in the Civil War period, and forty-seven in 1900, is now about seventy. The more than 20 million men and women over sixty-five today represent 10 percent of the population of the United States. The total population has increased threefold since 1900, but the ranks of the elderly have increased fivefold. For the weight of its numbers alone, that is a group to be reckoned with. The reckoning has been going on in the recent period, although not nearly fast enough.

Over the past fifteen years major efforts have been made to improve the welfare of elderly Americans, starting with the first White House Conference on Aging in 1961 and the establishment in the same year of the U.S. Senate Committee on Aging. In 1965 came the passage of the Older Americans Act and the creation under the Department of Health, Education, and Welfare of a central federal office, the Administration on Aging. Legislators are constantly considering new bills to benefit the elderly, although not passing many, and this consideration is not without some amount of self-interest. The over-sixty-five segment of the population, far from being disengaged socially or politically, is a powerful and articulate interest group, likely to register its opinions at election time. Studies of voting patterns consistently show that the turnout at the polls is higher for older voters than for very young ones.

The rising interest in the elderly is not limited to legislative circles alone. Programs for the elderly are featured in the popular press. Nursing home scandals make banner headlines. TV and documentary films are beginning to show the many faces of old age and making the general public stop and think about the needs of the elderly. Professionals in public and private agencies are trying to meet these needs and provide more supportive services. Social planners are contemplating more comprehensive health services and suggesting second careers to make the retirement years more meaningful, less empty. Even the building and architectural fields are dreaming up new communities geared to the lives of older people. Society is being forced to rethink former prejudices and biases which led to the neglect of the needs of the aged. Many of their needs are still unmet today, but the elderly at last are beginning to demand their rights, speaking out for themselves at the polls and through their own political pressure groups such as the Gray Panthers, the Congress of Senior Citizens, and the American Association of Retired Persons.

During these recent years, as the elderly are coming forward to center stage, the nuclear family—mother, father, and children—has also been given the spotlight, although not such a sympathetic one. The nuclear family has been accused of living in selfish isolation—as a tight exclusive unit involved only in its own interests, its own problems, its own daily life. Admittedly, some families do fit this description, and deserve the accusation, "Young people these days just don't care about their old parents." Such families are able to ignore the downhill slide of aging relatives, comfortably turning their backs on parents growing old on the other side of the country, five hundred miles away, or even across the park. An annual or even a monthly check, an occasional phone call, and birthday cards seem involvement enough.

But families cannot so easily be written off as uninvolved and uncaring. They generally prefer separate homes. So do their elderly parents. But that does not mean that they prefer separate, independent lives. Far from it.

Most of these families continue some involvement—often a close one—with the parent generation. Of the more than 20 million men and women over sixty-five, more than three quarters have at least one living child. A series of surveys made over the last ten years with national samples of the elderly all report similar findings: older people and their children (at least one child) usually maintain ongoing contact with each other. Furthermore—despite the assumption that children these days grow up, move far away from their parents, and then do not visit much—the studies report that 85 percent of the elderly with living children have at least one child who lives less than one hour away and that 66 percent of the elderly respondents saw one of their children the very day they were interviewed or the day before; only 2 percent had not seen any of their children within the past year.

Many families are willing and eager to help when aging parents, even grandparents, are in trouble. These grownup, often middle-aged children may be motivated by a sense of responsibility, of duty, and of guilt; they are motivated just as often by genuine concern and love. But when elderly parents become more dependent and the problems of daily living multiply, their children soon discover that "love is not enough."

But if love is not enough—what else is there? Millions of sons and daughters are asking the question. These millions will increase steadily in the future as extended longevity creates a further abundance of three- and even four-generation families. The millions concerned about their aging parents can be found anywhere and everywhere. Their problems are not limited to any one geographical location, any one class. Some are only in their early thirties, others much older. Some may even be in their sixties already, concerned about their own futures while still trying to help their parents, their children, and perhaps their grandchildren as well. They have low, middle, and high incomes, because although money helps, it rarely provides the complete solution. Sons may be laborers, farmers, hardhats, blue-collar or white-collar workers; daughters may be housewives, office workers, or career women. They are found in every ethnic group (with variations); they are urban, suburban, exurban, and rural. They are highly educated or barely educated.

The special middle generation has a membership in the millions, yet it has no organization or recognition. No one speaks for them, no one worries about them, and too often they feel they are groping for solutions alone.

This book is addressed to that large and still unrecognized group.

It does not pretend to cover every situation or touch on every problem, but the authors hope that the chapters which follow will help the readers to think through their own personal situations more realistically and to begin to figure out more effective solutions to their own individual problems.

While many of the solutions can be found in the outside community if families know where and how to look, other solutions may be found much closer to home. Sons and daughters naturally must understand their parents' needs before they can help them, but they must also understand themselves and their own feelings. Their own emotions are likely to confuse the picture, and perhaps even prevent them from helping effectively.

This book is therefore divided into two sections. The first section, "Taking Stock," presents an overall review of the range of problems which may complicate life for the elderly themselves and for their children: the emotions, conscious and unconscious, which color relationships between generations, the feelings between brothers and sisters which help or hinder when families try to work together.

The objective problems of the elderly themselves will be discussed: the inevitable losses of old age—physiological, psychological, and social—and the way some older people learn to compensate for these losses. Marriage in the later years will be examined as well as inevitable widowhood or widowerhood, the possibilities of remarriage, and the continuing sexual life of the elderly—an issue raised frequently by professionals but often viewed with uneasiness or alarm by the younger generations. The equally difficult and often unmentionable subject of death and the period before death is included, a logical final step in the stocktaking process.

The second section, "Taking Action," analyzes available solutions to the problems which have been raised in the earlier chapters. It considers first the ongoing relationships between children and elderly parents who are still managing independently. How much communication is necessary? How much is expected? How much visiting? Phoning? Is it possible to have too much communication? How can older people be encouraged to plan for future emergencies: disabling illness or accident? Supportive government programs and community services will be described—how to find them and how to pay for them, with particular stress on the ones which make it possible for older people to remain in their home communities. The question of whether to institutionalize or not will be raised. If this step is necessary, where to institutionalize, how to evaluate facilities, what will they cost, and who is going to pay for them? Ways to help a parent become a nursing home resident and ways to speed up the adjustment process once the move is made will be reviewed.

A quick glimpse will be offered of the future and what it holds for those who will grow old in the years ahead. Will the now-unmet needs of today's elderly population be met more successfully then? What can we hope for? What can we do?

The appendix contains a bibliography including directories of essential services, and an overall guide to specialized agencies and services, public and private, across the nation.

The pages that follow will not tell the whole story, because additional chapters are being written every year. A new character enters as each man and woman turns sixty-five. You may not recognize your own parents, but you are likely to recognize someone you know. A variety of answers will be suggested and many familiar questions raised. Among the most crucial are those asked recently by a young woman in her middle thirties:

❖ WHAT'S HAPPENED TO ME? I'm like the rope in a tug of war between my parents and my children. I always seem to be needed in two places at the same time and I'm never in the right one. When I'm with my parents I'm always asking myself, "What am I doing here? I ought to be with my children." And when I'm with my children I'm always asking myself, "What am I doing here? How can I leave my old parents alone so much?" It's awful to feel so guilty all the time. But do you know there's something even worse? It's that little voice inside my head that's always crying out, "What about me? When is there going to be time for me? Doesn't anybody care?"

Part 1
TAKING STOCK

2.

Facing Up to Feelings

❖ MARY GRAHAM WAS a devoted daughter—everyone said so. All her friends were amazed at the way she treated her old mother. . . . Such loving concern—such patient understanding! They knew that Mary phoned her mother every day, visited her several times a week, included her in every family activity, and never took a vacation without her. Her friends also knew that Mary's husband and children had learned to accept second place in her life years ago.

Mary herself knew that she had always done her best for her mother. Why did she always worry that her best was never good enough?

In times gone by, children who seemed loving and attentive to their parents were labeled "good" children, just as parents who seemed loving and attentive to their children were labeled "good" parents. The quality of the love and attention was not usually examined, nor the cost to the giver or the effect on the receiver. Things are no longer so black and white.

The behavior of family members toward one another is viewed today as a complex process governed by a wide range of feelings. In this context even traditionally "good" behavior is open to re-evaluation and tends to become suspect when carried to an extreme. "He gave up his life for his old mother" may have been considered the highest form of noble sacrifice several generations ago, but today such a sacrifice might be questioned. *Why* did he do that? Didn't he have a right to a life of his own, too? A sixty-year-old daughter still cowering in infantile submission before the rage of an autocratic ninety-year-old father may have symbolized the supreme example of "dutiful affection" to the Victorians, but current thinking would make us wonder about the deeper reasons behind such behavior.

It is important that sons and daughters take stock of their feelings about their aging parents, if they want to find some comfort for themselves and be better able to help effectively.

Enough concrete obstacles can stand in the way when sons and daughters want to help. They may live too far away. They may have financial, health, career, or marital problems which legitimately prevent them from taking a supportive role in their parents' lives. But sometimes there are no such concrete obstacles—life may be going along quite smoothly—yet a daughter may be incapable of reaching out to her mother, and a son may wonder why his friends seem able to help their parents more than he can help his. Such children often excuse themselves by playing the "it's-easy-for-them" game:

- They have so much money—*it's easy for them* to help John's parents.
- With that big house—*it's easy for them* to find room for Mary's father.
- Jane doesn't have a job—*it's easy for her* to visit her mother every day.
- All their children are grown—*it's easy for them* to spend so much time at the nursing home.

All these statements have the same unspoken implication, "I would be just as good a son [or a daughter] if only my life were different." But the unspoken implication would probably have greater validity if it substituted the words, "If only my feelings were different." Unresolved or unrecognized feelings can affect a child's behavior toward a parent, blocking any attempts to be helpful. Those feelings can also serve as catalysts for unwise, inappropriate decisions that can hinder rather than help to solve the older person's problems. Last, but equally important, unresolved feelings about parents can be very painful—sometimes really oppressive—for children. The well-being of both generations may improve once these feelings are understood, accepted, and acted on appropriately.

Feelings Which Spark an Emotional Tug of War

It is self-evident that human beings are capable of experiencing and acting upon a wide range of feelings. Different people, different situations obviously arouse all sorts of different emotions. It is less self-evident that one single human being can experience an equally wide range of feelings toward another single human being. That is exactly what happens, however, when a substantial bond exists between any two people. A whole variety of different (and often conflicting) feelings can be aroused at different times. When people are important to us we love them when they please us, hate them when they disappoint us, resent them when they hurt us. Love is not a twenty-four-hour occupation, and there can always be time out even within the warmest relationships for moments of irritation, envy, frustration.

It might be easier if our feelings toward someone we love were more clear-cut and consistent, particularly when that person is old and perhaps helpless, but consistency and clarity are rare qualities denied to most of us.

All feelings do not have the same intensity. The minor annoyance we feel toward someone we love can easily be controlled, just as the occasional, though surprising, moments of affection we feel toward someone we dislike can also be tolerated. When contradictory feelings coexist with equally high intensity toward the same person, however, a painful conflict results. "I wish I didn't love my mother so much, then I could really hate her," a daughter cries in anguished frustration. She is deserving of sympathy for her emotional tug of war. Her struggle might be less painful if she realized that both the anger and the love she feels for her mother may be closely related and can sometimes last a lifetime. She might also be relieved to know that she is not alone and that many people are offended and angered most by someone they love best, although they may try to remain unaware of their less acceptable feelings toward their parents. Psychoanalysis has taught us that when intense feelings are pushed down and hidden they only rise again in disguised form. Once admitted and accepted, they can more easily be placed in perspective and the person who bears them freed to behave more effectively.

Many of the feelings we have about our parents in their later years are the same old ones we always had about them. They were formed in childhood and a pattern was established to be carried through life. The intensity and immediacy of these feelings may have changed somewhat as we grew into adulthood. By moving out of our parents' house we also moved away from daily contact and interaction. Emotional and physical distance provided a wide buffer zone. While our parents remain active and self-reliant, they live their own lives with greater or lesser involvement with ours. The relationship with them may be pleasant and gratifying, or frustrating and abrasive.

Old feelings from the past can rise up to plague us again when our parents get older, feebler, sicker, or poorer, and are in need of our help as we were once long ago in need of theirs. We can no longer so easily maintain an emotional distance even when physically separated, and too easily fall back into old patterns, both the pleasant and the unpleasant ones: old affections may rise again, old wounds be reopened, old loyalties remembered, old debts revived, and old weaknesses exposed once more.

In addition to bringing old feelings into play again, our parents' aging—especially if they become dependent on us—may intensify feelings and attitudes which we have developed later because of experiences in our own separate adult lives. Some of these newer feelings, like the older ones, may seem rather unacceptable and we may prefer to ignore them. But ignoring them won't make them go away.

Because such a variety of feelings, some less comfortable than others, enter into the relationships between grown children and their aging parents, it may be helpful to examine a number of the most common ones—love, compassion, respect, tenderness, sadness, and then, anger, hostility, shame, contempt, fear, jealousy, and sexual feelings. Finally, we shall turn to the most uncomfortable feeling of all—guilt—which is worn like the scarlet letter by so many children of the elderly today.

Love, Compassion, Respect, Tenderness, Sadness

When some or all of these feelings are present in a relationship and are not too complicated by the simultaneous existence of powerful conflicting feelings, they serve as a vital source of support and strength for both generations. They provide comfort for the older one and enable the younger to reach out willingly to help. When these feelings have always existed between parents and children, they usually reflect a strong bond developed by a long-standing pattern of mutual caring.

While growing up, children look to those closest to them for models of behavior and tend to copy what they see. If both parents (or even one of them) show a young child love, care, unselfishness, and consideration, it is likely that the child as an adult will find it natural to show some of these feelings to his parents when they are old. Children who have never witnessed giving, reaching out, sharing, or tenderness in action often have no models to copy and never learn how to show or feel these emotions. Your parents' behavior to others, as well as to you, may have provided additional models. You may have seen them behave with respect and consideration to their own parents—your grandparents. Family traditions and patterns of behavior are often passed on from generation to generation.

But behavior is a complex process and many other factors besides family tradition and models set in early childhood can influence the positive feelings we have toward our parents when they are old. Their treatment of us as children may have been far from tender and warm. We may have seen them as distant, cold, and punitive and thought them unfair and unreasonable while we were growing up. But later in life when time, distance, and our own experience put a different perspective on past behavior, we may come to understand, as adults, what we could not understand as children: why our parents acted the way they did. Mistakes they made in the past may continue to rankle in the present, but the intensity of the resentment may be counteracted by a new respect we develop for the way they cope with life as old people. "He was a domineering tyrant when we were young," a son says of his father, "but how he's mellowed! He's great to be with now even though he's so sick—no complaints, no self-pity. I really admire the guy and I'll bet none of us do as well when we're his age." A daughter, raised in the Depression, remembers her deprived childhood: "We had to fight for everything we had. Mom and Dad seemed like misers—pennypinchers. But now that I've got my own family, I can understand what they went through to raise five kids then. I'd do anything to make things easier for them now." Strong feelings of love, compassion, tenderness, respect are likely to be accompanied by sadness, as the younger generations realize that elderly parents are no longer the people they used to be and that death is coming closer every day.

Indifference

Love, affection, respect, compassion, and concern can all exist simultaneously in any relationship between grown children and their aging parents. These emotions may all have equal intensity, or some may be stronger than others. It also may happen that one of these emotions may exist alone, without any of the others. A son may respect his parents and be concerned for them—because of these feelings he may be extremely helpful to them—but he may never have loved them, liked them, or felt much real affection for either one; instead, he may have felt apathy and indifference. That lack of feeling may be quite painful, and he may experience considerable remorse because of it, but even so he may still feel responsible for their welfare and concerned about their problems. It is well to remember that while love and affection are often effective catalysts to a helping relationship, they are not essential.

Love May Not Be Enough

Although love and affection are important catalysts to a helping relationship their usefulness may be diminished when they are not in partnership with concern and respect. A daughter's love and affection for her parents may spring from her own exaggerated dependency on them which she did not outgrow when she left childhood. It may never occur to her to be concerned about their welfare, only that they should be concerned about hers. A son's love for his parents may be counteracted by his lack of respect for their behavior, their narrow-mindedness, or their bigotry. He may find it easier to love them from a distance.

Fear and Anxiety

"She lies there like a fragile little doll—she couldn't lift a finger to hurt me. How can I still be scared to death she's going to be mad at me for something?" asked a middle-aged woman on one of her regular visits to her mother in a nursing home. She laughed as she spoke because she realized how ludicrous it seems to fear an eighty-pound, bedridden invalid. But she was serious, too. Some children live in fear of either or both of their parents even when these parents are weak, helpless, frail, or terminally ill. Children may be afraid of so many things—of disapproval, of losing love, of death, of the irrevocable loss of the older person and also of losing out on an inheritance. Chronic, irrational fear or anxiety in relation to a parent is likely to have its roots in dimly remembered early childhood experiences. Small children are totally dependent on their parents; without them they feel stranded, abandoned, alone. The parents, being bigger and stronger, are also the ones who set the rules and enforce the dictates of society. Thus, a child can fear his parents on three counts: abandonment, loss of love, and punishment.

As children mature and learn to take care of themselves, that rather one-sided relationship disappears and feelings of affection and trust emerge as between close friends. A filial bond develops which surpasses the parent-child bond. Children who never resolve or shake off that close, dependent relationship may continue to suffer fearful or anxious feelings in relation to their parents in one form or another throughout life.

Older parents themselves are often responsible for reinforcing fearful feelings in their grown children, unconsciously or even deliberately continuing to nourish old childhood dependencies. Weak old men and fragile old women often somehow find the strength to retain command, directing their children's lives from wheelchairs and sickbeds. A son may champ at the bit, longing for freedom from a domineering mother while simultaneously suffering constant anxiety that he will do something to displease her, that she will leave him or disown him. A child may also grow up in fear that he will not live up to his parents' expectations for him in terms of career, worldly success, or material possessions. He may also be afraid he will never be the kind of person they want him to be—someone they approve of. His struggle to win approval may continue through his entire life, even when he is in his sixties and his parents are in their eighties. He may fear he will only be loved if he measures up to their standards and that time is unlikely to come. "I've got a good business going," a middle-aged man complains. "I put three kids through college, I'm president of our Rotary Club, but my father thinks I'm a failure—his only son was supposed to be a lawyer. And you know what? Whenever I'm with him I feel like a failure, too."

Anger, Hostility, Contempt

Large-scale upheavals and tragedies obviously leave emotional impacts on children often affecting their future lives. Death or chronic illness of a mother or father, divorce, abandonment—such events can determine the kind of feelings children have for parents, feelings which can last a lifetime. "I hated my mother when she remarried," or "Our family fell apart after my father's business failed," or "My father walked out one day and left us alone." Such statements pinpoint causes and serve to explain the rise of hostile feelings. But even without such dramatic events, the development of angry feelings in childhood is unavoidably stimulated through the early years of day-to-day family living.

Just as the comfortable feelings of love and tenderness, as well as the uncomfortable feelings of fear and anxiety, are associated with close ties, so, in many cases, are angry, hostile, and resentful ones. Those are often most intense between persons most closely attached to each other. There are subtle differences among them. Anger is a transitory feeling, but if it becomes chronic it is usually referred to as hostility. Contempt describes the way a person feels toward someone he considers worthless or immoral. Children are likely to have moments, even longer periods, of all these uncomfortable emotions while growing up. Few relationships are free of them. But when occasional flare-ups become solidified into permanent attitudes, a complex relationship develops.

Oscar Wilde wrote in *Dorian Gray*, "Children begin by loving their parents; as they grow older they like them; later they judge them; sometimes they forgive them." He implied that the judgments are not always so favorably resolved. Childhood may seem an eternity away as people grow older and many memories are left behind, both pleasant and unpleasant. But the feelings developed in that early period are not so easily left behind; they tag along through life.

Once a resentful child begins to live his own adult life, he may forget how angry he used to be with his parents. But just as the helplessness and disabilities of their old age can awaken feelings of tenderness and compassion untapped for years, their new dependency can rekindle old feelings of anger and resentment long thought to be dead and buried. Buried—yes. Dead—never. Sons and daughters may remember all over again the way their parents neglected them as children, the way they punished them unfairly or too harshly, the way they scorned their abilities, belittled their accomplishments, and especially, the way they favored another sibling. Forty years later we can still be angry and resentful about our parents' failures in the past. The fact that they are now old and frail may not diminish these feelings particularly if they continue to behave in the infuriating manner we have disliked for so long. Our failure to help them now may be a form of unconscious retaliation: "You need *me* now. Where were *you* when I needed you?"

Sexuality, Jealousy, and Competitiveness

Sigmund Freud shocked the world nearly a century ago by claiming that very young children have powerful sexual feelings toward the parent of the opposite sex. The shock died down over the years, but there seems little question that most of us have tremendous difficulty thinking about our parents in a sexual context.

Sexual feelings of children toward their parents, rising from the earliest relationships, can account for either a strong identification with the parent of the same sex or an equally strong competitiveness with that parent. A little girl may be closely identified with her mother, or in constant competition with her for the affection of her father. Little boys have parallel conflicts and ties. These feelings of jealousy and competitiveness may last a lifetime and help determine how a middle-aged son or daughter treats an eighty-year-old mother or father.

The inability of children to admit that their elderly parents could have sexual needs has been traditionally reinforced by the attitudes of society, which ridicules any suggestion of sexuality in the aged. Today these needs are admitted and encouraged by some experts, but the subject is still taboo for much of the population.

Men and women may be completely unaware of these feelings and even deny that they could ever exist. The incest taboo is a strong one and leads many adults to banish the sexual attractiveness of one parent, as well as the competitiveness with the other, to the realms of the unconscious. Unresolved sexual feelings can perpetuate a lifelong pattern and be a major cause of younger people's denial of the sexual needs of the elderly.

Shame

This uncomfortable feeling comes in several forms and varying degrees of intensity. Everyone knows moments of shame; they come and go at different times throughout life in response to an endless number of causes. For the sons and daughters of elderly parents, shame can sometimes be an ever-present feeling. The simplest and most common form of shame comes when children feel they do not do enough for their parents. Perhaps a son doesn't visit his parents enough; perhaps he is unable to give them financial help; perhaps he allows a brother, a sister, or even a stranger to provide solutions to problems he feels *he* should be handling himself. He may have his own reasons for behaving the way he does, but nevertheless he feels deep inside that if he were a "better" person he would be doing a better job. Sons and daughters who feel ashamed for those reasons have plenty of fellow sufferers.

A second form of shame is involved when sons and daughters are ashamed, not of themselves for their own failings, but of their parents for *their* failings. A self-made man may be ashamed of his poor, illiterate parents and keep them in the background because he does not want his world to know where he came from. An intellectual woman may be ashamed of her uneducated father, a sophisticated city-dweller of her small-town parents. A son may want to keep an alcoholic father hidden—like other family skeletons—in the closet. When we are ashamed of our parents it is usually because we fear that their shortcomings will reflect badly on us in the eyes of other people whose opinions we value: our friends, neighbors, colleagues, church groups, social clubs, employers, even in-laws.

A third level of shame is a combination of the first two: we may be ashamed of ourselves *because* we are ashamed of our parents. This is probably the most painful form of shame and the most difficult to cope with. It stirs up great emotional conflict in sons and daughters, prevents them from offering constructive help to their parents, and forces them to bear a continual and heavy burden of guilt.

Special Reactions to Aging

While many of the feelings we have about our parents can be traced back to childhood sources, it is never too late to experience new ones. Successes and failures in adult life can also strongly affect the way we feel about our parents. New understanding can stimulate unaccustomed feelings of love and compassion we never knew before. New stresses can produce angry or fearful reactions we would never have believed we were capable of feeling. While the intensity of some feelings persists unabated through life, the intensity of others can fade through the years, leaving room for new ones, although it is often difficult to figure out where the new ones come from. Men and women may seem quite puzzled by their changing feelings: "I used to get along so well with my parents; why are they driving me up a wall all of a sudden?" or "I don't have any patience with them any more," or "I'd give anything to skip visiting Mother this week—I can't understand why she depresses me so much these days." Clues to the roots of these troubling feelings may be found in how the younger generation answers the following questions.

Can You Accept Your Parents' Old Age?

As old but active men and women begin to undergo mental and physical changes, their children can react with mixed emotions— shock (if there is sudden physical and mental deterioration), denial (if the deterioration is a slow slide downhill), anger, shame, fear, resentment—as well as the more expected feelings of sadness, sympathy, and concern. We may be surprised at our own reactions to our parents' decline and wonder how we could possibly be angry at them when we ought to be sympathetic. Anger is not as inappropriate as it may seem.

Most of us, as children, viewed our parents as immortal—strong enough to protect us forever. As we mature we learn we can take care of ourselves and in the process find out, with some regret, that our parents are not quite as perfect or infallible as we once thought. Somewhere inside us, however, remains a trace of the old conviction that our parents could still protect us if we needed them to—so their physical and mental deterioration is shocking. On an intellectual level we keep telling ourselves, "It's understandable— they're getting old, they're fading." But on the gut level we can still be sad, frightened, resentful as if they had broken a promise to us—a promise that had never actually been made. Every time we see them we have to be reminded of their mortality—and our own. The deterioration of a vigorous mind—loss of comprehension, confusion, disorientation, loss of memory—can be even harder to accept than the deterioration of a vigorous body in those families where intellectual activities and verbal communication are particularly meaningful. Nothing can be more painful than the realization that a parent no longer understands us, or even recognizes us. Why should we be so surprised that the realization makes us angry or that we try not to accept it?

Do You Like Your Aging Parents?

When this question is asked, it is rarely answered directly; rather, it is usually sidestepped. A typical reply might be, "My mother's pretty self-centered; she complains a lot and doesn't seem to appreciate anything I do for her. But she's *still* my mother." That, of course, does not answer the question, but most people find it almost impossible to admit that they really do not like one, or even both, of their parents. They may find it equally impossible to admit their dislike even to themselves.

It cannot be denied that, in addition to the infirmities and frailties brought on by age, some old people may also develop unpleasant personality traits that are hard for their children to take—harder still to like. They may have been charming and appealing when they were young, but their charm may vanish with the years. Or perhaps they never had either charm or appeal.

Older people have a right to adequate care, to have their needs answered, their security maintained, their pain diminished, their loneliness alleviated. They have no right to expect to be liked just because they are old—even by their own children.

Can You Accept a Different Role?

Although few old people return to "second childhood," which Shakespeare describes as the last in the seven ages of man, they frequently, because of increasing helplessness, need to depend on people who are stronger. When the family is young, the parent plays the independent, strong role and the child the dependent, weak one. When some parents age they may be willing to abdicate the power they once had, glad to pass it on to more capable hands. The "gift" may weigh heavily on some sons and daughters who prefer their old, familiar dependent roles. Others take the gift, use it well, but resent being forced to accept it. The acceptance in itself symbolizes the end of one longstanding relationship and the beginning of a new one.

A teacher, in her forties, described how shocked she felt one day when she heard herself speaking to her ailing mother in the cheery tones of the kindergarten: "Now let's hurry up and finish this nice soup." Later she commented wryly, "I have three children at home and twenty in my class at school. I certainly don't need another one. What I need is a mother, and I'll never have one again." She knew that she and her mother had to an extent changed roles forever, and accompanying the exchange were feelings of anger, resentment, fear, and sadness, all mixed up with love.

Can You Accept Your Own Aging?

So far this chapter has focused on relationships between children and their elderly parents, and the feelings generated by these relationships. But another set of feelings can be aroused independent of interpersonal reactions: the feelings people have about old age in general, and their own old age and their own mortality. The behavior of children toward their elderly parents can be profoundly affected by these feelings. Many people are reluctant to talk about their old age and mortality; some even prefer not to think about either one. Until very recently death and old age have been taboo subjects altogether, often denied until the zero hour.

Our attitudes vary, depending on whether we admire old people or secretly despise them, whether we feel older people deserve respect or consideration, whether we believe they can remain sexually or creatively active, whether we dread the day when we will be old or the day we will die. Not everyone can agree with the poet Walt Whitman:

Youth, large, lusty, loving—
Youth, full of grace, force, fascination.
Do you know that old age may come after you
         with equal grace, force and fascination?

The feelings we have about our own old age often have a direct bearing on how effectively we can help our parents during their old age, and how constructively we can plan for our own.

People who have a generally positive attitude toward old age in general—including their own—are more likely to be able to reach out to their elderly parents with concern, compassion, and constructive support. If old age appears as a time to be dreaded—and many features of modern society would suggest to us that it is—then our parents' decline may seem very threatening. Their aging seems to toll the bells for our own aging and our inevitable death.

At the funeral of an eighty-five-year-old man his gray-haired daughter was overheard saying sadly, "There goes our last umbrella." She explained later that she had always thought of the parent and grandparent generation as umbrellas, because even when umbrellas are broken and threadbare they can still give some form of protection and shelter from the elements. When her father, the last of the older generation, died, she mourned him because she felt, "Now we have no shelter left. There's nothing any more between us and what lies ahead for us. We're next in line."

Being next in line, of course, means being next in line for death. If we cannot contemplate our own mortality, how can we contemplate our parents'? It can be really painful, yet every time we see them we are reminded of the very thing we'd prefer to avoid thinking about.

An interesting parallel can be drawn between the way people look at childhood and the way they look at old age. One of the pleasures of watching their children grow involves, for many parents, the reawakening of childhood memories and the chance to relive the pleasures they knew when they were young. Similarly, as we watch our parents grow old we may see the shape of our own old age lying in wait for us. We may resent them because they force us to "pre-live" our own old age and death long before we need to. A Pakistani tale (similar versions of which are found in the folklore of other cultures, too) makes this point clearly:

An ancient grandmother lived with her daughter and her grandson in a small but comfortable house not far from the village. The old woman grew frail and feeble, her eyesight became dimmer every day, and she found it hard to remember where she'd put things and what people had asked her to do. Instead of being a help around the house she became a constant trial and irritation. She broke the plates and cups, lost the knives, put out the stove, and spilled the water. One day, exasperated because the older woman had broken another precious plate, the younger one gave some money to her son and told him, "Go to the village and buy your grandmother a wooden plate. At least we will have one thing in the house she cannot break."

The boy hesitated because he knew that wooden plates were only used by peasants and servants—not by fine ladies like his grandmother—but his mother insisted, so off he went. Some time later he returned bringing not one, but two, wooden plates.

"I only asked you to buy one," his mother said to him sharply. "Didn't you listen to me?"

"Yes," said the boy, "But I bought the second one so there will be one for you when you get old."

Are You Overburdened?

Children who are beset by a multitude of demanding problems in their own lives—health, finances, career setbacks, children, grandchildren, even their own retirement worries—may be so drained that they cannot begin to shoulder their parents' problems as well. They may try to do their best, feel ashamed they are not doing better, and, more likely than not, resent the older generation for giving them additional burdens to bear. The following phone call dramatizes this situation—a conversation between a mother and daughter *including* the younger woman's unspoken thoughts:

DAUGHTER   Hello, Mother. How are you? *(Don't let there be anything wrong today! I just can't take one more problem.)*

MOTHER   (small shaky voice) I nearly died last night.

DAUGHTER   (solicitously) Was your leg bad again? *(Oh, God! It's going to be one of those days again. I hope she doesn't keep me on all morning. I've got to get down to talk to Janie's teacher. Why is that child getting into so much trouble this year?)* Are you using the heating pad?

MOTHER   The pain was like a knife. I said to Mrs. Forest this morning ...

DAUGHTER   (cutting in—a little impatiently) Didn't you take that new medicine Dr. Croner gave you? He said it would help.

MOTHER   Don't talk to me about doctors! What do doctors care about an old person? It was a waste of my time going to him.

DAUGHTER   But you said he was such a genius. *(A waste of whose time! Does she have any idea what I went through to take her to that doctor? I changed my whole week around; Janie missed her dentist appointment. I got a parking ticket and Jack was furious. Jack's always furious these days.)*

MOTHER   Mrs. Forest said he was a genius. Mrs. Forest cares about how I feel—she listens to me. You're so busy all the time

—you don't really want to worry about me. You have your children and your husband to think about.

DAUGHTER (guilty but exasperated) Oh, Mother, stop saying things like that. *(Why does she always do this to me? I wonder if she'd care if she really knew what's going on with us now. One of these days I'll tell her; why shouldn't she know that Jack and I are fighting all the time and Janie's doing terribly in school and we have to borrow money to get the car fixed?)* You know how much I care about you!

It is never easy to take on another person's burdens, even when things are going smoothly, but there are some periods in life when it's almost impossible. Ironically enough, it very often happens that older people begin to need more support just at the point when their children's lives are the most complicated and their responsibilities are heaviest. A middle-aged woman is likely to have to deal with her children's adolescent crises and her parents' geriatric ones just at the time she is going into the menopause herself. Her husband may be going through the same midlife crisis. A middle-aged man may struggle to provide money for his children's college tuition and his parents' necessary medical expenses just when he has been passed over for a long-awaited promotion—which he now realizes will never come. His wife, if she is working, may have similar financial pressures and career setbacks.

If, in establishing their life's priorities, sons and daughters have not been able to assign first—or even second or third—place to their parents, they may never forgive themselves. But if they try to shoulder their parents' burdens as well as their own, they may feel continually resentful and put-upon, wondering as the days go by, "When is there going to be time for me?" No matter which course they decide to take, they are likely to carry an additional burden: guilt.

And Finally—Guilt!

Guilt has been left for last because it is usually the end result or the prime mover of many of the other uncomfortable feelings from past and present.

❖ JOHN WILSON IS ASHAMED of his parents. He feels ashamed of himself because he is ashamed of them and guilty because he is not helping them more. He then feels angry and resentful of them because he has to feel guilty and then anxious and fearful that some unknown punishment will be dealt out to him because of his anger.

Poor John. Because of one uncomfortable feeling, shame, he has to suffer the entire gamut of other uncomfortable ones. This is a frequent occurrence—rarely does one single emotion stand alone. The whole mixed bag of feelings is interrelated, one capable of setting off another. Love and tenderness can arouse sexual feelings, sexual feelings can arouse guilt, guilt can evoke resentment, resentment more guilt, and guilt more fear—an endless, self-perpetuating cycle. Pity the unfortunate human being caught in the middle!

Personal Guilt

Guilt is a hidden or exposed emotion which signals to us our own sense of wrongdoing in words or deeds or even thoughts. It is often accompanied by lowered self-esteem and a wish for punishment. Psychoanalysts differentiate conscious feelings of guilt from unconscious guilt which is manifested in a need for self-punishment.

❖ PHIL HAD PLANNED for some time to spend his only day off with his bedridden father. When the day came, it was so beautiful that he decided he had to go fishing instead. On the way to the lake he got lost twice on what had always been a familiar route, dented his car when leaving the gas station, and, when he finally arrived at the lake, found he had left his fishing tackle at home. That night he slept fitfully and dreamed that his father had died.

In present-day thinking, guilt feelings are often attributed to personal neurosis or wishes not rooted in the real world around us. But guilt is not always so buried. It should not be forgotten that people can also feel very guilty for things they have actually done or not done: objective sins of commission or omission. In that respect, guilt means an acceptance of responsibility for action taken or action evaded, and, within reasonable limits, can be a sign of emotional maturity. Our guilt may stem from the uncomfortable suspicion that we have not behaved responsibly to our parents and then, the more guilt we feel, the more difficult we may find it to behave responsibly. Responsible behavior usually flows more easily when we understand not only our parents but also ourselves and our feelings toward them.

A fifty-year-old man put this understanding into action recently as he carefully inspected a well-known nursing home and discussed his situation with the administrator.

❖ MY MOTHER AND I have never had an easy or a pleasant relationship. She's always been a difficult, cold, resentful woman. I can't forget the way she treated me when I was young . . . and I only had superficial contacts with her when I grew up. But she needs someone to take care of her now, after her stroke. I certainly can't bring her to live with me and my family—none of us could take it. But she *is* old and she *is* my mother and I want her to be as comfortable and as protected as possible.

Such cool, objective understanding is rare. The guilty feelings of grown sons and daughters are so primed and ready these days that they can be set off by the most insignificant stimulus. A sentence, even a gesture or a shrug, from an old mother or father can easily do the trick. Some statements are heard so frequently that they are often successfully included in comedy routines because they strike home so universally. "You young people run along and enjoy yourselves. I'm perfectly fine *alone* here by myself," or "You don't want me along. I'd only be in the way," or "I know how busy you are—I understand that you forgot to call me yesterday. Of course, I *did* worry." Shakespeare's King Lear pointed to the guilt of past, present, and probably future generations when he cried, "How sharper than a serpent's tooth it is to have a thankless child!"

Any discussion of guilt should include a reference, at least, to the guilt sons and daughters feel when they wish an elderly mother or father would die. Although not as universal as the "thankless-child syndrome," the "death wish" is felt more frequently than it is admitted. Most people who feel it also consider it too terrible to admit, particularly if they are angry with their parents. The death wish comes in two forms: the more acceptable form is reserved for a parent who is terminally ill, in constant pain, with no chance of recovery. A daughter says in genuine sorrow, "I hope Mother dies soon. I can't stand to see her suffer any more."

A less acceptable death wish is directed to a parent who is not terminally ill but merely difficult or incapacitated, sapping the physical and emotional strength of the family. A son or daughter most closely involved may feel (but rarely admit), "I wish she would die and then I'd have some life for myself at last." There are many instances where both these wishes are understandable, but since it has traditionally been considered "wicked" to wish death to another person, particularly to a parent, these wishes usually involve some burden of guilt.

The Guilt We All Share

The pervasive guilt so many of us feel today in connection with our aging parents is often generated by the knowledge that we cannot do for them as they did for us when we were young. We sense somehow that we owe a debt that we cannot repay. But in present-day society payment is often impossible. While some of our personal situations can be dealt with more effectively when we understand our own feelings, the problems often lie completely beyond our personal control. Their solutions can only be provided by society, and society often fails us and our parents . John Doe may be doing the very best he can to help his ailing mother, but he may know that he is not succeeding very well and feel guilty to be part of a society that has placed so little value on elderly lives. Numbers of other sons and daughters share this same guilt. Romantic, heart-warming stories of other days and other cultures—which gave greater support to their elderly—add to the guilt of today's thankless children. We sometimes hear even now of a helpless elderly relative being cared for at home by a devoted extended family. In these cases, usually in rural areas, old people are never cut off from family life. They are allowed to spend their days surrounded by familiar voices and tended by familiar hands until the end. It does not help those of us who struggle with our own guilt about our parents to know that the extended family still exists—under one roof in some circumstances—and still provides care that the nuclear family cannot deliver.

But the nuclear family, product of modern industrial society, has now emerged as the basic family unit, living separately from the older generations in most cases even while maintaining close emotional ties. For better or worse, bureaucracies and social organizations have taken over many of the functions that used to be private family affairs. Experts in nursing and medicine—although not nearly enough of them—know how to deal with the complicated ailments of the old. Competent nursing homes and intermediate care facilities can provide the day-by-day protective care some very feeble old people must have. The elderly themselves, in general, feel that the government, rather than their own children, should be responsible for their basic needs of food, shelter, medical care, and income.

This take-over by outside agencies does not necessarily diminish the strong bonds of affection and responsibility felt by many younger families toward their older members, but too often, because of inadequate facilities within the family and inadequate services in the community, well-intentioned children suffer the guilty burden, "We are not caring for those who cared for us."

Those are feelings of guilt which all of American society must accept, not just the children of the elderly. Society must admit, too, that it has little reverence for old age and that the elderly in great numbers are cast off, denigrated, ignored. This attitude does not automatically result from industrialization. In present-day Japan, for instance, where there is high industrialization and many of the elderly no longer live with the young, there is still a pattern of reverence and respect for old age. Youth-oriented American society has little room for these patterns. That may explain why older citizens find only meager services and insufficient supports when they look outside their families to society at large to meet their needs. Thus, whether we are related to the elderly or merely on-lookers, we all share the guilt of society's neglect. Some of us have to bear a double burden: our own personal guilt *and* our shared communal guilt.

What Untouchable, Unresolved Feelings Can Produce

Earlier in this chapter we stressed that there is room for all kinds of feelings in interpersonal relationships. Many people recognize this on an intellectual level, but even so, they find it difficult to express or admit feelings which have traditionally been considered immoral or "bad," tending to disavow unacceptable ones, pushing them underground to the unconscious level.

These feelings keep right on existing anyhow. Lock them up and throw away the key—they'll still struggle to get out. The struggle can distort our perception of ourselves and our relationships. Our ability to act responsibly and to make appropriate decisions may be affected by these submerged feelings. It does not necessarily follow, however, that every wrong decision is a result of unconscious distortion of the objective situation. Plenty of mistakes can be made from simple ignorance, and sons and daughters admit these mistakes every day:

❖ "We thought John's father would love the country and being with us, but he just sits and looks out of the window. We forgot what a city person he is."

*

❖ "I made my mother give up the house much too soon after Father died. I didn't realize she needed more time."

*

❖ "We didn't know Medicare would cover some of Mother's expenses in a convalescent home."

Errors can reflect lack of knowledge or know-how about an unfamiliar situation, but well-meaning mistakes aside, it is important to explore some of the typical pitfalls lying in wait when unresolved or hidden feelings direct our relationships with our parents and the decisions we make with them. Some of the most common ones are reviewed next.

Withdrawal

Mel Brooks's "2,000-Year-Old Man" can always draw laughter from his audience when he says, "I have 42,000 children and not one of them comes to visit me." That statement strikes home to many listeners. Lack of attention from children is a familiar parental complaint. Children avoid their parents for many reasons, and great numbers of them suffer only occasional twinges of guilt. But many want to be more attentive, and despite their conscious desire they find it difficult to visit, to phone, to write, and sometimes to keep in touch at all.

If, despite their claims that they *want* to be close and that they *try* to be, grown children find it almost impossible to keep satisfactory contact going, it may be that they are avoiding a confrontation which would arouse uncomfortable feelings they prefer to keep under wraps: anger, resentment, irritation, jealousy. They may wish they could behave differently and condemn themselves regularly— "What's the matter with me? Why can't I do better with them?"— and then withdraw still further.

Oversolicitousness and Domination

This pattern is at the opposite pole from withdrawal. Instead of removing themselves, children may come even closer, choosing a more acceptable type of involvement. By hovering over his parents, spending an abnormal amount of time with them, letting them become completely dependent on him before they need to be, a son may think he is acting out of love and devotion. This could be true, but it could also be *his* way of blocking out angry or guilty feelings.

Just as withdrawal may disguise fear, oversolicitous behavior may serve the same purpose. In that situation the fear lurking in the background may be fear of loss. It is not easy for an adult to accept the fact that he is still very emotionally dependent on his parents, that he has not grown up yet or proved to himself that he can stand alone. Such anxiety can be very painful and palliated by overprotective behavior which implies, "As long as I'm with them, nothing can happen to them," or conversely, "If I leave them alone for a minute they may slip away from me."

Faultfinding

Sometimes there is a job we feel we should do and we cannot manage to do it. Conscious of our own inadequacy, we may feel angry at ourselves and guilty. If we have to face the fact that we are shortchanging our parents, uncomfortable feelings may flow in two directions: toward our parents and toward ourselves. How much less painful it is, therefore, to divert these feelings in still another direction! What a relief it may seem to blame, not our parents or ourselves, but a third party!

When someone else is shouldering the responsibility for our parents' welfare—other siblings, other relatives, favored housekeepers, or nursing homes—a little voice may keep reminding us that we are not doing our share. That voice can be successfully drowned out by an endless barrage of criticism of those who are doing *our* job for us. We may accuse these "stand-ins" of being inconsiderate, inefficient, and inept, and point out how they are not showing the right kind of care or concern. Certain criticisms, especially those of nursing homes, may be valid, and it is wise to keep a close, watchful eye on anyone who is providing for the welfare of the elderly. But if *nothing* is right—*no* way, *no*where—then could it be that deep down inside we feel that something is wrong with us?

People frequently distort the world around them in order to make themselves feel better. The games are popular with many sons and daughters. By placing the blame elsewhere, they give themselves the momentary comfort that they have removed the blame from themselves. The comfort provided by faultfinding is almost invariably offset by angry feelings from other family members and the paid or volunteer helpers the older people are depending on.

Denial

It is not uncommon for children to deny that their parents have problems or need help. Sometimes the denial is so successful that these children are able to disbelieve what is going on right in front of them. If they cannot accept weakness in themselves they may deny the realistic symptoms of frailty in their aging parents. In Joseph Heller's recent book *Something Happened,* the hero, Bob Slocum, describes his behavior to his mother:

My conversation to my mother, like my visits, was of no use to her. I pretended, by not speaking of it, for my sake as well as for hers (for my sake more than for hers), that she was not seriously ill and in a nursing home she hated, that she was not crippled and growing older and more crippled daily. I did not want her to know, as she did know (and I knew she knew), as she knew before I did, that she was dying, slowly, in stages, her organs failing and her faculties withering one by one. . . . I pretended she was perfect and said nothing to her about her condition until she finally died. I was no use to her.

Children who need to deny longstanding sexual attachments to their parents, may also deny, when a mother or a father grows old, that either one could still have sexual feelings or needs. That distortion of reality can make it very difficult for even the most devoted children to accept comfortably a widowed parent's remarriage or extramarital relationships.

Denial is also closely tied in with fear of losing parents. A daughter may feel that if she can ignore the warning symptoms of her mother's physical deterioration, perhaps they will go away. The most dangerous part of this kind of denial is that the older person may not get medical help until it is too late to do her or him any good. But even when doctors are consulted, denial leads many children to unrealistic hopes for miracles from the medical profession.

Outmoded Role-Playing

Many a child discovers at a very early age that certain types of behavior produce enjoyable responses from his parents. Since these responses are so gratifying, he may repeat the behavior, and eventually it becomes expected of him. Ironically, by assuming a role and playing it successfully, he may get trapped in it and fear that if he ever stepped out of it no one would value him any more—particularly his parents.

A role can be assumed by a child in order to get along in the family, but a role may also be assigned to a child. Listen to parents discussing their children with friends: "Jim's the dependable one," or "Jane's the emotional one," or "Fran's so easygoing," or "Susie's the clown." All these qualities may be true about these various children from time to time, but every child has more than one emotional color and will be in trouble if expected to function only according to one.

If roles are perpetuated as part of family fun and tradition, they are not necessarily harmful. A gentle family joke kept alive through the years may be a warm and tender reminder of past closeness. But if roles are perpetuated out of anxiety or fear—if a daughter feels she must cling to hers in order to remain acceptable to others—then she may find it hard to step outside it, be herself, and deal constructively with problems affecting her parents' lives and therefore her own. Thus, if she still clings to the outgrown role of being the "child" to her parents, she may see herself as still dependent on them when in reality they are the ones who now need to lean on her. Her behavior is therefore inappropriate to the real circumstances. On the other hand, she may cling to an old role of being "the dependable one" in the family—the child who always did the most for her parents. She may be afraid to give up this role and may make unreasonable demands on herself even when her brothers and sisters are perfectly willing to share the burdens involved in caring for their parents. This kind of self-martyrdom will be explored in the next chapter.

Protracted Adolescent Rebellion and Blind Overinvolvement

When grownup people are still angry and rebellious toward their parents, it is legitimate to wonder if they ever as adolescents had a period of healthy rebellion which permitted them to mature successfully and assume separate adult roles.

There comes a time in the normal child's development when he needs to break away from close parental control, give his parents a hard time, disagree violently, try his own wings, make his own mistakes. Children need, in current adolescent lingo, to "do their own thing." This breakaway period has varying degrees of intensity, depending on the individual adolescent. The upheaval gradually quiets down, the struggle for independence becomes resolved, and eventually the stormy adolescent joins the adult world. But some children make rebellion a way of life. The skirmishes continue through the years, no decisive battle is won, and adult maturity remains elusive. A son who is still in constant conflict with his parents may also, in a perverse way, enjoy blaming them for preventing him from growing up. He may even project onto his parents tyrannical motives which he can rebel against. The anger he feels toward them may blind him to the fact that they are getting old and need him to grow up at last.

Those who never go through any adolescent rebellion at all are even more vulnerable. A child who has never been able to break away from one or both parents may never be able to see himself as a separate individual. The result, often masked as a loving, devoted relationship between parent and child, can in reality reach a point where the child cannot separate his feelings from those of his parents. This process may be particularly painful to bear, especially if the parents seriously deteriorate as they grow old. What a burden it can be for a son to live through his parents' old age with them and then have to face the same problems a second time when he gets old himself! Overinvolvement by a child can force an older person to be unhealthily stoic in order not to give his child pain, or a mother or father may be stimulated to more exhibitionist suffering by the knowledge that a child secretly enjoys being allowed to share the pain.

Scapegoating

The burdens and problems of our own lives, as mentioned earlier, can lead to an unfortunate type of behavior toward our parents: the process of scapegoating. Human beings often find it difficult to face up to the real things that trouble them: illness, failing resources, marital problems, troubles with children or careers. It is sometimes convenient to blame a totally innocent source (or person) for these problems and unload anger and resentment on something or someone else. Even if the older person is not actually blamed for the problems, he may have to bear the emotional outbursts generated by them. A campaign of television commercials for a well-known headache remedy a few years ago centered around the scapegoating of an elderly relative by a younger one. The series included a line that became famous: "Motherrr—I'd rather do it myself." It ended with the gentle reminder, "Sure you have a headache, but don't take it out on her." Substitute the words *unfaithful husband, bankrupt business, frigid spouse, disturbed child, bad investment* for *headache,* and the possibilities for scapegoating are endless—in every family.

Scapegoating is not usually done deliberately. It is a very human type of behavior, but when carried to an extreme it can be very destructive to everyone, particularly to the elderly.

It's not always easy to look at feelings and accept them. They may be unconscious, or may seem so shameful that it is easier to bury them. Many of us do not realize that there is room for such a wide variety of feelings toward the people we are close to: parents, husbands, wives, children, friends, enemies. But if those feelings are not faced and accepted, they can stimulate other feelings even more painful. Sometimes we cannot get in touch with our own feelings without the help of someone else, and just as we may turn to a counselor or psychotherapist when in turmoil about our marriage or our children, we can find similar help with our mixed-up feelings about our aging parents. Many people find it helpful to talk to their family physician, priest, minister, or rabbi. Others prefer to consult professionals, who are sometimes able to clarify problems after only a few visits. (Ways to locate professional help are listed in Appendix A, pages 254–64.) It would be unrealistic to suggest that elderly parents and their grown children will live happily ever after when their feelings toward each other are open and accepted. The best that can be hoped for is that problems will be faced directly and the most helpful solutions found—*under the circumstances.*

But the circumstances of old age are sometimes unhappy. Many old people carry into the later years the personalities that colored their relationships in their earlier years: selfishness, greed, cruelty, bigotry, hostility. And even in the best relationships there will inevitably be pain, and sadness. It is natural for children to feel these emotions when they watch their parents deteriorate and move every day closer to death.

But there can be pleasure and comfort even in these final days. This can be a time for looking back and looking ahead. The younger generation has one last opportunity to relive family history with the older one and understand—perhaps for the first time—the continuity of the life cycle. There is a chance for peace of mind even in the midst of sadness. This reward eludes children who continue to struggle with unresolved, troubled feelings until their parents' death—and afterward.

Death ends a life . . . but it does not end a relationship which struggles on in the survivor's mind . . . towards some resolution which it never finds.

Robert Anderson, *I Never Sang for My Father*

3.

The Family
Merry-Go-Round

❖ MARTHA WILLIS NEVER FULLY recovered from the severe bout of flu she suffered in the winter before her seventy-fourth birthday. Although she stayed on in her own little house, she could no longer take care of it or herself alone even with the help of a homemaker who came in several times a week. Her oldest daughter, Sylvia, who lived closest and whose children were teenagers, took on the major responsibility for her mother's care. Eventually, Sylvia found she was spending more and more time in her mother's house and less and less time in her own.

In the beginning everyone pitched in to help—her younger sisters, her husband, and her children—but as time went on Sylvia noticed that her sisters seemed less available, her husband less understanding, and her children more resentful, often accusing her of being more interested in Grandma than in them. Tensions built throughout the family and erupted frequently. In one typical week Sylvia screamed at her favorite sister over the phone, accusing her of "never doing anything for Mother." She had an ugly fight with her husband, who stormed out of the house and the next day forgot her birthday. In the same week her younger son was suspended from school for cutting classes and her older son had an asthma attack.

"Mother's the least of my worries," Sylvia complained bitterly to her best friend. "Since she got sick the whole family's starting to fall apart."

Of the nation's more than 20 million citizens over sixty-five, too many have no families to care for them or about them. In sickness, in trouble, and in poverty they have to go it alone, and their very aloneness makes their situation even more tragic.

But millions of other elderly people are not so alone. When their ability to manage independently seems threatened, plenty of relatives may be concerned—not only sons and daughters, but sons- and daughters-in-law, brothers and sisters, stepchildren and foster children, nieces and nephews. Concerned friends and neighbors may also become involved. In times of serious crisis a few close relatives usually assume the real responsibility, but any number of others—all of whom have some connection with the older person *and* with each other—may be drawn into the act, offering help, suggestions, advice, criticism. Their offers can be constructive and valuable, or—in some cases—misguided and destructive.

It may seem to you, if your own mother is deteriorating, that it is impossible to find a solution satisfactory to everyone—to her, to you, and to others in the family. Some situations undeniably defy solution. But it may be a mistake to jump too quickly to the conclusion that your own situation is in that hopeless category. Just as your feelings about your mother may make it easy for you to help her or stand in the way, other relationships can similarly facilitate or block effective behavior: your feelings about your brothers and sisters, theirs about you, and everyone's feelings about your mother.

Family Harmony or Family Discord

Throughout history countries have mobilized their efforts to deal with threats and disasters—wars, famine, disease—rallying together with greater unity than ever. And so with families. A shared crisis —a father's stroke, a mother's blindness—can bring out the best in every member, drawing everyone closer together. At such times brothers and sisters may get to know one another again as adults and be gratified by the new relationships. Husbands and wives may find hidden strengths in each other and be pleasantly surprised by the discovery.

❖ "I got married and left home when my brother was a teenager. I never realized what a great person he'd turned into until I spent all that time at home when Mother was sick. We're real friends now."

*

❖ "Jennie was such a helpless crybaby when we were little—who'd believe she'd be the one we all depend on now that Dad needs so much care?"

*

❖ "I really *talked* to my brother when we visited my Mother at the nursing home—we hadn't talked that way in twenty years."

*

❖ "Lizzie's sense of humor saved us. She could always make us laugh even when everything looked terrible."

*

❖ "My husband was always so quiet and unemotional. But he had what we needed when Mother got cancer. He was the one who kept things going— the rest of us just fell apart."

There are hidden benefits for everyone when the younger generations rally together to help the older ones. The elderly benefit if their relatives work together to find the best possible solutions to painful problems. The younger family members benefit if the crisis brings them all closer together again; old and valued relationships are often re-established, and new relationships may emerge, setting a pattern for the future.

But those benefits are only enjoyed in some families. The crisis that brings unity to one may lead to civil war in another, and the problems of the elderly may be further intensified by family conflict.

We tend to speak of families as homogeneous units. We refer to the Jones Family and the Smith Family and the Brown Family as if each one had a single mind and personality: "Oh, you can't count on the Davidsons," or "The Katers are so generous," or "The Phillipses are loud." But every family is made up of a number of individuals and a variety of personalities, capabilities, needs, ambitions, and frustrations. In order to function as a unit, family members, even when they are adults, may develop a certain balance in their relationships.

Frequently the unifying force in such families is the older generation, which maintains the balance, perpetuating ties between children. Elderly parents often serve as the family news agency: "Mother told me about your promotion—we're thrilled," a sister may write to her brother, or "Father wrote to us about your car accident so I had to call," says another sister, using the long-distance phone for the first time in months.

When a sudden crisis reduces an independent old woman to helplessness, or a slow deterioration finally disables a formerly self-sufficient old man, the news agency closes down. Brothers and sisters are thrown together again and must deal with each other directly, without a parent as intermediary. They may once again need to function as a unit as they have not done since childhood. The successful balance they may have achieved may be out of kilter. The family is forced to realign itself to absorb the changes.

Similar realignment may be necessary in marital relationships. A husband who has taken a back seat, staying carefully removed from his wife's family, may be forced by a crisis to take a more active role and contribute time, concern, advice, and even money. A wife who has managed a wary, though polite, involvement with her mother-in-law may eventually, because her husband needs her, be forced into an intimate, supportive relationship with a woman she never really liked.

Is Your Sibling Rivalry Still Showing?

The roles children assume or are assigned in childhood influence their relationships not only with their parents, but with their brothers, sisters, and other relatives as well. Some roles are accepted and admired by everyone and make for affectionate relationships which last a lifetime.

Many roles, however, while accepted or even encouraged by parents, are branded by others in the family as phony. A brother, aware of the admiration his sister always receives for being "the easygoing one," may always have been able to see through the role to her "real" self, which is actually fearful and manipulative. He may brand her as a fake and despise his parents for being so blind. "Don't pull that act with me," he may have said many times while they were growing up. "You'd like to stand up to Dad just the way I do, but you haven't got the guts!" Thirty years later he may still suspect her motives when she hovers anxiously over their ailing father.

A highly competitive group of brothers and sisters may continue to compete later in life, although not quite as directly with each other. But when their mother begins to age, they may resume open competition with each other over her welfare, particularly if she was the original source of their competitiveness. Each sibling may claim to be considering Mother's well-being, but the underlying motivation is winning out in a final family contest.

Sibling relationships can also be affected by the position held by each one in the family structure, and the age differences between them. The oldest may have always been expected to shoulder the greater responsibility when everyone was young, and that expectation may continue when everyone is grown up. But the opposite may happen. The oldest may marry first and, by making an earlier separation, leave the younger ones to deal with problems that remain. The youngest, as "the baby" in the family, may be seen as the one who is let off scot-free, while more was expected of the older ones. Conversely, the youngest, being the last to leave, may be left holding the bag because everyone else has gone. The varieties and mixtures of old relationships between brothers and sisters are endless.

These relationships do change and shift through the years. You may be amazed, when your parents are old, to find yourself depending on the sister who was the most scatterbrained or the brother who was most self-centered. Such switches may pleasantly surprise you, but you may be even more astonished to find out how few changes have taken place in all that time since childhood. What a shock to discover that your forty-year-old sister is just as selfish as ever, or that your sixty-year-old brother is still trying to boss everyone. Don't forget, they may be equally shocked that you haven't grown up much either. Even though you have all come together again to try to help Mother, she may be pushed aside while family history repeats itself all over again.

No One Can Ever Forget "The Favorite"

A particularly crucial childhood role—and one which often affects relationships years later—is the role of "the favorite."

When they are growing up, children often wonder about their parents' feelings, asking themselves, "Do they love *me* best?" or "Which one of us do they love best?" In some cases the favored relationship can be limited to one child and one parent: "Joey's always been closer to Mother, but Dad loves me best." In other families the role of favorite is conferred on one child and then passed on to another, depending on the stage of development of each. That unstable state of affairs can lead to further tensions as children compete for the prize, never knowing exactly where they stand. Parents usually loudly deny having favorites and honestly believe they love *all* their children equally, but their behavior may reveal their true feelings. "Look, Ma, no hands!" a triumphant four-year-old may shout, balancing for the first time in his life on a two-wheel bicycle. If his mother's response to this dramatic accomplishment is merely, "Be careful! Don't scratch your brother's bike!" the four-year-old may wonder what further act of bravery he will have to perform in order to gain the maternal spotlight. He may keep on trying all his life, hoping that one day he will do something to make his mother's face light up for him the way it always does for his brother. Like eager scouts, less-favored sons and daughters often push themselves through life to do more and more good deeds hoping for just that reward. But sad to say, no Brownie points are given out to middle-aged daughters and no Merit Badges to graying sons.

Favoritism is particularly hard to bear if the favorite seems to hold the crown for no valid reason. A ten-year-old sister (in second place) may wonder, "Why is it always Jennie? Why never me? Why can't they see how pretty and clever and kind I am?" Years later she may be asking the same questions: "Why do they always turn to her for advice—can't they see how greedy, cold, self-centered, neurotic she is? Don't they realize how much better off they'd be if only they listened to me?"

Oversolicitous behavior toward old parents may mask the anger a grown child feels for having to take second place, but it may also be a way of saying, "Look how good I am to you. *Now* won't you love me best?" or "By God, I'm going to be your favorite child *just once* before you die!" Indifferent, uncaring behavior may also be a way of saying, "You always loved Jack the best—he got the most —now let *him* take care of you." An uncaring son may be accused by others of taking a back seat and not coming forward to help his parents when they are old and need him, but he may merely be continuing to stay in the exact place they assigned to him when he was young.

Who's in Charge?

Your mother may have said over the years, "I will never be a burden to any of my children," but unless she has made some prior arrangements to cover all emergencies as she grows older, she may have no choice. She may be forced to turn to someone in her family for help. In families where there are several children, however, the big question is: *Who will that someone be?*

If you are the only daughter in the family, the chances are that it will be you, rather than one of your brothers. Experts in family relations feel that daughters (usually middle-aged) are more likely to take on the major responsibility for their parents' care. They and other female relatives are normally the ones who contact outside sources of support—family and community agencies—when they cannot cope with the responsibility alone. Even when their parents are getting along well and do not need help from anyone, daughters are usually thought of as keeping in closer touch than sons, who are more likely to become involved on special occasions or with major decisions and financial arrangements.

It could be argued that the behavior of daughters has been determined through the years because women have traditionally been at home and available, and also because housekeeping and nursing duties have always been seen as women's roles. It will not be known until the future whether this pattern will continue as more and more women become involved outside the home in careers, and domestic duties are shared to a greater extent by both sexes.

"The Caretaker" May Be Chosen

When there are two or more children in any family, one may be chosen by the parents to take care of them. Their preference may have always been known. One particular daughter (or son) may have always been called when problems arose, one who could always be counted on to answer any emergency, who keeps in touch on a regular, even a daily, basis. That relationship is often mutually gratifying and supportive to both generations over the years, with giving as well as receiving on each side. In the later years, when her parents have greater needs, that daughter may be willing, because of these strong mutual bonds of affection, to make sacrifices in her own life in order to make her parents' lives easier.

The child who is singled out by the parents as their main source of help may be the oldest, the youngest, the strongest, the weakest, the favorite, or the least favorite. One son (or daughter) may live close by, and that very proximity makes it natural for his parents to turn to him and his family. He may not even realize what is happening, but little by little he may assume more and more responsibility for his parents' welfare until one day he may wake up to realize he is "the caretaker." If he is married, his wife will probably share the role with him to some extent at least. In other families, as one by one children grow up, get married, and move into their own lives, one particular child (usually a daughter but sometimes a son) may be expected to stay around, her plans for her own future constantly influenced by the thought, "I'm the only one left—I can't leave them now." The unmarried daughter, mainstay of her parents' old age, was seen more frequently in the past, but she has not gone completely out of style today. Her life may become a series of postponements. She may hope to travel, to work in a foreign country. She may consider marrying Joe or Frank or Tom, but only after "Mother gets well," or "Mom and Dad sell the house and move south."

"I was always in the right place at the right time," an unmarried career woman explained. Specifically, her statement meant that whenever there was a crisis in her parents' lives she "happened" to be conveniently on the spot, while her brothers and sisters were conveniently (for them) miles away. After a number of years everyone began to take it for granted that she would always be there, and any plans for marriage or career advancement would always be indefinitely tabled. It never seemed to occur to the absent ones that they should disrupt their own lives and come home to help out. It *did* occur to their "dependable" sister as more and more years went by, but she was unable to extricate herself from a pattern everyone had allowed to develop—herself included.

"The caretaker" chosen by the elderly parents may not be their first or even second choice, but they may have no other one available. They may turn by default to the only son who is in good health, has a steady job, or has a wife they can tolerate (or who can tolerate them). Other brothers and sisters may determine the choice. Those who are married with children of their own may expect the childless couple to take the major responsibility. "I only wish I had as much time to spend with Mom as Mary does," a contented mother of three may say of her childless older sister. "But she's not tied down the way I am." Sister Mary may not agree that just because she is not tied down by children she should be tied down by Mom.

Being childless may, on the other hand, be a good excuse for avoiding responsibility. Brother Fred may say with genuine regret, "Phyllis and I would love to have Father live with us, but we're away so much—he'd be terribly lonely. Tom has all those kids at home anyhow, so Father's much better off with him." Brother Tom and his wife, already responsible for three children, become responsible for Father as well. The choice may seem logical and sensible, but neither brother may be completely happy, as Tom yearns for Fred's freedom and Fred envies Tom's closeness to their father.

A potentially explosive situation exists when parents divide their needs, accepting help and care from one child and advice and guidance from another.

❖ "I spoke to Larry last night. He doesn't think Dr. Parker's doing a thing for your father's arthritis. He thinks we ought to go to Dr. Larribee over in Beechwood Center," Mrs. Fuller said to her daughter Kate.

"But you've always liked Dr. Parker. He's known Dad for years. And Beechwood Center's miles away," replied Kate, who always drove her father for his regular treatments. She tried not to show the resentment she always felt when her brother had one of his "great ideas."

"Larry wants us to try Dr. Larribee," continued her mother.

"Then let Larry drive. He lives around the corner from Beechwood," snapped Kate, knowing exactly what her mother's next words would be.

"Oh, Kate. You *know* how busy Larry is. Surely you want to do what's best for Father."

Of course Kate wanted to do what's best for Father. Didn't she always follow through whenever Larry had a great idea? She dutifully took her father to Dr. Larribee, driving the extra thirty miles to Beechwood Center and back, gritting her teeth and hissing at herself, "Here you go again—doing Larry's work for him!"

"The Caretaker" May Volunteer

"The caretaker" may ask for the job. A son may realize that he is in the best position to help; a daughter may feel she can take care of her parents as well as her children. When their parents begin to deteriorate, these volunteers are ready to help out or to take over completely. But sometimes they are ready too soon—and take control of their parents' lives long before this is necessary. "Premature volunteering" by one of their children may accelerate an older couple's decline and make them dependent long before they need to be. The volunteer may then be suspected of assuming control more to satisfy his own needs than out of concern for his parents. He may have been waiting all his life for just this opportunity.

The volunteer may be the child who has always felt least loved and hopes finally to gain recognition and approval from everyone. For this reward he may be willing to make painful sacrifices in his own personal life—in his relationships with his wife and children, and in his career.

The favorite may also volunteer. He may feel forced by his parents' expectation that he will return to them the concern they have always shown him, or he may volunteer out of guilt that he has received so much more than the other children in the family and feels obligated to make it up to everyone. Or he may always have had a lurking worry that he did not really deserve his favored position, that he was unworthy of it, that it was conferred on him by mistake, or that he would never live up to it. When his parents are old he finally has a chance to convince them and himself that they were right to favor him after all.

The Pseudo "Caretaker"

Occasionally, a son or daughter volunteers as "caretaker" but functions in name only, wearing the title but performing none of the duties. Like a good general or clever executive, he is able to delegate responsibility to the lower ranks. He may use phrases like "Just this once" when he asks someone to pinch-hit for him, as if asking for the first time. "You *will* call Mother every day while I'm on vacation, won't you?" a pseudo "caretaker" may say earnestly to his sister. "What difference will it make if you *are* away? Don't I call her every day anyway?" she would be justified in replying.

The child who acts as pseudo "caretaker" usually has his own motives: to establish himself firmly in first place in his parents' affections, to gain admiration from the outside world, or perhaps to inherit the most from his parents—even if they have very little to leave behind.

Brothers and sisters sometimes seem to conspire to help the pseudo "caretaker" retain the title, knowing that efforts to unseat him would be futile or would cause pain to the parent who needs to perpetuate the masquerade. "I'm the meat and potatoes in my parents' lives, but my brother's the champagne," a sister admitted honestly. "I'm around all the time, but I don't do anything exciting or dramatic—just the ordinary little everyday chores that everyone takes for granted. But he breezes in and whisks them off to the country for the day—brings them some special treat or takes them to a restaurant or a show. He breaks that awful monotony for them. They can live on one of his visits for weeks. They even look younger afterward. I can't do that for them. I guess they need both of us."

"The Caretaker" as Martyr

Some aging parents place unreasonable demands on their "caretakers." In many cases when other relatives are really unable to help or simply prefer to keep a safe distance away, the "caretaker" is genuinely overburdened and justified in feeling there is just too much for one person to handle. But "caretakers," because of their own complex feelings toward their parents, often place unreasonable demands on themselves. They go overboard in their zeal, insist on carrying the entire responsibility single-handed, and discourage anyone else from sharing in it in any way. Brothers, sisters, and other relatives, initially willing and eager to help, will eventually back away when their offers are repeatedly rebuffed, at the same time resenting being rejected and shut out of their parents' lives. The "caretakers" may then complain bitterly to anyone who will listen about their heavy burdens and the selfishness of their families.

❖ "I'm everyone's slave, doctor," complained Sally Horgan, explaining during her physical examination why she was overworked and rundown. "After I've cleaned and marketed for my own family, I have to go over and do the same thing at Mother's apartment. And Mother's lonely—she needs company—so I have to visit a little, too. It makes her feel better. I fix her a little supper and then I have to go home and cook for all of us. I'm usually too tired to eat."

"You're an only child, then, Mrs. Horgan?" asked the doctor.

"No, doctor. I have a brother and sister."

"They live far away?"

"No, doctor—they're right here in Maplewood."

"Can't they help you out a little with your mother?"

"They always leave everything to me."

"Do you ever ask them to help?"

"They never offer."

"Do you ever ask them?" repeated the doctor.

"No, doctor, I guess I don't."

The one in charge who does not ask for help, or rejects help when it is offered, ends up alone. The burdens become heavier as time goes on, and eventually the "caretaker" is likely to become the family martyr.

Friend or Enemy?

The "caretaker" may be seen as the most valued member of the family or the most hated. Brothers and sisters are often genuinely grateful to the one who performs a job they are unable or unwilling to do, and are often eager to do whatever they can to make the "caretaker's" life easier. The "caretakers" are often equally appreciative and report that the additional help they are given makes their responsibilities bearable. "There must be ESP in our family," one sister claims. "Whenever everything's about to get too much for me—almost before I know it myself—my brother and his wife take over for a few days. I'm always surprised after all these years that they keep on appearing just when I need them most." A sister in California tells her friends, "I always fly home to Philadelphia every summer to be with Father for a month. My brother and his family take care of him the entire year—they deserve a break. And anyhow I'm glad to know that I can spend some real time with Father every year."

The one in charge may be hated instead of loved by the rest of the family, for using the position to keep everyone apart. Aging parents can become pawns in family power struggles. They may be used to settle old debts and rivalries between siblings. A sister, always jealous of her brother, may deny him the thing he wants most—the chance to be close to their parents and share the final years with them. "Mary acts as if Father is her private property—as if *she's* the only one who cares about him," he might complain —accurately—and then use every opportunity to draw his father over to *his* side. Poor Father, caught in the crossfire, is doubly threatened—by his own old age and by his own children.

The "Caretaker" Under Fire

In many families trouble may come from the most unexpected quarter: from the very child who seems the most remote from the parents, the least concerned, and the most willing to let everyone else take over. When plans have been put into action and seem to be working smoothly, an absent son or daughter may suddenly appear on the scene and imply to an elderly mother, "If I'd been around [or, if I'd been consulted] I'd never have let them do this to you." Mother, who may have been adapting pretty well to some new situation carefully worked out with the rest of the family, is likely to take several giant steps backward.

Well-run nursing homes, concerned with the future adjustment of a potential resident, know the value of consulting as many children as possible in the placement process. A daughter, making an application for her father, may find that the intake team discourages her unilateral decision, and asks to see everyone else involved.

A brother or sister may disapprove of a plan, not because the plan itself is ill advised, but because someone else thought of it first: "Bill would have approved of the nursing home if he'd selected it," or "Mary and John would have liked Mother's homemaker if they'd hired her."

Snipers and critics may not make real trouble, but they can be constant irritants. Rather than acknowledging how much responsibility the "caretaker" does shoulder, her siblings (and other relatives) may be quick to point out any omissions and mistakes. Aware that they aren't doing much for their parents themselves, they find it comforting to snipe at her.

Older Sister to Younger Sister:
"Mother was so disappointed when you didn't visit on Thursday, Kim. She was in tears when I called." Kim visited Mother every day of the week—she just happened that week to miss Thursday.

*

Younger Brother to Older Sister:
"How could you have let Dad gain so much weight since I was here at Christmas? Have you completely forgotten about his blood pressure?"

Dad had lived with older sister for four years. She watched his diet carefully, cooking special salt-free, low-cholesterol dishes. But Dad cheated, and she couldn't watch him every minute.

*

Younger Sister to Middle Sister:
"Aren't you *ever* going to get a new coat for Mother? She's been wearing that old rag for years. It makes me cry to see her looking so shabby." Middle sister did all Mother's shopping. She bought food, shoes, curtains, nightgowns, dresses, cosmetics, drugs. She just hadn't had time yet to look for a coat.

When the nursing home is the "caretaker," sons and daughters who still feel they ought to have taken care of their old mother or father themselves may make themselves feel better by constantly criticizing the institution: the staff, the housekeeping, the food, the activities. They may think they feel better doing this, but their continual sniping will understandably antagonize the staff and may even permanently prevent their parent from settling down comfortably.

"Caretakers" must also defend themselves against well-intentioned relatives and onlookers, ready with unsolicited advice or criticism. Your mother's friends may gently but sadly intensify your own anxieties and conflicts by casual comments: how much worse she looks, how depressed she seems. They may ask if you *really* have confidence in her doctor, and remind you that she's alone too much, doesn't eat enough, get out enough. You may already know everything they tell you and be doing the best you can, but these reminders usually carry the implication that you aren't doing enough, and if they had the job to do they would do it much better.

A Permanent Split or a Closer Bond?

"We've not seen each other since Mother died," a gray-haired matron answered sadly when asked about her older sister. "I guess we're not on speaking terms."

The wounds that are given and received during a parent's illness or period of dependency are sometimes so deep and painful that they can never be healed. Relationships between brothers and sisters can sometimes be permanently broken off. Often those wounds are only the final blows ending a relationship which has been distant or seething for years. The sister who has given up too great a part of her life caring for an elderly parent may, even when she is free of her burdens, never forgive her siblings for not sharing enough. A daughter burdened by remorse that she had never done enough for her father may, after his death, need to withdraw from the ones who did care for him. Siblings may resent the martyred caretaker who stood between them and their dying mother, making it impossible for them ever to resolve their feelings about her or to share her final days. Two brothers in Arthur Miller's play *The Price* voice their irreconcilable feelings toward each other while trying to dispose of their dead father's possessions:

VICTOR   *You came for the old handshake, didn't you? The okay? And you end up with the respect, the career, the money and, best of all, the thing that nobody else can tell you so you can believe it—that you're one hell of a guy and never harmed anybody in your life! Well, you won't get that, not till I get mine!*

WALTER   *And you? You never had any hatred for me? Never a wish to see me destroyed? To destroy me, to destroy me with this saintly self-sacrifice, this mockery of sacrifice?*

The split may be less dramatic, resulting more from apathy and attrition than from resentment. When the parent and the parental home goes, the unifying force in the family often goes, too, and there is no longer the same need for siblings to keep in touch with each other. One child may try to take over that central role. If the family had always gathered at Mother's for New Year's, Sister Ellie may try to preserve this tradition. But her New Year's celebration may be a conscious effort on her part rather than the spontaneous gathering it had always been when Mother was alive. Sister Ellie may succeed and establish a new family pattern, preserving it for the next generation. But she may fail, and the new tradition may never take hold. Next year, Brother Jack may say, casually, "You won't mind if we're not there for New Year's, will you? We've got a chance to go south for the week. We'd never have accepted if Mother were still alive. But it doesn't make much difference now, does it?" This will be the first defection, and others are likely to follow. Despite Ellie's efforts, brothers and sisters and cousins and nieces and nephews will, in the future, probably meet each other only at weddings—or, more likely, only at funerals.

Money—the Root of Many Evils

Money and material possessions—the abundance as well as the lack of both—very often provide the real underlying source of family dissension. Brothers and sisters have been competing over inheritances since the beginning of time. They are still doing it today, especially when their elderly parents have sizable estates to leave behind. But even when there is little money and only a few material possessions, these can still assume great symbolic worth. The struggle to win them may be out of all proportion to their value. "Mother's leaving me the silver candlesticks because I'm the oldest," or "I should get the silver candlesticks because I've done the most for Mother." "Doing" for Mother therefore is expected to pay off. But will this kind of "doing" really pay off for her?

Money can cause trouble when there is none. If Mother is barely scraping along on her small pension and Social Security checks, and her children are in a better financial position, who is going to contribute how much? Should they all contribute equal amounts? Or should the contributions be from each child according to his (or her) financial situation? Or from each child according to his (or her) emotional need? Will the contribution be given out of generosity or guilt? Will the gifts have strings attached? Will Mother have to subordinate her own wishes to the wishes of the biggest checkbook?

Money is therefore power: "I give Mother the most, therefore I have the right to decide what plans we should make for her." Does money ever buy that right? Many brothers and sisters say no.

Money can also be a substitute. A son who says, "I send my father a monthly check," may feel he has thereby discharged his total filial responsibility. Does his monthly check balance out equally with his brother's weekly visit or his sister's daily phone call? They may feel that their contribution has greater value, and no amount of money is a substitute for care and concern. Finally, money can be a contest. Competitive brothers and sisters who have money themselves may lavish luxuries on their elderly mother or father, not because either parent needs these gifts or even wants them, but to demonstrate which child has achieved the greatest worldly success.

❖ JASON NEVILLE WAS a successful man who prized success in others. His three children competed with each other through childhood to win his approval, and each one became successful as an adult. They constantly reminded their father of their success by sending him lavish gifts as he grew older and was often in financial straits.

When he was partially disabled by a stroke, they made arrangements for him to enter an expensive nursing home. They day he moved in, his daughter sent him an expensive bathrobe, his younger son provided a new radio, and his older son hired a limousine and driver to take the old man to the nursing home.

Eighty-seven-year-old Mr. Neville arrived in state—and alone. It was a full week before any one of his three children thought it necessary to visit in person to see how their father was adjusting to his new situation.

What About Your Own Family?

If you are involved with an ailing mother whose needs take up a lot of your time, your husband (or wife) and your children may give you great support, or resentment. They may share your problems, or add to them. Your conflicting loyalties may sometimes be unbearable.

Husbands, Wives, and In-laws

Husbands and wives react in a number of different ways when their in-laws need help. A husband may have no particular animosity toward his mother-in-law herself, but he may be jealous of anything or anyone who makes demands on his wife's time or concern. A wife who actively disliked her father-in-law from the beginning may be able to keep her feelings under wraps until he becomes helpless and needs something from her that she is unable to give. A mother may have made it clear through the years that she never approved of her daughter's husband. Can he be blamed for keeping his distance when she is old, or for resenting the amount of time his wife spends with her?

Your husband's (wife's) relationship with his own family also helps to determine how he behaves with yours. If he has always had a strong bond with his own parents, he may develop a positive one with his parents-in-law. A troubled relationship from the past, however, can affect his behavior in one of two opposite ways: he may, because of his conflicting feelings, be so neurotically tied to one or both of his parents that he has nothing left to spare for yours, or he may feel forced to separate from *all* parents—yours as well as his own—as if implying, "A plague on both your houses!"

Perhaps he came from an unloving family and hoped that your parents would make up for him all that he had missed in his childhood. He may come to resent them if they, too, let him down, fail to measure up to his expectations, and never become the parents he always wanted.

A son-in-law, as an outsider, may quickly size up the way his wife is treated by her family, and he may not like what he sees. She may have made her peace through the years and accepted the fact that her sister has always been the favorite, but her husband may never accept this. His feelings toward his wife's parents, therefore, may be determined by *their* feelings to *her*. How can he feel close to people who do not appreciate the person he values? A daughter-in-law, wife of the unfavorite, may never forgive her parents-in-law because they have been so blind and never recognized her husband's superior worth. She may retaliate in two ways when they are old: either by withdrawing and trying to pull her husband with her, thereby adding to his problems, or by devoting herself over-zealously to their needs. Her interest may be less in the welfare of the older people than in her continual desire to show up their favorite.

The wife of the favorite son (or husband of the favorite daughter) faces a different situation. She may have always known that her in-laws never considered her worthy of their son. She may always have to share him with them, or wage a constant and usually losing battle to win him away. When they are old and need to depend on him, she may sabotage his efforts to help them.

How Do Your Children Feel?

An endless variety of relationships are possible between aging parents and children-in-law: supportive, affectionate, caring, hostile, antagonistic. An equal variety is possible between grandparents and grandchildren.

Even though many people like to cherish the rocking-chair and Whistler's Mother images of grandparents, this image was probably more appropriate in the past. Grandparents these days, far from being white-haired and frail, are often vigorous men and women in their forties and fifties still pursuing their own careers and interests. Many are actually relieved to be free of child-care responsibilities and not too eager to take on babysitting and domestic duties again. They may not even feel comfortable in the role of grandparent and feel that it has been thrust on them too soon. Some may be pulled in a different direction, concerned about the welfare of their own parents, now great-grandparents in their seventies, eighties, and nineties. But even when grandparents are older, they may not behave according to the ideal image.

Bernice Neugarten and Karol Weinstein of the University of Chicago observed five major styles of grandparenting: grandparents who are "distant figures" (having little contact with their grandchildren), those who are "fun-seekers" (playing with and enjoying their grandchildren), the "surrogate parents" (taking over when Mother works or is ill), the "formal" or traditional grandparents, and finally, the grandparents who are "the reservoir of family wisdom." "Fun-seekers" and "distant figures" are more common among younger grandparents, while older ones (sixty-five and over) are more likely to follow the "formal" style.

The relationships that have developed over the years between the oldest and the youngest generation may determine how a grand-child will feel and behave toward a grandparent who is beginning to decline and needs help.

Occasionally, children see one particular grandparent as the per-son most important to them—more important than their parents. The relationship can be simpler, less pressured, less conflicted than between parent and child. A daughter may admit, "Mother's always driven me crazy, but Timmy won't hear a word against his grandma. He thinks she's great, and she is—to him!"

A granddaughter may depend on a loving grandfather, trust him, turn to him when she feels ill-used by the world, see him as a source of comfort, understanding, knowledge. He may have time to play with her when everyone else is too busy, time to tell stories, to make things, to go fishing, sightseeing, hiking. Grandfather, in turn, may thrive on this relationship, knowing he is still important in some-one's eyes, delighting in the audience he has for his old stories that no one wants to listen to any more. A sense of family history can be passed on from grandparent to grandchild, often skipping the middle generation. Those close relationships have prompted some observers to refer to the old and young as "generation-gap allies." When such grandparents grow old and feeble their grandchildren often share the family concern and try to do all they can to be supportive. Older grandchildren may even share "caretaking" re-sponsibilities, chauffeuring, sitting, housekeeping, even nursing du-ties. When several generations join together to help and comfort the oldest one, they usually comfort each other at the same time.

That closeness does not always develop. Your mother may never have been the ideal grandmother (or the ideal mother either), and when she needs help your children may not cooperate willingly. They may resent giving up their own interests and activities: "Why do we always have to go to Grandma's on Sunday?" or "Just because of Grandpa we have to miss out on our camping trip!" Some grand-parents are seen as stern or punitive figures, always disapproving of something: language, lifestyle, dress, manners, or friends. The younger generation, in turn, sees the older one as interfering, old-fashioned, bigoted, or even physically distasteful: "I don't want to kiss Grandpa. He smells," or "All Grandma talks about is constipation."

Such problems can be intensified, even reinforced daily, when a grandparent lives in the same house with growing grandchildren. There is little opportunity to relieve the tension or to let off steam. You may hear yourself saying again and again, "Shhh, Grandma's sleeping," or "Turn that stereo down—you know Grandpa hates rock music." Your older children may ask resentfully, "How can I bring my friends home when Grandma's always there bugging everyone?" and solve their problems by staying away from home as much as possible.

Young children may feel jealous or abandoned when their mothers and fathers have to be out of the house all the time "taking care of poor old Grandma" if she is still living in her own home. Occasionally, children may become fearful, anxious, and bewildered when a sick older person lives in the same house with them. They may wonder what really is going on: "How sick is Grandpa?" and "Is he going to die?" One granddaughter, now grown up, remembers all the years her grandfather lived with her and her family; she also remembers standing at his door every morning on her way to school, listening carefully to make sure she could hear him breathing before she left the house.

The Games Old People Play

Your behavior toward your parents when they are old is determined by so many factors in your own personal history and your own current life. But your behavior is also determined by *their* behavior.

Older people are just as capable of playing games as younger people; in fact they may become even more skillful over the years. Some children learn how to play the same games and win, but usually their parents come out on top, because of long years of practice.

Manipulation

A mother who has always played games with her family will know from long experience exactly how to manipulate her children in order to get what she wants from them when she is old. She may know she can go only so far with one but that the tolerance of another is limitless. She may vary her strategy accordingly with each one.

❖ "SHE'S A BRAVE OLD GIRL," a son will say admiringly of his crippled mother. "She's going through hell, but she always manages to sound bright and chipper when I call."

"And how often *do* you call?" his sister may snap back bitterly. "I talk to her every day, and the minute she hears my voice she sounds like the end of the world is here. I have to drop whatever I'm doing and rush over there to see what's wrong."

Denial of Infirmities

By pretending that they have no problems and refusing to admit that anything so terrible is going on, some disabled old people force their children into playing the same game.

❖ "EVERYONE TELLS ME I ought to go into a Home," says Millie Farkas pleasantly. "What do I need with a Home? I'm doing fine here in my nice old apartment. I've got good children—we're a close family—they're happy to give a little help to their old mother once in a while."

Mrs. Farkas doesn't stop to define "a little help" or "once in a while." If she did, she'd have to revise her statement. She's not doing fine and her children know she's not. Jack stops by on his way to work most days to see that Ma has breakfast and doesn't burn herself making coffee. Francie usually comes in at lunchtime, brings groceries, and cleans up a little while she's there. Grandson Billy brings dinner over every evening before he goes to night school; his mother, Laurie, has cooked it. When Mrs. Farkas is ill, her three children take turns sleeping over at her house. By denying her incapacities she has made the lives of three adult families revolve around her needs.

Exaggeration of Infirmities

The rules of this game require older people to exploit their age, insist they cannot manage, play for sympathy, and demand attention. The elderly players use their physical infirmities to control everyone. Loud music, late parties, family arguments must be ended quickly if Grandpa has palpitations or Grandma has one of her dizzy spells. When no one is looking Grandpa doesn't hobble quite as painfully and can climb the stairs pretty well. Grandma can read the fine print of the TV schedule to find her favorite program even though she tells everyone "my eyes are gone."

❖ EIGHTY-ONE-YEAR-OLD GRANDPA ALLEN, living with his son, used his age as an excuse to avoid any activity he disliked. He would have liked to have helped his daughter-in-law around the house, but his legs weren't strong enough any more. (He had always hated any form of housework.) ''Make my excuses to the minister,'' he would say to the family on Sunday. ''Tell him I can't manage to get to church any more.'' (He had always hated church.) ''Make my excuses to Aunt Cissie. Tell her those family gatherings of hers are too much for an old man.'' (He had always hated family gatherings *and* Aunt Cissie.)

But when his oldest friend moved back to town and suggested they go fishing, Grandpa packed his gear efficiently, rose at dawn one day, and was off. His daughter-in-law stood at the window watching him leave and muttering to herself, ''Okay, Grandpa—but don't play your games with me any more.''

Self-belittlement

The elderly themselves can contribute to society's generally negative attitude toward old age. An older woman may deliberately draw everyone's attention to the miseries old age has inflicted on her. ''Look at these crippled hands!'' or ''Have you ever seen so many wrinkles?'' or ''I was beautiful once—would you ever believe it now?'' She may reject herself before anyone else rejects her, answering all invitations, ''Who wants an old woman like me along?'' or ''I'd only spoil your fun.'' The younger generation is then expected to respond to such statements, ''Now, Mother, *of course* we want you to come, don't we, children?'' The elderly may use self-belittlement to gain sympathy, to manipulate their children, but also to quiet their own anxieties about their deterioration.

Money

Some older people use money as others use love (or the withdrawal of love) to control their families. They may try to buy attention, implying that certain behavior will be rewarded and other behavior will be penalized. Threats and promises which have price tags attached can keep entire families in line, bowing to the wishes of one frail old parent.

When old people play games with their children, it sometimes seems as if they always win. But their gamesmanship often backfires. It may create such resentment in their families that, when they really need help, everyone's judgment is so distorted that no one can function at all.

Family Paralysis

When tensions and conflicts run high, family members may be so tied up with their own emotions that they may be immobilized, too paralyzed to act. Some may withdraw completely or become ill themselves, often with psychosomatic conditions: ulcers, migraines, high blood pressure. Unable to act in concert on Mother's behalf, they may find it easier to ignore her deterioration.

To admit they are unable to deal with her situation would be to admit failure. Better, therefore, not to notice it—or to notice it and then argue about what to do about it: Is she or isn't she getting worse? Whose doctor is more reliable? Should she or should she not live alone? Whose suggestions are acceptable and whose are worthless? Everybody's talking about Mother's problems, but nobody's doing anything about them. While all this goes on, Mother is probably getting steadily worse, until one day the family is forced into action by a crisis that cannot be ignored. Something must be done. In all likelihood it will be a sudden, ill-planned placement in an inadequate nursing home—the only place with a bed available at that moment. Even if the placement is in a reputable home, Mother is unlikely to make a good adjustment, because the family battle will probably follow her there.

Can Old Patterns Be Reversed?

Family history can never be rewritten. Brothers and sisters cannot return to earlier days to heal old wounds. Husbands and wives cannot start married life all over again, this time loving their in-laws. The lifetime personalities of older people cannot be turned around, either, nor can their old relationships with their various children. But attitudes and perspectives can be shifted slightly—problems approached in different ways may become easier to deal with.

Lack of communication often produces deadlocks. Families may not realize they are not communicating with each other—they may feel they are communicating too much. But sniping, complaining, recriminating is not communication. How can it be when everyone is talking and no one is listening?

Being willing to hear someone else's point of view, acknowledging that there may be other opinions besides your own, allowing room for other feelings—all these processes are capable of working wonders. It's certainly worth giving them a try.

Husband to Wife: "I know I've spent every weekend over at my folks' house—someone's got to be there to give Marion a break. But I know you're angry I'm gone so much. How can we manage better?"

*

Mother to Children: "I've left you alone too much and I feel terrible. We don't seem to have any fun any more. But you know how sick Grandma is. Let's try to think how we could make things easier for all of us."

*

Brother to Sisters: "Nothing's gone right since Pop's operation. We're all furious with each other. It's not doing Pop any good and it's certainly not good for us. Can't we get together and talk about it?"

Such family forums, if they work successfully—and some do not— offer everyone a chance to air personal grievances. You may come to see that your friction with your husband over your parents' care was not caused—as you kept insisting—by *his* unreasonable jealousy, *his* hostility or perversity, but by *your* treatment of his parents, *your* disregard of his feelings, or *your* neglect of the children.

Similar family conferences can give brothers and sisters the same opportunity to say what is on their minds. If you are the "caretaker," they should give you a chance to list your burdens. But if you are willing to listen to them in return, you may learn how your behavior has seemed autocratic and rejecting to them. It may even begin to dawn on you that they have not been doing their share because you have not allowed them to. Together you may find a new approach that allows everyone a share.

❖ AFTER MUCH HESITATION, Sonia Kepple finally told her two brothers that she couldn't go on any longer carrying the main portion of their father's care. Not only was she in daily touch with him, superintending his apartment and visiting him several times a week (despite the fact that she had a part-time job), but every weekend she brought him to her own house to stay while his homemaker was off.

She and her husband were worn out by the endless routine; her children were becoming increasingly resentful. Sonia's brothers were immediately concerned. They had always wanted to share their father's care but had never felt there was anything they could do—Sonia had always seemed to manage so well. Now they had an opportunity. They quickly agreed to rotate weekends, each one taking their father in turn.

But on the first weekend with his younger son, the eighty-six-year-old man, waking up in a strange place, became confused, turned on all the lights in the house, woke the children, and tried to get out of the front door in his pajamas. On the second weekend, the older son started out to pick up his father but on the way he skidded on wet leaves and drove his car into the ditch.

Rotating weekends seemed doomed to failure. Sonia's brothers were unable to do things the way Sonia had always done. But they were determined to help, so they decided, instead, to share the cost of a weekend homemaker for their father.

By not insisting that things always had to be done *her* way, by allowing her brothers to do things *their* way, Sonia and her family were able to have two out of three weekends free.

Gaining new insights is the first step; developing new approaches to problems affecting a number of family members is the second. There may be a certain amount of trial and error. The new approaches may not work at all, or it may take time before they work smoothly. You may feel uncomfortable with your new relationships; they may seem forced, artificial, unnatural. You may, from time to time, slip back into old patterns. But after a while the strains may begin to lessen, and in addition, by working together for the first time, you may come up with solutions that never occurred to any one of you when you were searching alone.

4.

What Have They
Got to Lose

❖ FRANK BARRETT LOST a lot in the ten years after his retirement. As the cost of living rose, his income became barely adequate, arthritis prevented him from enjoying the active outdoor life he'd always loved, and finally, when he was seventy-four, his wife died. Even so, he still continued living his own life. His two married children who lived in the same city were devoted to him, and they did help. They shared his period of mourning with him, helped him to give up his house and move into a small, efficient apartment. They were relieved when they saw he was keeping himself busy. He visited his friends, although their numbers were dwindling. He sat in the park, worked at his hobbies, spoke to his children several times a week by phone, ate dinner with them frequently, and even babysat for his grandchildren occasionally. His children were proud of him—and of themselves—feeling that, all in all, their father's situation, if not happy, was at least pleasant and satisfactory.

But shortly after Frank's seventy-ninth birthday his children began to feel uneasy; they noticed little things at first. One day his daughter arrived and found the water running and overflowing the bathtub. Later that week she noticed that her father had forgotten to lock the door of his apartment. Then there were bigger things. A pot boiled over, extinguishing the flame and escaping gas was filling the apartment when Frank's son arrived to pick him up one evening. Two days later his children were horrified at a long, nasty burn on their father's arm, but even more horrified that he didn't seem to remember where it came from—nor did it seem to bother him. He seemed increasingly confused and often forgot what day of the week it was, which meal he had just eaten, and what his children had told him yesterday. He began to be irritable when they corrected or contradicted him and defensive when they questioned him. The day he fell and broke his hip, his children had already come to the realization that their "satisfactory" situation was no longer workable. Even if their father managed to walk again, they could not let him live alone any more. And so began their search for a safer, more protected kind of living. Then their real problems began.

Frank Barrett's story is being replayed by numbers of elderly people all over America and will be rerun even more frequently in the future as modern medicine prolongs life expectancy for additional thousands. Your parents and elderly relatives may be living out similar scenarios right now.

Their problems, like Frank Barrett's, although disturbing to everyone in the family, may be relatively simple and straightforward. You may know exactly what kinds of solutions to look for even though these solutions are often difficult to find. But things are not always so clear. Perhaps, instead, you are quite confused about what's happening to your parents. Perhaps you cannot put your finger on any one single difficulty, even though you are aware that *something* is wrong. They may seem weaker, more tired, less alert— or withdrawn, full of self-pity and complaints, dissatisfied with everything—and everyone. But even though you know that things are not right, you may not have the slightest idea how to make things better. How can you find answers if you don't even understand the questions?

Just as you may find it helpful to consider all the various emotions involved in your relationship with your parents in order to answer the question, "How do you really feel about them?" it can be equally important to consider all the various changes in their personal world in order to answer the question, "What's really happening to them?" You may never have stopped to wonder how old age has affected their overall lives.

Misconceptions and Misinformation

Despite popular belief, most older people adjust quite well to the changes in their lives. Your parents may be in this adaptable majority. Old age of itself is not a problem. It is the final stage in the cycle of living. Like every stage, it has its share of pleasure and pain, but unfortunate misconceptions and stereotypes prevail, perhaps accounting for the existence of "ageism" in many places and the prejudices against old age and old people held by many Americans. The old are viewed generally as poor, lonely, useless, inactive, and sick. But the facts of aging, once they are known, can quickly prove these assumptions false. In the area of health, to take one example, although problems do mushroom during the later years, they are not nearly as universally incapacitating as many people suppose. Most men and women over sixty-five are healthy enough to carry on their normal activities—only 15 percent are not. Less than 5 percent of the elderly are in institutions, nursing homes, or homes for the aged at any one time. Our elderly population averages less than fifteen days a year in bed because of ill health, and even after sixty-five, illness and disability does not have to become chronic but can frequently be cured or at least arrested. So much for the idea that the old are sick. The aged themselves, in contrast to younger generations, give a far more optimistic report about old age, not only in matters of health but in other areas as well. Their views have been repeatedly confirmed by scientific surveys. After questioning a national sample of noninstitutionalized men and women over sixty-five, investigator Louis Harris, in *The Myth and Reality of Aging in America,* concluded:

> . . . while serious problems of not enough money, fear of crime, poor health, loneliness, inadequate medical care and getting where they want to go indeed exist among certain minorities of older people, they are by no means as pervasive as the public thinks. Nor should having a problem be confused with being a problem. . . . Such generalizations about the elderly as an economically and socially deprived group can do the old a disservice.

The young, with most of life ahead of them, understandably have a different view of the future than the old, with most of life behind them. The present may be even more precious because the future is limited. While physical and emotional suffering are possible in every stage—childhood, adolescence, maturity, and middle age— except where fatal accident or terminal illness occurs there is "always a tomorrow." The ugly duckling becomes a swan, teenage acne usually vanishes, an ungratifying career can be changed, a bad marriage dissolved.

In old age there is a finality. It is the period that inevitably leads to the natural end of the life cycle: death. The comforting clichés of previous ages are inappropriate now and sound emptier: "It'll be better in the morning," or "Things should be looking up next year," or "My time will come," or "When my ship comes in." Prosperity is *not* just around the corner. The only thing just around the corner is death. But death, the inevitable fact of life, is the only certainty in the final stage of the life cycle. Everything else in old age is subject to chance variation and individual interpretation. Dr. Robert Butler, the well-known gerontologist, writes in his book *Why Survive? Being Old in America,* that the elderly are

> as diverse as people in other periods of life and their patterns of aging vary according to the range they show from health to sickness, from maturity to immaturity, activity to apathy, useful constructive participation to disinterest, from the prevailing stereotype of aging to rich forms of creativity. . . . Under suitable circumstances, the present

remains very much alive and exciting to them; but they also turn to a review of their past, searching for purpose, reconciliation of relationships and resolutions of conflicts and regrets. They may become self-centered or altruistic, angry or contrite, triumphant or depressed. . . .

However, if any one word can sum up the varied catalogue of problems that do appear in old age, it is the word *loss.* A seventy-year-old woman may have had very little during a long and deprived life, but it's amazing how much she still has to lose as the years go by. Loss seems like a simple concept, but it often works in mysterious ways.

Children are usually quick to recognize obvious losses and to respond sympathetically to them. When Father is widowed, everyone expects him to mourn. If Mother's arthritis seriously cripples her, it's easy to see why her daily life is so difficult. But loss is not always so glaringly apparent. When a seventy-nine-year-old woman considers it a tragedy that she cannot drive any more, her family may be quite impatient with her. "What's she making such a big deal about? Can't she understand we'll take her anyplace she needs to go? Why does she act as if the world's come to an end?" They may not even begin to realize that *her* world *has* come to an end because she has lost what she valued most: her ability to go her own way and her independence. When aging Michael Parker's canary died, he could not be comforted. "It's only a bird," his children kept repeating in disbelief. "He wasn't this bad when Mother and Aunt Ellen died." They were right that their father had been able to recover more easily from greater losses in the past, but they did not realize that his canary's loss may have been one loss too many. While he mourned for his pet, he may also have been mourning for Mother *and* Aunt Ellen *and* his childhood friends *and* his fishing companion *and* his eyesight *and* his good digestion—*and* his teeth.

Loss comes in so many different forms. It can be a single blow: the death of a spouse or a sudden stroke. Or it may be multiple: loss of work, combined with loss of social status, combined with loss of health, combined with loss of favorite activities. Your parents' ability to adapt to loss—single, double, multiple—is perhaps the key that determines whether they experience a satisfying old age, an unhappy one, or a totally dependent one.

It's a High-Risk Period

Despite the generally positive attitudes held by those who are experiencing old age firsthand, there is no denying that the years after sixty-five contain a considerable number of negative possibilities. More of the elderly suffer from chronic illness and disability than younger groups. Physical decline is often the underlying cause of other familiar problems of aging: mental illness, decrease in intellectual functioning, slowed-up reactions, and reductions in the gratifications and satisfactions of living. Even when the elderly are in relatively good health they have greater physical vulnerability, and that vulnerability may in turn affect many other aspects of their lives. The old definition of middle age as a time when "stairs become steeper, print becomes smaller, lights become dimmer, and people are always mumbling" is no longer a laughing matter for many of the elderly but stark reality.

If the potential losses of old age were merely physical they might be easier to deal with, but in our complex modern society, physical problems are usually interwoven with emotional and social ones. Throughout history men have been searching for the fountain of youth, but never with greater frenzy than in the period following World War II:

> Crabbed age and youth
> Cannot live together:
> Youth is full of pleasance,
> Age is full of care.

If these words were true in the sixteenth century when Shakespeare wrote them, how much truer they seem to ring today in the second half of the twentieth. The emphasis on being young, looking young, acting young, feeling young has grown more intense in this period and reached its peak in the youth culture of the 1960s and the famous slogans "Never trust anyone over thirty" and "Over the hill at forty." Your parents have been told so often by the media and the fashion industry that they are out of step with the world that it's not surprising when they seem to believe it, too.

The spotlight seems to be shifting now and no longer is directed exclusively on youth, but there is still enough in our culture today to persuade older people that society's needs can be met only by the young and the middle-aged. One quick look at the mandatory retirement age in many industries and professions produces evidence enough that the calendar and the clock determine usefulness, rather than an individual's ability to function and produce efficiently. Society tells its senior citizens that old age is a problem long before they would be likely to find it out for themselves. The psychological and emotional problems which spin off from that arbitrary eviction notice are sometimes enough to cause quite vigorous men and women to age ten years between their sixty-fifth and sixty-sixth birthdays. Some people's parents are able to adjust without much trouble to the losses they suffer. Other parents cannot do the job alone. Whether they are then helped by you or someone else, it may be useful now to review the major areas of loss that can accompany old age, sometimes singly but more often in combination. Your parents may be experiencing one or more of those losses at this very moment.

The Loss of Physical Health

The Irreversible Changes

If some genius in the medical profession were to discover a cure for all chronic and disabling disease, he would, of course, be removing some of the greatest problems that beset the elderly and would deserve worldwide gratitude and honor. But the process of aging would still keep right on, because some physiological changes are inevitable. Fortunately or unfortunately, there is no built-in chronological timetable determining when these changes will begin, how fast they will take place, and how much damage they will do. Your father may show them early, your mother much later, or vice versa. There is tremendous individual variation and no two people are likely to follow the same schedule—some seem to show little deterioration at all.

Each organ system of the body, including the brain, is made up of millions of cells, and each system loses cells with advancing age. We can even watch this process taking place, since it is visible in the progressive wrinkling, drying, and sagging of the skin. Another visible evidence is diminishing height. Some older people actually seem to shrink because of the narrowing of the bones and the increased curvature of the spine.

Each of the sense organs suffers some loss. Although only 15 to 18 percent of the elderly have poor vision, the lens of the eye loses elasticity, making it difficult to focus clearly. We have all seen older people trying with difficulty, when they come in from the dark, to recover from the glare stimulus of a brightly lit room. Many of us can remember the eighty-year-old poet Robert Frost, at John Kennedy's inauguration, trying to shield his script from the glare of the bright winter sun so he could manage to read the poem he had composed especially for the occasion. An older person's eyes may take eight or nine times longer to adapt to glare than a younger person's.

The ear suffers its own tissue and cellular changes, and hearing impairment is noticed first by the elderly in the higher frequencies. Sensitivity of the taste buds becomes duller, making it difficult to discriminate among foods. Sensory changes, handicaps in themselves, are often particularly difficult for the elderly to cope with emotionally, since these losses can so radically affect the pleasures of their daily living.

Cellular and tissue change can also affect the nervous system and reduce sensitivity and perceptual abilities. You may have noticed a cut on your mother's hand or a large bruise on her leg, and been surprised, even irritated, that she seemed unaware of either. Frank Barrett's children reacted that way to the burn on their father's arm. Reduction in pain response—its exact site unknown but lying somewhere in the brain—may make it harder for older people to perceive pain within themselves. Other familiar signals transmitted by the nervous system, which formerly alerted them to the part of their body in trouble, may no longer come through loud and clear. The doctor may tell you that your mother has "walking pneumonia" or has suffered a mild heart attack that went unnoticed some time back. You can't blame her for not taking care of herself. Blame her nervous system for sending out inadequate signals.

There is continuing loss of brain cells throughout life, and that decrease as well as other tissue changes can have decided effects on an elderly person's thinking and behavior. While the relationship between brain cell loss and the mental and behavioral problems of older persons has been grossly oversimplified by both experts and the lay public, and too often consigned to the catch-all phrase *senility*, there is little doubt that brain cell loss is significant in many older persons and in combination with other factors can seriously affect their ability to remember, to comprehend, and to think clearly. *Osteoporosis*, a condition in which the bones of the elderly skeleton become thinner and more brittle, makes older people more susceptible to fracture. Think about the number of times you hear of an elderly relative or friend breaking a wrist, a shoulder, or an ankle, or spending months in the hospital recovering from a broken hip.

The body must adapt to other reductions: the excretion ability of the kidney diminishes, the speed of the conduction of nerve impulses slows down, there is a decrease in heart output which does not necessarily imply that the heart is diseased. Decrease in muscle tissue may produce a decrease in strength, and lung capacity may be reduced, perhaps because the muscles no longer work efficiently. Digestive functions also slow down: the flow of saliva and gastric juices, the action of the stomach, and the contractions of the intestines—factors leading to constipation.

There is also likely to be some alteration in the overall functioning of the nervous system which plays an important role in coordinating the interaction between muscles, glands, and blood. That may also account for a decline in muscle strength, and since so many acts of daily life depend on this three-way interaction, when all three do not function smoothly together older people may find simple, everyday activities affected: walking, sitting down, dressing, and housework.

When the impairment of vision, hearing, and reaction time is taken into account, it is not surprising that the elderly have more accidents than younger groups and sustain more injuries, especially from falls.

Perhaps the most devastating reduction of all is the depletion of the back-up reserves which determine the human body's ability to fight off or recuperate quickly from disease. Your father may take a week to recover from the same virus that you and your children threw off in twenty-four hours. How much longer, therefore, and more precarious is the recuperation period from a more serious illness!

As of this year, with the present state of scientific research and knowledge, the aging processes taking place in your parents' bodies right now are inevitable and irreversible. But it is obvious that people are living longer and in better physical shape than ever before in history.

Geriatrics, that somewhat recent medical specialty devoted to the problems of aging, is continually studying all the irreversible trends, and some specialists in this field believe that certain changes, if not all, may eventually be withstood or at least delayed by preventive medicine taken in earlier decades. They know, for instance, that people who have drunk large quantities of milk when they were growing up seem to suffer less from osteoporosis of bones.

New discoveries may appear in time to help you in your own aging, but no matter how soon they come they will be too late to help those who are already old. There is no known way now to prevent or stop the irreversible changes taking place in their bodies, nor is there any real explanation for the individual variation in timetable and intensity—why some changes occur more slowly in some people, begin later, and never progress as far.

There Are Compensations
and Sometimes Improvements

Losses, even severe ones, are not always unbearable. Older people are often able to compensate in many ways, and the final stage of life has its special meanings. Your parents may have found this out for themselves already and discovered how to adapt. Many older people are very successful. Look at the partially blind who turn to large-type reading matter, "talking" records, or Braille—or the deaf who learn how to rely more exclusively on eyesight, the arthritics who search out more sedentary activities to replace their formerly active ones. There are even those with memory loss who learn to keep a pad and pencil handy to jot down everything that needs to be remembered.

Memory loss should not be confused with overall mental decline. Psychologists have found that while memory may decline with age, judgment often significantly improves with age, and the ability to comprehend what is seen also improves with experience. When rapid response is required, older people do not react as quickly as younger ones; they do not seem able to process as much information per unit time. But this slow-down is normal, and is not a sign of mental decline. Some brain syndromes, formerly considered irreversible and included in the catch-all diagnosis *senility,* are not necessarily chronic or hopeless. Reversible brain syndrome, showing a variety of symptoms—confusion, disorientation, stupor, delirium, or hallucination—may result from any one of a number of causes: malnutrition, anemia, congestive heart failure, drugs, or infection, among others. If diagnosed quickly enough before too much damage is done, reversible brain syndrome can be treated successfully.

Surprisingly enough, some physical problems become less serious in old age: for example, duodenal ulcers seem to decrease in severity. High blood pressure and obesity are less threatening in the old, and cancer grows less rapidly in elderly bodies. Older people have been found better able to survive acute heart attacks even though they may suffer as many as younger people.

Modern scientists—engineers, physicists, medical and dental specialists—have provided a variety of inventions to compensate for the losses of the aged, although—let's face it—they have not provided nearly enough. Geriatric problems have never been given a Number 1 priority rating in these professions any more than in society at large. But some attention has been given; more must be given in the future.

Hearing aids in some instances can be excellent substitutes for lost hearing, although much more research is needed to perfect and refine them. Too many elderly people complain of static and unfortunately reject the instrument hands down, although trying out different sets has been found to be successful. Cataract surgery and the substitution of lenses have been very successful in prolonging and maintaining sight. Prosthetic appliances are endless, from the cane to the walker to the wheelchair. Granted, many of these were developed for different age groups, but an appliance devised for a paraplegic war veteran can be adapted perfectly well to the needs of an octogenarian partially paralyzed by a stroke.

Some Physical Problems *Are* Treatable

It is important to keep in mind that many physical problems afflicting aging bodies can be treated; some are even reversible. Disease and illness must be separated from the inevitable changes, although undoubtedly these changes make the elderly more vulnerable and less resilient. Except in terminal situations, illness or disease is assumed to be responsive to treatment and by that definition must not be considered irreversible. In this area medical science is making great advances, and it is gratifying to know that some conditions once considered part of the inevitable process of aging can now be safely classified as diseases and therefore responsive to treatment.

Arteriosclerosis (hardening of the arteries), for example, until recently was considered to be part of the aging process because doctors found it more frequently in people the older they became. It also seemed to become progressively more severe in some particular individuals as the years went by. Today, however, it is seen as a complex metabolic disturbance and, thanks to major advances in drug therapy and dietary restrictions, is subject to treatment and alleviation.

A few words of caution are necessary, however. If the condition has been present in various organs in an unrecognized form for a long period, it may have had time to produce damage which can never be reversed. In those cases, arteriosclerosis and all other chronic diseases have the potential to produce irreversible harm in an elderly body. Furthermore, diseases in the elderly are often of multiple origin, and it can be difficult to recognize and treat each one, but it is somewhat reassuring to know that chronic disease, while not curable, may be controllable.

Admittedly, the threats of disability and death from long-term illness become greater in the older age group, despite medical advances, although the same threats are always present even in younger groups. The leading causes of disability in men and women over sixty-five are coronary heart disease, stroke, arthritis, hypertensive vascular disease, neuritis, lung disease, accidents, diabetes, cancer, and diseases of the eye and ear. (For a more detailed description of these and other chronic diseases of the elderly, turn to Appendix E, pages 315–19.)

The list may sound like an overwhelming catalogue of catastrophe, but we must face the fact that illness and disability cannot be completely avoided with the passage of time, especially after the sixtieth birthday. But another side of the picture may be comforting. There is good evidence to indicate that with adequate medical care, relatively stable health can be maintained for years, even allowing the irreversible changes to take their toll, and elderly people can expect to function and carry on their normal schedules, some with greater and others with less success. The statistics quoted earlier in this chapter bear out this expectation and are worth repeating: *Only about 15 percent of the elderly are physically incapable of continuing their normal activities.* That small percentage, however, translated into people, becomes 3 million incapacitated men and women, a number equal to the total population of the state of Connecticut or the state of Washington.

Why Some Function Better than Others

Except in severe situations, then, the physical losses of the elderly should not be considered insurmountable problems. They become problems when they interfere with an individual's ability to function, to live a somewhat "normal" life, and to carry on familiar routines.

Plenty of younger people go through life afflicted with one ailment or another, but rarely need to stop their activities except momentarily. As a matter of fact, many mature and middle-aged people seem to carry their own special physical ailments as marks of distinction. Haven't you heard them announce almost with pride, "My allergies are terrible this month," or "My back's acting up again," or "I've got one of my migraines." It's the same with the elderly. Most of this group should be able to function at least adequately, and many do, but some do not. The irreversible processes of aging or the associated diseases may be compensated for beautifully by one elderly person while his neighbor, similarly afflicted, may be just barely getting along. Watch the progress of two patients recovering from the same long illness. One takes his medicine, follows the doctor's orders, and seeks out rehabilitative training, while his roommate gives up and retires into semi-invalidism without making even a half-hearted try.

Arthritis may have turned your friend's father into a crippled shut-in who hesitates to leave the house. Why is it that your own father, no less arthritic, moving a little more slowly than before and possibly needing a cane, still travels in the same circles he has always enjoyed? Your mother may refer to herself as "half-blind" and consider herself seriously incapacitated while your colleague's mother, with equally deficient vision, tells the world that she's lucky her sight is holding up so well—and believes it, too.

To the despair of their children, many elderly people are unable to make satisfactory adjustments and seem unwilling to try; they almost perversely reject other people's suggestions. Listen to the conversations at the next social gathering you attend—cocktail party, sewing club, lodge meeting—it's almost predictable that you'll hear the same old familiar refrains: "Mother's a diabetic but she won't stick to her diet," or "John's Mom won't consider a cataract operation," or "Father's got a walker but he's never tried to use it," or "We bought Ginny's Dad a hearing aid but he's never worn it once."

Certain losses may be more difficult to bear for individual, personal reasons. A vain and narcissistic woman may be able to compensate successfully for impaired hearing, but she may be totally devastated by her wrinkled skin which another woman might accept as a natural, although unwelcome, fact of life. Your parents' feelings, attitudes, psychological make-up, and personalities are often the factors determining whether or not physical losses are seen as overwhelming problems.

Loss of Social Contacts

Just as cell loss inevitably takes place in your parents' bodies, almost as inevitably do social losses occur in their world, particularly in the later years. Patterns of living, of working, of communicating, of socializing, built up over all the earlier stages of their lives, often break down completely or are harder to maintain. The universe of the elderly tends to become a smaller, more confined place, less crowded with familiar faces: friends, relatives, co-workers. As widowing takes its toll, husbands are left without wives and wives without husbands.

There are always exceptions: because of some unusual event or accomplishment of their own or the rise to prominence of a son or daughter, men and women in their seventies or eighties may find their horizons expanding and discover new faces, new experiences, and even new geographical locations. That is far from the norm. In general the social world of the elderly is a shrinking planet.

Here again, as with physical loss, the variation among the elderly is tremendous—and mysterious. For some, the social losses can be devastating. For others the impact is not unbearable—they may have been self-sufficient always. Severe physical impairment and financial privation can produce the greatest social hardships, but your parents' ability to accept their social losses depends (as it did with their physical losses) on a number of factors: their own personalities developed over a lifetime, the stability of their marriage, their relationship with their children, their roots in their community, the plans made in earlier years for their retirement period, and their own attitudes toward age and even death.

Changes in Human Relationships

Physical problems are difficult enough to cope with, but the social problems that result from severe physical decline can be additional traumas. If your father has been immobilized by arthritis or paralyzed by a stroke, if he is confined to bed or even just confined to the house, if he can no longer board a bus or take a walk by himself, if he cannot even go out with you in your car, then his world will become no larger than his own apartment or house. It may even be no larger than his own room, if he is bedridden. Then, in addition to the physical pain he is suffering, he will also suffer the pain of social isolation. Your mother, if she is still alive and healthy, will inevitably share some of this isolation. Because of *his* incapacity, *her* life will also become more limited. A constant stream of relatives and friends can help to bring the world to the invalid. A few concerned neighbors who drop in regularly can prevent social isolation. For the less fortunate, with no relatives and friends nearby, social isolation can be relieved only by planned visits from social workers and nurses, priests, ministers, and rabbis, and occasional impromptu contacts with the milkman, the newspaper boy, neighborhood children, and dogs who may drop by.

Social isolation also occurs when older persons can no longer communicate easily with the world around them because of blindness, deafness, and even loss of the ability to speak. Here again, the more physically active partner suffers some of the same isolation. When familiar social patterns, formerly shared by both husband and wife, are lost for one, they are often lost for both.

But social isolation comes not only from physical causes. It can come from death of close family members: husband, sister, brother, friend. Even more tragic for the elderly is when death strikes younger generations: children, nieces, nephews, even grandchildren. When those ties which have been so close for so long have been broken, how can they ever be replaced? Some old people live long enough to see their entire generation disappear and every close relative and friend they have ever known. There may be no one left in the world to call them by their first names. The only human voices they ever hear may be those of the grocer, the doctor, the minister, and the disembodied voices coming from the radio and the TV.

Changes in Environment

Social isolation may also result from changes in familiar patterns. Ours is a mobile society; friends and children (even loving and devoted ones) may move far away for jobs or a preferred style of living. Thousands of miles may separate parents from children, friends from friends, although relationships can still remain close even when no longer face-to-face. The telephone, the tape recorder, and the movie camera can keep contacts amazingly alive. Friendly neighborhoods change, too. They become more built-up, less cared for, less residential. Familiar faces disappear off the streets and are replaced by unfamiliar ones. Favorite stores where shopping was a comfortable, even a sociable process, change hands and merchandise, and cause bewilderment to elderly customers. Mr. Malatsky's little delicatessen on the corner may have been replaced by a new modern supermarket, but for your elderly mother nothing will replace Mr. Malatsky. Many children try arguing, shouting, pleading, in vain attempts to dislodge elderly parents or a widowed father or mother from an apartment or a house situated in a neighborhood that is run-down and unsafe. "It was good enough for your father and me for forty years. It was good enough for you as a boy. It's good enough for me now," is a typical response, and nothing short of abduction or a crowbar will budge the speaker.

Because they risk being mugged, robbed, or beaten if they are alone on the streets, older city-dwellers often fear to go out at all. They become shut-ins or limit their outings to certain "safe" times of day. "I rush to be home every day at four thirty P.M. My son calls me to see that I'm home," is a typical statement from an aging urban resident. Being inside, however, is not necessarily much safer than being outside. One elderly woman interviewed by a *New York Times* reporter about crime in her neighborhood described the system she had invented to burglar-proof her apartment:

> *I now have my valuables, if there's anything a little valuable which I haven't got much of any more, hidden away in a place where nobody will look. My television I have covered up with blankets and a pillow. It looks like a day bed. Or I put it in the bathtub with a load of clothes on it. I do it every morning. It's like a baby —I put it to bed.*
>
> *When my son came in he said, "Where in the name of God did you put the television I gave you?" I said, "It's there." "Where?" "It's in the bathtub." He said, "I didn't see it." I said, "You weren't supposed to."*

To the despair of their children, elderly parents often cling to familiar walls even though an alien country lies right outside their front doors.

Loss of Familiar Roles

The elderly cannot escape undergoing some changes in their customary roles, all the various patterns of behavior that accompany an individual's numerous positions or statuses in life—behavior that others expect from him and he expects from himself.

In the course of a lifetime people assume a multitude of roles. They take on the role of parent, breadwinner, homemaker, spouse, church member, athlete—even black sheep. But then, as individuals age in our society, they lose or voluntarily give up a number of their earlier roles, in extreme cases all of them. Here again there is variation. Some roles are given up easily; others are more painful to lose. Older people no longer fulfill a parenting role unless they live with their children and grandchildren, and even then they may have to take on a less direct role and are rarely encouraged to interfere. The role of meddler is not usually acceptable. Because of mandatory retirement age, the breadwinning role is given up somewhat early. Eking out a small pension as babysitter or watchman does not replace the prestige of the role of breadwinner.

In other times and other societies, the elderly who no longer were able to perform their former roles could turn to auxiliary ones and continue to be, as well as feel, useful and needed in their communities. Among the polar Eskimos, old couples helped in summer to store the winter's supply of bird meat; old women too feeble to travel stayed indoors doing household chores and repairing clothing. They tanned leather, chewing it to make it soft. Elderly men made seal spears and nets. There is a shortage of meaningful auxiliary roles for the elderly in our society.

The one role left for many older people is the role of householder. "My own place," whether a house or an apartment, can symbolize the last rampart, and it can become crucially important to defend it. That may be one reason why older people so often refuse to leave familiar neighborhoods and are far less likely to move than other younger Americans. Even the final role of householder is removed when the elderly need to enter a home for the aged or an institution. Here they can only fulfill a dependent role: the role of patient or resident is rarely satisfying.

Many do make successful adjustments to role loss. Some actually thrive on being relieved of burdensome demands, and find greater contentment in the final years than in the previous ones. "I'm an old lady and glad of it!" insisted one active grandmother on her eightieth birthday. "I don't have to prove anything to anyone any more. No more competing, no more pretending—I can just be myself now." Those who hold on to some threads of a career, who manage to keep some job identification, usually suffer less, and some who find it painful to lose the parent role may derive compensatory satisfaction—sometimes even greater satisfaction—from the role of grandparent. Some older people maintain their sexual identities, their male and female roles, through a continuing active sexual life. But even taking these successful examples into acount, loss of an important role can be a painful blow to the self-regard and emotional well-being of some of the elderly population.

Loss of Financial Security

The financial problems of the aged affect every aspect of their lives: physical, social, and emotional. For the elderly—able or disabled— diminishing financial resources or inadequate financial resources present serious problems. Persons over sixty-five are the most deprived group in the nation, with the exception of racial minority groups. A very tragic aspect of this situation is that most of the elderly poor are poor for the first time in their lives.

In other times and places the elderly could expect that the struggles and labors of their earlier years would be rewarded in their later years by comfort and security. "I shall cherish your old age with plenty of venison and you shall live easy," was the customary assurance of an Iroquois son to his father. Even poor Job, afflicted for so long by trial and tribulation, could relax when he became old!

So the Lord blessed the latter end of Job more than his beginning: for he had fourteen thousand sheep, and six thousand camels, and a thousand yoke of oxen and a thousand she asses.

There are many growing old in America today who cannot expect such comfort and security ahead. Too many learn that to grow old is to grow poor.

The purpose of the Social Security Act, passed in 1935 as part of President Franklin Roosevelt's New Deal, was to guarantee basic economic security to older Americans. In the words of Supreme Court Justice Benjamin Cardozo, "The hope behind this statute is to save men and women from the rigors of the poorhouse as well as from the haunting fear that such a lot awaits them when journey's end is near."

Although Social Security has gone a long way to relieve the economic plight of the elderly, today, nearly forty years after the act was passed, the "haunting fear of poverty—and poverty itself" is a daily reality for too many. Some 15 percent of those over sixty-five live at or below the poverty threshhold defined by the government in 1975 as $2,572 annually for a single person and $3,232 for a couple (monthly: $214 single, $269 couple).

Most people who have been active in the labor force face mandatory retirement. Overnight their incomes are severely reduced. The postretirement income for millions of retirees consists only of their monthly Social Security benefits, which in July 1976 averaged $221.00, the exact amount depending on how much they had paid in prior to retirement, supplemented for some by pensions which are not much higher. Alone or even in combination these amounts rarely approximate a retired person's former income. In addition, increases in Social Security payments and pension checks cannot keep up with the inflationary spiral of the present. In 1970 there were substantial increases in Social Security benefits, and the number of elderly Americans below the poverty level declined for several years. But now inflation has caught up with the increased benefits and eroded them completely. In 1975 there was no decline in the poverty figures among the elderly. For lack of other sources of income, those over sixty-five are forced to augment inadequate incomes by using savings built up with struggle over the years, or they may turn to their children or fall back on public assistance. Many still reject this solution because of the stigma that they feel is carried with it, and they scrape along on a subhuman level. "Somebody's cat is eating well," said the cashier to the little old lady piling up cans of cat food on the check-out counter. "I'm the cat," she replied.

A retired mechanic probably once could feel somewhat secure as his nest egg piled up in his savings account, but now he watches with dread as the inflationary spiral turns a tidy sum into an insignificant pittance. In the face of today's cost of living, a few thousand dollars in the bank will not provide warmth and comfort for many winters.

For some mysterious reason government economic experts seem to think that older people have fewer needs than younger ones. The Bureau of Labor Statistics has worked out a series of sample budgets for a variety of families, and all of these budgets reflect the assumption that older people need less for clothing, home furnishings, travel, even for their pets. Whether the old need to spend as much on clothing, travel, entertainment, or furniture as the young is open to argument but there is no argument about the fact that the old have greater medical expenses and account for one fourth of the nation's expenditure on health. Those over sixty-five spend on the average three times as much for prescribed medicine alone as those under sixty-five. The Medicare and Medicaid programs administered under the Social Security Act cover many health costs, but there are significant loopholes in both programs, so that extreme financial burdens often fall on the very people these programs were established to protect. Costs that are not covered by Medicare must be shouldered by the individual and his private insurance, if he is fortunate enough to have any.

Earlier in this chapter we mentioned that some people seem able to compensate better than others for the variety of losses experienced in old age. It is not always easy to explain these differential reactions but in light of diminished finances they are more understandable. An older person living on a small Social Security check and a small pension may desperately need orthopedic appliances to compensate for progressive arthritis, but he simply does not have the financial ability to purchase them. If compensatory devices are not provided under Medicare, they might as well not exist. The financial limitations of life are among the most severe obstacles blocking elderly people from compensating for the problems of aging.

Financial insecurity and money problems do not vanish above the poverty level. Fear of reduced income may realistically haunt even middle-income elderly couples and individuals who have substantial assets, a car, an unmortgaged house, and many personal possessions collected over a lifetime. When regular salaries and incomes stop coming in, healthy seventy-year-olds with thousands of dollars' worth of assets are not unrealistic when they worry, "When this is gone, what will happen to me?"

Financial curtailment, if not financial hardship, is a fact of life with most elderly people, except in the small highest-income groups. When one half of the urban elderly are living below the poverty line, it may seem difficult to sympathize with the comfortable elderly matron who bemoans the loss of her servants, her trips to Europe, and her country home. But they are real losses in her life, and she may have great difficulty adjusting to them. Her emotional health may be threatened, if not her physical existence or her daily bread. Furthermore, money in our society represents not only purchasing power, but social power as well. It brings prestige, respect, control of others. It may also provide for immortality. Some older people are reluctant to spend their money or see it dwindle away, because they hope to leave legacies to younger family members. If they have no money to leave, they fear they will not be remembered after they die.

Financial insecurity—whether absolute, as in the poverty levels; relative, as in the more affluent levels of society; or even imagined, as among the wealthy—can produce severe emotional consequences which make it additionally difficult for older men and women to make satisfactory adjustments.

Loss of Independence and Power

The combination of some or all of the losses described in the previous sections—loss of physical health, familiar roles, social contacts, and financial security—can precipitate several other losses which have particular meaning in our society: the losses of independence and power, qualities which are highly regarded personal assets today, particularly for men. The loss of either or both can be a stunning blow to an older person's self-esteem.

Increased dependency is forced willy-nilly on the severely disabled elderly. They must accept help, which can pose severe problems for themselves and for close family members who must care for them. Severe problems are also created for the larger society, which is expected to provide medical, nursing, and protective care. Increased dependency can affect all the invalid's social relationships. The disabled ones may overreact to their needs and become too dependent and too demanding. They may try to deny their dependence or mask its magnitude by "showing who's boss" and ruling their relatives, wives, and children, curtailing everyone else's freedom and independence. We've all heard these relatives commenting helplessly from time to time, "We try to do everything Mother wants, but it never seems to be enough!"

Conversely, the disabled ones may try vehemently to deny their dependency by insisting, in the face of all handicaps, "I can manage perfectly well," and refusing the willing offers of help essential to maintaining health. Independence can be admirable, but when carried too far can lead to trouble. The loss of financial security, especially if it is severe, also contributes to the loss of independence. Many older people are just about able to scrape along on Social Security benefits even when these are supplemented by meager pensions. They must live from check to check, each month's activities determined by carefully allocated dollars and cents rather than by personal preferences and inclinations.

You may be financially able, willing, and eager to provide additional funds for your parents. You may even insist on doing so. But when forced to accept money from their children, many older people feel that they are surrendering, in return, much of their independence, so the extra income may prove to be at best only a mixed blessing. Your monthly check may be a sweet and loving gesture on your part, but it may be received as somewhat bitter medicine by your parents, who had grown accustomed through their lives to earning their own money, paying their own way, feeding and educating their families—and taking care of *you.*

If the day finally comes when an older person finds it impossible to manage on his own financially or physically, and must accept institutional living, the greatest sacrifice he may have to make is the final portion of his independence. Institutionalization, by its very nature, seems to symbolize that ultimate loss and probably explains why so many older people prefer inadequate, isolated living conditions to the protective care of even the best institutions.

A sense of personal independence—autonomy—is considered to be such an essential positive value that many forward-looking professionals are currently searching for ways to maintain this feeling among their patients even within the institutional framework.

No one would suggest that the elderly are a powerful group in our society, although their reawakened awareness of their own numbers, and therefore their power at the polls, is presently increasing their political clout. Their voices are being heard through groups like the Gray Panthers and the Congress of Senior Citizens. In our culture, however, groups who are in general financially less well off, whose social contacts may be fewer, and who include greater numbers of severely disabled individuals—blind, deaf, handicapped— have less power and therefore can safely be disregarded by society. Those groups may be justified in feeling, "Who listens?" or "Who cares?"

That disregard is best dramatized by the heavy concentration society places on the needs of our children. We should, of course, be deeply concerned with the health, education, and welfare of our young, although admittedly some of our more fortunate young receive a larger share of our concern than others do. But this wholesome regard for the young seems to carry with it an unwholesome disregard for the elderly. A more even-handed show of concern is possible and can be seen in some of the more socially advanced countries of Europe, such as Sweden and Denmark.

The treatment of the blind population in America offers a perfect example of how our society views its priorities. In the 1960s there were more than eight hundred agencies and programs for the blind. It was estimated then that nearly two thirds of these catered exclusively to the young. Some 60 percent of available funds are earmarked for blind children and adults who are not aged. Yet about half of the total blind population in America is over sixty-five and only one third under fifty-five.

More than 20 million elderly citizens in this country have managed to remain generally unnoticed for too long. Even though their needs are beginning to be recognized now, much more concern will have to be shown by the year 2000, when their number is expected to rise even more dramatically, particularly in the later decades. So many of their plain, simple, ordinary, everyday needs are unmet in modern society today. Until recently medical and other related professional schools have placed little stress on the importance of training specialists equipped to deal with geriatric problems. The transportation needs of the elderly are rarely considered, and there is a real lack of public conveyances fitted to their physical requirements. Look at the high steps on buses and the long flights of stairs into the subways. Our automobile-dependent society is particularly hard on the elderly, who have been forced to give up their cars because of limited vision or slowed reflexes. Many rural and suburban areas, where one-, two-, and three-car families prevail, have discontinued all forms of public transportation, so elderly citizens without cars become cut off and socially isolated for still another reason. Medical needs may be neglected when regular visits to doctors or clinics are difficult to arrange. Nutrition may be inadequate when there is no market within easy walking distance.

Adequate and appropriate housing for the elderly has not been generally considered to be important. Few apartments are designed to provide the safety measures necessary for older people trying to live independent lives: such as hand rails in the bathrooms or safe kitchen appliances. Even the manufacturers and advertisers have shown a cavalier disregard for this large group of potential customers, granted their dwindling incomes keep them from heavy spending. Hardly a product is advertised on television which might ease the life of an older person, except Geritol, and even that product is being pushed further and further down in order to appeal to a younger, more affluent "buying" public.

Modern America does not regard its elderly very highly, and the elderly are fully aware of this. They seem to be a low-status group and they know it. Prevailing attitudes are damaging. According to Louis Harris in *The Myth and Reality of Aging in America*,

> they confront older people with a society who sees them merely as a problem and not as part of the solution to any of society's problems. Such problems as the public perceive among the elderly can only generate a sense of guilt and pity among the young, and not a sense of appreciation for the talents and energies that older people can still contribute to society. As a result, older people are not likely to find themselves the recipients of opportunities to pitch in and help solve the problems that affect our society as a whole. As a group for whom there is little social and economic demand, the older population also may lose self-esteem with deleterious effects.

Loss of Mental Stability

You may have noticed that the discussion of each of the areas of loss examined in the preceding pages ends with the mention of the psychological ramifications: the effects on the emotional well-being, the egos, the self-esteem of the elderly. Psychological problems resulting from losses, as well as those triggered by other threats, real or imaginary, are often the most difficult to handle. In dealing with your own parents you may have already discovered that their psychological problems place the heaviest demands on your own emotional resources. Physical incapacity can present enough problems; they become even more difficult to deal with when they are accompanied by increased dependency, financial hardship, and social isolation. The physical picture grows more complex when psychological problems are added. Those problems can be very perplexing for the children of the elderly, especially when the emotions of both generations become intertwined. It is not unusual for a family to report that an elderly relative has undergone a real personality change: "He's not the same person he used to be," or "I just don't know my mother any more." Surprisingly enough, some personality changes are for the better although many, admittedly, are for the worse.

As your parents begin to age, psychological difficulties may appear for the first time, developing in direct response to their physical and social losses. But those psychological difficulties may also be continuations of lifelong emotional problems which, successfully held in check at earlier times, become intensified in old age, and therefore more difficult to control.

What Are the Psychological Problems?

They include a familiar list—depression, anxiety, hypochondriasis, psychosomatic disorders, alcoholism, unwarranted suspiciousness, and sometimes severe neurotic and psychotic reactions. There's nothing really new or special in this list. These are the psychological problems of all ages—the young as well as the old—but statistics reveal that some appear with greater frequency in the population sixty-five and over. This greater frequency occurs, in part, because of the higher incidence of depression among the elderly, and also because of the organic brain disorders of the elderly which produce their own special symptoms, including disorientation, loss of memory, confusion, and wandering.

There is no doubt that psychological problems are closely related to the physiological losses of aging. But physiological damage to the brain or sense organs is only one cause. All the areas of loss, as well as other stressful changes confronting the older person which have been discussed earlier, can individually or in combination trigger psychological problems.

It is always important to remember that older people do not necessarily react in the same way to the same loss. What is stressful to one may not be stressful to another. Some also have a far greater capacity to withstand stress, although the elderly in general are less equipped physiologically to handle stress than younger people. Old people do not come naked into old age—they bring with them the accumulated experiences of a lifetime. It is generally believed that if people have developed successful capacities to deal with change and difficulty at earlier stages of life, they will more easily face the insults and injuries of old age. Rich experiences and resourceful capacities accumulated throughout life can be priceless treasures to draw on in later years. Studies in which old people have been followed from earlier ages to later ones have shown this continuity. The same loss which is devastating to some becomes for others a new challenge to face and overcome.

Certain patterned psychological responses to loss are commonly seen in older persons and, while upsetting to relatives and difficult to deal with, must be accepted as within normal range. Other types of behavior are so extreme that they must be considered pathological.

"Normal" Reactions to Loss

It is completely normal to react to loss emotionally. The emotions your parents feel in their old age are no different from childhood emotions, young adult emotions, and middle-aged emotions. The infant faces loss when giving up the close dependent relationship with its mother; the adolescent when breaking away from parental authority; the middle-aged adult when facing the loss of youth. The elderly react with the very same emotions to the physiological and social losses accompanying old age as well as to the indignities and neglect imposed by society. The latter are particularly hard for some older men who find the experience of helplessness especially painful. Since losses appear with greater variety and frequency in old age than in any other stage of life, anxiety and depression, fear and anger and guilt, can be anticipated. They are normal, even appropriate, emotions. You would certainly be surprised if an older person who had suffered a severe loss did *not* seem to be sad or angry— if he did *not* grieve. More damage can be caused when the mourning process is circumvented. "We shouldn't leave Mother alone today —she'll only sit and think about Dad," may be an understandable, well-meant, loving reaction from concerned children shortly after a father's funeral. Yet perhaps that's just the very thing Mother *needs* to do for a while before she's ready to do anything else. Oversolicitous relatives can sometimes cause as much harm as neglectful ones. Mourning plays an essential part in making a healthy adjustment to the loss of a beloved person. It helps those who mourn to work through their grief and redirect their energies to new interests in life.

Anxiety and fear play equally useful roles. There's nothing abnormal about an older person's fears for his future—he's got every right to be afraid within reason. If a person's eyesight is failing, it is perfectly realistic for him to wonder how he will manage for himself and to feel a diffuse sense of foreboding. It's also realistic for someone who has already had one heart attack to be concerned about his health or even to fear approaching death.

Anger is also to be expected as a normal emotional reaction to loss. When you've suffered an injury or an insult, what's wrong with being angry? After all, anger is an emotion of retribution, a way of striking back at whatever has caused an injury. Just as a young child gets angry at the hammer with which he has smashed his own finger, an older person may get angry at the gods or the fates or whatever he believes may have caused a particular loss. Your father may even direct his anger at you for lack of a better target and feel guilty as a result. There's no need to be alarmed when your parents exhibit fear, anxiety, grief, or anger. They are not pleasant emotions—no one claims they are—but they may be necessary, even therapeutic, at certain periods. Your parents should not have to feel guilty if they show those emotions, nor should you feel guilty yourself. There is room for those feelings in the total context of life.

Older people, like younger ones, develop special behavior patterns which help them to ward off anxiety, depression, or a fear of uncontrollable rage. These behavior patterns are important to their own sense of survival. They may be within a "normal range," although you may, on occasion, find them bewildering, frustrating, even infuriating. It is important to note that these patterns of behavior are used by all ages, although the old may rely on some of them more than the young.

One of the most potentially effective behavior patterns employed by the elderly, yet misunderstood by their families, is *living in the past.* As death approaches, many older people spend much time reminiscing—going through a life-review. Remembrance of things past can be a painful process, but it can also be comforting. It can provide meaningful significance to the final years and help to reduce fear and anxiety. Living in the past is often mistakenly seen as a symptom of brain damage: "What's the matter with Father? He can remember the name of his first-grade teacher, but he can't remember his neighbor's name or whether he's had lunch or not!" At best the tendency to live in the past is viewed as unnecessary nostalgia —an unfortunate disengagement from the present—or as self-preoccupation. You may despair that your parents always seize every opportunity to discuss their past life with you or with anyone else who will listen, but it may be an indication of health rather than a sign of deterioration. If so, it should be encouraged, not stifled.

Some older people, while not seriously depressed, do not bounce back from a period of mourning and are never again ready to contemplate new directions. Mourning can become a lifestyle, best described as *preparatory mourning.* It can be seen as a protective pattern of behavior and is often reflected in a morbid interest in death, a fascination with obituaries, and a preoccupation with funerals—even those of strangers. All of us know people who, even in the prime of life, turn first to the death notices of the daily paper. Some older people find this their favorite section.

One testy seventy-year-old used to horrify his grandchildren at the breakfast table by chuckling cheerfully as he scanned the obituary page of the newspaper every morning: "Well, I see another old friend of mine has made headlines today!" Preparatory mourning can be seen in the widow who refuses to discard her black clothes years after her husband's death. She still mourns for the past, but also for her future losses. Preparatory mourning is exhibited in the gloomy interpretation of all events, even happy ones, including the activities of younger family members: "She's a lovely child. I do hope she doesn't inherit her grandmother's weak heart!" or "What a beautiful day—there are sure to be a lot of accidents on the highway!"

"Old Mr. Jones is really showing his age these days, isn't he?" commented Mr. Smith to his daughter. Mr. Smith himself is eighty years old, bent with arthritis, walking with a cane, and increasingly hard of hearing. Yet he is only able to notice the signs of aging in others—not in himself. His own old age and impending death are not conscious realities to him. He uses *denial*—a common defense —to ward off facing his own advancing years and the painful feelings accompanying this advance. Denial, used in moderation, is a necessary and useful mechanism for maintaining a sense of stability and equilibrium. If it is carried too far, however, it can become hazardous. The elderly may deny pain and physical symptoms until they are beyond help; they may deny dependency, deafness, blindness, and confusion, thereby jeopardizing their safety. Denial need not be limited to physical symptoms or sensory losses and may be used in relation to other losses as well. A seventy-five-year-old widow seemed to take the drastic reduction in her finances after her husband's death with remarkable good will—or so her children thought, until they discovered that she had simply denied her financial problems and continued to spend her dwindling capital and to use her charge accounts as if there had been no change. Denial is not uncommon, nor is it dangerous in itself. Only if it interferes with reality and prevents sound decisions can it then be legitimately considered a serious problem.

You may sense that your father is becoming increasingly suspicious as he grows older. That is quite possible. *Mistrustful behavior* is sometimes used by the elderly. Some forms of this behavior stem from an unconscious process and arise when the elderly project their own uneasy feelings elsewhere—away from themselves. Having unconsciously attributed these uneasy feelings to other people, they then may be consciously fearful of these people. Mistrustfulness which has no visible roots can be bewildering and upsetting to families and may, if carried to extremes, be considered a mental illness.

Some mistrustful behavior can be more easily understood and clearly grounded in reality. It may be realistic and self-protective. A frail old man can be at the mercy of other people who are stronger. He may become a prime target for abuse and exploitation. Caution and suspicion may be the only weapons he has with which to protect himself. Sometimes the elderly are not mistrustful enough!

Other forms of mistrustful behavior, although unwarranted, are rooted somewhere in reality and stem from the anxiety aging men and women feel as independence slips away from them. Once able to care for themselves independently, but now increasingly dependent on someone else, they begin to wonder if that "someone" is really doing right by them. They feel they must watch out for their own interests or "someone" will take advantage of them: cheat them, rob them, hurt them. You may find it quite painful when that suspicious "someone" turns out to be you. The concerned child who is trying hardest to help may accidentally become the target for mistrust and the focus for the anger which can accompany it.

"Stubbornness" and *"avoidance of change"* are two particularly successful and related adaptive patterns of behavior used by the elderly. Both are likely to be extremely frustrating to children, close friends, and other relatives. "I can't budge him!" is a familiar cry from a long-suffering son or daughter trying in vain to help an aging father. "He won't listen," "won't move," "won't see a doctor," "won't watch his diet." Stubbornness is also used as a magical solution to fight the forces which disrupt life, and it's remarkable how strongly a frail one-hundred-pound old woman is able to resist the combined weight of hundreds of pounds of concerned relatives. So many changes and losses are forced on the elderly, as the years go by, that they may often try to control their lives in such a way that they can avoid change whenever possible. To that end a whole way of life may be developed. When your parents insist on remain-

ing in a familiar house, apartment, or neighborhood, even though they agree with you that the neighborhood is changed, the house is too big for them, and the apartment is too isolated, they are obviously avoiding change, although you may see this as "stubbornness."

A pattern of avoidance can also operate more subtly. It can explain fear of travel—fear of even leaving the house—or refusal to consider new activities, meet new people, or try new doctors or new medicines, even though they know the old ones are not doing them much good. Avoidance of change and stubbornness can often be used by the elderly as a kind of protective armor that wards off the changes well-meaning children or relatives would like to impose.

❖ MR. THOMPSON ALWAYS thought of taxis as extravagant, and he had lived frugally all his life. But it was unsafe for him to walk home alone at night. His children begged him to take taxis, but he refused to pay for that extravagance or let his children indulge in it. He could not allow himself to change the frugal habits of a lifetime. He found it easier to risk the danger.

*

❖ MRS. GROSS BECAME a quasi shut-in. She only went out for occasional emergencies. Her children made superhuman efforts to dislodge her, urging her to "come to dinner," or "come to the movies," or "come for a drive." "It's for your own good," they insisted. But she turned down all invitations. She was, however, very sociable, always delighted to have visitors and to serve light meals very hospitably. Mrs. Gross did not ask her children for help and was contented with her life.

Admittedly there are cases where parents do act out of spite, refusing to change a lifestyle that disturbs their children *just because* it does disturb them. They may find this a successful way to produce guilt among those closest to them. By clinging to a disturbing pattern they seem to say, "See how miserable my life is!"

Closely connected with avoidance of change is a passionate, although often inappropriate, *worship of independence.* Many older people see independence as another weapon with which to protect themselves from outside interference. To the horror of family, friends, and social agencies, aging men and women often reject safe and protective surroundings, and endure drab furnished rooms, inadequate nourishment, and irregular health care, in order to preserve that treasured state. It is painful to accept the fact that when independence is weighed against protected living in a child's home, independence often wins. But painful as that is, relatives should understand that when such a value is given to independence, its loss could trigger a devastating emotional reaction.

Overdoing it is a very common defense among the elderly against depression, anxiety, and other painful conditions. "When in trouble, keep busy," is the rule they appear to be following.

❖ JOHN PARKER, after his retirement, had adapted to a fairly leisurely and involved way of life. That included a little volunteer work, puttering around the house, visiting his cronies. But most of his time was spent with his wife in a variety of shared pursuits, particularly traveling. After she died from a cerebral hemorrhage, John Parker threw himself into his volunteer activities, running for office as the head of the local senior citizens' club, spending many hours in his activities, and seeming to relish it. Keeping busy was good medicine in John's case—it warded off painful depression and gave him the leeway he needed to work slowly through his grief over the death of his wife. But his children were undoubtedly concerned that by "overdoing it" he was jeopardizing his health.

You may feel that your mother has become a slave to routine, that she wants everything to be "just so," that every move—coming in, going out, dressing, eating, going to bed—seems to involve a whole series of regular steps. She's probably involved in *ritualistic behavior*. Some people behave as if repetitious ritual has the magical power to ward off evil and the threat of future loss. That kind of behavior also helps the handicapped to compensate for sensory and memory losses and thereby bolster their command of their environment. So even though you tap your foot impatiently as your mother spends ten minutes putting out these lights and putting on those, and checking the windows, the gas on the stove, the jewel box, and the refrigerator before she is able to put on her sweater and go out for a walk, remind yourself that she's not necessarily losing her grip but rather reinforcing her sense of security.

Extreme Reactions

Behavior patterns and feelings—"normal" when kept within limits—become serious when they go out of bounds and interfere with your parents' overall ability to function. Someone who is still mourning after more than a year, and showing no signs of recovery, may be suffering from a depressive reaction. Someone who is continually anxious about his health, even though a competent doctor has pronounced him in fine shape, may have a psychiatric problem. Someone who gets angry for an inordinate amount of time and, even worse, directs his anger broadside at anyone in his path— engaging in verbal, even physical, violence—is certainly showing an emotional problem. Grief, anger, anxiety—all "normal" emotions— can lead to severe difficulties which may require psychiatric attention when they are unremitting and intense. Other severe problems may develop independently of those intense reactions to loss and stress—organic brain disease is one cause. For the most part, however, those intense reactions play an important role in mental disturbances of the elderly. Here are several of the more common ones.

Depression

Depression as a mental disorder is quite different from the temporary moods almost everyone experiences from time to time, moods which we describe by saying, "I feel so depressed today." The symptoms of a real depression go beyond "blue" feelings and are not always obvious. Prolonged periods of insomnia, fatigue, lack of appetite, agitation or various psychosomatic ailments may all be indications of depression, although the correct diagnosis is often overlooked.

So-called depressive reactions in later life often can be related to earlier experiences. A person who has lost a great deal as a child, or has never worked through the conflicts of childhood satisfactorily, may suffer periods of depression repeatedly throughout the life cycle. Depression, mild or severe, may return when there is a reminder of early childhood trauma—the loss of a parent, the rejection of a parent, illness, deprivation. The onslaughts of aging can be such grim reminders of earlier losses that they can trigger acute depressive states. Depression can also be an extension of unresolved mourning. Extreme depression is one of the causes of the high rate of suicide among the elderly, particularly among elderly men.

Depression can mask other conflicts: severe guilt, shame, or unacceptable anger. If a person cannot accept these feelings he may turn them inward, bringing on an apparent state of depression. Loss normally produces some depression and anger, but if a person in any way feels responsible for the loss he has suffered, he may suffer as well the painful feelings of guilt and shame. That is especially true when death comes to someone who has been very dependent, very troublesome, or very unloving. The partner who survives may feel all the more guilty. (The same kind of depression may afflict grown children when a difficult, troublesome parent dies.)

Hypochondriasis

Hypochondriasis, a neurotic reaction, is an excessive concern with health accompanied by unfounded physical complaints. In mild forms hypochondriasis can be acceptable, even useful. Older people should be encouraged to take care of their health. However, when carried to an extreme and turned into an all-consuming activity, this type of behavior can be a major problem. Hypochondriasis has a number of meanings. Some professionals say that older people tend to withdraw their interests from the world around them and, in preparing for death, turn their interest inward—to their bodies. Others say, conversely, that the world of the elderly becomes so limited that, lacking other interests, they focus on themselves. Hypochondriasis, as a form of behavior, can be an excellent attention-getting device for someone who feels neglected or left out, as the elderly often do, or it may be part of an individual's life history. Hypochondriacs are found in every age group, and young hypochondriacs are likely to grow into old hypochondriacs. This behavior is sometimes used to identify with a lost loved one, or as a means of self-punishment. Whatever the cause, intense bodily preoccupation can prevent otherwise normal, healthy older people from living satisfying lives. In addition, it can rub off and interfere with the normal living of everyone close to them.

Psychotic Reactions

When people lose contact with the world around them, psychotic reactions may occur. They may see, hear, or think things which have no basis in reality. Overanxious, depressed, and angry feelings can precipitate psychotic reactions, which can also result from severe impairment to the sense organs and the brain. Loss of hearing can affect mental stability—the deaf often turn to their own inner world for sensory clues. Unable to hear what is going on around them, they invent explanations. Furthermore, brain impairment can interfere with an older person's ability to process information from the real world, thereby setting off or compounding a psychotic reaction. Paranoid states are a type of psychotic disorder involving delusions of thinking, and false beliefs of persecution and victimization.

Chronic Organic Brain Disorders

Less amenable to treatment are the chronic organic brain disorders. Closely akin to the irreversible physical losses of aging discussed earlier in this chapter, these disorders alone or in conjunction with other mental disorders can result in serious behavioral and emotional difficulties for older persons. (Chronic conditions should be differentiated from reversible brain syndromes, which are often the result of other physical conditions and are amenable to treatment.)

Organic brain disorders are mental conditions caused by or associated with impairment of brain tissue function. Their distinctive features include disturbance and impairment of memory, intellectual function or comprehension, judgment, orientation, or the presence of emotional instability. All those signs may not be present except in the most advanced stages of organic brain disease, and even then they may come and go from day to day. Older people with very advanced conditions, in addition to suffering mental impairment, may also be incontinent. (While incontinence is often associated with damage to the nervous system, this is not the only cause. It also can be the direct result of other physical conditions.) For the families the most upsetting aspect of advanced organic brain disease may occur when an elderly relative no longer recognizes anyone, even those who have always been nearest and dearest.

It is important to note that there is no absolute relationship between the degree of organic damage an older person suffers and the actual way in which he functions. Additional important factors that enter into his ability to function are his physical and emotional health, his own adaptive capacities, and other resources accumulated over a lifetime upon which he may draw. Very often, the older person is written off as hopeless or "senile" because of the presence of brain disease. Other contributing conditions which may be amenable to treatment and help are too quickly overlooked. For example, experimentation is now going on with chemical and mechanical means to increase the supply of oxygen to the brain. It has been found that improving the blood supply to the brain through the use of electronic cardiac pacemakers in elderly patients often results in improved mental status and behavior.

Indirect Psychological Problems

Psychological reactions among the elderly are not always expressed in extreme emotional states or difficult behavior. Like the brain and nervous system, other organ systems depleted by cellular loss and tissue change can show physiological breakdown as a result of psychological stress. Anxiety in particular has been shown to be related to cardiovascular difficulties. All the various systems of the body—the neurological, the cardiovascular, the gastrointestinal—depleted by age, may no longer have the backup reserves to withstand headlong attacks from the emotions.

It may seem that this chapter has opened up a Pandora's box of catastrophes—a terrifying catalogue of afflictions the mind and body are subject to as the aging process goes on. But we have tried to separate the inevitable from the reversible, the normal from the abnormal, the routine from the exceptional. Old age is full of endless possibilities—long-suffering acceptance, dreary monotony, grim misery, high tragedy—as well as deep satisfaction, unexpected gratification, serenity, and even fun.

5.

Marriage, Widowhood, Remarriage, and Sex

Like my father, I've learned that the love we have in our youth is superficial compared to the love that an old man has for his old wife. "My old gray-haired wife," my father used to call my mother. And I can still remember her saying as she passed the food around the table on their 50th anniversary, "I thank God for giving me this old man to take care of."
Interview with philosopher Will Durant, *New York Times*, November 6, 1975

Will Durant was celebrating his ninetieth birthday on the day of this interview. He himself had been married to his wife, Ariel, for more than sixty-two years. The public responds with delight to such stories of marital longevity and contentment. Pictures in magazines and newspapers of a white-haired couple cutting the cake on their golden anniversary are sure to arouse pleasant emotions. No words are necessary—those pictures evoke images of love, tenderness, fidelity, companionship, and mutual support. In some cases these images are true. In others they are not.

For better or for worse, old age affects not only each husband and wife individually but also their life together—their partnership.

The institution of marriage has been examined, probed, and analyzed by scholars, professionals, and the clergy. Much attention has been focused on marital problems in the early and middle years, but little of that scrutiny has been turned on marriage in the later years. Part of this neglect in the past may have been because of the lower life expectancy. Few marriages continued intact with both partners alive in their seventies and eighties.

But there are many of these durable marriages today. There will be even more in the future. In 1955 there were 6.9 million men and women over sixty-five still living with their spouses; in 1970 the number increased to 9.4 million, and it is undoubtedly higher today. (The figures include remarriages as well as the original ones.) The growth of the population in general, as well as current extended life-expectancy, accounts for the dramatic rise in recent years.

Marital Adjustment
in the Retirement Years

After thirty or forty years of life together, then, it would seem that two people would have come to know each other as intimately as possible and, assuming that the marriage has been a relatively stable one, there would be few surprises left. But there may be plenty of surprises in the postretirement period, the greatest one probably being that they do not know each other quite so well after all.

In the middle years—particularly if there are children in the family, but even when there are not—husbands and wives usually function independently of each other much of the time, even in the closest of relationships. When they both work, each one goes off every day to separate places. Even if they share all household tasks equally, they are physically in each other's presence only in the evenings, on weekends, and on holidays. When the husband is the sole breadwinner and his wife cares for home and children, there are also many hours of separation. The two may thoroughly enjoy the time they do spend together, yearn for more, steal occasional weekends away, and resent the stresses of life which prevent them from being together more. But the fact remains that their hours together are limited.

In the postretirement years, their hours together are limitless. Unless they have prepared themselves in advance with activities and routines to share together or ones which will take them in different directions for some time at least, they may face each other twenty-four hours a day, seven days a week, Saturdays, Sundays, and holidays. Like children on rainy afternoons they may say, "There's no place to go. There's nothing to do."

When both husband and wife have had careers, each one at some point past sixty may have to develop a new, different (sometimes even more rewarding) lifestyle for the retirement years. But the housewife and mother whose children are launched by the time she is in her early fifties or younger usually faces her midlife crisis—sometimes known as the Empty Nest Syndrome—much earlier. She may face her menopause at the same time. Her husband, still in his mid-fifties and probably still in mid-career, may remind her, with understanding and compassion (or possibly with irritation and ex-asperation), that she has always wanted to "eat dinner at a civilized time," or "go back to school," or sell real estate, volunteer at the hospital, spend time at a club, go into politics. He may even wonder how she can be depressed when she finally has the time to do all the things she always complained she had no time for. She may go ahead and do any one of these things, or instead devote herself to domestic routines, gardens, close involvement with children or grandchildren. During the next ten or fifteen years, while her hus-band is still actively involved in his own work, she may establish a very satisfactory way of life for herself. But suddenly one day, after the gold watch has been presented and the farewell dinner for her husband is over, she may find she suddenly has a constant companion sharing or possibly interfering with that new way of life.

She may watch her husband go through some of the same confu-sion and uncertainty she herself had known years before and may say to him as he had said to her long ago (also with understanding or exasperation), "You always wanted to go fishing," or do more carpentry; take up golf, painting, sculpture; learn a foreign lan-guage; work in a settlement house. Many men—sometimes joined by their wives—do develop new interests by enrolling in adult education classes or university courses. But often the same activities which, in their working days, seemed to promise relaxation and satisfaction, now lose their appeal for the retirees and appear more as idle puttering and meaningless time-filling.

Sweden, which prides itself on its elaborate network of social and economic care which covers its entire population from birth to death, provides its elderly population with great financial security. Yet the government, recognizing the psychological hazards of retirement, is trying to set up a system in which workers can move into retirement slowly, tapering off their working hours between the ages of sixty and seventy so that when they stop working completely, they will have made their adjustment to a new lifestyle.

The United States has no such tapering-off period, but many men and women prepare themselves by thinking through alternative patterns for the future and developing compromises that will satisfy both partners in a marriage. Such advance preparation is usually the best insurance against the apathy, depression, anger, and interper-sonal conflict that lies in wait for many couples.

Retirement can hardly be considered as a shock. Except for the self-employed, retirement is a fact of life. Every worker knows it lies ahead, yet many react to the inevitable with anger and surprise. Your parents may not have planned ahead—or perhaps their plans do not work out as expected. Your father may seem to go downhill after his retirement.

The breadwinner (usually the husband) often feels that by losing his job he also loses his valued role and therefore his prestige, purpose, and self-respect. He may feel aimless, rejected, cast aside, excluded, forgotten, and often reacts with depression, anger, resentment. If he directs those emotions toward the person who is closest to him—his wife—a great strain will be placed on their marriage. You may notice that your parents disagree and bicker as never before. Some newly retired men age dramatically in the first years of inactivity or go through a period of depression—fertile ground, according to some experts, for premature disease and deterioration.

Personalities may clash as they have not done since the early days of marriage. Tastes and interests may be in constant opposition. Your father may want to make the most of his new freedom: to adventure, see the world, rent a camper and gypsy for six months, or sell the house and move away. Your mother may be thoroughly content in the new life she has built for herself and reluctant to leave it—or her children or grandchildren.

Conversely, your mother may be the one with the wanderlust. She may have been waiting all these years for a chance to "live a little." She may be constantly frustrated by your father's preference for a quiet life and resent his inclination to putter around the house, watch TV, lick the wounds caused by his retirement. She may appeal to you in desperation to "help him snap out of it."

After all those years of knowing how to spend weekends and holidays together, a retired couple may seem virtual strangers to each other on weekdays. "Is that what you eat for lunch?" a husband asks his wife as she spoons out cottage cheese. Married for nearly forty years he may not have the slightest idea what she normally eats for lunch or what goes on in his house for eight hours every weekday. "I never knew your father was such a busybody," your mother may sigh to you. "He's into everything I do. He's forever asking me what I'm doing, why I'm doing it, and then telling me how to do it better. I don't have a minute's privacy. Who does he think has been taking care of this house all these years, I'd like to know?" She may complain on a regular basis that he intrudes on her kaffeeklatsches with her friends, insists on buying the groceries, and monitors all her conversations. "The next time he says to me, 'What in God's name do you and Flora have to yak about every day?' I'm going to throw the phone at him."

You may find yourself drawn into their disagreements and be tempted to take sides, either with the parent you are most closely attached to or with the one who seems to be most ill-used. If your father is withdrawn and apathetic, you may criticize him for giving your mother so little pleasure: "He's burying her alive! He doesn't want to do anything himself and he won't let her do anything either." Or you may take his side against her: "Why can't she let him alone? He's worked hard all his life. Doesn't he deserve a little peace now?"

Instead of taking sides with either, you may be critical of both of them and quick to tell them all the mistakes they are making and what they ought to do instead. You may even come up with a variety of wonderful ideas which appeal to you tremendously but might not give them the slightest satisfaction. If, instead of pushing your own solutions, you are able to show some concern, patience, interest, and understanding, they will probably in time work out their *own* solutions—in their *own* way.

Some couples, confused and disturbed by their unaccustomed incompatibility, turn not to their children but to friends, ministers, doctors, and other professionals. "Imagine me—at sixty-seven— going to a marriage counselor!" a retired salesman said sheepishly, at the same time admitting that he and his wife really needed someone to help them smooth out the fraying edges of their forty-four-year marriage. Not infrequently, couples, finding life in the later stages as difficult as in the earlier stages, are turning to professional help. Marriage counselors report what many couples find out for themselves in time: that if a marriage has strong bonds and a firm foundation, it is likely to weather the postretirement crisis and come out intact. Any marriage which has lasted more than forty years has undoubtedly weathered its share of crises in the past.

In Sickness and in Health—for Richer, for Poorer

In addition to adjusting to the changes in daily life produced by retirement itself, many older couples may also have to adjust at some point to each other's failing health, and the dwindling of their joint financial assets. The famous words of the wedding ceremony are really put to the test when husbands and wives live on together into their seventies, eighties, and nineties. Poverty and ill health may come separately or in combination, since the more frequent or chronic the physical disability, the more money must be spent on medical expenses.

Reasonable, well-thought-out plans for retirement can be disrupted overnight by the sudden illness of one partner or the gradual decline of both. Your mother and father may have developed an enjoyable pattern of living, pursuing some activities independently and sharing others, but what if your father has a stroke or a heart attack, or crippling arthritis? He may need constant care. The new life the two have made together may come to an end, yet another pattern has to be developed. Your mother may be ready and able to care for your father, but at the same time, whether she admits it or not, she may resent being so tied down. The strain may affect their relationship with each other.

Illness can also reverse longstanding behavior patterns. A wife who has always been dependent and submissive may find herself forced to take control when her invalid husband can no longer run the show. If a domineering wife is incapacitated she may, for the first time in her married life, have to turn to her henpecked husband, expecting him to manage everything *and* take care of her. Frequently those formerly submissive spouses rather enjoy their new-found power and flourish, despite the burdens they have to assume. They may even turn the tables completely, becoming dictatorial and autocratic, to the amazement of their children, their friends, and their relatives.

Dwindling financial resources, inadequate pensions, Social Security checks which cannot keep up with the nation's rising inflation rate, or heavy medical expenses—all can strain marital relationships, particularly in marriages where money—or the lack of it—has always been a source of conflict. An elderly couple may have to give up their home because of increased rents, higher taxes, or rising maintenance costs, and cramped quarters may contribute to irritation. If they are able to hang on where they have always lived, there may be no money at all for entertainment, relief from monotony, or occasional escapes from each other. Medical expenses may erode their food budget; their health, emotional as well as physical, may deteriorate from inadequate nutrition.

Couples who were always in greatest conflict when life was easier may be drawn closer together by the harsh problems of ill health or poverty. Their days are devoted to fighting off the enemy at their gates, concentrating their energies, husbanding their resources, and caring for each other with greater determination than ever.

The Final Years

As they get older and physically less active, some couples become even more closely involved with each other, zealously watching over each other's health, protecting each other from excitement, sparing each other exertion. At the pace they establish for themselves they may read, walk, market, do the housework, watch TV, listen to music, garden, take their medicine—always together. Relatives and friends may report with admiration, sometimes mixed with irritation, "They don't really need anyone else. They're only interested in each other," or "They think alike, they talk alike, they even look alike."

If the elderly wife in such couples ages more rapidly or is more seriously incapacitated than her husband, he may try to assume full responsibility for her care. The wife may respond in the same way to her invalid husband. A parent-child relationship can develop; if it has always been present in the marriage, it may become more intense.

Those relationships can become so totally interdependent that in time they can tolerate no separation at all. Not infrequently, the death of one spouse is followed within a short time by the death of the other, who may have seemed in comparatively good health. One doctor reports that he was obliged to place a ninety-four-year-old man in intensive care after a severe stroke even though his eighty-nine-year-old wife begged to be allowed to take care of him at home. Two days after her husband was hospitalized, she died of a heart attack.

The family may be understandably concerned when an elderly relative insists on nursing her bedridden husband. Everyone may try to persuade her to institutionalize him or hire a nurse, saying, "You've got a right to live, too." But that may be the only way she wants to live. One seventy-seven-year-old wife, persuaded against her will by her children to place her paralyzed husband in an excellent nursing home, agonized constantly that he was not getting the right care: "They don't shave him the way he likes," or "They always forget the pillow he needs under his legs," or "He'll starve with that slop they feed him." She could not enjoy a minute of her new freedom. "But, Ma," her children kept saying, "He's better off in the home. You would have killed yourself if you'd gone on any longer." She had only one answer: "I should have died trying."

When the stronger partner in a marriage dies, the weaker one is often incapable of continuing alone. Such dependent survivors have few options open to them and must either live with a child or accept some form of institutional life.

Discord in the "Golden Years"

Your parents may not have such an exclusive relationship. Instead of turning to each other they may turn to you, trying to involve you and their other children in their conflicts. Hearing them fighting or complaining about each other may make you very uncomfortable. You may remember that they fought all the time you were growing up, but somehow you may have expected all this to stop as they grew old together. The answer to the question "How can they still be fighting, at their age?" is "Why should they stop now?"

For forty-seven years they had been married. How deep back the stubborn gnarled roots of the quarrel reach, no one could say—but only now, when tending to the needs of others no longer shackled them together, the roots swelled up visible, split the earth between them, and the tearing shook even to the children, long since grown.

Tillie Olsen, "Tell Me a Riddle"

There is no reason to expect tempers and personality clashes to fade away with the years. Occasional conflict is to be expected in any close relationship. It can provide a catharsis, a release. Conflict may even arise for the first time in the later years, as couples struggle to cope with the stresses and difficulties caused by their aging. When there is a strong bond between husband and wife at any age, periodic quarrels can serve to cement rather than destroy a relationship. But some couples—perhaps your parents—make quarreling a way of life.

A young child is often terribly upset when his parents fight, particularly if they carry on directly in front of him. Even if they try to keep their conflicts private, he can be just as upset knowing that something terrible is going on the house. Years later he may be upset all over again when they attack each other and may need to withdraw for his own protection. "I'm nearly fifty, but I still get that old sick feeling in the pit of my stomach when I hear Mom and Dad fighting," a daughter admitted to her mother's doctor, trying to explain why she visited her parents so rarely.

A successful writer claims that he invariably falls asleep at the theater when the scene onstage involves a marital battle. As a child he had always used sleep to escape hearing the thing he hated most: his parents fighting. They are in their eighties now and still at war. Their son visits them, although infrequently, and after he visits he usually goes home and sleeps.

Some stressful marriages which have held together during the middle years "for the sake of the children" feel free to break up when the family is launched. Couples separate, divorce, start afresh with new partners at fifty, sixty, even seventy. Other, seemingly shaky pairs, while using their children as the rationale for staying together, remain intact permanently because of their mutual dependence on each other. Despite constant threats to separate through the years, they never follow through, to the surprise of their children, who report, "We grew up expecting our parents to get divorced—we almost still expect it now—but they're still together and still at each other's throats."

❖ THE VAUGHAN'S MARRIAGE had always been a battleground. No one had heard Philip Vaughan refer to his wife by name for years—only as "THAT WOMAN." Even when they grew older their conflicts continued, and they frequently spent long periods of time refusing to speak to each other. In their later years they often communicated to each other by making long-distance calls to their daughter, Edna, who had moved far away from her parents. "Tell your father to see a doctor about that cough of his," Mrs. Vaughan would say to her daughter, who could hear her father coughing in the background. Edna, in New Hampshire, would then speak to her father when he got on the phone in Iowa and urge him to see a doctor. In reply her father would shout, "Tell 'THAT WOMAN' to stop worrying about my health all the time."

At least the Vaughans, despite their bickering, managed to keep a close watch over each other's physical well-being, but other couples may remain so wrapped up in their conflict that they no longer communicate about anything else. Each one may keep quiet about a disturbing physical symptom, refusing to admit to the other that something hurts somewhere. Thus they may keep their fears to themselves until it is too late.

Children, friends, and relatives even go so far as to recommend divorce or separation to an elderly couple who battle on a daily basis. An outsider may not realize that along with all the anger there are also strong bonds holding the two old people together, and beneath the conflict they may be very attached to each other.

❖ SEVENTY-NINE-YEAR-OLD MAVIS WOOD had been threatening to leave her husband, who was a year older, for most of the six decades of their marriage. In her mid-seventies her threats were somewhat idle, since she was confined to a wheelchair and dependent on his help. When a double room became available in a nearby nursing home, their children, tired of being drawn into their conflicts, urged their parents to move in. Jack Wood was reluctant for one reason only: "She'll leave me when she has someone else to take care of her." But he was persuaded, and the two moved in carrying their conflicts with them. Now they involved the nursing home staff as well as their children.

After some time, the staff, tired of the situation and convinced that the two would be better off separated, offered to move Mrs. Wood to another room. When the move was made she was delighted: "You never believed I'd ever leave him, did you? Well, I did!" she gloated to everyone. Her children and the staff were relieved at the peaceful period which followed, but their relief was short-lived. Within four days Mrs. Wood was back in her old room with her husband once again, ready and eager to resume their old combative relationship once more.

Widowhood

A marriage may remain intact, in harmony or in conflict, for forty, fifty, or sixty years, but sooner or later it will inevitably be broken by death. Unless they die together in a plane crash or other disaster, one partner will have to face life without the other for some period of time. Of all the losses which must be faced in old age, the loss of a partner is often the most cruel and disruptive loss of all.

In most cases the wife will survive her husband. According to current statistics women can expect to live seven years longer than men. Since women tend to marry men older rather than younger than themselves, the likelihood that they will survive their husbands is even greater. One fifth of all men sixty-five and over are widowers, and more than one half of all women over sixty-five are widows: two thirds of those sixty-five to seventy and more than three quarters of those eighty and over.

In addition to the grief and upheaval caused by the loss of their husbands, numbers of elderly widows living alone (along with other elderly single women) face dire financial privation. Some 51 percent fall below the poverty line.

Because most wives are aware of the strong possibility that they will outlive their husbands, some go through a kind of "preparatory widowhood" in the later years, talking to their children about what lies ahead, thinking through specific plans, working out budgets, or concentrating their efforts on protecting their husbands' health and well-being. Even if they prefer not to think about the future they cannot avoid the fleeting thought, "Am I next?" as more and more of their friends become widows. Husbands, by contrast, are generally not prepared for the possibility that, despite the statistics, they may be the ones who survive, and give little or no thought to the idea that one day they, too, could be alone. Widowers may be even more shocked and helpless than widows in the initial stages.

But prepared or not—even if death follows a long period of illness, even if it is expected, almost hoped for—the loss of a partner is almost always a devastating occurrence followed by some period of grief and disruption. Mourning usually involves a number of emotional reactions—numbness, apathy, longing, sorrow, remorse, and guilt—as well as physical symptoms of weight loss, insomnia, irritability, and fatigue. But there is great variation, depending on the individual, in the intensity of the emotional and physical reactions and their duration. It may be hard for you to predict in advance just how your own mother or father will react.

When a surviving husband has always been particularly dependent on his dead wife (or vice versa), it is understandable that he will feel utterly lost without her.

But dependency in marriage is often a very subtle process. You may have always thought that your father was a very independent, self-sufficient, dominant type who ran everyone's life. Why should he seem so shattered by your mother's death? It is worth remembering that the most independent of husbands may, underneath, be very emotionally tied to their wives and dependent on them, although heaven forbid they should ever admit it! You may not believe your father could ever feel dependent on anyone—he may not even believe it about himself. The realization may only dawn on the day he is widowed, and his reaction may shock everyone.

On the other hand, you may have always underestimated the strength of your surviving parent. Although your mother may have seemed docile and passive, inner reserves you never saw before may surface when your father dies. You may have a sneaking suspicion after a while that she actually seems somewhat relieved, which is quite surprising and inappropriate under the circumstances. But once the funeral is over and the mourning period is past, some widows and widowers experience an unexpected sense of freedom rising above their feelings of loss. If a dead husband has been truly dominating, a kind of parental figure, his wife may be quite relieved to be free of his control. She may need some time before she can reactivate her rusty old self-sufficiency, but she may surprise everyone, including herself, by her ability to think and act as an independent person.

A similar sense of freedom may be felt by widows and widowers who have spent long years caring for physically or emotionally dependent spouses. A husband who felt duty-bound to care for his invalid wife, who never could bring himself to gain his freedom by institutionalizing her, will be freed by her death—and not through any deliberate act of his own. He may then find he still has time to make use of his new freedom, although for many it comes too late.

If relief seems to be an unexpected emotion, you may be just as surprised if one of your parents reacts to the loss of the other with calm tranquillity. Some widows and widowers, after a short time, reflect this quality in the midst of sadness. They seem able to pick up their lives and carry on, even start afresh if there is still time.

Disruption Is to Be Expected

Widowhood for elderly men and women, almost invariably involves disruption which may last longer than the grief itself. An elderly widow is no longer anyone's wife, anyone's companion, anyone's sex partner (for the time at least). She has no one to care for or to run a house for except herself. With no one to cook for, she may not bother to cook at all and may become further weakened by malnutrition. She may have to change her level of living completely because of reduced income. If her husband has always been the handyman, finance officer, and business executive in the marriage she will have to grapple with those unfamiliar roles. Widowers face similar disruptions in habitual patterns of daily life.

If the couple's social life has always been carried on together, that, too, will be disrupted temporarily—or permanently. Widows and widowers often report that they don't "fit in" any more, that they are no longer as comfortable or as welcome in their old social niches, although widowers are more likely than widows to be sought out and included by friends. A widow often senses (rightly or wrongly) that her old friends are uncomfortable with her grief, that they feel depressed around her, or that she has become a fifth wheel in couple-oriented activities. Widows are more likely than widowers to discover that if they do not drive or can no longer afford former forms of entertainment, their social life begins to fade away. Older widows have one compensation denied to younger ones: since it is unusual to be widowed early, young widows often feel out of step with their married contemporaries while older widows, because of their numbers, can often find kindred spirits among their contemporaries. A steady diet of female companionship may not be completely satisfying for most, but for some widows it beats loneliness.

Loneliness itself is not a simple feeling and can mean different things to different people. When your widowed mother tells you she is lonely, you may not understand exactly *how* she is lonely. Helen Lopata, in *Widowhood in an American City*, reported that the widows she interviewed defined their loneliness in a variety of ways: some were lonely because they missed everything about their dead husbands; others were lonely for companionship, for someone to organize their days around, for escorts, for someone to love or to be loved by, for someone to share activities with. Widows and widowers have to learn how to live with their own individual variety of loneliness.

Unless totally dependent on others because of ill-health or prolonged depression, your widowed mother (or father) is likely to adjust eventually to the disruption in her life and develop a new pattern which may go on for many years. Things will never be the same for her again. Life will certainly be different; it will probably be bearable; and it may—as it is in some cases—be even better.

When Mourning Goes Out of Bounds

While shock, pain, depression are not only normal emotions during the mourning period, but actually necessary ones which make it possible for survivors to work through their grief and eventually resume life again, some widows and widowers never recover.

Prolonged mourning was more obvious in the past when the process was more ritualized. Some widows refused to give up their "widow's weeds" and lived on, shrouded in black, never letting themselves or the world forget their loss. Although less visible, prolonged mourning is not unknown today.

While experts agree that the survivor of a marriage is more susceptible to physical and mental illness in the early days of widowhood—a higher rate of suicide is reported in this period—they also report that the intensity of those emotions and physical symptoms normally eases with time. Those who remain in a state of perpetual grief may have conflicting feelings about their dead partners or have been known to have had depressive episodes in the past. What seems to their families to be a state of perpetual mourning may actually be a state of severe depression, set off, but not caused by, the bereavement itself. Simple remedies which help to ease normal grief will not work. Some form of professional help may be needed.

Queen Victoria gave the world a classic example of prolonged mourning. Victoria, as queen of England, was one of the most powerful figures of her time. No one could possibly say she did not have enough to keep her busy. Yet in 1861, after the death of her husband, Prince Albert, she retired, at the age of forty-two, into seclusion at Windsor Castle. For three years she never appeared in public and did not open Parliament again—an annual duty for British monarchs—until 1866. Even though she lived another forty years after her husband's death, she never let her country forget her loss. The poet Rudyard Kipling suffered permanent royal disfavor when he dared refer to his queen as "the widow at Windsor."

The Death of a Parent:
The Effect on You

The previous discussion has focused on your parent's reactions to his or her widowhood, but your own personal ones cannot be ignored. When your father dies, you may feel some responsibility to help his widow (your mother or your stepmother) recover from her loss. But you may have a hard time behaving in a cool, level-headed way yourself, because her loss is yours as well. She has lost a husband, it's true, but you've lost a father. If your father is widowed, he mourns for a wife while you mourn for a mother. When sympathy goes in two directions, when the older generation is able to acknowledge that the younger one is suffering, too, it is easier for everyone. But that does not always happen. A mother may complain to everyone, "Carol carries on so! You'd think she'd lost a husband. Can't she think what it's like for me?" But Carol may tell a different story: "Mother acts as if she's the only one who misses Dad. Doesn't she remember that I loved him, too?"

Even if both generations recognize each other's grief, they may mourn in different ways. Your mother may turn to religion after your father's death, taking her comfort in ritual and prayer, visiting the cemetery, lighting candles, wearing black. None of these rituals may be at all helpful to you—they may even seem distasteful. Many families are in disagreement about the entire mourning process, starting with the funeral itself. Some members may want a lavish ceremony, a constant stream of condolences, and find comfort when the world seems to share and witness their grief. Others can mourn only in privacy. If you find no comfort in the rituals which comfort your mother, there is no reason why you should be forced to do everything her way—but no reason, either, to prevent her from taking comfort where she finds it.

You may be so shattered by your own grief after your mother's death that you find it painful at first to talk about her at all, even to mention her name. Your father may need to talk about her all the time. For your own sanity you may need to withdraw a little and let others do the listening.

A particularly painful situation exists when a son or daughter has had a stronger bond with the parent who has died and greater conflict with the surviving one. If you had an especially close feeling for your father, his death may be devastating to you and you may find it almost impossible to comfort your mother. You may even resent her for still being alive while he is dead, and also for never —in your opinion—treating him well enough or appreciating him enough during his lifetime.

Although it has always been customary to speak well of the dead, children are frequently amazed at the way the surviving parent manages to remember the dead one. Widows and widowers often seem to find comfort in idealizing relationships which were actually far from satisfying and are quite skillful at rewriting their own marital histories. Relatives may listen in disbelief as a widow describes her dead husband as "the gentlest soul on earth," when everyone knows he was tyrannical and demanding. A widowed father may remember his wife as "selfless and saint-like" after her death when in reality she had been self-centered and hot-tempered. Families at such times quickly come to believe Sigmund Freud's comment: "Consideration for the dead, who after all no longer need it, is more important to us than the truth."

What You Can Do to Help

Your involvement when one of your parents is widowed depends on your mutual relationship, your desire to help, how many other people are available, and where you live. Obviously, if you live far away you will not be able to do much more than return for the funeral (or possibly during a final illness), and help out with the arrangements and initial problems. You may be able to continue to help from a distance by keeping in touch by phone and visiting more frequently, especially in the early period.

It is important to keep in mind that mourners go through many different stages on their way to recovery, and some of those stages may be difficult to deal with. Your mother may be full of self-pity at one time and anger at another. She may withdraw from you and your siblings this week, and accuse you of neglecting her next week. Those stages may be surprising and burdensome but are likely to pass.

Mourning takes time, and since older people are likely to move more slowly in all situations, they cannot be rushed through their grief or accept changes before they are ready. "We can't let Mother stay here alone. Everything here reminds her of Dad. We'll have to sell the house," may seem like a logical statement, but Mother may be worse off and her recovery permanently jeopardized if her home is sold out from under her and she is bundled off to a strange environment. Familiar surroundings as well as familiar faces are very comforting, although temporary changes of scene can be helpful.

When elderly widows or widowers are initially helpless and bewildered because of their grief, children may be tempted to rush in with impetuous invitations. "Come live with us—you can't live alone here," may seem like a kind solution at the moment, but unless it has been considered carefully from all angles in advance, it may turn out to be far from kind for anyone: your mother, persuaded to become dependent on you before she has given herself a chance to test her self-reliance, may forfeit her independence forever, while you and your family may come to resent the unnecessary and uncomfortable adjustments you have to make in your own lives.

The elderly themselves, in an attempt to escape their grief, may be the ones who rush into impetuous decisions. They may ask or demand to live with you. A widow may decide to sell her house and move into a one-room apartment or a hotel. Once the move is made, she may regret it. A widower, thinking he cannot face a winter alone in a cold climate, may pick himself up with little notice and move to a warm place where he knows no one. You may be able to forestall radical moves which may boomerang in the future by agreeing with the idea in principle but suggesting alternative approaches. "I can see why you don't want to stay here alone, Dad, but why sell the house? Why not rent it this winter and see how you like living in Arizona? If you don't like it there, you'll always have a place to come back to."

Even if a widowed mother does not seem to need anything from her children, it is usually helpful for her to know they can be depended on. Dependability and availability are important, so is sympathetic listening and genuine concern. It is equally important to help widowed parents build up their self-confidence and to encourage them to take their first independent steps. Your first instinctive reaction to your widowed mother may be to protect her in every way. "Don't worry about a thing, Ma, we'll take care of everything," may be a well-intentioned offer but may only make her more dependent than ever. A more effective approach would be to reassure her that she is perfectly capable of taking care of herself but that you're ready to back her up when she needs you.

On occasion widowed parents who no longer have partners to share their lives focus all their attention—and their demands—on one particular child. A daughter may be expected by her father to take the place of her dead mother, or a son to replace his dead father. (Children themselves sometimes try to assume these roles, and are hurt and angry when their attempts are rejected and their parents prefer to be self-reliant.) The only way to prevent those expectations from taking hold is to set firm boundaries from the beginning: "No, Mother, I can't spend Saturdays working in the garden with you like Dad used to do. You know I coach Jim's Little League team on Saturdays. But we'll be over to see you after church on Sunday as usual." Or: "No, Father, I can't get over every day. You know how much I have to do at home. But don't forget you're spending the weekend with us." The situation is more difficult to handle when the requests are less specific. It is harder to set boundaries when your mother wants you to be responsive to her emotional needs just as your father always was.

Remarriage

Older men and women, widowed or divorced, may remarry, even in their eighties. It will be impossible for anyone to predict after your father dies just *what* your mother will do. You can't be sure and neither can she. A categorical *never* can only be said in cases where individual survivors are seriously incapacitated. Widows and widowers often swear during the mourning period that they will never marry again. Their children usually believe them, often finding the mere idea inconceivable. You may share this view. Yet your widowed mother may surprise herself—and you, too.

The chances of remarriage are obviously greater for older widowers than for widows, because single women over seventy-five outnumber men of the same age 3 to 1. The field, therefore, is wide open for the widower, and his selection is not limited to women in his own age group. His new wife could be ten, twenty, thirty, forty years younger than he is. Women, because of social mores, are less likely to marry men who are much younger. Winston Churchill's mother, Jennie, was a famous exception. After she was widowed she had two more husbands, both younger than her own sons. Such exceptions seem to be on the increase today, although they usually cause quite a furor.

Some older widows and widowers are unable to contemplate marrying again because they feel it is somehow improper, undignified, or frowned on by society. Their children frequently agree and voice even greater opposition, adding a new concern of their own: money. When a father remarries, who will inherit from him? His children or his widow? If he marries a younger woman, he may have children with her; who will be his heirs? His first set of children? Or his second? Or will the inheritance be less for everyone because it has to be shared? Prenuptial agreements are sometimes made by an elderly pair to reassure the children on both sides that their "rightful" inheritances will not be lost.

You may approve in principle of the idea of remarriage for older people but find it appalling when your own father remarries. Your reasons for thinking it is ill-advised, in his particular situation, may seem to be valid. His new wife may be after his money; she may be from a different background, have different interests, less education. Her health may be poor, and you may be concerned that he will have to take care of her or possibly that you will have to take care of both of them. But actually, if you are completely honest with yourself, you may admit that these are not your real reasons for opposing his marriage. You may be against it because you feel it is disloyal to your mother. It may be too painful to you to think of another woman taking your mother's place in your father's life, using her things, sleeping in her bed. You may be jealous that your father prefers another woman and is not content to depend on you. Finally, you also may feel that remarriage at his age makes him look ridiculous—and therefore makes you look ridiculous, too.

But unless elderly men or women are seriously disturbed and not responsible for their actions, their children might be better advised to consider the consequences of opposing a remarriage. A son who seriously opposes his mother's marriage is telling her that she is better off living with her loneliness than with someone *he* considers inappropriate. Is she really better off? Can he be sure?

Although you initially opposed the idea, once your widowed parent has remarried it may become easier for you to accept. The closeness you once had may be gone, however. The new remoteness you feel may be obvious if you refer to the woman your father has married as "my father's wife" rather than as "my stepmother." Many children are never reconciled and continue to feel hurt and resentful because a father treats his new wife better than he ever treated them or their mother, or a mother seems to show more affection for her new husband than she ever showed for their father.

Although remarriage after the death of a spouse, particularly soon after, may appear to children and close friends as disloyalty to the memory of the dead man or woman, it actually may be the reverse. Some experts claim that when there has been a good, solid, mutually gratifying relationship in a marriage, there will inevitably be pain and grief after one partner dies, but the survivor will eventually be freer to start life again and even to contemplate marriage again. A widow or a widower whose former married life has been gratifying may want "more of the same" and hope to continue, in a new marriage, patterns enjoyed in the old one.

When the marriage has been difficult, conflicted, and unsatisfying with elements of dependency, anger, and resentment, the death of one will not wipe out those emotions for the survivor. The grief that follows may be intense and as conflicted as the marriage itself. Those conflicts may prevent the survivor from making a new life or a commitment to marriage again. Even though the marriage was generally happy, a widow may reject remarriage if her husband had been ill for a long time before his death and she had carried the major burden of his nursing care. "I never will go through that again," she may say when the subject of remarriage comes up.

A woman (or man) remarries late in life for a variety of reasons: to gain companionship, to share common interests, for financial security, to have someone who cares about her or someone she can care about, to satisfy sexual needs.

Elderly widows and widowers, even those who have all these needs, may fail to remarry for many reasons: fear of making a mistake, family opposition, lack of desire to resume marital responsibilities, and lack of opportunity. But they may find alternative ways to satisfy their needs. Just as young people are turning to more unconventional lifestyles, so may their grandparents: group marriages, shared living arrangements, communes, and homosexual or lesbian relationships. Their financial situation frequently makes marriage economically unwise, and they may decide to live together without legal ties in order to protect their assets. This situation is uncomfortable for many elderly men and women but is forced on them by Social Security regulations, which provide less benefits to married couples than to single individual recipients (see Chapter 7).

Such unconventional living arrangements, difficult enough for the elderly themselves to accept, may be hair-raising for their conventional sons and daughters, who may already be having a hard time accepting the unusual lifestyles of their children. Consider the discomfort of the conservative middle-aged citizen who is forced by current mores to refer to "the girl my son is living with" or "the boy who shares my daughter's apartment" at a social gathering. How much greater his discomfort will be if, in addition, he has to include "my father's mistress" and "my mother's roommate"! He may prefer to withdraw from both generations.

Sex After Sixty-five—Myth Versus Reality

Many children like to ignore the fact that sex plays a part in their parents' lives at any age. That possibility can be ignored even more easily when their parents are old because of the prevailing assumptions that sex is not possible, necessary, or nice in the later years, and furthermore, that it can be hazardous to the health! You yourself may never have given a conscious thought to your parents' sex life or have discussed your own with them, and may accept the belief passed on through the centuries that while the other appetites last indefinitely and must be satisfied, sexual appetites die young.

... at your age
The hey-day in the blood is tame ...

said Hamlet to his mother, Queen Gertrude. He could not understand why she married with such "indecent haste" after his father's death and denied that a woman of her age could be motivated by love or passion. Yet Gertrude's age was probably less than forty-five.

It's easy enough to smile at Hamlet's naïveté, to point out that knowledge of human biology was very limited in Shakespeare's time, and to say that things are different now in our own liberated century. But are things really so different?

❖ IN THE SPRING OF 1975, a young doctor, graduate of a famous medical school and with advanced training in a great teaching hospital, cautioned his patient, Mary Walters, against continuing to use The Pill because of her high blood pressure. When Mary objected, reluctant to give up the convenience and security of The Pill, he reviewed the dangers again and added kindly, "At your age, Mrs. Walters, is it really *so* important?" Mary Walters was forty-eight—echoes of Hamlet four hundred years later!

Popular attitudes, supported by some members of the medical profession, are not so radically different today, despite the advances in scientific knowledge. The facts concerning sex and the later years continue to be distorted by old myths and false assumptions.

Many young adults are proud to be liberated from the sexual inhibitions of Victorianism and puritanism. Well-informed about all aspects of sex, they discuss with ease the pros and cons of contraceptive devices, open marriage, group sex, Gay Liberation, and abortion. Yet that same uninhibited, "well-informed" group may also still believe that a woman's libido vanishes after the menopause and that impotence lies in wait for middle-aged men.

Plenty of aging men and women, of course, know from personal experience that those myths are false. Their own continuing sexual activity is all the proof they need. But plenty of others share the beliefs of the younger generation. If they feel any sexual drives or suffer any sexual difficulties, they often worry that something is the matter with them, hesitating to seek advice about their anxieties for fear of looking foolish. In addition, they are constantly reminded by the media that to be old is to be undesirable—another way of saying *sexless.*

Any example of passion and sexual potency still surviving in the later years is considered unusual enough or "abnormal" enough to be newsworthy: the marriage of a seventy-nine-year-old man and a thirty-year-old woman, fatherhood at eighty, an affair between an older woman and a younger man, or a crime of passion.

Paris, November 29, 1975 (Reuters)—An 80-year-old man, Charles Bouchet, who served 27 years in the Devil's Island penal colony for manslaughter, was under close guard today, charged with having stabbed to death a rival of his own age for the love of a woman in a Paris home for pensioners.

Such stories should make people question their old assumptions but public response is most likely to be, "Oh, yes, but these are the exceptions."

Modern studies of human sexuality have shown that sexual activity among the elderly is far from unusual. Nearly thirty years ago Alfred Kinsey's first studies showed that while the frequency of intercourse declines steadily among men through the years, the majority continue some pattern of sexual activity. A number of men are sexually inactive at seventy, but a greater number still have intercourse with some regularity at the same age or older. (Kinsey's sample included one seventy-year-old whose ejaculations were still averaging more than seven a week, and a man of eighty-eight who had intercourse with his ninety-year-old wife anywhere from once a week to once a month). Kinsey also reported that the sexual capacities of women show little change with aging.

Masters and Johnson and other present-day researchers confirm Kinsey's earlier findings. Their studies show that men and women can, and often do, remain sexually active at sixty, seventy, eighty, and beyond, and furthermore, that older couples who maintain sexually gratifying lives are usually continuing the pattern of a lifetime. Sex may be less frequent, possibly less intense, but just as meaningful in their old age as it was when they were young. Similarly, single men and women—widowed, divorced, separated, never married—who have always been sexually active are likely to seek out sexual relationships when they are old, although partners are increasingly difficult to find as the years go by. (Kinsey found that among previously married women masturbation became more important with age, possibly as the only available sexual outlet.) Far from dying out with age, sexual feelings, if they have been strong and satisfied through the years, may be intensified when an elderly man or woman is alone and lonely.

Sexual patterns of behavior may start early and continue late but only be considered socially acceptable in the earlier years. A young man who sows wild oats at twenty may be admired and envied; but he would be branded a roué at fifty, and a "dirty old man" at seventy, for the same behavior. "Mother, you were flirting with the butcher!" a daughter may say reprovingly, but the white-haired old lady may merely shrug off the reproof: "I can't change old habits at my age."

Eyebrows are usually raised when an elderly man marries a younger woman. People are quick to assume that she married him for his money, or for security, or for social position, or because she needs a father, and that he needs someone to take care of him. But their assumptions may easily be wrong:

❖ FRIENDS AND RELATIVES were happy when old Phil Richter married his fifty-year-old housekeeper a short time after he was widowed. "How nice for him," they said. "He was so lonely. Now he'll have companionship at least." They were quite upset some time later to learn that the marriage had not worked out and that the newlyweds had separated. Rumors circulated that the trouble was caused by sexual incompatibility. "Of course," everyone quickly assumed, "she was too young for him—not sixty yet. She still needed a physical relationship. Poor old man—how sad—he probably couldn't satisfy her."

Those closest to old Mr. Richter knew that the situation was reversed. The younger woman had always found sex distasteful and was glad to marry for companionship, convinced that nothing more would be expected from her. Mr. Richter had other ideas. He had maintained a high level of sexual activity all his life, not only with his wife, until she died, but with a series of mistresses as well. Now in his eighties and widowed, he needed companionship, but he needed a sexual partner, too, and expected to find it in the younger woman he married.

Age, therefore is not a barrier to healthy, ongoing sexual activity. The barriers come rather from physical disability, mental disturbance, longstanding sexual maladjustments, and—more frequently —lack of an appealing or willing sexual partner.

The Elderly May Be Misinformed, Too

Scientific research has broken down many of the myths that have surrounded the subject of sex and the elderly, but many older people still do not fully understand the changes taking place in their own bodies as they age. Temporary setbacks in their sexual performance may quickly revive the old myths. Their anxiety may then make temporary setbacks permanent. A woman may know intellectually that her libido will not be affected after the menopause even though her ovaries stop functioning, but she may not be aware of other possible changes: thinning of the vaginal walls, and decrease in elasticity and lubrication, resulting in painful intercourse. Those conditions can usually be treated, but unless she gets good medical advice she may decide by herself that her sex life is over.

A man may be concerned that his sexual potency will be gone after prostate surgery or may worry merely because his reactions are slower, and because it takes him longer to achieve an erection and an orgasm. He may be anxious that he is becoming impotent, and his very anxiety may make the impotence a reality—a self-fulfilling prophecy. Many problems, not necessarily related to age, can cause periods of impotence in younger as well as older men, such as drinking, fatigue, worry, fear of failure, or boredom. Careful physicians are often able to pinpoint the problems, suggest ways to overcome them, and reassure elderly patients that impotence is not necessarily permanent. But sexual failure seems so shameful to many men that they are reluctant to admit the problem. If they decide to consult a doctor they are often told, "Don't worry about it—it's to be expected at your age!"

Modern medical thinking has exploded another old myth: that sex is hazardous to the health of older people. Many doctors are convinced that the opposite is true, even for the elderly with heart conditions and arthritis, and that sexual activity can actually be therapeutic in reducing tension, heightening morale, and maintaining a sense of well-being. Nursing home rules until recently required the segregation of the sexes, or permitted only married couples to share a room. But today, the more concerned institutions, realizing the importance of sex to the adjustment of elderly residents, are making it possible for unmarried couples to have privacy together. This innovation, while producing great happiness for the residents concerned, often produces even greater consternation among their children.

What Will the Children Say?

Laurence Olivier, in a recent interview in the *New York Times,* discussed a new play, *The Seagull,* and its author, the elderly British playwright Ben Travers:

> Travers is well into his 90's. It's a very naughty play indeed. He discovered sex very late in life. He was thrilled by it and quite ashamed of the play. He put it in a drawer. He didn't want to shock his children, all of whom were over 60. We persuaded him that they would be able to take it.

Perhaps Ben Travers's children were able to "take it," but children are not always so open-minded. They may accept a widowed father's remarriage to the elderly woman who was their mother's best friend, or a mother's remarriage to a kindly old man everyone loves. If sex is considered at all in these marriages, everyone may like to assume that the elderly couples maintain separate bedrooms or at least separate beds.

But what if you cannot make any such comfortable assumptions in your own father's situation—or your mother's? What if the behavior of one or the other makes it perfectly clear that a sexual relationship is going on? A special set of feelings may be aroused and suddenly, although you firmly believe that sex is normal and appropriate for other people's fathers and mothers, it may now seem highly inappropriate for your own. You may try to prevent what you feel is an "unwise" marriage or break up a relationship that does not seem "right." You and others in the family may insist that "he is making a fool of himself," or that "she doesn't know what she's doing." You may even consider that your elderly parent is becoming mentally impaired. It is dangerous to jump to such conclusions. Although older people who are seriously deteriorated—mentally or physically—may lose the defenses they once had which inhibited inappropriate sexual acts, you may have a hard time deciding if your father's behavior is *truly* inappropriate or if it just *seems* inappropriate to you and simply makes you uncomfortable, or ashamed. Perhaps you want your father's or your mother's affections to be exclusively yours and are jealous when someone else comes between you. Perhaps you cannot bear to see your once very proper parent—who cautioned you against sexual display—exhibiting open sexuality.

When children feel ashamed or jealous of an elderly parent's sexual relationship—one which is appropriate and gratifying—it is the children's problem and not the parent's. The children may deal with their problem by learning to accept the relationship or by staying away from it as much as possible. Worrying, "What will the children say?" often makes older men and women hesitant to remarry and also prevents them from establishing new relationships, forcing them to settle instead for unnecessary loneliness and abstinence.

6.

Facing the Final Crisis

"He is certainly of an age to die." The sadness of the old; their banishment. . . .
I too made use of this cliché and that when I was referring to my mother. I did not
understand that one might sincerely weep for a relative, a grandfather aged seventy
or more. If I met a woman of fifty overcome with sadness because she had just lost
her mother, I thought her neurotic: we are all mortal; at eighty you are old enough
to be one of the dead. . . . But it is not true . . . the knowledge that because of her
age my mother's life must soon come to an end did not lessen the horrible surprise.
                         Simone de Beauvoir, *A Very Easy Death?*

The death of an elderly mother or father inevitably touches the
children who are left behind, whether they are just grownup, middle-aged, or nearing old age themselves. Even if it is expected because of a hopeless illness, even if it is welcomed as an end to
suffering, even if there is remoteness or estrangement between the
generations, the death of a parent cannot be a casual event.

Any review of life in the later years must therefore include a
consideration of death. Death becomes more and more of a reality
with every passing year. Its closeness touches not only those who
are about to die but also those who love them and will survive them.

According to the laws of nature, the younger generation shall
survive the older one. But the process is not necessarily without
pain. A son expects to survive his father but also expects to mourn
him and to feel some amount of sadness, regret, loneliness. He may
also realistically expect to feel a certain sense of relief when the
burden of caring for an invalid is lifted, particularly if the invalid
has been difficult, demanding, or suffering. Many children respond

in just these ways when their parents die. Others surprise themselves and wonder why they respond with more painful emotions: inconsolable grief, anger, fear, guilt, and a sense of abandonment when someone who has been old, sick, helpless, and no longer able to enjoy life finally dies.

Painful reactions should not be so surprising. Parents are crucial figures in our lives when we are children. If they live on into their seventies, eighties, and nineties, they may continue as integral parts of our adult lives, too; we and they may even grow old together. When a mother dies at eighty, her children at fifty or sixty may learn for the first time the meaning of life without her. Each one of us has only one mother or father to lose, and when either or both die, some part of us dies with them.

Our personal being is in some way, to a greater or less extent, diminished. A strong force linking us to our past is gone. As our parents' lives end, an eventful chapter in our own life history ends, too. It may not have been a particularly good chapter for us, but it is finished and can never be revised or rewritten. There will never be an opportunity again for reconciliation, for explanation, for understanding, or for saying things left unsaid for years: "I'm grateful," "I'm sorry," "I love you."

Psychologist Clark E. Moustakas, in *Loneliness*, described the thoughts of a son watching his dying mother:

> *This was my mother; and the word 'mother' brings on a flow of feeling and past experiences and years of living together, loving together, and hating, too. The fighting and conflicts do not seem important any more, the arguments and intense pains and emotions that clouded the relationship have evaporated. This was my mother, and I realize the uniqueness of our relationship. It was not an impersonal fact of someone having cancer and dying, but it was a basic relationship that can never be repeated, a piece of eternity, never to be the same any more.*

A story, fact or fiction, was repeated recently about a sixty-year-old man who, when asked to indicate on an insurance form whether he was married, widowed, or divorced, wrote in the appropriate blank, "orphan." While this word did not describe his marital state, it did describe the state of his feelings. Many of us have a similar feeling, if only for a fleeting moment, and the old fear of abandonment is remembered from childhood. As long as our parents live we are always somebody's child no matter how old we are. Whenever they die we are orphans for life.

Most of us are unprepared for this feeling. If we sense it in advance we are likely to laugh at it and ourselves for being ridiculous. We certainly are not likely to discuss it with our parents who are close to death, yet undoubtedly they must know something about it—after all, they have probably been orphaned, too.

The Conspiracy of Silence

As a matter of fact, we are likely to talk to them about very little that relates to their deaths, and more likely to stop them from bringing up the subject. Families with deep religious faith may be able to deal with death more directly, to talk about it and what comes after, but the subject of death—like sex, only more so—has been generally taboo in modern society. Freud discussed that taboo in his essay "Obscure Thoughts on War and Death":

> . . . we were of course prepared to maintain that death was the necessary outcome of life, that everyone owes nature a death and must expect to pay the debt—in short, that death was natural, undeniable and unavoidable. In reality, however, we were accustomed to behave as if it were otherwise. We showed an unmistakable tendency to put death on one side, to eliminate it from life.

For some, not only the subject but also the word is taboo. Euphemisms are used instead: "passed on," "gone," "departed," "lost," "at rest." Not wanting to be reminded of the inevitable, people find it safer to avoid the topic; if they talk about it at all, they tend to do so in general, impersonal terms with no names attached. A wall of silence, therefore, can grow up between those who are about to die and those who care about them most. That silence can deprive both sides of help, comfort, and support just at the time when those elements are needed most. In *I Knock at the Door*, Sean O'Casey writes of a dying old man:

> And here he was now reclining in a big horse-hair covered armchair, shrinking from something that everyone thought of, but no one ever mentioned.

The same taboo which makes it difficult for us to discuss death with the dying makes us uncomfortable with mourners. "What can I say?" you may have asked every time you sat down to write a condolence note or went to visit friends in mourning. A few conventional, stilted words of sympathy—and then on to pleasanter, safer topics. The subject uppermost in everyone's mind is the subject that is hardest to bring up. Children, as Freud himself noticed, uninhibited as yet by social taboos, often spontaneously break the conspiracy of silence and refer point-blank to the thing that terrifies them.

❖ WHEN FRANK AND ELEANOR THORNE returned with their two children after a three-year assignment in Japan, their homecoming was a sad one.

Eleanor's father, who had always lived with them, had died at eighty-two while they were all overseas. He had been extremely close to his daughter, his son-in-law, and his grandchildren, and they were all acutely aware of his absence when they came back to the house he had shared with them for so long.

Friends who dropped in to welcome the family were also aware of the pain of the homecoming and were determined to be helpful. A succession of visitors came and went, each one full of bright chatter and careful to avoid any reference to the missing person. The Thornes were surprised at first when no one mentioned Grandpa—they would have liked to talk about him—but they decided it would put a damper on their friends' efforts to be cheerful, so they kept silent, too.

At the end of the day a small boy arrived with his parents, surveyed the piles of luggage scattered all over the house, spotted a giant duffel bag standing upright in the corner, studied it with fascination, and then, to the horror of his mother, asked in a shrill voice, "Is *that* where they keep the grandfather?" The silence was broken.

Man has orbited in space, harnessed nuclear power, and walked on the moon, but death remains undiscovered territory, terrifying in its mystery. The motto observed by many is, "When terrified— hide." So they try to hide in silence, but that does not always provide real shelter. Without a word being spoken, our parents' aging forces us to acknowledge the fact we are trying to ignore. Their increasing frailty, their whitening hair, their fading vision, their advancing birthdays can be daily reminders of their mortality and, by extension, our own. No wonder many of us react with anger and impatience if, on top of those visible reminders, they want to *talk* about dying, too. They are likely to find themselves cut off before they have a chance to begin:

ELDERLY PARENT   I'm not going to be around forever.
SON/DAUGHTER   Nonsense! You'll outlive all of us!
                      (The subject is closed.)

*

ELDERLY PARENT   When I'm gone . . .
SON/DAUGHTER   Oh, Mother, stop talking that way.
                      (The subject is closed.)

*

ELDERLY PARENT   I've had a good life, but I . . .
SON/DAUGHTER   Don't act as if it's over. You've got years to go.
                      (The subject is closed.)

These are all direct references to death, but some older people make more indirect allusions which sensitive sons and daughters are quick to catch and resent:

❖ DAD ALWAYS HAS his affairs in order. His drawers are all neat and tidy. He's always reminding me where his papers are and which keys fit which locks. He used to be like this when we were kids before he went off on a trip. He always seems packed for a trip these days and ready to go. Whenever I visit him I feel like I ought to say goodbye. I hate it.

*

❖ EVERY TIME THERE'S A SALE—sheets or underwear or stockings or towels —I always ask Mother if she needs anything and she always says, "No, I have enough to last me." Why does she have to keep on reminding me all the time that she's going to die?"

Some People Need to Talk About Death

If death were not so taboo, if it could be talked about more freely, those direct and indirect references might stimulate rather than abort discussion. The discussions would not be likely to go on indefinitely, or to monopolize all conversation. The elderly are not usually preoccupied with thoughts of death every minute. Thoughts and fears come and go. When they come, it can be comforting and reassuring to voice them occasionally. Not much is required of the listener except listening and a few words: "I know," or "I understand," or "I remember, too."

Your father may be looking for a chance to talk to someone about himself—to reminisce—about what his life has meant to him, what certain people have meant to him. He may wonder what he has meant to others—to you. He may want to talk about his accomplishments, mistakes, regrets—or perhaps his fears not only of death but of the process of dying. He may hope to be reassured that he will not die alone or be in pain. He may also want reassurance that he will be remembered, that he will be able to leave some kind of a legacy behind for future generations.

He may want to discuss his will and the distribution of his material things, his feelings about funerals and burials. His concerns may be not only for himself but also for those he will leave behind, people he worries about: you, or your mother, or your brother, or a grandchild. He may not expect to find answers to all his questions, but talking about them can be therapeutic if only there is a willing listener.

Children frequently look back on lost opportunities after a parent has died and wonder why they did not listen more, both for their parent's benefit and for their own. One daughter said regretfully:

❖ I'D GET PRETTY BORED when Pop rambled on about the old days and what happened before I was born. But he always seemed to catch me when I was busy—I'll admit I hardly ever listened. But I wish I had. Who is there left now to tell me the name of the town in Scotland where my great-grandfather is buried? Who remembers Aunt Tessie's mother's maiden name? Why should I care about such silly little unimportant things? But I do. And he'll never know I do.

Direct and indirect references to death are often ignored, but sometimes the subject never comes up at all; there seems no way to open it. You may feel you would like to talk to your mother when you realize she is failing and may sense that it would help her to talk to someone, but both of you may be uncomfortable and uncertain how to begin. There may be awkwardness and reticence on each side. It's easy enough to say to her, "Listen—before you take off for California is there anything we should go over together, anything you need me to do for you?" It's harder to speak so freely when she is not going to California but is going to die. Much, therefore, is likely to be left unsaid by both of you.

> Do not go gentle into that good night,
> Old age should burn and rave at close of day;
> Rage, rage against the dying of the light

wrote the Welsh poet Dylan Thomas, opening one of the best-known contemporary poems about death. According to those who knew him, Thomas wrote those words for his dying father but never could bring himself to read them to him because of the great reticence in their relationship. The poem has been read by countless strangers instead of by the one dying man for whom it was written.

The conspiracy of silence has generally included not only the relatives of the dying, but the healing professions as well: physicians, scientists, and technicians, who by training are more concerned with fighting death than with helping their patients to meet it more easily. Their professional life is dedicated to avoiding, preventing, or at least postponing death and to developing life-preserving procedures: antibiotic therapy, chemotherapy, transfusions, infusions, transplants, and life-sustaining machines. By machine, lungs can now be kept breathing, hearts kept pumping, kidneys kept functioning. In the past human organs had had no such miraculous support systems, and without them greater numbers of people died and died younger. The only possible benefit offered the dying then was that more of them died at home in a familiar atmosphere with people who loved them nearby.

The patient dying in the hospital today is in an alien environment made more alien if he has to be surrounded by strange tubes, bright lights, machines, and monitors—with teams of experts and skilled technicians, all strangers, concentrating their efforts on preventing death. While so much necessary intensity is concentrated on physical needs, there is a danger that the dying patient as a person may be forgotten, his other needs brushed aside.

Intensive care procedures often save lives, and those whose lives have been saved are thankful, but some speak later about the sense of personal isolation they experienced. They could hear voices, but the voices did not usually talk to them; they were touched by gentle, capable hands, but the hands, busy with tubes and wires, usually transmitted impersonal messages. After surviving a critical illness, the recuperating patient is able to resume human contacts again, but many of the elderly remain isolated until death.

Breaking the Silence

The conspiracy of silence is not as pervasive as it once was. Among certain groups of people it is currently being discussed openly and examined freely. It is the subject of books, articles, seminars, institutes, workshops, and public lectures. Concern for those who are about to die is coming not only from physicians, but also from psychiatrists, social workers, philosophers, scientists, theologians. Popular books, magazine features, and TV programs are making the general public aware that more can be offered to the critically ill than medical procedures alone to make the process of dying easier and less painful.

Thanatology, the study of death, is an emerging field of science, its name derived from *thanatos,* the Greek word for "death." Particular concern has been focused by the growing number of professionals in this new field on the emotional needs of those who are nearing death. Dr. Elisabeth Kübler-Ross, a psychiatrist, best known to the general public for her book *On Death and Dying,* observed after years of close contact with numbers of terminally ill patients that they usually go through a series of emotional stages —denial, isolation, anger, bargaining, and depression—before they finally can accept the fact of their own deaths. Some may not have time to work through all these stages, and many have difficulty working through them alone without the help of someone who understands and who cares: a relative, a friend, a professional. In some hospitals and nursing homes today staff members are given special training to make them more responsive to the needs of the dying and to the feelings of the dying person's family.

It has been generally assumed that the elderly fear death less and face it with greater equanimity than the young. This may be true for many old people. They undoubtedly have had plenty of experience with death. Most of them are forced by their advancing age to acknowledge their own mortality, and their awareness is constantly reawakened as, one by one, close friends and relatives die. But even though they may fear death less, that does not mean that they are not afraid. Many are fearful until the end and never reconciled, continuing, in Dylan Thomas's words, to "rage, rage against the dying of the light." Kübler-Ross is convinced that most dying people go through the same stages, perhaps with some variation in the intensity and duration of each phase, regardless of age. The old may even begin to work through these stages prior to the period when they are actually dying, beginning in some cases when they have endured too many losses, when they become seriously incapacitated, or when they must enter an institution. Sons, daughters, and close relatives of the elderly may go through parallel emotional stages before they, too, can accept irrevocable separation.

Telling the Truth to the Dying

Those who have been working closely with the dying are convinced that frankness and honesty about their physical condition is usually essential before patients and their families can begin to work through the stages of dying. A dying man has the same right to know, whether he dies at forty or at eighty. While that may be the best approach in most cases, there are always exceptions. It may be necessary to take a somewhat more cautious approach with the elderly who are confused or mentally disturbed, and there will always be some older people—just as there are younger ones—who do not want to hear the truth, rejecting it and denying it when it is offered to them. There obviously can be more than one approach to death and truth should not be forced on anyone; neither should it be denied to those who ask for it or are willing to receive it.

You may think, as many loving children do, that you are protecting your mother, whether she is at home or in a hospital or institution, when you urge her doctor not to tell her the facts about her physical condition. You may honestly believe it is kinder to lie to her. But how kind can it be to keep her completely in the dark about what's wrong with her? How can she understand why she feels so terrible? How can she explain her aches and pains? How can she accept her limitations? Nothing is more confusing to an older person

—or a younger one—than to sense that something is seriously wrong and then to be told by everyone that it's nothing—just a minor problem that should go away soon. Yet relatives and doctors have been equally timid about being honest, not realizing that uncertainty, confusion, anxiety, distrust are usually much more damaging than the simple truth.

❖ WHEN LILY SIMMONS, a nursing home patient, complained of abdominal pains at eighty-two, her physician in consultation with her family decided not to tell her the diagnosis they had made—carcinoma of the stomach—but told her, instead, that she had an allergic condition. That did not really satisfy Mrs. Simmons, a bright, alert woman, since it did not explain the severity of her pain or her sense of forboding.

One day, as she was signing some Medicare papers, she noticed that the diagnosis of her condition—carcinoma of the stomach—was filled in on the form. She went immediately to the nurse on the floor to ask the meaning of the word, and when she was told that it meant cancer she demanded that the nurse tell her the truth. At first she was angry and resentful of both the doctors and her family, but eventually she understood their motivation. During the next weeks she went through a variety of emotions similar to the stages described by Kübler-Ross, but in time she began to reconcile herself to her condition. Since her cancer progressed slowly, because of her advanced age, she found herself once more taking an interest in the world around her and decided there were things she could still enjoy before she died. Until the last months, which came several years later, she remained quite actively involved in life around her.

Although it is important that your mother understand the truth about her condition and its implications, it is not necessary to go into great detail or to keep on referring to it continually. Once she knows what's going on she can begin to prepare herself, ask questions, raise her fears, and receive reassurance. She may wonder how much pain and discomfort lies ahead and how these can be alleviated. It is not necessary, either, to tell her she is dying in so many words, because she may not be dying at the point the diagnosis is made. Her cancer may be inoperable and it may cause her death one day, or her heart condition may be serious and her next attack may kill her, but she may surprise everyone. There are all kinds of terminal illnesses, and many make slower progress in elderly bodies than in younger ones. Cancer may be detected in an eighty-year-old man, but he may die of a massive stroke before his cancer has had a chance to do much damage.

Professionals are reluctant to pinpoint months and years. The dramatic "death sentences" so popular in drama and fiction—"You have three months to live" or "one year at the most"—are less likely in real-life situations today. The future is unpredictable even for the elderly. There is evidence to suggest that those who are about to die can sometimes, in some mysterious way, postpone their deaths in order to remain alive for some particular occasion or until some particular piece of work is finished. It is not uncommon to hear families report, "Mother was determined to live until Billy came home from Vietnam," or "Father wanted to see Mary and Jack get married," or "He managed to stay alive until he finished his book."

Just as there are disease factors governing death, so social and psychological factors play important roles. Statisticians, demographers, and social-psychologists have documented the existence of a phenomenon which they have termed the "death dip," in which the death rate among certain groups of people drops prior to a special occasion and rises shortly afterward. A recent study reported in the *British Medical Journal* suggested that, among the elderly, an approaching birthday can be a motivation for survival since research showed that fewer older people died in the two months before their birthdays. An earlier study of more than three hundred famous Americans, whose birthdays were of national significance, revealed the same pattern.

The death dip has also been noticed prior to less personal occasions, such as Thanksgiving and other holidays. In two separate studies of big cities with large Jewish populations, a death dip was documented among Jews in the period immediately preceding Yom Kippur, the most solemn day in the Jewish calendar.

In this Bicentennial year it is appropriate to mention that Thomas Jefferson, at eighty-three, and John Adams, at ninety-one, both died on the Fourth of July, 1826, the fiftieth anniversary of their country and of the signing of the Declaration of Independence which they had both shared in drafting. The words of the doctor who was with him document the fact that Jefferson was aware of the significance of the date until the end:

> *About seven o'clock of the evening of that day, he (Jefferson) awoke, and seeing me staying at his bedside exclaimed, "Oh, Doctor, are you still there?" in a voice, however, that was husky and indistinct. He then asked, "Is it the Fourth?" to which I replied, "It soon will be." These were the last words I heard him utter.*

> Merrill Peterson, *Thomas Jefferson and the New Nation*

Should Life Be Prolonged?

That question has been asked over and over again. Many people would give the old familiar answers: "Life must go on," or "While there's life there's hope." But is there hope for the hopeless? Must life go on in any condition? The right to die is a controversial issue, becoming even more pressing in the recent period as more and more life-sustaining procedures keep alive men and women—old and young—who would have died fifty years ago. But there is a great difference between "being kept alive" and "living." It is possible through "heroic measures" to prolong life, but it is much more difficult to assess the value of the life that is being prolonged.

The controversy over the right to die has been making front-page news recently with dramatic cases involving young and hopelessly ill people, but the controversy has been ongoing, although less publicized, over the old and the hopelessly ill. It is possible to prolong the life of a seventy-five-year-old man in a coma for months. It is possible to keep an elderly woman alive even though a stroke has condemned her to a vegetative existence. It is possible to extend life for someone over eighty with one operation after another, each one causing additional suffering. But is life worth prolonging under these conditions?

Opinion today is divided about the right to die. Some deny that right, abiding by religious teachings and secular law or because they believe that life itself must be valued regardless of its condition. Others are convinced that life without meaning and dignity has little value. The controversy is not new. As long ago as the sixteenth century, in England, Sir Thomas More, sometimes called the "Father of Euthanasia," wrote in his *Utopia:*

> *If the disease be not only incurable, but also full of continual pain and anguish, then the priests and magistrate exhort the man that . . . he will determine with himself no longer to cherish that pestilent and painful disease. . . . And in so doing they tell him he shall do wisely, seeing by his death he shall lose no happiness, but end his torture. . . . They that be thus convinced finish their lives willingly, either by fasting, or else they are released by an opiate in their sleep without any feeling of death. But cause none such to die against his will.*

Euthanasia for the aged was not uncommon in certain primitive cultures. Some peoples because of the rigors of their life—particularly in nomadic tribes—were forced to abandon their very old who were helpless and ill, leaving them alone to starve or freeze to death. Some Eskimo groups left their aged to die on ice floes. But other groups found euthanasia more humane than abandonment. As one Chukchee, a reindeer-herding nomad of Siberia, put it:

> *Why should not the old woman die? Aged and feeble, weary of life and a burden to herself and to others, she no longer desired to encumber the earth, and claimed of him who owned nearest relationship the friendly stroke which should let out her scanty remnant of existence.*

Leo Simmons, *The Role of the Aged in Primitive Societies*

Today even those who believe in the right to die are not unanimous in their feelings about it. There are the advocates of "active euthanasia," the ending of life for the hopelessly ill and disabled, and the advocates of "passive euthanasia," the withdrawal of all life-saving medications and interventions without which life cannot go on. Whatever the logic and reason in either approach, one crucial question remains unanswered: "If such decisions are to be made, who will make them?" Who will decide what condition is hopeless? Who will decide when life is no longer meaningful? Will it be the relatives of the dying—those with the closest emotional ties? Or will it be the doctors—those with the best medical judgment? Such power over life and death may be too great to be entrusted to any single person or group of people, who might use it irresponsibly or for personal gain. Dr. Robert Butler suggests that a panel of experts be established—including not only physicians but also psychiatrists, social workers, and legal advisers, as well as family members —to judge each individual case.

Many older people feel that they themselves are the only ones who should have the power over their own lives, and many are careful to let their feelings be known clearly in advance. Some discuss their desires with their families, exacting promises that no "heroic measures" be taken on their behalf. Others feel safer when they put everything in writing; just as they specify certain funeral arrangements or bequeath their bodies for medical research, in the same way they may leave written instructions about their desire to die with dignity or sign a "living will." Such a document, although not legally binding, is addressed "To my family, my physician, my lawyer, my clergyman. To any medical facility in whose care I happen to be. To any individual who may become responsible for my health, welfare or affairs." The document states:

> If the situation should arise in which there is no reasonable expectation of my recovery from physical or mental disability, I request that I be allowed to die and not be kept alive by artificial means or "heroic measures." I do not fear death itself as much as the indignities of deterioration, dependence and hopeless pain. I, therefore, ask that medication be mercifully administered to me to alleviate suffering even though this may hasten the moment of death.

By 1972, fifty thousand copies of the living will had been distributed by the Euthanasia Educational Council.

Occasionally the elderly are not content to put their trust in others, and they make their own decisions on when and how to die, choosing to end their lives by suicide. The public, as well as philosophers, scholars, and theologians, usually responds with shock to the act of suicide, which goes against most religious and moral teaching. Yet in 1975, seventy-eight-year-old Dr. Henry P. Van Dusen, a world-famous theologian, and his wife committed suicide together. Ill for several years and knowing they would both soon become completely dependent on others, they felt there would be little meaning or dignity in the life ahead for them. In the letter they left behind, the Van Dusens wrote, "Nowadays it is difficult to die. We feel this way we are taking will become more usual and acceptable as the years pass. Of course, the thought of our children and our grandchildren makes us sad, but we still feel this is the best way and the right way to go." In commenting on their suicide in the *Saturday Review,* editor Norman Cousins asked, "What moral or religious purpose is celebrated by the annihilation of the human spirit in the triumphant act of keeping the body alive? Why are so many people more readily appalled by an unnatural form of dying than by an unnatural form of living?"

A Time for Emotional Daring

Kübler-Ross, in *Questions and Answers on Death and Dying,* described her answer to the question, "How do you, if you do, protect yourself emotionally in your relationships with terminally ill patients?" Her reply was, "I dare to get emotionally involved with them. This saves me the trouble of using half my energy to cover up my feelings." The conspiracy of silence about death, the awkwardness so many feel about it, their discomfort, often makes those most closely involved with the dying do just that—waste their energy covering up their feelings—the very feelings which could provide so much comfort and support.

But sometimes there is little opportunity for this closeness. Babies in the past were born at home, with fathers and close relatives hovering nearby. The dying died in the same environment. Birth and death were events not to be experienced alone, but to be shared. In that intimate atmosphere emotions could be shared, too, the painful as well as the joyous ones. Birth and death in this century have moved out of the home into institutions. The moves were essential in order to provide the greatest protection for the new lives and old ones. But in this highly efficient and highly sterile atmosphere, strangers may usher in life and usher it out, while those with the deepest personal ties can feel like trespassers. There is a growing trend—encouraged by some doctors, nurses, and hospitals, and by young parents themselves—to reinstate the family in the process of birth. In some hospitals fathers are allowed to be with their wives during deliveries so that the ones most intimately involved can share the first minutes of life. The same kind of closeness could be allowed during the last minutes of life. But this is not always possible, as one middle-aged son discovered:

❖ I WAS ALWAYS very fond of Tom's father and really shaken when I heard he had a brain tumor—an inoperable one. But I learned a lot from his family. When they learned that nothing more could be done for him in the hospital, they—his wife and his children—decided to bring him home to die—to the house by the lake which he had inherited from his father. This was what he wanted, and they knew it. I thought it would be terribly hard to visit him, but it wasn't—even when he got much sicker. He lay there in his room, looking out over the lake which he had always loved, and he could hear his family in other parts of the house—his wife, his children, his grandchildren—preparing meals, playing games, talking to each other. He could hear laughter and music. They didn't hover over him, but they didn't leave him alone much either—every once in a while someone would stop by his room to talk a little, to read, or just to sit quietly with him. Even the littlest children came. I thought then, "What a wonderful way to die, with your whole life around you—past, present, and future." I hoped my father could die this way, too.

But he didn't. My father had a massive heart attack when he was eighty-three and we had to rush him to the hospital. They did everything they could to save him. We were there with him, but there was no place for us. We were only allowed to see him for a few minutes at a time—never long enough to say much. We didn't know what to say anyhow. We were in the waiting room when somebody came out and told us he was dead. I wonder if he knew we weren't with him when he died—and that he was dying alone.

Part 2
TAKING ACTION

7.

Helping—When They Can Manage Independently

❖ MARIAN FRANKLIN—seventy-two, widowed, somewhat arthritic, and mildly diabetic—continued to live in her old neighborhood that had gone dangerously downhill. Her children, comfortably settled in pleasant suburbs, were frantic. They worried when their mother went out alone and worried when she stayed home alone. They complained that she "exhausted" herself with volunteer work at her church and were upset every fall when she went apple-picking at a friend's orchard. She kept telling them that she was fine, steadily refused their offers of help, and rejected their repeated invitations that she make her home with one of them. She was reasonably content with her life.

Eventually, her children found the opportunity they needed when an elderly woman was brutally mugged in the lobby of Mrs. Franklin's building. All the other tenants were fearful and understandably upset, including Mrs. Franklin herself, and therefore her children were able to persuade her that she was unsafe in her apartment. Within a short time they helped her move out to live with her younger son in a room they redecorated especially for her. They were delighted that they were finally able to "give Mother a good life," but wondered why she didn't seem to enjoy it the way they expected she would. She was somewhat bewildered during the move, remained apathetic and uninvolved in her new surroundings and physically frail. Everyone was heartbroken when she died of pneumonia less than a year later. They all continued to believe that they could have prolonged her life if only they had insisted she make the move earlier.

It could be said that Mrs. Franklin was fortunate. She had loving children, eager and able to help her as she grew older. Many old mothers and fathers would envy her. It could also be said that she was unfortunate, because those loving children were unable to understand the kind of help she needed. With the best of intentions, they weakened rather than supported her.

Help sounds like a simple four-letter word, but many steps are involved in the helping process, and being ready and willing to help is only the first. A second step is knowing the right kind of help to give. Many well-meaning children take the first step easily but never are able to take the second, or else they fail in the process.

Help for the elderly can be undermined by the younger generations because of ignorance, lack of understanding, or total misunderstanding. In many instances they jump to false conclusions about what is best. Too little listening is done, too little attention paid to the desires and inclinations of the older person. Too little time is taken to understand him and to evaluate the adaptation he is making to his old age and its accompanying losses. Understanding in and of itself can be helpful. But understanding can go further and produce a realistic assessment of what kind of help—and how much—an elderly person actually needs in order to get along.

Although the term *elderly* is used to describe the sector of the population sixty-five and over, that sector is far from homogeneous. Using the term makes things simpler from the point of view of legislation, but in the process one label is pinned on a very diverse group of people. *Sixty-five and over* may cover a thirty-year timespan. In addition to the tremendous diversity among the elderly as a group, aging men and women as individuals may go through many different stages. A more accurate approach, taken by some experts, would be to think of the elderly as three separate groups: the young-old (up to seventy-four), the middle-aged-old (seventy-five to eighty-five), and the old-old (eighty-five and over). Your father may live one kind of life at sixty-five, another at seventy-five, another at eighty-five, and still another at ninety-five. His needs will change accordingly. The young are inclined to forget the diversity, and to forget that needs of older people are determined not by chronological age but by the ability to manage independently.

In the next chapters we shall consider the help and understanding likely to be supportive to the elderly at strategic points along the dependency scale, ranging from the totally independent to the totally dependent:

- Older people who can manage alone and know it
- Older people who can manage alone but think they can't
- Older people who cannot manage alone

The members of each of these three categories have all suffered, in varying degrees, the losses and stresses of aging. Many are able to make successful adaptations and find at least some compensations. Others give up without a struggle. The elderly are capable of an amazing assortment of adaptations, and their capacities can be strengthened by the effective support of their children—or weakened by their children's well-meaning interference—although in some instances, where parents are particularly determined, children have no effect at all.

"I'm Okay"—Those Who Can Manage and Know It

Because the plight of the elderly who cannot manage is so heart-rending and tragic, it is easy to forget that a large proportion of older people adapt to aging fairly successfully. A surprising number take the cumulative losses of old age in their stride, are somewhat content with their lot, and would be justifiably offended if anyone were to suggest that they were not competent to handle their own daily routines by themselves: cooking, cleaning, dressing, shopping. In addition, they feel perfectly able to take care of their own finances, entertainment, and health. They still consider themselves functioning members of society, perfectly capable of making their own decisions and deciding what is best for themselves—by themselves.

When it comes to needing help, those capable older individuals usually know when they need it, how much they need, and what kind. They can be quite definitely outspoken when they do not need any help at all. A self-reliant octogenarian has a real sense of pride and personal dignity; he may even delight in flaunting his age and letting the world know he's not finished yet. An energetic older couple may insist on roughing it on camping vacations and take pleasure in disregarding the anxious pleas of younger relatives that they vacation instead in a safe and comfortable motel.

If your parents fall into that enviable group, the best approach to take is to give them quiet support. Let them know that you accept, even admire, the lifestyle they have chosen for themselves. Jumping in with unsolicited advice or offering unwanted help may only rock the valuable equilibrium they have established, or create bad feelings. A good rule to follow here would be to let it be known that you are willing to help if they want you to help. Even though they don't want to be dependent, they probably like to know that you are dependable. Lewis Carroll made this point clear in *Alice's Adventures in Wonderland:*

"You are old, Father William," the young man said,
"And your hair has become very white.
And yet you incessantly stand on your head—
Do you think, at your age, it is right?"

Father William was not asking anyone's help to stand on his head; he managed successfully by himself. His feat may have been unusual, but if he could still perform it, how could it possibly be considered wrong? If your parents have established a way of life they feel works for *them*, it would be foolish to try to impose a different lifestyle just because *you* feel it is more appropriate.

It is easy enough to take this live-and-let-live philosophy when your parents adopt a way of life that is socially acceptable, or even admirable. It is no hardship to encourage your parents when they have found a satisfying life in a retirement village and are in a safe, comfortable environment with plenty of congenial companionship. It is even easier to applaud an elderly relative who views old age as a time of renewed vigor, creativity, vitality, and curiosity. There are numbers of remarkable old people who chart new courses for their lives after seventy and experience a kind of rebirth. Stories appear frequently in the press of seventy- or eighty-year-olds who have just completed the requirements for a high school diploma, a college degree, or even a graduate degree. It is not unusual today for a retired businessman to start a new and successful business venture at a time of life when many contemporaries are in wheelchairs. Those admirable examples are endlessly pleasing and reassuring to the younger generation, who can say to themselves, "That's what I'll be like when I'm old." The world loves a "wonderful old man" or a "fabulous old lady."

Quiet support for those lifestyles comes naturally. But what about the elderly who also get along completely independently but in less acceptable, less socially approved ways? It may well happen that your parents develop a lifestyle in their seventies or eighties that satisfies them perfectly well but that you find terrifying, unsatisfactory, or embarrassing. What if you fear for their safety (as did Mrs. Franklin's children), despise their hobbies, disapprove of their friends, or look down on their interests? What if your father still pursues an active sex life and your mother talks about her dates and going dancing? A live-and-let-live philosophy may not be so easy then. But if your father's lifestyle seems to be working for him, although it makes you uncomfortable, you may have to keep reminding yourself that it's his life and not yours. It does not matter that you would *prefer* him to live differently, nor what the neighbors say to your face or behind your back. If he is able to take command of his own destiny, he deserves a willing go-ahead.

Parents of adolescents or young adults often face a similar dilemma. One family decides that the older son will be a doctor, or a lawyer, or an accountant. But that son may have different ambitions for himself. Parents may wring their hands when an artist daughter paints—and starves—in a garret. "This is no life for her," they cry. But this may be just the life that stimulates and excites their daughter.

And so with older parents. It may be embarrassing to admit that your mother is obsessed by some offbeat spiritual cult, that she swears by an astrologer, that she accepts money for baby-sitting, mending, or ironing (even though you'd be willing to double that income for her), that she hurries off to pick fruit at harvest time. But as long as she is able to manage her own daily routine, and as long as she chooses to live this way, it is better to forget your embarrassment. No one would suggest that you have to follow your mother's spiritual leader or abide by her astrologer's prediction, but don't try to make radical changes. Enough changes will have to be made when she can no longer manage to live so independently. A well-meaning but interfering daughter might do well to ask herself before she tries to redirect her father's life, "I'm asking him to give up everything he's always known, but what am I offering him instead?"

Children court trouble for themselves not only when they try to interfere with a lifestyle that works well for their parents, but also when they try to modify behavior patterns which their parents find useful. These patterns, related to the defensive behavior discussed in Chapter 4, may be worrisome, infuriating, depressing, and irritating to the young, but can be very supportive for the old, helping to offset the strong emotional reactions brought on by the losses of aging. They may enable your parents to maintain some measure of equilibrium. If a certain behavior pattern works well, like it or not, there is no reason to interfere with it. If it does not work well (if your mother uses denial to ignore a dangerous physical symptom), then some interference may be necessary.

The Pseudo-Helpless—Those Who Can Manage but Think They Can't

In contrast with the resolute, independent elderly who insist on managing their own lives, stands another group of their contemporaries who present a totally different set of problems to their children.

While your friend down the street worries about his independent mother who won't let him take over any part of her life, you may have the opposite situation to cope with. Your mother may be in relatively good health, enjoying relatively solid finances and relatively pleasant living conditions. She may be managing perfectly well. But the problem is, you can't convince her that she is doing fine. Unable to adapt to the losses of aging, she shows increasing self-pity and inordinate anxiety, while demanding unreasonable amounts of time from you and your family. Sometimes this behavior is short-lived, following a time of crisis, but it may become chronic.

The elderly who feel they cannot live through their old age by themselves often tyrannize their children. Chapter 3 described how one particular child may be chosen or may assume the role of "Mother's support," sometimes becoming a martyr to Mother's old age. Many of the pseudo-helpless elderly like to claim that they can manage, but the minute the focus of attention is drawn away from them, they will cry for help. They often have a sixth sense of the exact moment when the child they depend on is particularly involved elsewhere.

❖ JOHN FARNETTI'S MOTHER managed quite well some of the time but could turn helpless overnight, particularly when her only son and his family were about to leave on a trip, when a new baby was about to arrive, or when a particularly important business deal was pending. John could always expect at every crisis in his life that the phone would ring (usually late at night) and he would hear his mother's voice saying faintly, "You're going to be very upset with me." This was the dreaded but familiar opener: the overture to a new crisis that would demand John's immediate attention. He was expected to let his personal affairs simmer on a back burner while he made an emergency trip to another state to settle his mother's problem. It must be admitted that John allowed his mother to run his life and his family's.

The elderly who engage in this type of behavior do so for many reasons. One is fear or anxiety due to lack of understanding or knowledge. Some people do not understand the normal aging process. Ignorance leads them to exaggerate the danger of each physical symptom. Given greater understanding, they may be able to take their physical losses with greater equanimity and revert to less demanding behavior. In some cases, when logical explanations and reassurance are given by a child, a nurse, a doctor, or a social worker, anxiety can be allayed and episodes of panic prevented.

Reassurance and understanding do no good at all to others in the pseudo-helpless group, who make self-pity their way of life, exploiting their old age and their incapacities in order to gain an inappropriate amount of time and attention.

❖ EIGHTY-YEAR-OLD Jack Forbes was obsessed with his failing hearing and had been for years. His daughter, who had been helpful and sympathetic for a whole decade, was relieved when he finally agreed to a hearing aid, but she could not enjoy peace for long. Within the next few months, when his hearing improved, he began to complain of intestinal pain and sinus trouble. By moving on to new symptoms, he could regain the attention he lost when his hearing improved.

If life histories were to be taken of the pseudo-helpless, it would most likely become clear that they had always been dependent or self-centered. Old age merely provides the golden opportunity to exploit these needs more openly. Helpless behavior may also be a continuation of guilt-invoking behavior, which a parent may have used throughout life with various family members. The old ploy "I brought you up and now you leave me out in the cold" is a favorite and familiar type of guilt-producer, as is the commentary "One mother can take care of ten children, but ten children cannot take care of one mother." Such simple statements can activate ulcer-type pains and depression in quite sturdy children.

These statements, admittedly, are often rooted in reality, and many children deserve the accusations, but the words are just as frequently used as ammunition against the most devoted children, who keep asking themselves, "What more can I do?"

When to Say No

Just as unreasonable demands on the part of young children, teenagers, and adults can and should be turned down, there is no reason to give in to unreasonable demands from your parents. That is especially true if the demands add severe and unnecessary burdens to your life. The resulting bitterness, tension, and resentment that build up may make you completely ineffective when your parents legitimately need your help at some future time. Some children, who have never learned to say no firmly, find their only solution lies in cutting loose completely and disappearing from their parents' lives, a potentially guilt-producing act in itself. There is no reason to grit your teeth, penalize your children, or wreck your digestion while trying to satisfy your mother's unreasonable demands. Your pulse will be steadier, your intestines quieter, if you can learn to say no. Once you've said it, you may be surprised to see that it is often accepted with relative equanimity and less argument. Your mother may be relieved to know where you stand and exactly what she can expect of you. She also may catch a supportive message which tells her, "We will not treat you like a baby, because you aren't a baby. You are not helpless—you're doing all right on your own." There may be initial bitterness, but if you can live through this period, the ground rules for living will be firmly established for everyone.

"I Can't Say No"

You may not want to say no to your parents in their old age even if their demands are somewhat unreasonable and they are really getting along well. You may feel they deserve to be indulged, telling yourself that they worked hard all their lives and deserve to be pampered. But it would be a good idea to think things through less sentimentally and consider the long-range effects on yourself and the rest of the family. You could also consider the debilitating effect on your parents themselves when you allow them to be prematurely and unnecessarily dependent on you. A greater gift to them might really be to say no to unreasonable demands and refuse to allow yourself to become a partner in behavior which makes them grow old prematurely.

You may be equally reluctant to say no because you are inhibited by all sorts of unresolved conflicts. Guilt, shame, anxiety, anger always seem to get in your way—so you say yes rather than having to cope with these unpleasant emotions directly.

If you find it impossible to say no directly, it may help to make a quick run-through of the consequences to your life if you say yes.

- "How can I say no when Mother suddenly announces she wants to spend the summer with us?"

❖ IF I SAY YES and let her come, we'll have to give up the camping trip to Canada which we've been planning and saving for all year. Jenny won't be able to have her best friend spend August with us because there won't be enough beds. The dog will have to be boarded because Mother's allergic, and I'll have to give up coaching the softball team because Mother hates it if I'm out at night.

After looking at the results of giving in to Mother, a better question to ask yourself might be, "How can I say yes?"

- "How can I say no when my father says he doesn't want to live alone in the big house any more? But he won't give it up and he wants us to give up *our* apartment and move in with him."

❖ IF I SAY YES it will mean that Jim will have to commute an hour longer to his job, the kids will have to change schools, I'll be tied down with extra housework, I'll have to give up my hospital work, and I'll have to cook two sets of meals because of Dad's low-fat diet.

How can you say yes?

*

• "How can I say no to Mother when she begs to come to live with me? She's afraid to live alone even though she's managing quite well."

❖ IF I SAY YES we'll both go under. Mother is eighty-five and I'm nearly sixty. I'm having enough problems of my own. If she comes to live with me I'll never be able to take care of both of us.

Saying no to Mother will be kinder to her and to yourself.

Saying no doesn't mean that the subject is closed and that the desires of the older generation are ignored. A different approach can be taken: "I'm sorry, Mother (or Father), I know things are hard for you now, but your idea just won't work. Let's try to figure out a different way that's better for all of us." By rejecting the unreasonable demands of the pseudo-helpless, the younger generation need not always be accused of callousness, selfishness, or indifference. The firm no can ultimately be the greatest blessing to both generations.

Prepare for the Day When They Can't Manage

Whether your parents can manage and know it, or can manage but *think* they can't, there is no guarantee that the situation will continue. While they are still living independently is the time to look into the future and explore what will happen if and when their independence runs out.

Some of the blows of old age are beyond all remedy, and no amount of advance planning can soften them. But many can be averted completely or made easier to bear. Preventive care is probably one of the most important and most neglected areas of help for older people. That may be why so many of us are caught unprepared when a crisis occurs in our parents' lives.

It's great to be able to boast with pride about a parent's independence, good health, and varied activities. It's wonderful to be able to say, as some fifty-year-old sons and daughters can, "Mother's eighty but she looks sixty-five and does everything for herself. Last year she traveled to Europe alone." The strong possibility is that this eighty-year-old will run into difficulty before she's finished unless a massive stroke, a fatal heart attack, or a plane crash makes it possible for her to die with her boots on.

Serious difficulties may lie ahead for even the most active parents, partly because of their physical and mental vulnerability and partly because tragic gaps exist in the support which society provides. The sad results of insufficient advance planning are seen over and over again in hospital emergency rooms or in substandard nursing homes where families literally have to "dump" elderly relatives who could no longer manage. Such a tragedy might have been avoided if someone had given any advance thought to what would happen to them. The family usually feels the greatest sense of failure when problems occur because of lack of planning, but the older person who has not thought ahead himself should share the blame. Careful anticipation of future crises by all concerned can offset the shock, grief, disruption, and guilt which accompany them. When it comes to planning for old age, a stitch in time saves more than the proverbial nine— it can save whole families.

Planning ideally should start in young adulthood, although few young people make any such moves other than entering a pension plan. Certainly, planning should begin by the middle years. But it is never really too late to begin, and if your parents are in their sixties now, they may still have quite a future ahead for them. A 1974 Metropolitan Life Insurance Company study shows that men who have reached the age of 65 can expect to live until 78, and women who have reached 70.5 years can expect to go on until 83.5.

Perhaps the most effective help you can give your parents while they are still independent is preventive help: planning along with them to avoid tragedy in the future. Although easier said than done, the best way to initiate planning is in the context of open, respectful, relaxed discussion. Some parents bring up the subject spontaneously with their children or with one particular child whom they consider—sometimes mistakenly—to be the most level-headed or caring. They want to talk about what they will do if they become sick, if their money runs out, or when one of them dies. They may just want to talk and have someone listen, or they may ask for help, suggestions, guidance.

Others will play their cards closer to the chest, clinging to secretiveness about their resources and about any thoughts they have for the future, becoming angry and insulted if you insinuate there could be trouble ahead. Of course, underneath the anger may lie their own fear that they cannot face. Some will close any discussion about the future with the flat statement, "Don't worry about me. I'll be gone soon enough." Or they may loudly deny that their health could ever fail them.

❖ EMMA DEXTER at seventy-seven was admired by her younger relatives and friends. Widowed and still living alone in her comfortable apartment, she dined out, went to theater and concerts, traveled, and continued to work as a volunteer in her favorite hospital. It dawned on her suddenly that some of her younger colleagues avoided discussing any subject with her that was related to old age, even the tragic problems of some of the elderly patients —sensitive that they might be personally upsetting to her. As soon as she realized this, Emma quickly reassured them at a coffee break.

"Don't worry about my feelings," she said. "Old age isn't a touchy subject with me. I never believed I'd enjoy it as much as I do. I love talking about it—even the problems I have. Ask me anything you want."

"Are you sure, Emma?" asked a young volunteer tentatively.

"Of course," she replied.

"Well, then, I've often wondered when one of these awful stroke cases comes in—does it worry you? Do you think about yourself and what could happen to you?" the younger woman said.

"*That,*" replied Emma, turning on her heel and walking out of the room, "is a subject I never think about."

Your parents may share Emma's feelings, and if they have any plans for their old age tucked away in the back of their minds, they may refuse to talk about them. Their feelings should be respected and they should not be forced too suddenly into a discussion of the future. But the subject need not be dropped completely. You deserve to know what they are thinking, particularly if you are likely to figure in their plans, and you may be able to open up the touchy subject by making casual references to it from time to time.

When the casual approach does not serve to open a real discussion of your parents' plans, or their anxieties about the future, a more direct approach may be necessary:

❖ "DAD, JEAN AND I HAVE been doing a lot of thinking about you and Mother. You're doing fine now and we hope things stay this way, but you never talk to us about what you'll do if either of you got sick. We'd like to know what you're thinking and what you'd like us to do."

If nothing works and your parents steadily refuse to share their plans with you or even to plan at all, you can do some planning on your own, so that you will be ready with some reasonable alternatives when a sudden crisis descends.

Future planning for your parents should focus on three major areas of their lives: their health, their social world (including the big question, "Should they live with you?"), and—what may be the most crucial area of the three—their finances.

Health Care Planning

Even if they seem to be in excellent health, all aging individuals should have frequent regular medical checkups. A seemingly healthy seventy-year-old may have an undetected condition which can lead to a catastrophic illness or further physical deterioration. Early detection and early treatment can prevent some conditions from progressing further. Once the symptoms become obvious, it may be too late to reverse the disease. Incipient diabetes and high blood pressure, for instance, can be brought under control if they are detected early. They do not need to become fatal or incapacitating.

Some basic health education is essential for everyone. Many people, old and young alike, are unaware of the danger signals of cancer, or the symptoms of a heart attack. Health education includes nutritional guidance. Medical studies repeatedly show that poor nutrition is the cause of many problems formerly attributed to the aging process. Since older people living alone tend to eat only the foods that they like and that are cheap and easy to prepare, eventual deterioration may come as much from inadequate diet as from age. They may hardly eat at all if they have no one to eat with. When they become seriously ill and are hospitalized, they often not only recover from their illness during their stay but also regain much of their former vitality. The balanced diet offered by hospital dieticians can often reverse the process of deterioration in the very patients who frequently complain loudly, "The food here is so terrible I wouldn't give it to a dog!"

Basic instruction in bodily care and personal safety is equally essential. Older people may not know about new developments in hearing aids and eyeglasses. Regular attention should be paid to teeth and gums as well as to the care of hair and nails (particularly important to the diabetic). Safety measures should be considered (hand rails, unwaxed floors, protection against slipping in the bathroom), special clothing (elimination of tight garters and corsets), the use or abuse of medication, and the effects of alcohol, drugs, and tobacco. Some discussion of sexual matters may be included. None of this information is readily available at present, and there seems to be a need for a manual describing for the elderly the necessary steps to take to protect their health and safety.

Focusing on the whole range of health and hygienic needs can be of double benefit to the elderly. They will understand something about preventive medicine and at the same time understand more clearly just what is happening to their bodies as they grow older. Emotional preparedness can often forestall or minimize the anxiety and depression that accompanies serious physical losses. You may recoil from discussing their possible physical deterioration with your parents, fearful that such ominous predictions will depress them. (You may also recoil because these predictions depress *you*

and make you anxious about *your* own future.) Rather than producing negative reactions, however, a full and thorough knowledge of
possible afflictions of old age can have the opposite result for the
elderly. Fear of the unknown can be more frightening. Open discussion also works against denial and the childish game many old
people play: "If I don't think about it [some alarming symptom] it
will go away." Many young people play the same game, but with
the elderly, "it" is not likely to go away and is likely to get worse.
Denial prevents care and cure and leads to further deterioration.

Any discussion of future health care has to touch on the dreaded
subject of catastrophic illness and physical incapacity. Either situation will make it impossible for the older person to care for himself.
That is the most painful area to open up, and some parents cannot
face it at all. Your mother may be touching on the subject when she
talks to you about how she will live "after Father is gone." But she
may not be able to move further ahead and discuss what could
happen if she has a stroke "that paralyzes me." The younger generation may be equally reluctant to contemplate these possibilities.
One parent may open up the discussion, only to be turned aside by
the child: "When the time comes that I can't walk any more," a
severely crippled mother may begin, and then be quickly inter-
rupted by her daughter with, "Oh, Mother, don't talk that way. It's
not going to happen."

Her mother may have done a lot of thinking about the future. She
may have some strong feelings about her preferences and really
want to voice them. These preferences should be explored whenever possible. Some older people decide that a good nursing home
will be the best solution. They may turn to their children to help
in finding a suitable one. (Chapter 9 deals with nursing home selection.)

Others, who dread the idea of nursing homes, admit they hope
to remain right where they are. An investigation of how much
outside care is available in a given community could be reassuring
and establish whether this hope is realistic. (Chapter 8 reviews
community services.) Your parents may imply they hope to move
in with you or other relatives or a special friend. If you already
know that such moves will be impossible, make it clear as soon as
possible and move on quickly to alternative plans. Promises that
can't possibly be kept should be avoided, as should deathbed promises. Unless you have considered the possibility carefully, instead of
just emotionally, you may rue the day that you promised your
dying mother, "Of course, I'll bring Dad to live with us," or "I
promise never to put you in a nursing home." Deathbed promises
can produce the same chain of disastrous consequences as the ques-

tion "How can I say no?" They can put a stranglehold on the living. When such promises are broken, a son (or daughter) may be accused of bad faith by the rest of the family and by a more severe judge: himself.

Nothing is lost by anticipating future problems and making a tentative plan of action. Like insurance that may never need to be used, the plans are comforting to have in reserve. They may never need to be activated if your parents are spared disabling illness, but if disaster does come, you will not have to go through the additional insult of being caught unprepared, floundering helplessly, and having to resort to makeshift, unsatisfactory solutions.

Once you have opened up the whole painful subject of possible deterioration with your parents, you also have an opportunity to help them consider what will happen if, eventually, they have to give up some of the activities they enjoy the most. The active sixty-five-year-old who still spends hours on the tennis court may need to review other outlets which do not require such physical stamina. Similarly, progressive arthritis may be a painful blow to a woman who is known for her fine embroidery. Failing eyesight may disrupt the life of the book-lover, and loss of hearing end hours of contented listening for the music-lover.

Much more is known today about the activities that can be undertaken successfully by handicapped older people, and the elderly are continually contradicting the old adage, "You can't teach an old dog new tricks." Sixty-, seventy-, and even eighty-year-olds are proving it is not necessarily ever too late to take up a musical instrument, a paintbrush, yoga, meditation, sculpture, indoor gardening, or creative writing. An instructor in a correspondence school for writers reports that many of her students are sixty-five and older, and some in their eighties—and that the senior group are just as productive and just as eager as their junior classmates. Senior citizen centers in the community often provide a variety of activities.

Now is also the time for your parents to investigate—by themselves or with your help—organizations which actively promote the welfare of the elderly: the Gray Panthers, the American Association of Retired Persons (AARP), and the Congress of Senior Citizens. Opportunities for paid or volunteer work may be found through government programs or groups like Retired Seniors Volunteer Program (RSVP). (See Appendix B, pages 304–5.) There is a lot of time to be filled in the later decades, even when energy is limited, and finding gratifying activities can have a positive effect on the total health and well-being of the elderly.

Social Preparedness

The future well-being of the elderly is also greatly dependent on the social supports they will be able to rely on. Advance planning should also consider whether continuing contacts will be possible with friends, family, and other meaningful groups or individuals. Who will be around in the future for your parents to turn to for affection and companionship, as well as for help with chores, transportation, and small emergencies? How accessible is their housing to church or temple and community recreational activities? Would moving to a different location provide greater safety and easier social contacts? These questions about social supports are often tied in with health and financial problems. If disabled physically or financially strapped, the elderly may not be able to visit friends easily or have friends visit them. Furthermore, if they live far from medical services, it may one day cost too much in physical and financial terms to get essential medical care.

Although it may be clear to you that one day your parents may have to move, you may have a hard time convincing them. They may refuse to listen when you point out that their friends are slowly vanishing, that their neighborhood is going downhill, that the house is really too big for them, or that they may not always be able to maintain it. Their home may mean so much to them that they cannot contemplate living anywhere else. Some old people willingly suffer social isolation, loneliness, serious inconvenience, and unsafe conditions in order to stay right where they are. Although you may find more appropriate, safer places for them to live right in their own community, even around the corner, they may keep on insisting that there's no place like home for them. (Special housing for the elderly is discussed in Chapter 8.)

Even if they are willing to give up their home, they may have a hard time deciding where to go. Moving is not always advisable, and any move, particularly a distant one, should be weighed carefully. You may be able to point out potential difficulties they had not considered: A retirement community several thousand miles away may make sense for the immediate moment when your parents are "young-old," but what of the more remote future when they become "old-old"? What if they are incapacitated far away and need your help? What if they need a nursing home and there is none convenient in their new location? What if you want to bring them back again from two thousand miles away to be near you again, and they have lost their residency rights in your state and may no longer be eligible for certain services?

Before your parents make a move to a distant place, or even to a new location nearby, that would isolate them from familiar social activities or necessary health facilities, it is important to voice your reservations in advance. "It's your move," you might say pleasantly, "and I'm not going to stop you. But remember, if you're way out there I can't promise I'll be able to drive you as many places as I do now—and you'll hardly ever be able to see Aunt May and Uncle George."

Should They Live with You?

It is often painful for a son (or daughter) to admit that he cannot ask his mother or his father to live with him. He may have legitimate reasons, such as insufficient living space, ill health, or no settled home, or the reasons may be purely personality clashes: "She'd drive me crazy in a minute," or "My marriage wouldn't take it." But how much more painful it is to take such an irrevocable step, invite your mother to live with you, and then find out later that it just plain does not work. It may make you feel better to try living together, even though you fail, so you can comfort yourself later by saying, "Well, I did my best," but what a price you may have to pay later in terms of your subsequent relationship with her and the responsibility you feel for having disrupted her life!

If you are feeling that you ought to ask your mother to live with you, even though you are reluctant to, it might be some comfort to know that other people share that reluctance. National surveys consistently show that the majority of adults in the United States —young and old alike—think it is a bad idea for elderly parents and their children to live together. It might be reasonable to assume that the strongest opposition to such living arrangements comes from the younger generation, but it is not true; the surveys show that the older the individual, the less likely they are to favor living with their children. Older people particularly do not want to be burdens.

Rather than asking a parent to live with them permanently, some children think a part-time invitation is the best solution: "Mother lives with us in the summer, and then she goes to my brother Bill until New Year's. She's at Jeannie's all spring. We've decided that's the best arrangement for all of us." It may well be a good arrangement for the children but what about Mother? Older people usually function best with stable roots and less change. Mother, in that case, must have felt she was on the road all the time. A more permanently satisfactory situation could have been worked out by her three children.

Two- and three-generation families, so frequently seen in the past and in other cultures, do come about today for a number of reasons:

• A parent is widowed (or divorced) and, although physically independent, is emotionally dependent and too fearful or helpless to live alone.

• A parent, physically incapacitated and incapable of living alone, wants to be cared for by a child rather than strangers or a nursing home.

• Parents and children decide to pool their finances so that both generations can live more comfortably, or they may live together because they get along well and choose to have a combined household.

• An older but somewhat active parent escapes a lonely life by living with a child but at the same time fills a useful function, such as babysitter or housekeeper, freeing the child (usually the daughter or daughter-in-law) of many household chores and making it possible for her to pursue a career or a special talent.

Many parents aware of the pitfalls or reluctant to give up their independence, state flatly long before the issue comes up that they will "never, under any circumstances," live with any of their children. Some parents even mean it. Ironically enough, it is often the children of those very parents who press the invitations most strongly. But even if your mother hints subtly, asks directly, or even pleads to live with you, sentiment should not dictate your decision. Instead, base your choice on cold, careful analysis of your own situation, the wishes of the rest of your immediate family, and the history of your past relationships with her. Consider these questions:

1. How does your husband (or your wife) feel? (This is perhaps the most important.)
2. What kind of financial arrangements are being considered?
3. What kind of living space will there be for everyone? (Cramped quarters can wreck the best relationships.)
4. Will she depend completely on you and your family for companionship and entertainment? What about other friends, relatives, contemporaries? What about recreational and religious needs?
5. Can you really, honestly expect to live comfortably together? Do your personalities clash? How have previous visits gone? How often, during these visits, did you (or your wife or husband) have a migraine headache or an ulcer flare up?

6. When she visited you in the past, did you always count the days until she left?
7. Can she take a back seat in the running of the household and the rearing of the children? Of course promises can be made, but will they be kept?
8. Would she by temperament, education, or social experience feel continually out of place in your home—with your friends?
9. Will you be able to provide ongoing, accessible, competent medical care?
10. Do you treasure your privacy?

Those questions make up a rigorous test and should be taken by both generations. If you and your mother manage to pass it well—and that can happen—you have a good chance of creating a successful two- or three-generation family. If you fail the test, it is better to know it before you find yourself tied into a situation which is unworkable for everyone. All these questions can be faced and pondered before any crisis strikes and one of your parents suddenly needs a new place to live. Do not move into the future on the basis of unspoken or poorly considered assumptions.

❖ KATHLEEN GRAHAM LIVED comfortably with her husband until his death. She was left financially well off and remained healthy enough to keep her own apartment herself, but it was generally assumed by her children and relatives that she would move in with her only daughter if she ever became incapacitated. At least that was assumed by her three sons. Julie, the daughter, by remaining silent, seemed to share the family assumption. In reality, Julie was far from eager for the move, and her husband and children were equally against it. Whenever she visited, Mrs. Graham usually managed to tangle with her son-in-law and upset her grandchildren. To complicate things, Mrs. Graham had a hidden competitive relationship with her daughter which made it difficult for Julie to accept comfortably her role as mother and wife.

But Julie kept quiet out of her sense of duty, her guilt, and her concern over what everyone else would say. No alternative plans were made, therefore, and when Mrs. Graham suffered a paralytic stroke, she was brought to live in Julie's house after she had made a partial recovery. Her presence caused all the problems that Julie had anticipated and feared previously, as well as new problems caused by her mother's illness. Eventually, with bitter, guilty feelings, Mrs. Graham had to be resettled in an excellent nearby nursing home. The old lady felt betrayed as long as she lived, and Julie never completely recovered from her feeling of failure.

Financial Preparedness

Money can be a touchy subject, even in the closest of families. Men are often unwilling to discuss their finances even with their wives. Widows may be equally secretive with their children. There are still people who claim proudly or smugly, "We don't discuss money in our family." That may have been another sign of good breeding in Victorian days, but now, one hundred years later, it can be a prelude to disaster.

The elderly may be secretive if they feel—and sometimes they are correct—that the younger one is always trying to find out what inheritance can be expected. They also may be secretive if they are ashamed they have so little. But your parents may be willing to explore their financial future with you. There is no need to imply that you question their ability to manage intelligently, but you may be able to point out pitfalls ahead that they have not considered, or benefits that are due them which they had not heard about. Some older people are fully aware of the economic realities, but others may not realize that an ever-increasing proportion of their limited income will have to be devoted to health needs as time goes on, or be fully aware of the rate of inflation and the limitations of a fixed income steadily decreasing in buying power. It is also important to consider how they will be able to cope with the cost of a serious illness, and to find out exactly how much of the cost will be covered by insurance.

If they are unwilling to discuss the dollars and cents of their own personal income and assets, you may find it helpful to inform yourself about the variety of financial supports available at present for the elderly in America. Once you know what these supports are— the range of their payments, who is eligible for them, and how they are administered—you may have a more realistic understanding of your parents' current and future financial situation. But always remember that what you learn today may be changed tomorrow. The entire financial picture for the elderly is in a state of flux. Costs and benefits change from one year to the next. It is hoped that benefits will continually change for the better, but there is always the danger that cutbacks will be made if economic conditions worsen. In 1975, 46 percent of those sixty-five or older were dependent exclusively on retirement benefits: Social Security, and public and private pensions. Some 29 percent continued to earn money by working, 15 percent had income from assets, 4 percent received public assistance, and 3 percent veterans' benefits; 3 percent had outside sources of support, such as contributions from their families.

Social Security

You may feel somewhat reassured if your parents tell you that they are receiving money both from Social Security and from pension funds. But even though the intent of the Social Security Administration when it was established in 1935 was to provide ongoing financial security for Americans after retirement, for many inflation has turned that dream into a pipe dream. Pension checks and Social Security checks, even in combination, cannot keep up with rising prices. The dollars and cents on most monthly checks confirm this story. Your father's Social Security check from age sixty-five onward depends on his average earnings over a period of years prior to his retirement. During that time both he and his employer were contributing equal amounts to the Social Security trust fund. If he retired before he was sixty-five (this is permitted after age sixty-two), his checks were reduced accordingly. If he delayed retirement until after sixty-five, his benefits are slightly higher.

If your mother is still alive and has been working, she is entitled to her own Social Security. If she did not work and make independent contributions, she then qualifies as your father's dependent and collects an amount equal to half his check. In other words, two people are entitled to one and a half payments. If a wife who has worked finds that the Social Security benefits she would receive as her husband's dependent are higher than her own benefits would be, she may choose to be considered his dependent. This means, however, that she forfeits all contributions that she and her employer have made to the Social Security fund. (The same is true for a husband who chooses to be considered his working wife's dependent.)

If your father keeps on working after retirement, he is allowed to earn up to $3,000 annually without affecting his benefits. That does not include nonwork sources of income: dividends, interests, or pension payments. If he earns more than that, $1 is deducted from his Social Security check for every $2 he earns over $3,000. The figure is not cumulative throughout the year, and he is entitled to full benefits in any month that he does not earn more than $250. If he takes seasonal employment, therefore, he is not penalized in the months he is not working unless his annual total exceeds the limit. One small note of comfort: at age seventy-two he will be permitted to return to full-time employment without any reduction in his benefits: *if* he lives that long, *if* he is healthy enough, and *if* anyone gives him a job.

What does all that mean in cold cash? Not very much today, unfortunately. The *maximum* monthly retirement benefit paid to a retired worker who turned sixty-five in 1976 was $412.70. However, the *average* benefits paid in July 1976 were $221.00 to single workers, $377.00 to couples, and $210.00 to widows. It is important to remember, in noting these amounts, that the poverty threshold in 1975 was set at the annual figure of $2,572.00 for a single person and $3,232.00 for a couple. (Calculated on a monthly basis, the poverty threshold is $214.00 for a single person and $269.00 for a couple.)

The moment your mother is widowed, her financial situation almost automatically goes downhill unless she has independent assets. If your father died before retirement age, having accumulated, but never collected any of, his Social Security benefits, your mother can collect 100 percent as his dependent when she reaches sixty-five. If she is already collecting her own benefits, she has a choice: she can either continue independently or collect as your father's widow, whichever amount is higher. She cannot collect both. If your father had already been collecting before he died, according to a formula which takes into account the length of time he has been collecting, your mother's benefits will be reduced.

If your mother has been collecting her own benefits and decides to remarry, her checks will not be affected. But if she has been collecting as your father's widow, she again has two choices: she can collect as your dead father's dependent receiving half his benefits but losing her widow's status—which probably provided a larger amount—or she can collect as the dependent wife of her second husband. She will obviously choose the system which pays better. But she may decide to choose neither and turn down a second marriage because it costs too much and she cannot afford the luxury. Unwilling to lose her widow's benefits, she may instead set up extramarital housekeeping with the man she would like to marry and, by pooling resources with him, gain a somewhat greater state of financial security. Such a decision is particularly hard on conventional, self-respecting older people, but according to current Social Security regulations, no matter which way the pie is sliced, women who did not work come out receiving the smaller share. Any confusion that you or your parents feel about their benefits, entitlements, or eligibility can usually be cleared up by a phone call or a visit to your local Social Security office, listed in the telephone directory under U.S. Government, Department of Health, Education, and Welfare, Social Security Administration. A staff member should be able to answer your questions and also to supply you with a variety of free pamphlets explaining the workings of Social Security.

Pensions

Unless your parents have other assets, the only way they can get along reasonably well is if they have Social Security and adequate pension benefits. (Many pensions are far from adequate.) A variety of retirement systems do provide reasonable incomes for retired personnel: the Federal Retirement System, the Teachers Insurance and Annuity Association, veterans' pensions, and many union and company plans. There are also a number of private pension plans for self-employed men and women.

But many workers arrive at retirement age with no pensions at all or find when they near age sixty-five that the pensions they had been counting on vanish before they can reap the benefits. The faithful worker is not always rewarded when he retires. An Assistant Secretary of the Department of Labor testified at a congressional hearing in 1969: "If you remain in good health and stay with the same company until you are sixty-five, and if the company is still in business, and if your department has not been abolished and if you have not been laid off for too long a period, and if there is enough money in the fund, and if that money has been prudently managed, you will get a pension" (Thomas R. Donahue, quoted in the *Washington Post,* November 24, 1970). The statement is still true today. Factories and plants may close down leaving employees near retirement and unprotected. Pension rights may be lost if an elderly worker is laid off, retires too soon, or transfers to another job. The money such workers have paid in to a pension fund may be forfeited. Pension reform legislation was introduced with the Employee Retirement Income Security Act of 1974, popularly known as the Pension Reform Act, which established an Office of Employee Benefits Security under the Department of Labor to investigate questions and complaints from individuals about their pension rights.

At present there are 16 million retirees collecting some pension income. But *some* does not mean enough. The median monthly amount is $99. Private pension payments in themselves are usually not enough to insure a decent standard of living even when combined with Social Security payments. Also, few pension plans provide for survivors' benefits, and most of those that do so pay less to the ex-worker, which means that most people refuse that option.

Supplemental Security Income (SSI)

What can be done if your parents' monthly income is inadequate? They can—if they are not doing so already—apply for additional income under the federal Supplemental Security Income program, which provides additional funds for blind, disabled, and aged people with inadequate resources.

Your father, at sixty-five or over, is eligible for minimum SSI benefits if his monthly income falls below $177.80 or if he and your mother together have a monthly income below $266.70 (as of July 1977). They do not have to be destitute in order to apply. Certain personal and household possessions will not be counted against them. They may own a house, up to a value of $25,000 ($35,000 in Hawaii and Alaska); they may own a car with a retail value up to $1,200, and only the portion of the value above $1,300 will counted against them. A car will not be counted at all if it is used as transportation to a job or to regular treatments for a specified medical problem. They may have cash resources of $1,500 for an individual and $2,250 for a couple. The first $20 a month of their retirement check is not counted; the first $65 of their earnings and half of the remainder are not counted either.

Eligibility requirements can be determined at your local Social Security office, and it is important to check with them, since SSI does not operate uniformly in every state either in eligibility qualifications or in amounts of benefits. Some states add money to the federal allotment; some states allow applicants to retain more assets than other states.

The states that did *not* add to the federal monthly minimum SSI payments to people over sixty-five living by themselves were, as of July 1976, Alabama, Arizona, Arkansas, District of Columbia, Florida, Georgia, Indiana, Iowa, Kansas, Kentucky, Louisiana, Maryland, Mississippi, Missouri, Montana, New Mexico, North Carolina, North Dakota, Ohio, South Carolina, South Dakota, Tennessee, Texas, Utah, Virginia, West Virginia, and Wyoming.

The remaining states added extra amounts which varied in size. Eleven states added monthly supplements of $50 or more for individuals, and ten states added monthly supplements of $100 or more for couples.

Example: John Doe is sixty-six in 1976. He does not work, and he lives alone in a small house he owns. He has $1,500 in the bank. He has no pension and no contributions from children. His *only* income is his monthly Social Security check.

Social Security check	$150.00
Less deductible	20.00
Countable income	$130.00
SSI minimum	$167.80
Less countable income	130.00
Federal SSI check	$ 37.80
Social Security check	$150.00
SSI check	37.80
Total monthly income	$187.80

If John Doe lives in one of the states listed above, his monthly income is $187.80. If he lives in California, which adds a $108.20 monthly supplement, his monthly income is $296.00. If he lives in Illinois, which adds $7.20 a month, his monthly income is $195.00. If he lives in Oklahoma, which adds $21.90 a month, his monthly income is $209.70. Those state supplements, effective July 1976, are of course subject to change.

A sizable number of older people, however, although eligible for SSI, do not make use of it. Sometimes they are completely unaware of its existence. Sometimes they have modest savings tucked away —just enough to make them ineligible. But many are too proud and independent, unwilling to accept the assistance. While SSI was intended to be a supplement to Social Security rather than a welfare program, it does not seem to have been able to shake off the stigma of welfare, and some older people therefore refuse to apply for it.

How Are Social Security and SSI Similar?

Both programs are run by the Social Security Administration of the Department of Health, Education, and Welfare of the United States government.

People can get both if they are eligible for both.

Anyone who is dissatisfied with a ruling under either program has a right of appeal through the Bureau of Hearings and Appeals of the Social Security Administration. (Ask for details at your local office.)

How Are They Different?

Social Security benefits are paid from contributions of workers (income up to $16,500 a year is taxed as of 1977), employers, and self-employed people. As of 1976, employees and employers must each pay 5.85 percent of the employee's wages. Self-employed people pay 7.9 percent of their income. The money for SSI assistance comes from general funds of the U.S. Treasury: personal income taxes, corporation taxes, and others.

Social Security is uniform throughout the United States. *SSI* varies from state to state.

Social Security is a program of insurance wherein benefits depend on average earnings over a period of years. *SSI* is a program of *assistance* wherein benefits depend on need.

Indirect Noncash Supplements

Some financial aid is provided for the elderly through programs which offer them not money itself but opportunities to save money.

Title VII of the Older Americans Act makes funds available to the states (in proportion to the population sixty and over) for projects providing meals for the elderly: hot lunches, congregate meals (meals served in a central location), and some home-delivered meals for the homebound. (See Chapter 8.) Everyone over sixty is eligible, and the cost is determined by the individual's ability to pay. Unfortunately, there are only a limited number of these projects serving a limited number of meals in a limited number of locations.

Government Food Stamps and the Commodity Distribution Program (under the U.S. Department of Agriculture) also help to defray food costs, but here again the needs of the elderly far exceed the available supply of stamps, which must be shared by the needy of every age.

The elderly are allowed some benefits under the taxation regulations. The federal income tax laws (and some state income tax laws) allow double exemptions for those sixty-five and over, and in a number of states and local communities tax relief or rent assistance is given to elderly homeowners and tenants.

Depending on where they live, the elderly may find a variety of different ways to save money. Some communities give out half-fare or free transportation cards; some supermarkets issue their own food stamps providing a 10 percent reduction on total costs; some movie houses offer half-price tickets at certain hours. There is no overall, nationwide policy on those noncash benefits, which vary greatly from location to location. Information about your parents' community can be found through their State Office on the Aging. (See Appendix A, pages 248–53.)

Who Pays the Medical Bills?

Your parents may be hale, hearty, independent, and contented at the moment. You may be amazed at how well they seem to get along, even though you are pretty sure they do not have much money. But that reassuring situation is not likely to continue if either one—or both—develops a chronic condition, a general state of poor health, or a serious illness, and begins to need to see a doctor more frequently, and to spend more on drugs (the largest single medical expenditure) and other health-related items. No other expense is more draining for the elderly, more potentially disastrous, than medical expense. Government and private insurance programs, while helping to meet some of the costs, are by no means able to cover all of them. There are always loopholes and gaps in the coverage for acute illness, and there has been almost no insurance for the elderly to offset the calamitous cost of chronic illness requiring ongoing care.

Your parents, like the majority of older Americans, probably rely heavily on one of two government programs which help to defray medical costs: Medicare or Medicaid, both established under the Social Security Administration. They may also carry some additional private medical insurance to fill some of the gaps left uncovered by Medicare.

MEDICARE

This is a federal health insurance program for the elderly and for some younger people who are physically disabled. The Medicare program is divided into two sections: *Part A, Hospital Insurance,* helps to pay medically necessary inpatient hospital care. It also covers posthospital recuperative care in a skilled nursing facility for up to one hundred days. Under certain circumstances a limited amount of convalescent care at home is covered. Medicare's optional *Part B, Medical Insurance,* helps to pay for doctors' services, outpatient hospital services, outpatient physical therapy, speech pathology services (often necessary after strokes), and other medical services and supplies. In some instances it can help to pay for part-time skilled nursing care at home for a limited time when the hospital insurance (Part A) cannot pay for this.

Contrary to popular assumption, a Medicare membership card does not arrive on your parents' doorstep, along with the birthday cards, the day one of them turns sixty-five. They must apply for membership. Medicare is *not* automatic and it is *not* free. Each eligible individual must pay a monthly sum of $7.20 for Part B (cost as of July 1976). Medicare does not cover all medical expenses, nor does it move in immediately to cover expenses that are allowed. Every recipient is responsible for a deductible amount under Part A, which is roughly the average cost of one day's hospitalization, and for co-payments toward the cost of hospital and nursing home stays. None of that personal liability seems to add up to a fortune in money, but if your mother is a widow trying to manage on her Social Security check alone, the costs of medical care over and above Medicare can be a burden indeed. If she is admitted to the hospital in 1977, she will be responsible for the first $124 of her hospital bills, up from $104 in 1976. Her co-payments will be $31 per day from the sixty-first to the ninetieth day of hospitalization, up from $26 in 1976.

The average yearly medical bill for someone over sixty-five is $1,218. Of that, Medicare pays only $463. That is not only attributable to the deductibles and co-payment. Medicare regulations contain a number of "nots": Medicare does *not* cover care that is "unreasonable or unnecessary" (as determined by a Utilization Review Committee or a Professional Standards Review Organization of a hospital). Medicare does *not* cover custodial care, homemaker services, meals delivered to the home, eyeglasses, dental care, drugs, or routine foot care. Medical bills may be disallowed if your mother or father receives care from persons or organizations whose services are not approved. You or your parents can check Medicare status by asking directly or by sending for a *Directory of Medicare Providers and Suppliers of Services,* which costs $2.70 and is available from the U.S. Government Printing Office.

Confusion is rampant about the way Medicare works, what services are covered, and even how to fill out a Medicare form correctly. The Medicare carrier in Florida reports that 30 to 40 percent of the claims received for payment from older people are incomplete or incorrectly filled out. The Florida Medicare carrier, therefore, is conducting seminars on Medicare form filing. In Indiana, because of a similar confusion, the carrier distributed how-to leaflets on Medicare claim-filing procedures.

If you and your parents share this general confusion, you are likely to find some clarification in "Your Medicare Handbook," a pamphlet describing the details of the entire program, available free at any Social Security office. Here you will find spelled out which services are covered, the range of payments allowed, how to submit insurance claims, and the addresses of all organizations in the country selected by the Social Security Administration to handle the claims.

Medicare members may be surprised to find out that they have rights and do not have to accept without protest decisions which they feel are unfair in their individual circumstances. They have the right to appeal through the Bureau of Hearings and Appeal under the Social Security Administration. You can find out at your local office how to ask for a review, but the procedures can be time-consuming, and it may be months before the outcome is known.

PRIVATE HEALTH INSURANCE

Because it was originally assumed that Medicare coverage would carry the major burden of medical expense for the elderly, many health insurance policies cease when insured individuals reach sixty-five or when they become eligible for Medicare. But the gaps in Medicare coverage proved to be so costly that whenever possible many elderly carry supplementary medical insurance to help defray the cost of Medicare gaps: medical deductible and co-insurance costs, extra inpatient hospital days, outpatient services, and extra posthospital days in skilled nursing facilities.

Supplementary health insurance policies are available to the elderly from a number of insurers to fill the gaps that Medicare leaves or to pay for services not included in the federal program. (See Appendix D.) In various states, supplemental coverage is called "65-Special," "Medicare Tie-In," "Supplemental Coverage," and the like. It is usually covered by the same organizations which handle the Medicare claims and whose names and addresses are in the back of "Your Medicare Handbook." For a monthly charge ($11 with some companies), supplementary insurance will cover the Medicare deductible and co-insurance, extra inpatient hospital days, outpatient services, and extra posthospital skilled nursing facility days.

The extra coverage, while it helps, does little to offset the catastrophic cost of serious chronic illness, which is capable of wiping out the assets of entire families. Most major medical policies which cover catastrophic illness terminate at age sixty-five, although some companies do issue lifetime coverage on a guaranteed renewable basis. As of 1973, 12 million people sixty-five and over had some private health insurance, but only 1 million in that group had major medical protection. Medicaid assistance is available to those without major medical protection, but only when most of their assets have been used up. Health insurance plans other than those third-party payment arrangements are of two main types: those which offer services on a prepayment or insurance basis to the subscribing public of their general area, and self-insured employer-employee union plans. They may also be classified into plans that provide service through group practice units, and plans that provide a free choice of physician (or dentist) on a fee-for-service basis.

The service through group practice units known as "Health Maintenance Organizations" are one-stop medical shopping centers that offer a broad range of health services for a fixed monthly or yearly premium. The payment can be high—as much as $300 or more a year. But in return, according to *Consumer Reports*, the subscriber gets probably the greatest depth and breadth of protection there is. However, HMOs are not widely available and most do not accept persons over sixty-five who are not previous subscribers.

There is an urgent need at present for increased health protection for the elderly, not only to extend existing coverage but to pay for services that are as yet not covered at all: vision care, dental care, prescription drugs, and home health care. The American Association of Retired Persons and other action groups promoting the welfare of the elderly are seeking reforms in that direction.

MEDICAID

This state-administered program for the financially needy draws on state and federal funds. Each state designs its own individual program within the broad framework of federal regulations, so there is great state-to-state variation.

In *all* states an individual eligible for SSI is also eligible for Medicaid and other state social services, but it is not automatic. The elderly must apply for Medicaid assistance at their local social services office, listed in the telephone directory under the Department of Welfare or the Department of Social Services.

Twenty-nine states in 1976 also have Medicaid programs for the "medically needy": those who do not qualify for SSI but are unable to meet some extraordinary medical bills. In some states partial Medicaid coverage is allowed when need can be proved. In addition, *some* of the items that Medicare does not allow are covered in *some* states by their Medicaid programs for which *some* people are eligible. That all sounds very confusing—and it is! But experienced people in local welfare offices and state departments of welfare are able to review each individual case and determine who is eligible for what.

Every state Medicaid program receiving federal funds must supply certain basic services: inpatient hospital care, outpatient hospital services, lab and X-ray services, skilled nursing facilities, and some home health care. A wide variety of optional services may be available in the state where your parents are living. They can include clinic services, prescribed drugs, dental services, prosthetic devices, eyeglasses, private duty nursing, physical therapy, emergency hospital services, optometrist services, podiatrist services, chiropractor services, care for persons sixty-five or older in institutions for mental diseases and tuberculosis, and institutional services in intermediate-care facilities.

Medicare and Medicaid Are Similar

Both programs are designed to help defray hospital and medical bills.

Both programs are part of the Social Security Act.

An individual may be eligible for both programs.

Medicare and Medicaid Are Different

Medicare is a federal program. *Medicaid* is a federal-state program.

Medicare is uniformly administered by the Social Security Administration throughout the U.S.A. *Medicaid* programs vary from state to state within federal guidelines and are administered by local social service departments.

Medicare is an insurance program available to everyone sixty-five and over. *Medicaid* is an assistance program available to certain needy people of all ages according to standards of eligibility set by each state.

What Can You Do?

In the past children who had some financial means were held legally responsible for their elderly parents' support by laws of filial responsibility. Heartbreaking stories were reported of entire families wiped out by the illness of one elderly relative. Money set aside for Johnny's education sometimes had to be used to keep Grandma in the old age home. Federal regulations prohibit relative responsibility as an eligibility condition for Medicaid with the exception of spouse or the parents of individuals under twenty-one. In administering SSI, however, states *may* hold adult children responsible for their parents. That has been difficult to enforce, and there is a right of appeal to the Bureau of Hearings and Appeals of the Social Security Administration.

Whether "filial responsibility" has a legal hold on you or not, you may feel it anyhow and wonder what you can do to help when your parents are living under financial privation. If you have plenty of assets, you may be able to take over and support them, but even if you have financial problems of your own, there are a number of ways to help.

- Keep them informed. If you inform yourself on available programs, you may be able to show them how they are eligible for greater benefits.
- Override their pride. The older generation, particularly the current one, is often too proud to apply for assistance that is due them, fearing the hated stigma of welfare. You may be able to convince them that supplements are not "handouts" but returns from their own contributions as taxpayers.
- Encourage them to work. Your father and mother may be forced to retire, but there is no reason to stop them from taking a second job or starting a second career. If they want to try this, instead of dissuading them, explore with them the possibilities of part-time employment which could provide them with a necessary financial boost without overtaxing their energies. Opportunities are limited, but a few communities have employment agencies dealing exclusively with retired applicants, and a recent amendment to the Older Ameri-

cans Act established the Community Service Employment Program, which makes funds available to projects employing the elderly. (See Appendix B, pages 304–5.)

• Make small regular contributions of your own. You may be afraid it will hurt their pride if you offer them financial help. They may refuse it, but you may be able to persuade them to accept small amounts from you and others in the family. Life at the poverty threshold is grim for anyone at any age, and it is especially grim for the aged. A few extra dollars a month contributed by family members could make day-to-day living a little less dismal, but those extra dollars may be considered as income when Medicaid or SSI eligibility is being determined.

What About Your Own Preparedness?

You may have been giving serious thought to your parents' old age and anticipating their future needs. But have you at the same time given any thought to your own? You may be in fine shape now at forty or fifty, but your parents may live another ten, even twenty, years. How much extra money or energy will you have to share with them then? You may be single or childless now and in a position to do a great deal for them, but what if you marry or have your own children? Perhaps you have told your parents they can count on your financial help in the future. What if you were to die young? The current extended life-expectancy of older people creates the serious possibility that they will outlive their own children, a tragic but not uncommon occurrence.

If, when you contemplate your own situation ten or twenty years from now, it seems unlikely you will be able to do much for your parents, it would be better to discuss this openly. If you remain silent, they may assume they can count on you and make no alternative plans for themselves. Adult children too frequently play games with their parents. They send out the message that they know their parents want to hear rather than the one that is true. An inability to send the correct message may stem from a child's need to be a "good parent" to his own parents, or from his need to prove that he is a better parent to them than they ever were to him.

❖ THE DODSONS WERE a well-to-do couple with an apartment in Boston and vacation homes in Newport and Palm Springs. They suffered financial reverses in their later years, so at the time of Mr. Dodson's death, his widow was left literally penniless and quite resentful of her dead husband. Her son, however, was able to recoup a smaller part of the family fortune through his own ingenuity and for ten years was able to support his mother in an elegant apartment hotel with a live-in companion-housekeeper. After a time, the son suffered his own financial reverses and his health deteriorated. He continued to support his mother, although he could barely support himself and his family. Because of his own strong need not to seem a failure to his mother as his father had been, he never admitted the financial drain she made on him. But eventually he was forced to tell her that he was incapable of supporting her any longer. His mother was bitter and resentful, feeling, with justification, that if she had been told of the problems earlier she could have made better plans for herself.

Preparedness Versus Interference

This chapter began with a strong warning against interfering with the successful lifestyles your parents may have developed. It may seem that a contradictory position has been taken in suggesting that you help your parents plan for the future. There is actually no contradiction here. Preparation does not imply that changes must be imposed on older people against their will.

The preparedness that has been discussed suggests that families can enter into a kind of partnership with an elderly relative. Children can help gather information and guidelines, suggest alternatives, raise cautious warnings, and express concerns. The older person, of course, will make the final decision.

It can happen that your own mother and father may view your efforts at a partnership with distrust and resentment. They may rebuff any seeming intrusion into their private lives. But they are just as likely to respond positively—respecting, even welcoming, your opinions—although even the most receptive may not be ready to start planning at the same time you are. It may take them more time, but eventually they may be willing to share the planning process with you—or take it over for themselves. If not—if all attempts fail and you make no progress at all—you will at least have the small comfort of knowing that you have thought through some plans of your own and will therefore be better prepared yourself to know what has to be done if the day ever comes when they cannot manage on their own.

8.

Helping When They Cannot Manage— Community Solutions

❖ "TIMMY, IT'S BATH TIME. Did you pick up all your toys?"

"Yup."

"Timmy! You did not! What's all over the floor?"

"Nothing—just a couple of marbles. I picked up my cars."

"Get those marbles, too. Right now! You know Grandma's coming at six o'clock to sit with you. Come on! Hurry!"

"Awright, awright! I'm doing it as fast as I can. What's the big deal about a couple of little marbles?"

One of Timmy's marbles did make a big deal. Grandma stepped on it as she walked in, turned her ankle, lost her balance, and fell. That night, instead of Grandma sitting with Timmy, Timmy's family sat in the hospital while Grandma's broken hip was set. Before the marble she had been a self-sufficient seventy-year-old, ready to help out whenever one of her children needed her. Afterward, the tables were turned, and it was clear to them that she needed their help for the first time. But that was the only thing that was clear. It was unclear how much help she would need, what kind of help, and for how long.

The story of Timmy's grandma is not unusual. A widow or a widower, or an elderly couple, may move along through the years functioning reasonably well and presenting few if any problems to their children, who probably accept the status quo and give little thought to its impermanence. But suddenly one day a crisis can occur with little warning. A stroke can render an older person partially or totally incapacitated in a matter of hours. Even light falls can result in serious fractures.

More often than not, however, an approaching crisis gives off warning signals. Telltale signs appear months, possibly years, in advance, and all too often are ignored or denied by everyone. (As noted in the previous chapter, when the signals are picked up early, some crises can be averted.) Your father may be suffering from a number of diseases which limit rather than incapacitate him, although it is obvious to everyone that his normal resiliency is declining, his social world closing in, and his friends dying off. He may also have hidden clinical conditions that only surface after a serious accident, a physical trauma, or an emotional one. Common crisis-producers are the death of a spouse, an acute illness (pneumonia or a severe bout of flu), a serious fracture, or a frightening experience (a car accident or a mugging), even though no injury is sustained. Crises are frequently overcome and many elderly people return to independent living, but for others the crisis is the last straw. It does irreversible damage, and independence is gone forever.

Diseases are not necessarily crises in themselves. The crisis develops when a disease interferes with an older person's ability to manage. The day that your mother learns she has cancer may be agonizingly painful for everyone, but the real crisis will come when her illness begins to interfere with her normal routine and her ability to manage. An old man can live with his diabetes for years, but one day the disease may develop to the point where amputation is necessary. Arthritis may eventually make walking impossible; glaucoma may advance to partial or total blindness. Mental disorders must be evaluated in terms of the disability they produce. Your mother's occasional loss of memory may disturb her and upset you without seriously hindering her ability to take care of herself, but if she becomes increasingly forgetful or disoriented, it may one day become unsafe for her to continue to live alone. The amount of help the elderly need is largely determined by the extent of their physical and mental incapacities.

The extent of permanent disability left after acute illness or accident is equally unpredictable. The recuperative powers of two convalescents may be very different. One may return to semi-autonomous life within a matter of months, while the other may retire into a permanently dependent state.

Disease, disorder, and accident do not always dictate terms for the future; the future depends just as frequently on the physical and emotional resiliency of individual elderly patients as well as the supports available to them within their families and their communities.

Putting All the Pieces Together:
The Assessment

Neither the elderly nor their children can look into a crystal ball in times of crisis and see what lies ahead. The safest way to judge the future is to find out as much as possible about what is going on in the present. What does Mother have going for her? What does she have against her?

While your mother is recuperating from a fractured hip, an important job for you to do, if you are the responsible relative, would be to collect as much relevant information about her overall situation as possible. The process can be compared to putting together a jigsaw puzzle. Her future is made up of a number of separate but related pieces, and when all of them are fitted together a clear picture emerges. The pieces in your mother's case include her hip itself and how it is healing, her general physical condition, her emotional strengths and weaknesses, her personality, her motivation, her finances, and, perhaps most important of all, how and where she lives. Even if there is every reason to believe that she could make a good recovery, she will undoubtedly need some amount of help during the recuperative period. She may never be able to manage completely alone. Her future depends to a great extent, therefore, on the range of help she can find in her community. When the help she needs is not available, her only alternative may be to enter a nursing home. (The variety of vital community services making it possible for older people to avoid institutionalization will be described later in this chapter.)

The best way to understand all the pieces in your mother's situation, and how they fit together in the total picture, is to arrange for a comprehensive assessment of the many aspects of her life. After that, you will have a clearer idea of the care she is likely to need and be better able to plan accordingly. If you and she had done any contingency planning, as discussed in the last chapter, you may now be ready to put some of those plans into action. Others will have to be revised and adapted to meet her current needs. The same kind of comprehensive assessment is helpful for older people who are not in the hospital but are having serious difficulty at home. Although lengthy medical procedures cannot be done in the home, most of the assessment can be made there, and much insight can be gained in that way. When an elderly man is seen in his own home setting it will be easier to understand how much help he will need if he is to remain there.

The Physical Pieces

After an illness, an accident, or a general physical decline, an old man may wonder, "What's happening to me?" and his wife and children may ask themselves, "How much damage has been done?" "Is he getting worse?" "How long can he go on like this?" "What can we do to help him?"

A complete physical examination is the first and most crucial step to be taken before any answers can be given. But you may hit a snag right there. Since the medical profession in general has given low priority to the problems of the elderly, it is unsafe to assume that every physician is familiar enough with geriatric medicine to make an accurate diagnosis. The diseases of the elderly, as pointed out earlier, are often so closely intertwined that they can present a confusing picture, difficult to interpret unless a physician has special knowledge and experience.

Illness does not always show the same familiar signs and symptoms in the old as in the young. Diagnosis is often more difficult. Unfortunately, there are doctors who, because of lack of geriatric training in medical school, lack of experience with the elderly, lack of time, or lack of interest, tend to attribute an endless variety of symptoms to one cause—aging—and look no further. It is easy but dangerous to pin the hopeless, catchall term *senile* on confused, disoriented, even hallucinating older patients. They may in reality, as Dr. Robert Butler points out, be suffering from a treatable—reversible—brain condition resulting from any number of causes.

It may be hard for your mother to stand her ground with a doctor and insist that her questions be answered, her condition explained, and its treatment mapped out. It could be just as hard for you to speak for her if she cannot speak for herself. But there is a growing movement today urging the patient's "right to know." If you are dissatisfied with the answers you get—if they seem casual, unconcerned, fatalistic—you may be able to find more convincing answers at another consultation.

Your father may be fortunate enough to have a competent, interested family doctor who has known him for quite some time. A longstanding close relationship with an older patient can be particularly helpful in assessing his overall physical condition. Your own knowledge of your father's medical history can be useful, too, and added into the assessment. You may also be an important source of information when your father sees new doctors. He may forget his symptoms, or give an incomplete history. You may be a more accurate reporter with a clearer memory. But if he does not have a doctor you both trust, and you don't know who to see, there are better ways to go about finding a competent opinion than searching the Yellow Pages or asking a friend, neighbor, or Aunt Emma. There may be a nearby medical school, a hospital with a medical-school affiliation, or even a reputable local hospital where you can find the names of doctors with geriatric experience. The county medical association or a local social agency may also have names on file (see Appendix A, pages 254–64). A few communities—about thirty in the country—have compiled directories listing cooperating physicians and including information about their training, credentials, fees, office hours, and Medicare and Medicaid participation. By writing to the Health Research Group, 2000 P Street, Washington, D.C. 20005, you can find out if there is such a directory covering your own community.

The Psychological Pieces

The impact of illness and disability on an older person's emotional state is often ignored even though this can sometimes cause as much damage to the patient as the physical condition itself. Some, but not all, physicians are careful to take that vital element into account as part of a general physical examination. The incidence of psychiatric disorders increases greatly with age. If your mother's problem seems clearly a mental one involving any of the extreme reactions discussed in Chapter 4, then obviously a psychiatric examination is necessary, but sometimes it is hard to distinguish between primary and secondary conditions. The elderly may react with severe anxiety or depression to a physical or a mental loss; the anxiety and depression may in turn precipitate further physical deterioration.

❖ JACK WILSON'S FAMILY knew he was worried about his failing sight. What they did not realize was that his semiblindness triggered a depression which affected his appetite, disturbed his sleep, and intensified his anxiety. What was his real problem? His eyesight or his depression? Nothing much could be done to offset his approaching blindness, but his depression, once it was recognized, was lifted by psychiatric help.

Jack Wilson was lucky to find the help he needed readily available. There is a great lack of psychiatric services for the elderly in many parts of the country. People over sixty-five have a high incidence of psychological and emotional problems, yet they often can find no one to turn to for help.

You may have a number of sources to consult in your community. Psychiatrists, psychiatrically oriented physicians, social workers, and nurses can be helpful in evaluating the significance of emotional factors in your mother's condition. The county medical society and your local hospital, family service agency, and public health or visiting nurse associations are usually good sources for referrals.

The Functioning Pieces

Physical and psychological factors only fill in part of the total picture of an older man or woman in crisis situations, since physicians are usually interested mainly in diagnosis or treatment. They can tell you what's wrong with your father, what caused his problem, what other conditions contribute to it, and what procedures will modify it, but they may fail to consider carefully enough how the problem is likely to affect your father's own personal life and his day-to-day functioning. "Be sure he keeps to his diet and takes his medication. Call me if you have any problems, and I'd like to see him again in three weeks," a doctor may say pleasantly as you leave the office with your father. You may have no cause for alarm about his physical symptoms, but other considerations may concern you. If he lives alone, all or some of the time, will he be able to resume his daily routines, shopping, cooking, dressing, bathing, toileting? Will he be alert or coordinated enough to protect himself from all the potential hazards in his environment? Can he manage the stairs, pay his bills, take his medicine regularly, keep to his diet? Will he call you or someone else if he is in trouble? Even more important is his motivation to regain independence. If he has lost motor skills, will he be willing to relearn them through exercise or physiotherapy? Is he receptive to using compensatory devices, such as wheelchairs or walkers? Registered nurses, occupational therapists, and trained social workers, especially if they make home visits, can be helpful in assessing how adequately a disabled person is likely to function in daily routines. Local hospitals and family service agencies may be able to help you contact these professionals.

Without this evaluation, you may too hastily assume during a crisis that your father is more permanently disabled, plan accordingly, and make him more helpless than he really needs to be. Or you may underestimate the extent of his disability, provide inadequate supports, and invite serious accidents to happen.

The Social Pieces

Some missing pieces in the total picture can be found by evaluating the social environment in which older people are living. Will they be able to remain in familiar surroundings? How much help will they need in order to stay there? Some families set up schedules, take turns, and share the responsibility of caring for a disabled mother or father. One particularly devoted relative may be available or willing to take on the job. Older people who are rich may hire the necessary help, or a wealthy son or daughter may provide it. Friendly neighbors may be willing to pitch in and provide the extra support necessary. Essential help may be found outside the close circle of family and friends through public or private agencies in the community.

Knowledgeable social workers can be particularly helpful in sorting out the options available in each individual case. That valuable source of information is rejected hands down by some families reluctant to turn to outside professionals, preferring to keep family matters within the family itself. But in addition to providing an accurate description of services readily available in a given community, and explaining eligibility rulings and the real costs involved, a social worker, in a home visit, may be able to size up the older person. Although many independent-thinking fathers and mothers are suspicious of strangers and refuse to allow any outsiders to enter their homes to help them, a competent social worker may be able to persuade even the most reluctant to allow such outsiders as homemakers, home health aides, and visiting nurses to invade their privacy.

A social worker can also serve as a middleman when there is a communication problem between the generations in a family. A lack of communication may have a longstanding history in some families, or it may become a problem only in times of crisis. Children may be unable to tell painful truths to their parents, or the parents may refuse to listen. Someone outside the family can often provide the objective viewpoint that is missing and provide supportive counseling to the upset older person.

The Financial Pieces

Financial realities must always be included in the total picture, because money—or the lack of it—can be a crucial factor in the recovery process, speeding it up or blocking it completely. When a special or even an adequate diet is called for, elderly convalescents may or may not be able to pay for it. If they cannot, they then may suffer further malnutrition and deterioration. Rehabilitation can often be accelerated by physiotherapy, special retraining procedures, or the use of certain prosthetic devices, but everyone cannot afford such so-called luxuries. So Mrs. Jones, because of her adequate monthly income, may return to semi-independent life, while Mrs. Smith, struggling along at the poverty level, is never able to leave her wheelchair again. Money also determines whether enough extra household help can be hired to enable a semi-independent older man or woman to remain in the community. When adequate help cannot be provided free by relatives and friends and cannot be paid for, that fact alone may force a family to consider some form of institutional placement.

Who Puts All the Pieces Together?

Even though an overall assessment makes sense in principle, it may be close to impossible to obtain in reality. You may have trouble finding any competent help at all. Again, the stumbling block is society's historic lack of concern for the problems of the elderly. The professions are at present ill-equipped to offer the thorough physical, psychological, and social work-ups needed by millions of older citizens in trouble, even though individual competent professionals know how valuable those work-ups can be.

In many locations across the country, unless you are able to turn to a team of professionals, you may be able to work up your own team or fit the whole puzzle together yourself with assorted bits of information, insights, and advice. It may be little comfort, when you are forced to settle for makeshift compromises, to know that more concern for the welfare of the elderly is shown in other parts of the country—where unfortunately you do not live—or will be shown in the future—when unfortunately it will be too late to help your own parent.

Professional interest in the over-sixty-five sector of the population is growing. More facilities for information, referral, guidance, and treatment are opening up. Some of the better-staffed nursing homes across the country currently offer full assessments to the elderly who come to them for help. Visiting nurse associations make functional evaluations in the home. A few community agencies and clinics offer medical, nursing, psychiatric, and social assessments. A number of hospitals provide assessments to elderly patients before they are discharged, sometimes as part of an aftercare program.

Your own need for an assessment of your mother's condition may come, as it does for many families, while she is still actually in the hospital recovering from some acute episode. If you are bewildered about what to do when she is facing discharge, you may be referred to the hospital social service department, where a social worker will help you find the advice you need. The social worker may also be able to suggest appropriate arrangements to make after the assessment is completed. But things do not always go that smoothly. There may be no competent social service staff at your hospital; it may be difficult to set up the assessment; the general hospital policy may be to recommend institutionalization as the simplest course of action; or your doctor may resent anything which he considers outside interference on his private cases.

If you find out, as many people do, that there is nowhere to turn for a thorough professional assessment, the best way to proceed is slowly, deliberately, watchfully. If you do not panic, you yourself may be quite adept at figuring out what is happening, since you've known your parents longer and better than anyone else. Obviously, workable arrangements must be made to care for a disabled person adequately during an emergency, but they should not be solidified too quickly into permanency. They should be subject to revision until the situation stabilizes and its long-term implications become clear.

❖ JENNY FRANKLIN LAUGHS a little sheepishly today when she remembers all the terrible thoughts that galloped through her mind whenever she looked at her crippled father in the early weeks following her mother's sudden death. "I couldn't bear to look at him. He seemed ten years older. All the progress he'd made in getting around after his car accident vanished overnight. Someone had to lift him from the wheelchair to the bed. He hardly spoke, barely listened to anyone. I kept wondering, How could he go on? Not alone here! He'd have to move in with us! I'll have to quit my job to take care of him! But I can't do that! A nursing home, maybe? Never! Not that! But what? I found myself wishing he'd died, too. What was left for him?"

Lucky for Jenny that she did not know which way to turn and therefore did nothing. She took time off from work to help her father through the first devastating effects of her mother's death. Then slowly everyone noticed he seemed to be getting stronger, moving around a little better every day, eating more, taking notice, responding. A few months later it became clear that with some additional help—granted, that was a problem to arrange—he would be able to live a somewhat independent existence. When he remarried a few years later, Jenny was a little ashamed that she had predicted such a dire future for him just a short time earlier.

Pessimism may, on the other hand, be warranted. Jenny's father was lucky, but many are not. Emergencies may pass, leaving older people totally incapacitated. Radical changes must be made then, and families will be consoled by the certainty that they had no other alternatives. They will be less likely to torment themselves months later with guilty self-accusations, all beginning with phrases like, "If only we'd realized . . ." or "We never should have . . ." or "Why did we. . . ."

What Kind of Care?

Since crises vary in severity, in duration, and in extent, there are several different ways to cope with them. During the acute phase, older people, like younger ones who are seriously ill, need intensive care. But once that phase has passed, other types of care are often more appropriate. It is important to find the right balance in your own situation. Too little care can make your mother overanxious and helpless. Too much care can make her overdependent and infantile. Either extreme may lead to additional problems.

"Off-and-On" Care

This level of care is neither continual nor intense. It is required when older people cannot really manage alone and need help off and on. It would be ideal if off-and-on care were available to all the elderly, even those in comparatively good health, as part of preventive care, but it is especially important to the numbers who can manage some, but not all, of the time. Your parents may only need outside help during special periods: minor illnesses or accidents, the death of a loved relative or friend. When an emotional flare-up is triggered by some crisis, they may need occasional periods of support provided by casework counseling, or individual or group therapy. Temporary care should be available for just the amount of time it is really needed—no longer, no shorter.

Undoubtedly, the best place to find such care today, as in years past, is still within the immediate family. That does not mean that you have to be around your parents all the time; you don't have to take them into your own home or consider nursing home placement. Simply knowing that you will be available when they need you can be all the reassurance they need in order to manage for themselves the rest of the time.

Sons, daughters, and in-laws, as well as sisters, brothers, nieces, and nephews, are usually quick to respond to a close relative's crisis if they are in any position to respond at all, and not only when that relative lives with them or around the corner. Assuming there is a basically affectionate relationship between the generations, close relatives provide an all-important ingredient often missing in off-and-on care from outsiders: the loving comfort that gives the extra boost to an older person's recovery.

❖ EIGHTY-YEAR-OLD Maude Evans had a cardiac condition and high blood pressure, but had managed to live by herself for ten years. When she was feeling well she was able to manage her small apartment, cook for herself, and visit her friends and relatives. Periodically she suffered cardiovascular flare-ups which required close medical supervision and a good deal of rest. At times the flare-ups made her anxious and depressed; at other times they were precipitated by an emotional upset. During those episodes her daughter would visit her daily to take care of the house, prepare meals, and do necessary chores. Occasionally during an acute phase a twenty-four-hour home health aide was hired to stay with her, but as soon as her condition improved, Mrs. Evans was eager to have her house to herself again and ready to return to her former pattern of living. Just knowing she had someone to turn to for help, if things went wrong, made her able to manage alone when life was smooth.

The family is not always in a position to respond even to a temporary emergency, and substitutes may be found to provide temporary care. A close friend or a neighbor may be able to stop in. The necessary care may be arranged, if possible, through social or health agencies, which will be described later in this chapter and which are increasing their services to the elderly in some locations. If, because of complications in your own life, you sense in advance that you will be unable to provide off-and-on care for one of your parents, you may decide to prepare for that situation in advance and look into the outside help available in your parent's community. You will feel relieved to know there is someone they can call when problems arise, and they will be reassured, too. Self-reliant though many elderly people may be, they are usually willing to give up some portion of their treasured independence. When off-and-on care is not available, either from a social network or from community services, its lack can be the crucial factor leading to nursing home placement.

Protective or Supportive Care

This is middle-range, second-level care needed by the elderly who do not alternate between independence and dependence. Many older people have chronic disabilities which permit them to function in some areas but not in others. They are not likely to improve, but they are often able to get along well, despite their handicaps, if ongoing care is provided in specific areas. Your father's heart condition may prevent him from managing his apartment alone, but if someone comes in to prepare at least one meal a day for him, and do the marketing and the heavy cleaning, he can probably remain where he is—and where he may vehemently insist he *wants* to remain.

Supportive care may be required by the elderly who are arthritic, crippled, partially blind, or partially paralyzed, but it may also be necessary for those who have no one specific infirmity but are just generally weakened by advancing age. Although no longer able to manage any physical chores, they may be perfectly capable of thinking clearly, making their own decisions, knowing exactly what they want, and saying so loud and clear. Supportive care may also be necessary for those who are physically sound but, because of minimal mental impairment, need someone to help them manage their routines or their money, or make complicated decisions. Their ability to make decisions for themselves in some areas, however, should never be underestimated. Only when there is evidence that they are endangering themselves or others should their ability to make their own decisions be questioned.

As in the case of temporary care, supportive care can be provided by children and close relatives, but it is long-term, ongoing, and sometimes very demanding. Many families may find it too heavy a burden. Since it is always possible for any machinery to break down when outside help is used—a housekeeper gets sick, a doctor is unreachable, transportation to an essential treatment does not show up—the disabled person should ideally have a permanent contact with someone, either in the family or in the community agency, who will respond to an SOS. Individuals responsible for supportive care may get sick, take time off, or go on vacation, but the care itself cannot be allowed to lapse; stand-ins and understudies should be available.

Long-Term Intensive Care

Eventually, for some older people, the time does come when halfway measures are no longer enough. One day, after a stroke, a heart attack, or severe mental deterioration, your mother may no longer recognize you or anyone else, or she may be permanently invalided. Your father may not know where he is, or he may have lost control of his bodily functions. People in those tragic conditions require twenty-four-hour care. Some, whose overall condition may not be so hopeless, are still disabled enough to require constant medical attention and skilled nursing. That is the point at which many families feel forced to consider institutionalization, which may now become the only solution. But intensive care is also possible either in an older person's home or in a child's home.

❖ PRIOR TO HER STROKE, seventy-eight-year-old Gina Tarrant had lived with her daughter and her daughter's family. She had been a good-humored, cooperative person who blended well into the family, helping when needed and rarely interfering. She was an excellent babysitter, and shopped and took care of the house while her daughter and son-in-law went to work every day.

Her stroke left her paralyzed on one side of her body, and unable to handle any of the activities of daily living, including bathing, dressing, feeding, and toileting. At times she was incontinent. But following her hospitalization the family decided to bring her home. They bought a hospital bed and other equipment to make nursing care easier and hired a home health aide to come in every day from nine to five. A visiting nurse stopped by regularly to check on Mrs. Tarrant's condition, and a local doctor made occasional house calls. Her daughter and son-in-law took over in the evening and on weekends, but other relatives came in regularly to relieve them when they needed a break.

Fortunately, there happened to be a number of other relatives willing to share the responsibility, and no one individual was seriously overburdened. Mrs. Tarrant, although partially paralyzed, remained in her familiar setting, aware of her family and the love and concern that surrounded her.

Gina Tarrant was fortunate that outside help was available in her community and that so much "inside" help was offered by her extended family. Intensive care can be provided under less favorable conditions. One family member—a daughter, a daughter-in-law, a niece, a sister—may be willing enough and strong enough and dedicated enough to assume the major responsibility. But no one should volunteer impulsively without a full understanding of the rigorous demands of the job. If you are contemplating caring for your mother or father yourself, you might discuss the case first with a registered nurse at a hospital or a visiting nurse in your community, and find out as much as you can about the necessary routines. (A textbook on home nursing published by the American Red Cross is listed in Appendix F.)

It is essential to remember in advance that when a patient needs intensive care it must be available round-the-clock, seven days a week. You will be able to take time off, of course, but only if the care is provided in your absence by someone else. Beds must be made several times a day, baths and sponges given, bedpans emptied, medications administered. Special care must be taken of the skin to avoid bedsores. Any minor skin condition may be aggravated by incontinence. You may have extra laundry duties and kitchen duties. Nutritious meals—sometimes involving special diets —must be served three times a day, as well as periodic snacks. Orders from the doctor are to be followed and reports on the patient's progress turned in to the doctor. Efforts should be made to encourage a patient to take care of himself whenever he can: grooming, shaving, feeding. His morale must be considered, too. The life of a shut-in or a bedridden invalid can be endlessly dreary and lonely. Some kind of recreation and entertainment must be provided—handicrafts, books, music—and visitors encouraged to stop by. Patients can be difficult, discouraged, irritable, demanding, suspicious, or resentful, but nursing care is still expected to be performed with cheerfulness, compassion, understanding, and caring.

Helping the Mentally Impaired

When caring for an older person with some degree of mental impairment, it is essential to have some ongoing psychiatric and medical supervision. Medications may be prescribed for some agitated elderly patients, and a calm, structured atmosphere with a regular ordered routine is usually the most effective. Too much stimulation and excitement can be overwhelming and confusing.

If intensive care of a physically disabled parent is a rigorous job, the care of a mentally impaired one is equally taxing, even if it is not round-the-clock. You may find it particularly draining because of your close emotional involvement. Dealing with your mother's confusion, disorientation, loss of memory, and possibly delusions day after day can be nerve-racking, and even though you understand that she cannot help the way she behaves, you may still feel hurt and rejected when she does not even recognize you.

The best approach, which involves an almost superhuman effort for many children, is to remove yourself as much as you can from your personal feelings and try to help her hold on to some threads of reality. Although you find the endless repetition agonizing and frustrating day after day, she may be less confused if you repeat quietly simple factual statements: "Yes, you've had your lunch," or "No, it's not morning, it's bedtime," or "Today is Thursday. Tomorrow is Friday," or "This is Jane—your sister." Big calendars, large clocks, even photographs of relatives, can be ever-present silent reminders of everyday realities. Older people with only partial mental impairment frequently suffer only brief periods of disorientation, slipping into confusion and then out again. The more concrete clues they have available, the less likely they will be to lose their grasp of reality.

The same detached calmness can be helpful for the mentally impaired who distort reality. Arguing about what is real or imagined will not help, but will rather make them more anxious and compound their confusions or delusions. There is no advantage to be gained by a pitched battle with your mother when she anxiously insists, "The mailman has a gun!" or "The delivery boy is a thief!" "The homemaker is poisoning me!" Better results will usually follow if you can ignore what she says and pick up the feelings accompanying her words. When your first impulse is to snap back impatiently, "Nonsense! How can you say that nice little Billy Forse is a thief?" try taking a deep breath and saying instead, "You're frightened, aren't you, Mom?" If your father keeps angrily insisting you have a lover, your husband has a mistress, and everyone is talking about your immoral behavior, he'll never believe your denials. But he might respond if you ask him, "You're angry at us, aren't you, Pop?" Eventually, you may find that oblique responses on your part come more spontaneously.

Despite its demands and frustrations, the care of the very sick can be very rewarding if it is provided with devotion and high competence. But regardless of the success you have with your patient, regardless of your ability to handle the routines, it is absolutely essential that you arrange for regular periods of relief—respite time —from a job that goes on round-the-clock and weekends, too. Friends and relatives may be willing to take over for you at regular intervals. Public health and visiting nurses and health aides may also provide some respite and may be invaluable in showing you more effective nursing techniques.

Even if you are confident that you can manage the job with all its physical and emotional demands, one final question must be answered before you take it on: What does everyone else in the family feel about it? Is it possible that although you do not resent your demanding job, others will resent it? Their freedom will probably be curtailed in some way, too. You may end up devoting all your energies to one member of your family while neglecting everyone else. Think of the additional burden you may then have to carry— your guilt that you are neglecting them and your resentment that they make you feel guilty!

If your decision to keep your mother or father at home is predicated on help you expect from others in the family, then their wishes should be considered in advance. If you do not choose to involve them earlier and make a unilateral decision, they may not choose to pitch in and help you later. When the situation has been discussed freely in advance and all individuals have been allowed to say how much responsibility they are willing to accept, family disruption can be avoided, and the resulting family unity can work wonders.

In their recent book *Gramp,* photographers Dan and Mark Jury have put together a pictorial record of the last years in their grandfather's life—years during which the old man became seriously deteriorated and incontinent. Nevertheless, he remained in his home, cared for by his loving and devoted family. The Jurys admit that they were able to keep Gramps with them until he died, partly because of the genuine feelings they all had for him and partly because there were enough of these loving people in the family to take the ongoing care in turns. No one person was victimized or martyred. Great satisfaction can be gained by caring for a deteriorating but well-loved relative at home—a satisfaction that often is compensation enough for the heavy investment of time and energy required from everyone. The Jury family and others like it stand as modern examples of the old Iroquois Indian precept, "It is the will of the Great Spirit that you reverence the aged even though they be helpless as infants."

What Does Mother Have to Say?

So many problems must be dealt with when crises arise in the lives of elderly parents. Sons and daughters frantically search for solutions while simultaneously trying to keep their own lives, their business affairs, and their children functioning smoothly. Although all the confusion may be caused by Mother's crisis and all the searching centers around "What's best for Mother?" Mother herself may be the forgotten woman. No one may remember to tell her what's going on and what's being done for her, or—worse yet—to ask her what her wishes are and what *she* thinks would be best for her. The omission, while humanly understandable, may be the very thing that causes carefully made plans to boomerang. Here again, as in most dealings between the generations, shared decisions are likely to produce the best results.

As caretaker, you may want to take matters into your own hands for efficiency's sake and dictate terms to your parents "for their own good." But if you do, don't be surprised if your terms are not accepted, or if they are accepted reluctantly and then deliberately torpedoed. Even if your terms work out and your parents *do* manage, you may find that they resent you more. Some semblance of a partnership can continue to operate between the generations even when the older members are quite sick and plead, "Tell me what to do." Attempts should be made to involve them whenever possible in decisions, and a frank discussion of why some options are open, and others are not, will ultimately help to convince them that they are not being willfully railroaded by their children.

You May Not Be Quite as Important as You Think

When off-and-on care or supportive care is necessary for one of your parents, *someone* must be around to provide it, but that someone does *not* have to be you, or your younger sister, or your older brother. Because society has provided such limited assistance to the elderly, they have been forced to turn to their children for lack of anyone else to turn to. Even today, when more services are becoming available, your mother may have no idea where to look for help outside of her family. You may not know either and feel obligated to take the responsibility for the care yourself.

Finding someone else to share a burden is not buckpassing or shirking, although it may be labeled that by other family members, friends, or neighbors, who may tut-tut when they see a stranger coming in every day to take care of old Mrs. Grenville or an outsider taking old Mr. Packer to have his leg brace adjusted. They may enjoy gossiping about Mrs. Grenville's "unfeeling" daughter or Mr. Packer's "no-good" son. Meanwhile Mrs. Grenville may be quite content that she has someone to take good care of her, and Mr. Packer may be relieved that his brace can be adjusted regularly without bothering his busy son. Both old people may prefer to have their children around when there are fewer chores to do and more time for them to talk and enjoy each other.

Modern sons and daughters, so accustomed to feeling guilty about their parents, may overestimate their own roles in their parents' lives. Studies suggest that the older generation, even when it has close ties with their children, sometimes prefers a measure of separation. Why else do so many choose, as one report shows, houses or apartments in retirement villages with no extra bedrooms? This choice may be made not only because of cost or convenience but also to prevent lengthy visits from children and grandchildren.

Your mother may have been "on your back" all your life, but if she was never that way when she was younger and only in her old age burdens you with endless phone calls, requests for rides, and constant attention, it may be not that she is deliberately burdening you, but that she has no one else to call. If she could Dial-a-Ride or Dial-an-Aide when she needs transportation out of the house or help inside it, she might not have to call on you so often.

❖ "I'd love to come visit you and the children," an elderly aunt living in a one-room apartment in a retirement village said pleasantly when her niece called, "but it will have to be next month. This month I'm too busy. I go for physiotherapy every day, I've promised to read to my neighbor who's blind until her regular reader comes back, and I've found someone to help me get to that concert series I wanted to hear." All those activities were being undertaken by an eighty-year-old who needed a walker to get around. Her niece, who had felt guilty for weeks because she had not made the effort to invite her "poor old aunt" for the weekend, hung up the phone feeling surprisingly unnecessary.

What Does the Community Have to Offer?

The ideal community, particularly for the elderly, should be able to offer basic health resources: family doctors (willing to make house calls on the homebound), specialists—including psychiatrists—twenty-four-hour emergency care, dentists, and a nearby, well-equipped general hospital with provisions for psychiatric emergencies and short-term treatment. Somewhere in the larger community there should also be a psychiatric hospital and some well-run nursing homes, as well as social service agencies and a variety of other helping services offering in-home and out-of-home assistance. But the ideal community does not actually exist. It is probably safe to state that *no* community at present can take care of all the needs of its elderly.

Some communities have quite an extensive variety of services for the elderly; others are disastrously poor, lacking even the most essential ones. A 1972 study made for the U.S. Senate Special Committee on Aging showed that 54 percent of all American communities, some with populations of more than 50,000, have no home health services at all. More time, energy, and money will have to be invested by politicians, professionals, and concerned citizens before that day will come.

Older people living in communities lacking in services may be unlucky, but those in communities with many services are no better off if they have no idea how much is available and how to make use of it all. In many places it can take some real detective work to track down the right services for each individual situation. When you or your parents wonder how to begin to find the help you need, the best way to start is to contact someone who knows the overall community set-up. Those informants can be found in a number of public and private agencies.

Information and Referral Services

Some areas have special information and referral services (publicly or privately funded) to guide residents of all ages to appropriate local services. (See Appendix A-2 for selected list.) Here you can usually find out exactly what services there are and which ones your own mother or father is eligible to use. When there is no independent information and referral (I & R) office, similar information can be found at local sectarian or nonsectarian family services agencies or senior centers whose staffs of professional social workers are usually well briefed on the community. These professionals may also arrange for an assessment for one of your parents, advise on the type of care necessary, and refer you to other specialized services. You and your parents may also be given the name of one specific social worker to call on when further problems arise.

When no family service organizations are listed in your phone book, you can write to the Family Service Association of America for the agency closest to your parents' community. The personnel of their local Social Security, Medicaid, or Welfare offices are usually familiar with the range of services offered and may be particularly reliable in knowing which ones your parents will be financially eligible to use. Physicians and clergymen are also likely to have a general idea of what goes on in the community. Further information can sometimes be found by consulting special groups, such as the American Cancer Society.

Caretakers often feel particularly helpless or overwhelmed when facing the heavy responsibility of caring for their ailing parents, and it can be a tremendous relief to discover that there are other helping people around to shoulder some of the burdens.

When services bring help directly into their homes or make it possible for them to leave their homes, the elderly usually find that life seems better. The anxiety and depression so many of them feel because of their disabilities may be alleviated. The loneliness and isolation, so much a part of old age in America, can be partially counteracted.

At-Home Services

A number of services bring help directly into the home, and are particularly important to the homebound. Information and referral offices, and social workers at family service agencies, can tell you which ones operate in your parents' community, and can make the necessary arrangements unless you or your parents prefer to make the arrangements yourselves.

A few words of caution are necessary here. While similar services may be found in communities across the country, there may be great variations in quality and performance. There may be scandals, mismanagement, inefficiency, incompetence at any point. General, overall standards may be lacking, or there may be no one available to monitor and supervise every local facility.

Visiting Nurse Services

Most communities have some nursing professionals—registered nurses, public health nurses, and licensed practical nurses—if they have any health services at all. Nursing staffs are often limited in number and must cover nursing needs at every age level, so it may be impossible for them to meet the needs of the elderly group adequately. The elderly have so many needs!

Regular supervision by a registered nurse, usually referred by a physician, is particularly important for older people with chronic illnesses, but the visiting nurse is also vital for bedside care during acute illnesses and the convalescent period that follows.

The schedule of visits varies. Sometimes the nurses come in every day or several times a week, for a few minutes or for longer. They supervise medication, carry out special procedures, provide nutritional counseling, give general guidance about household management. In addition, they frequently take a personal interest in the older patient's ongoing daily life, directing homemakers and home health aides and teaching families how to make life easier for themselves as well as for the patients. They are often invaluable in dealing directly with mentally disturbed old people and in helping relatives to make their dealings more effective.

Visiting nurses represent to the elderly a crucial link to other community services. They keep up to date on new services being set up and the most direct means of making use of old ones. Local visiting nurse groups are usually run by voluntary organizations and have a sliding scale of fees—sometimes, but not always, covered by the Medicaid and Medicare programs. Visiting nurse fees vary according to location and the individual patient's ability to pay.

Homemaker–Home Health Aide Services

It is difficult to say which is more important to the ongoing well-being of the disabled elderly: the visiting nurse or the homemaker.

The nurse takes care of vital medical problems (along with the doctor), but the homemaker makes life move more smoothly every day. When homemakers are available they may make it possible for families to avoid institutionalizing an elderly relative or at least to postpone placement. In 1963 there were three hundred homemaker–home health aide services across the country, and in 1973 an unpublished directory of homemaker services prepared by the National Council of Homemaker–Home Health Aide Services, Inc., listed over 1,700. Numbers have increased steadily in the past decade, but the demand is constantly greater than the supply, which the elderly must share with all the younger groups. (See Appendix B-1, pages 265–71, for a selected list of homemaker—home health aide services.)

Homemaker–home health aide services are sometimes hospital-based, provided by hospitals for their ex-patients, but more frequently they are community-based, sponsored by private or public agencies. The charges are on a sliding scale and vary according to the status of the sponsoring agency, whether it is public, voluntary (nonprofit), or proprietary (profit-making). Health insurance, Medicaid, and Medicare may cover the services of health aides, but only with specific provisions and limitations.

Homemaker–home health aides are trained in household and personal care and usually work under the direction of a nurse, social worker, or other health professional. The majority are women (on occasion men are available) and are trained to be more than housekeepers; in some areas they are given special orientation for working with the elderly. They can take on partial or full responsibility for running a house as well as the care of the older person living there. Health aides are primarily trained for patient care but may assume some household responsibilities as well. They must not be considered as professionals (nurses) or as servants (maids). The amount of care necessary in each individual situation is usually determined jointly by the family and the sponsoring agency; it may be once or twice a week, every day for a few hours, or round-the-clock in special cases for short periods.

Families hoping that a homemaker will be a miracle worker must always be aware that there may not be one available at the time they need one. There are an estimated 30,000 homemaker–home health aides to meet an estimated need of 300,000.

But even if one is available, there is no guarantee she or he will be competent, kind, efficient, capable. Homemaker–home health aides are not licensed and may, in some locations, have no professional supervision. Quality and standards vary greatly from one local service to another. If you are uncertain how to go about evaluating the service in your own community, turn to the checklist in Appendix C-2, page 310.

Meals on Wheels

Although adequate nutrition is a vital ingredient in the total health of the elderly, malnutrition, which aggravates physical and mental problems, is the fate of many. Poverty is a major cause of malnutrition, but another is the inability of the elderly to prepare adequate meals for themselves. Low-cost or free meals are offered more frequently now to both the poor and the disabled, although here again the need far exceeds the supply.

The federal government shares in the cost of a limited number of meals delivered directly into homes, particularly where older people live alone. Most Meals on Wheels programs, which also deliver to the door, are funded and operated locally by voluntary organizations. Commercial (profit-making) home-delivered food services also can be found, but they are usually cost-prohibitive for limited budgets. Here again, as with other services, there is great variation in cost. In one Indiana community a hot meal served five days a week costs $1.75 per meal, and in one Connecticut town where hot lunches and cold suppers were served three days a week, the charge is $2.50 per day.

When a hot meal is delivered every day, it provides not only nutritional benefits for the elderly recipients, but a side benefit as well. The volunteer delivering the meal is sometimes the only daily contact the homebound have with the world outside. They can look forward every day "at meal time" to a friendly chat and a little human concern, which can be as satisfying to the spirit as the nutritious meal is to the body.

Telephone Reassurance Programs

The telephone represents a lifeline for many of the elderly living alone, but even when there is a phone they may not be able to get to it to make an outgoing call for help in the event of an accident or acute illness. Both they and their children often worry about those possibilities. A daily phone call by a regular caller at a prearranged time can serve as the best reassurance that all is well, for one more day at least. Children often set up their own systems, calling every day at the same time to say, "Hello, Mother, how are you?" and the elderly themselves sometimes set up "buddy" systems in which two or more friends will call each other. But children may live too far away, making daily long-distance phoning too costly; buddies may vanish or die off. Then a volunteer or commercial telephone checking service charging moderate fees can be used instead. Here again the older person receives an added bonus, the chance to hear the sound of a human voice every day: "Hello, Mrs. Gavin. How are you today?" If Mrs. Gavin does not answer her phone, help will immediately be sent to her home, and if she does not answer her door, a neighbor, friend, or nearby police or fire station is asked to check in person and see if anything has happened to Mrs. Gavin. Lives have often been saved that way.

Escort and Transportation Services

Because they are afraid to go out of the house alone—afraid of getting hurt, getting mugged, or getting lost—even semi-independent old people are forced, too soon, to be shut-ins. Little has been done to adapt public transportation to the physical limitations of the elderly. Stairs are too steep in subways, steps into buses and trains too high, curbs too low, signs too confusing or too hard to read. After trying to deal with all the hazards of going out, an older man or woman may just give up. It may be depressing and demoralizing to be isolated inside four walls, but at least it's safe.

The elderly have traditionally depended on their children, close relatives, and friends to accompany them, but escort services sometimes providing transportation can now be found in some, although not many, communities. When your mother leaves her home with an escort, both you and she will have some sense of security that, despite the hazards and complexities of the transportation system, she is likely to arrive safely at her destination.

Chore Services

Some older people are able to take care of themselves in their own homes, but they are unable to take care of their homes alone. For lack of physical strength or lack of money, they are unable to handle repairs and maintenance. They need someone to come in to fix leaks, put up storm windows and screens, mow lawns, and do other household repairs. Funds are available in some communities for projects which provide necessary assistance at reduced cost. In a number of communities vigorous and capable older men and women are willing to act as handymen and chore people for their contemporaries who are incapacitated.

Friendly Visiting

Even when escort help is available, many older people are too incapacitated to leave their homes and therefore have no escape from
homebound life. Friends and relatives can relieve the isolation,
boredom, and loneliness, but when there are few nearby, friendly
visiting, often described as organized neighborliness, can take their
place. Friendly visitors may be university students, volunteering
their services or charging only small fees. The International Ladies
Garment Workers and other unions include friendly visiting programs among their services for their retired employees. In many
places friendly visitors are elderly themselves, but active and self-
sufficient enough to visit and help contemporaries who are shut-ins
or severely handicapped. These visitors stop in on the homebound
on a regular schedule, one or more times a week, and do whatever
any other concerned guest might do: play chess or cards, write
letters, help with mending and picking up around the house, run
local errands, make telephone calls, sit and chat and, perhaps most
important of all, *listen.* The continuing companionship is the best
antidote to the loneliness and endless silence which are so built into
the life of a shut-in.

Sitting Services

"Who's going to watch out for Grandpa when I go out?" a harried
daughter often wonders. The answer may be found at a local sitting
service, which lists sitters of all ages for all ages. Some are vigorous
older people willing and eager to help less fortunate contemporaries
and earn a few extra dollars at the same time. But added now to the
list of teenage job possibilities—babysitting, lifeguard duty, yard
work, paper routes—is a newer category: Grandma and Grandpa-
sitting. Young people, particularly those living in age-segregated
communities where they rarely see anyone over sixty and may
hardly know their own grandparents, can find real gratification as
well as sitting fees from their first close relationships with really old
people.

Out-of-Home Services

Some old people are luckier than the shut-ins and are able to leave
their homes more easily, but they often find, once they go out, that
they have no place to go. Some communities have little to offer,
while others have a great variety: educational and religious classes

and meetings, health services, occupational physical and psychological therapy, as well as recreational and social opportunities.

Congregate Meals

In 1972 Congress passed the Nutrition Program for the Elderly (Title VII of the Older Americans Act), and funds were made available to provide low-cost, nourishing meals to the elderly (sixty and over) in centrally located centers—schools, churches, and community and senior centers. The nutrition program has two aims: to improve the nutrition of older people, and at the same time to offset the isolation so many of them suffer. Too many elderly men and women hardly bother to eat because they have no one to eat with. Meals are served in the various centers five days a week. Participants do not have to meet financial eligibility requirements.

Senior Centers

Originally established several decades ago to provide social activities for the elderly, senior centers may now offer a much broader range of activities, some of which are designed to help their members cope with the many problems of old age. Depending on where your parents live, their center may offer information and referral offices, social casework assessment, counseling, medical and psychosocial diagnosis, home health care, financial management, legal services, transportation and escort services, and hot lunch or other meal programs (which may be used in addition to Meals-on-Wheels at home). The elderly members have a chance to enjoy the companionship of contemporaries as well as younger volunteers and professional workers. As one staff member of a busy center commented recently, "Some of our people are senile, some in wheelchairs, and some are just plain old. But there is no reason for them to be sitting around the house or in bed every day."

Senior centers for elderly residents are sometimes found in public housing projects; they sometimes are freestanding and sponsored by public or volunteer agencies. A directory of senior centers in the United States, published jointly by the Administration on Aging and the National Council on Aging, listed twelve hundred centers in 1970. (See Appendix D, page 312.)

Transportation Services

In addition to escort services particularly important to the disabled, safe transportation is crucially important, though sadly neglected, for the elderly who are less handicapped but find the regular services difficult or frightening to use. Volunteer groups appearing under a variety of different names, such as Dial-a-Bus or Dial-a-Car, and often sponsored by religious and social clubs, make convenient transportation available in private cars or buses. Occasionally those groups provide specially equipped buses or vans with ramps for wheelchairs and walkers. Some communities provide half-fare cards to older citizens, and a few offer free transportation.

Day Hospitals and Day Care Centers

Just as a sitter these days may sit for the very old or the very young, day care centers cater to either age group. There are still very few for the elderly, but since they fill such gaps in community care, more are likely to be established in the future. These centers cover the needs of older people who need help, but not round-the-clock— who are too dependent to manage alone and too independent for nursing home placement. Day care centers, providing excellent supportive care for the chronically or temporarily disabled, are attached to nursing homes, clinics, or hospitals (in which case they are known as day hospitals), although some are independent. Medical, nursing, therapeutic, and psychiatric services may be included, as well as recreational programs and hot meals. Round-trip transportation is often available. Elderly men and women can spend the day at the center and return home at night, thereby enjoying the advantages of both institutional and private life. There is some Medicaid funding for day care, and we hope it will increase. Such centers are especially important for older people who are afraid or unsafe in their own homes, but they may be equally important for the elderly who live with their children and who may easily sit alone all day while the rest of the family is at work or at school.

❖ INOPERABLE CATARACTS had made eighty-six-year-old Fritz Hoffman almost blind. Nevertheless, he was still alert, well oriented, and able to enjoy his record player, radio, talking books, friends. Unable to shop, prepare his meals, clean his house, or go out alone, he was dependent on others for protection and supportive care. Since he loved getting out of the house, his daughter, who lived an hour away, arranged for him to go to a day care program—funded by Medicaid, for which her father was eligible—at a local nursing home. Every day a bus picked him up early in the morning and delivered him home in the late afternoon. A homemaker–home health aide came in twice a week to help him with household chores and shopping. His evening and weekend meals were delivered by a Meals-on-Wheels program from a nearby church.

At the day care center, Mr. Hoffman was given rehabilitative help to handle his blindness, medical and nursing care when he needed it, and the opportunity to have a social life he enjoyed. All of this could have been provided for him twenty-four hours a day at the nursing home next door, but it was important for him to preserve some portion of his independence and remain for some part of his life in his own home.

Legal Services

Older people sometimes have their own lawyers to turn to with their legal problems—when they are threatened by landlords, exploited by unscrupulous people (sometimes their own relatives), or in need of other legal advice. But too many old people have no one to advise them on their rights or to safeguard their assets. Help can usually be found through local legal aid societies, which provide low-cost advice for all age groups. In some localities there are special legal services for the elderly poor.

Special Housing with Special Care

Many of the services just described can be used by the elderly living in a variety of settings: their own homes, their children's homes, foster homes, and boarding homes. Those who are prosperous may find some of these services in cooperatives, retirement hotels, condominiums, retirement communities, and apartment complexes specially adapted to the needs of older people. In addition to providing some meals and recreational facilities, these living arrangements may also have homemakers, home health aides, and sometimes nursing care available. Without that readily available care, many of the elderly tenants would be forced to enter nursing homes.

The elderly who are partially disabled and with few financial assets beyond their Social Security checks have no such range of living arrangements to choose from. They are forced to rely on either stopgap measures or institutional placement. In a few scattered locations throughout the country, special living arrangements are being set up which enable a few low-income, elderly men and women, although partially disabled, to remain in their communities and to continue to live semi-independent existences. Those living arrangements, sometimes called domiciliary housing, congregate housing, adult homes, boarding houses, or assisted residential living, all provide a number of protective services as well as food, shelter, companionship, and recreation.

Some homes approved by the state are reimbursed at a flat rate by the federal government (under Supplemental Security Income) for the total cost of their services to individuals. The quality of these services is seriously in doubt, however, and unscrupulous profit-making interests are creating a national scandal akin to the crisis in nursing homes. Furthermore, some of these homes are serving dis-chargees from state hospitals desperately in need of more protected psychiatric settings. While there are undoubtedly a number of spe-cial housing arrangements under SSI that are very suitable for older persons, families are cautioned to investigate those facilities with the same precautions they would apply to nursing homes (see Chapter 9).

In the 1960s, the federal government funded some small-scale experiments in alternative housing in Ohio, Georgia, Nebraska, and South Dakota. They are still in operation, but similar projects are being funded today by private social agencies which either build special housing units, rehabilitate existing structures, or merely rent space. The units may be occupied by single residents or shared by a number of disabled people, but everyone has access to a number of services: homemakers, housecleaners, transportation, hotlines for medical emergencies, visiting social workers, live-in aides, and some provision for meal preparation. The total expenses range from under $100 to $350 a month, depending on the financial situation of each individual resident. The sponsoring agency provides funds to make up the difference, but even so, the costs for such projects are far less than the costs for institutional care. Despite the smaller costs in-volved in the satisfaction gained by the individual residents, such projects are few today and solve the living problems of only a handful of elderly people.

The truth of the matter is, however, that there are tremendous inadequacies in all kinds of specialized housing for the elderly. The United States has lagged far behind many western European coun-tries and Israel. No overall plan for housing for the elderly by public, private, nonprofit, and private-profit sponsors exists. The total level of multifamily public housing units specially designed for the needs of elderly residents—whether already occupied, under construction, or approved for construction—as of 1973 was only 450,000. Half a million units for a population of over 20 million! (A directory of housing for older people is listed in Appendix D, pages 313–14.)

When You Are Far Away

Nothing is more alarming for children than getting word that a parent who is far away is in trouble. Whether the trouble is a minor crisis or a major one, it can produce frantic anxiety. Of course, families who have planned ahead carefully may be better prepared to cope with these crises long-distance, but even careful planning cannot take care of every possible contingency.

If you live on the East Coast and your parents on the West, you may fly out on occasion to help, but if their difficulties are ongoing you will not be able to spend your life in the air shuttling back and forth across the country. An information and referral service or a family service agency in *your own* community may be able to tell you where your parents can turn in *their* community to find the help they need.

❖ DORIS MINER and her daughter had a mixed relationship, warmly affectionate when they were separated and constantly abrasive when they were together. When Mrs. Miner, who lived in Texas, became frail, she made almost daily calls to her daughter, who lived near Boston—reporting a new problem day after day. After several difficult trips to Texas, her daughter called her local I & R office which located a family service agency in her mother's town. A social worker was contacted there and stayed in close touch with Mrs. Miner, making arrangements for her as she needed them: homemakers, escorts, transportation, and medical appointments. All those were important to Mrs. Miner's general well-being, but more important to her was the knowledge that she had someone nearby to call when she had problems—someone who would listen and then *do* something. Her phone calls to Boston became less frequent.

Legal Steps for Managing Your Parents' Financial Affairs

You may need a lawyer if one of your parents seems incapable of handling financial matters alone. While you may be able to offer periodic help from time to time, that may not be enough to prevent financial chaos. If your father one day is obviously unable to handle his funds or pay his bills—if he goes on irrational spending sprees or is easily exploited by swindlers—he needs protection. He may realize this himself and ask you to take over, but if not, you or another responsible person may have to take legal procedures to assume management of his financial affairs. Procedures differ from state to state, so you may need a lawyer, a legal aid service, or a social agency to tell you how things work in your state.

You will also need a lawyer to help you to take appropriate legal action. You may be advised to select one of three procedures most commonly used: power of attorney, joint tenancy, or inter vivos trust. All three require that your father is sufficiently alert to enter into a contractual agreement.

1. *Power of attorney* is used most frequently. If your father gives you power of attorney, he thereby allows you to manage his funds, but only as long as he is able to enter into any contract you make. Once he is incapable, the power of attorney must be terminated.

2. *Joint tenancy* is also frequently used and does not have the same limitations as power of attorney, since each party has total control over the funds regardless of the competency of the parties involved. If your father is able to enter into a joint tenancy contract with you or another responsible person, and deteriorates thereafter, the joint tenancy continues.

3. An *intervivos trust* is the most sophisticated of the three and provides the greatest flexibility. Using that procedure, your father may create a trust for himself, naming himself as trustee, but at the same time providing for a successor trustee (you or another person) to take control if he becomes incapacitated.

Each of these legal procedures has its own drawbacks and limitations, all of which should be reviewed with a lawyer. They may also be costly, but the most important problem to be faced is that most old people are reluctant to turn over all or even a portion of personal control of their own personal financial affairs. You may be caught in the middle of an uncomfortable dilemma if your father is reluctant to accept any help from you. Either you insist on helping him, thereby antagonizing him and making him feel more powerless than ever, or you sit back and do nothing, watching him squander his money or be exploited by others.

The Painful Process of Incompetency Proceedings

The day may come when your father's mental condition deteriorates to such a point that he is no longer capable of managing his affairs at all. He may be too disabled to enter into any contract, and the only way open to your family may be to have him declared incompetent by the courts. Incompetency proceedings, like many other legal proceedings, vary from state to state, but they usually involve certification by physicians or psychiatrists of the older person involved, and appointment of a guardian to manage his affairs and provide for his needs and well-being.

Many families find the mere idea of incompetency proceedings too painful to consider. There is still much shame and stigma attached to any kind of mental illness in our society. New York State recently enacted a conservatorship law designed to avoid the emotional burden normally involved in incompetency proceedings. That law provides for the appointment of a conservator to take over the financial affairs of anyone who becomes too impaired because of advanced age, illness, infirmity, or mental deterioration to manage alone. If your father is seriously mentally deteriorated and psychiatric hospitalization is necessary, he may refuse to commit himself. You may have to have him committed involuntarily, a procedure usually requiring the endorsement of several physicians.

Protective Services

Painful legal proceedings or commitment might be avoided altogether if an adequate array of community services can be provided for the mentally impaired older person. They would include legal, medical, psychiatric, nursing, homemaking, and home health aide services, coordinated by a social worker skilled in helping the often resistant older person. "Protective services" such as these are sometimes provided by local welfare offices and voluntary agencies.

What If They Won't
Be Helped—by You or Anyone Else?

There are legal steps to take in cases of mental incompetence, but in cases of physical incompetence the course of action is less clear. Most older people are willing to ask for help and to accept it when they cannot manage, but some may refuse any help of any kind from anybody. Although it is obvious to everyone else in the family that Mom and Dad are incapable of taking care of themselves, Mom and Dad think they are managing very well and resent any suggestion that they are not.

"I'm perfectly fine. Stop worrying about me!" an eighty-year-old crippled father may shout at his son for the fiftieth time. "I can still manage my own affairs," a half-blind mother may insist. But he's *not* fine, and she *can't* manage. Many older people ask for too much help; others ask for too little. Some won't accept any. They may refuse to accept the limitations made by their age, their physical deterioration, and their financial plight. They will not listen to logic and reason, nor will they be coaxed, bribed, or cajoled into changing their lifestyles.

Sometimes both your parents may be in that position—refusing all offers of help, rejecting any alternative living situations, and insisting on staying right where they are even though their house is an unsanitary shambles and full of hazards. If you take matters into your own hands and make arrangements for them, they are legally within their rights to fire summarily any outside help you bring in. There is not much you can do except wait for the day a serious accident or illness incapacitates one or both of them. Surreptitiously helping behind their backs may make you feel better but at best will only postpone, rather than prevent, disaster.

Occasionally, if they will not listen to you or anyone else in the family, they may listen to someone they trust who is not a relative: a minister, a rabbi, a priest, a social worker, a doctor, or even a close friend. But if they will not accept any compromise in their living arrangements, if all pleading and shouting and cajoling cannot shake their stand, the most you can do is firmly state your own feelings and the limits of your own involvement: "I can't keep on visiting you every week or seeing you living this way."

Although children are urged to give quiet support to their parents' lifestyles, no child is urged to support a pattern which threatens life and health. Your warning that you may have to withdraw from your close relationship with them may seem cruel, but it may be the only way you can get through to them. It is likely that you carry a more valued weight in their lives than their independence.

❖ MARY AND FRANK VISCONTI were not managing. Their daughter knew it, their friends knew it, but they would not admit it. Money was not a serious problem, but no outside help was allowed to remain for long. They were both undernourished, their clothes and bodies uncared for, and their apartment littered. Their daughter went back and forth between her town and theirs trying to bring order out of the chaos and hoping each time to persuade them to accept some compromise. Their son-in-law finally stepped in to settle the situation. He did not give orders; he was not dictatorial; he allowed the old people to be involved in future plans. He gave them three choices: All they had to do was select one.

"All right, which will it be? Come and live with us. Go to a nursing home together. Or STOP FIRING THE HOUSEKEEPER!"

A Realistic Afterthought

This chapter has described the variety of ways children may be able to help their disabled, aging parents and the variety of services that may supplement or replace their help.

In many communities—perhaps yours—a reassuring number of services are available. But do not relax too quickly if the Yellow Pages of your phone book list homemaker, escort, transportation, and other helpful services. Your reassurance may not last long if all the homemakers are busy just at the moment your parents need one, all the escorts booked, and all the cars spoken for. Visiting nurses may be overworked, social workers may be carrying heavy caseloads, and there may be long waiting lists at the health services.

We hope a greater number and a greater variety of services will develop across the country during the coming years, offering the elderly and their families a wider variety of options and opportunities for support and care.

9.

Helping When They Cannot Manage—the Nursing Home Solution

❖ THE SECOND STROKE did not kill eighty-year-old Peter Vorman, but it severely paralyzed him. He lived—but he needed care twenty-four hours a day. Someone had to be there all the time to feed him, bathe him, dress him, take him to the bathroom, and medicate him. Neither his wife, a semi-invalid herself, nor his children, who were married with families of their own, could give him the care he needed. There were only limited community services in the small town where they lived. The family made a careful study of available nursing homes and settled on the one they felt would suit Mr. Vorman best. Once he had moved in and was comfortably settled, his family left relieved.

But Mrs. Vorman could not forgive herself for "abandoning" her husband, and the children never lost the feeling that they had failed their father, "locked him up," "put him away."

The Vorman family is not alone. The very term *nursing home* conjures up a series of unhappy, even terrifying images in the minds of old and young alike. The words suggest coldness, impersonality, and regimentation at best—at worst neglect, mistreatment, cruelty, loneliness. Unfortunately, negative images can legitimately be used in describing some institutions. But they cannot be used broadside. While there are too few excellent nursing homes and too many disgraceful ones, the majority lie somewhere between these two poles.

No nursing home can work miracles. No nursing home can make the old and feeble young and vigorous again. No nursing home menu will ever please all elderly palates—sensitivities vary and taste buds are often duller. No nursing home will solve the various roommate problems or prevent friction between residents—communal living has its built-in stresses. Dissatisfaction is predictable in some areas of nursing home life.

When nursing home placement is necessary for an elderly parent, realistic sons and daughters must face an imperfect situation and at the same time face two other painful realities: the irreversible deterioration of a person they love, and their own inability or unwillingness to care for that person.

Institutionalization, although often a tragic step, is not tantamount to dying. It is a step closer to death, admittedly, but there still may be some gratifying living ahead. Nor does institutionalization necessarily imply family rejection. But those are widely held suppositions often reinforced by the elderly themselves. "No matter what happens," a dying mother may say to her children, "don't ever let your father go into a home," or "Promise me you'll never put me in one of those places."

The statistics are misleading. While it is true that at any one time less than 5 percent of the nation's elderly are living in institutions, 25 percent of that group at some point in their later years spend time in one, either temporarily—until they recover from a serious illness —or permanently—until they die. It may surprise those who share the prevailing antipathy to learn that a number of old people decide to enter a nursing home voluntarily; they are not pushed in, cast aside by rejecting relatives, or locked up against their wills.

❖ WHEN RETIRED ACCOUNTANT George Brody realized a few years after his wife died that in addition to his severe hypertension his sight was fading, too, he found an intermediate care facility he liked, moved in, and became a permanent resident, while his family stood aghast at the decision he made. But after considering the alternatives open to him for his remaining years, he decided that the institutional solution was the best for him. Mr. Brody had his reasons for the decision he made.

"My daughter says, 'Live with us, Pop.' She's a good girl and that's a bright boy she's married to. But they rush around all day— all night, too. And those grandchildren! Sure I love them, but there's no rest when they're around. My son wants me to stay in my apartment. He'll pay for a companion, he says. What do I want with a companion telling me what to do? We'd drive each other crazy, just the two of us all alone together all day."

Mr. Brody did not share the popular belief (or misconception) that institutionalization inevitably signifies the end of it all. There are some, but not many, Mr. Brodys around. Most families have two obstacles to hurdle prior to accepting a nursing home solution: they must overcome both their own aversion and the opposition of the potential nursing home resident. It is hard to pinpoint the exact moment when institutionalization becomes a necessary move—

what provides the tipping point forcing the decision. In cases of severe incapacity, the need for such an action is more obvious. But the tipping point may also come from a combination of factors: partial incapacity, combined with inadequate help in the home, combined with increasing personality conflicts. The tipping point may arrive sooner for an elderly relative who is difficult, demanding, and uncooperative, or in families who are burdened with their own problems. But for most families, whenever the tipping point comes—whether it is early or late—it is painful to accept, for it may represent failure to them and a finality in terms of their parents' lives.

The Breath of Scandal

The nursing home scandals of recent years have reinforced the negative attitudes of the general public, adding new dimensions to these attitudes by exposing specific institutions where inhuman treatment and criminal misappropriation of funds have been going on for years, providing astronomical profits for the owners. The majority of nursing homes in the United States are privately owned and run for profit-making interests. But that is the only quality they have in common, and their other qualities vary greatly. At the top of the scale are excellent facilities, forever aware of the human elements, constantly re-evaluating and upgrading the care they offer their residents. Unfortunately, there are too few of these top-quality homes.

At the bottom of the scale are institutions oblivious to the human element, operating solely for the profit to be made. Professional staffing is meager, little attention paid to the screening of applicants, little interest shown in determining whether nursing home placement is appropriate in a given case, and little attention paid to an applicant's adjustment once the admission has taken place. A deliberate selling job is often done on the older person and his relatives, usually just at the time when the entire family is most vulnerable, desperate, and helpless.

Blame for the existence of such inhuman places lies with greedy, unscrupulous owners, willing, in the words made famous during Watergate, to "walk over anyone's grandmother" in order to build a financial empire. Blame also lies with government agencies, whose lax monitoring has allowed such disgraceful institutions to remain open. But the nation at large is not blameless. The existence of so many substandard homes dramatizes society's amazing ability to turn its back on the elderly, ignoring their rights. Now that public opinion is focused on nursing homes, mismanagement, misappropriation of funds and mistreatment of residents are less likely to pass unnoticed. First steps in controlling the country's nursing homes have been made, but more must be taken by society at large, by law, and by individual family members keeping watchful eyes on the ongoing welfare of their institutionalized relatives.

The glare from the scandals taking place in some institutions should not blind public opinion to the benefits offered by other ones. A patient-oriented, professionally guided, intelligently operated nursing home often is the most humane alternative open to many old people. Far from being a waiting room for death, nursing homes can even represent, for some, a new and meaningful phase in their lives.

A Planned Option or a Forced Decision?

The longer people live, the greater is the likelihood that they will develop disabling conditions requiring protective or skilled care. That care can, of course, be provided outside the institutional setting. Some old people can stay right where they are if enough money is available in the family and enough services in the community. But often neither money nor services can be found and institutionalization is the only solution. Many families prefer to ignore the future, coasting blithely along as if no such grim possibilities lay ahead. Such families may spare themselves anxiety by not dwelling on a disaster that may never happen, but consider the odds: at some point, *one out of every four* older people will enter a nursing home. Those who have investigated nursing homes in advance will be in an infinitely more advantageous position to make a sound choice.

When there is no immediate crisis demanding solution, there is time for a thorough review of all possibilities, as well as a thorough analysis of the preferences and attitudes of the older person involved. Nursing home placements made on the basis of impulsive, frantic decisions usually produce disaster all around. The mother or father in question may feel bewildered, coerced, infantilized, and rejected. In addition, rushed placements allow no time to investigate the quality of an institution or to find the one offering rehabilitative, restorative, and supportive services. "Who's got room for Mom right away?" is the only question there is time to ask, rather than, "Which is the best place for Mom? Where will she be happiest?" An essential ingredient in all of this planning is to make sure that

Mom is involved step by step. She, after all, has the ultimate right to make the final choice if she is still capable mentally.

Deliberate and careful planning for a placement has the further advantage of giving both families and parents sufficient time to prepare themselves emotionally. The feelings stirred up by placement can be so intense that counseling may be invaluable to everyone during this time. Your mother may need someone to whom she can express her anxiety over the separation which placement will bring and her feelings of perhaps being unwanted. Since placement is usually a less socially acceptable solution to a problem than remaining in one's own home, it can create feelings of anger, sadness, and guilt, all of which need to be aired if the transition is to be smooth for all concerned. (A list of counseling services is provided in Appendix B, pages 272–303.)

This chapter will summarize important steps to follow in selecting nursing homes. It will offer guidelines for the actual admission and sketch a brief review of institutional life itself as it affects those inside and the relatives who remain in the outside world. The selection process is bewildering for most people. One novice reports:

❖ "JACK AND I prided ourselves that we were so smart in sizing up new situations. When we moved to the suburbs, we cased each one—covered all the possibilities—so when we decided we'd found the right place and made the move we felt pretty sure we knew what we were doing. It was the same with schools for the kids and summer camps. But when it comes to finding the right nursing home for Jack's mother—we're hopeless. We don't know what to look for—what we expect to find. We don't even know where to start."

Not knowing where to start is the quandary shared by many families when they first approach the unexplored territory of nursing homes. "How do we go about the whole thing?" they ask helplessly. There are thousands of nursing homes in the country, varying in capacity from twenty-five to more than one thousand beds. In some geographic locations the choice is limited; in other areas there are dozens to choose from. There are also three different types of sponsorship:

1. Voluntary—nonprofit, sectarian or nonsectarian, governed by a lay board
2. Proprietary—private, profit-making
3. Public (very few)

In the wake of the nursing home scandals, public and private agencies in some locations have drawn up lists of acceptable nursing homes in their particular areas. Local information and referral services, social service agencies, ministers, doctors, and nurses may know if such a list has been compiled for your parents' community. Even if no such list exists, the same sources can usually tell you something about the local nursing homes. A directory of accredited voluntary homes, listed by state, may be obtained from the American Association of Homes for the Aging, the national organization of nonprofit homes and housing for the aging (see Appendix D, page 312, for details).

But knowing what's available is only the beginning. A series of logical steps must then be taken in order to find the answer to the crucial question, "What is the right home for Mother?" or "Which is the best home for Father?"

Step One: Understanding How Money Determines Your Options

Unfortunately, as in every other aspect of the lives of the elderly, dollars and cents must be considered in choosing a nursing home. The financial picture today is not as bleak as it used to be before the establishment of Medicaid, but it is essential to determine before choosing a nursing home whether it is approved for Medicare and Medicaid, assuming your parents are eligible for either. Medicare only covers care in an approved skilled nursing facility for one hundred days post-hospitalization and for specified conditions. Medicaid covers the cost of care for eligible persons in approved skilled nursing facilities for as long as their condition merits it.

If your parents have no money, several agencies can guide them through the steps that must be taken to apply for Medicaid coverage of nursing home placement (refer to Chapter 7 for Medicaid eligibility): their local Department of Social Services (Welfare Department), their local Medicaid Office, and their local Social Security Office. The nursing homes themselves can be helpful, too, and if there is one particular nursing home your parents prefer, they can find out directly from the admission department there if residents are admitted under Medicaid. If so, the home will help with the necessary applications.

Be prepared to discover, however, that many homes do not accept residents who cannot pay at least some initial period of time and therefore will not accept anyone who must be admitted on Medicaid funds from the beginning. When your parents have no money at all, their options are limited in every area of their lives—including nursing home selection.

Private nursing home care is very expensive. Without government subsidies, it can be financially crippling to even comparatively wealthy families. In New York State homes the annual rate can exceed $20,000 a year per person, and in Alabama, which has one of the lower nursing home rates in the nation, the cost is close to $8,000.

Relative Responsibility

Children used to be held accountable when their parents needed nursing home placement, but today, under Medicaid regulations, children are no longer held legally responsible. Husbands and wives, however, are still held legally responsible for each other's nursing home bills in *every* state of the union.

Because of that *spouse responsibility,* a dangerous situation lies in wait for elderly couples. Suppose your mother needs nursing home placement. You may feel your father can support her there easily, since he is worth over $200,000. But consider what may happen if he has to support her in the nursing home for a number of years, while still maintaining himself in his own house. When the family funds run out, your mother will be unaffected: Medicaid will take over her nursing home expenses, but at that point your father could find himself virtually bankrupt. Spouse responsibility jeopardizes not only those who have plenty of money, but also those who have little. Even though your parents' only source of income is their combined Social Security check and even though your mother qualifies for Medicaid coverage if she needs nursing placement, your father can still be held financially liable to some extent. He must contribute to her care from his limited income which may, as a result, place him below the poverty threshold (thus making him eligible for SSI; see pages 158–60 for details). Because of this unfortunate situation, couples—rich and poor—may refuse nursing home placement, even when it is necessary. A frail old man may struggle to care for his wife at home (or vice versa), to his own detriment and hers, in order to avoid the specter of destitution. It is also not uncommon for an older couple to arrange a divorce so that one will not be financially wiped out by the nursing home bills of the other. While conserving assets or a small pension check, such a move can be devastating emotionally.

Careful financial calculations and projections are essential before any nursing home placement can be made, even when children feel they are in a position to pay for their parent's care. You may feel you do not need to worry about finding a Medicaid-eligible home for your father. Between his assets and your own, you are confident that there will be plenty of money to cover a completely private placement. But will there really be enough? What if he lives another ten years? What if you have a heart attack and must retire early? If your father should outlive you, will there be money enough to protect him, as well as your widow and your children?

Step Two: Understanding the Kinds of Care Available

Once financial questions have been answered, other questions must be considered. What kind of care do nursing homes offer? Do they all offer the same kind? How do they differ from hospitals? In choosing a nursing home it is important to remember that all facilities are not alike, that they offer different levels of care, and that under the federal laws regulating Medicare and Medicaid, two types of facilities are recognized: the intermediate care facility and the skilled nursing facility. You may wonder which facility is the right one for your father.

The Skilled Nursing Facility

Although there has been some confusion about the dividing line between the two levels, a skilled facility is usually considered necessary for someone requiring intensive care: twenty-four-hour-a-day supervision and treatment by a registered nurse. Residents of skilled nursing facilities, if they qualify, are eligible for Medicaid coverage in all states of the union.

Intermediate Care Facilities

When round-the-clock nursing by an R.N. is not considered medically necessary, an older person may be eligible for an intermediate care facility, which provides twenty-four-hour-a-day unskilled care under the supervision of a registered nurse. Intermediate care is covered by Medicaid in most states as of 1975 at about half the cost of skilled nursing care.

Homes with Both Levels of Care

Many institutions offer both levels—skilled and intermediate. A resident may only need the intermediate level this year, but next year his condition may deteriorate—or his condition may improve, and the nursing homes utilization and review committee may decide that he can be moved to a lower level of care. When both levels are available in the same place, shifting from one level to another can be done smoothly and is less traumatic to both the older person and his family than a move to another institution. If you are uncertain about which level of care is necessary for your father you can ask for an assessment of his needs from your doctor, an intake team at a hospital or nursing home, or a qualified medical social worker or nurse.

This is the time to make sure that nursing home or intermediate care is really the right solution. If placement is made incorrectly, there is always a danger that your father may be shifted to a different level of care or even back to the community.

Step Three: Evaluating Quality

A review of the dollars and cents of nursing home finances and the levels of care offered is the preliminary ground work preparing the way for a thorough investigation of individual nursing homes. That investigation is the most important step in finding the answer to the crucial question, "Which one will be best for Mother?"

Finding the ultimate answer involves making up a list of possibilities in the desired geographic area, checking the opinions and judgments of knowledgeable people, and then inspecting each one in a personal visit. Whenever possible, it is recommended that the prospective resident be encouraged to take the initiative, or at least share all the steps including the inspection tours and the final decision.

A Journey into the Unknown

It is not hard to make up a list of nursing homes or to gather opinions about them, but visits to nursing homes—particularly the first ones—are often bewildering, depressing, even terrifying experiences. One visitor reported, "I felt like a stranger in a foreign land. Nothing looked familiar, not even the people. It was terrible—all I wanted to do was RUN!"

That reaction is not unusual, nor is it surprising. The world of the nursing home is unknown territory to the general public. Unless involved professionally or because of a relative in residence, the average person manages to stay blissfully ignorant about these places, almost unaware of their existence. Until recently there has been little to call public attention to them, and the recent interest has centered mainly on the scandals involved.

The TV screen takes viewers into submarines, jails, drug centers, jungles, mountain peaks. Hospitals, thanks to the various media, are as familiar as neighborhood backyards. Drs. Kildare, Casey, and Welby, and an army of their colleagues, have brought examining rooms, therapy rooms, operating rooms, emergency rooms into the living rooms of the nation. European writers took their readers into TB sanitaria in the past. Solzhenitsyn did the same with the cancer ward. But who has opened up the doors of the nursing homes for the elderly and invited the public in? The country knows more about life on the moon than it does about life in those institutions. How ironical it is—only a handful of us is ever likely to walk on the moon or orbit in space, yet most of us are likely to grow old. For some reason the media have allowed the nursing home world to remain clothed in mystery. No wonder people find it painful and frightening when they penetrate this mystery for the first time by actually visiting an institution.

That mystery—that not-knowing-what-to-expect—accounts for much of the initial shock so frequently reported by visitors. Perhaps the main shock-producer for the novice visitor is the nursing home population itself. This may be the first time old age has ever been encountered en masse. You may know your own mother well, understand her problems, ache for her pains and her losses. Because of your involvement with her you may even consider yourself quite a geriatric expert. But in a nursing home you must face everyone else's elderly parents, and all the range and variety of deterioration that old age has to offer, although residents of intermediate care facilities look much healthier than residents of skilled nursing facilities. On your first visit you may only be struck by negative impressions: people in wheelchairs, in walkers; disoriented old men, weeping old women. Your immediate reaction may be, "My mother doesn't belong here—not with these people." If your mother happens to be along with you on the first inspection tour her reaction may be similar: "This is no place for me."

Later on, in subsequent visits to other institutions or even on a return trip to the first one—when the initial impact has lessened, you may come to accept the wheelchairs and the walkers and the disorientation—and be able to see beyond them to other residents enjoying a variety of activities and busily participating in the daily routine of "their home." A second visit or even a third may be necessary in order to sort out the bewildering kaleidoscope of impressions and come to a final decision.

You Can Learn a Lot from Your Reception

While it is true that first impressions about a given nursing home are sometimes incorrect and need revising, it is usually possible to sense immediately and correctly a nursing home's attitude toward your visit. Is there a friendly welcome? Are you encouraged to tour freely, ask questions, talk to residents and staff? If the staff seems defensive, reluctant to let you tour, or insists on showing you only what *they* want you to see, you would probably be right in supposing that there is something they want to hide. Openness is usually a clue to quality and all parts of an institution should be open to you. Potential residents and their relatives are consumers shopping for a way of life. They have a right to know down to the last detail exactly what kind of a life they are buying.

Since the privacy of residents should always be respected, certain specific areas of any nursing home may be in use and closed to you when you visit. If you are particularly interested in seeing those areas, it may be necessary for you to return at another time. Return visits can be time-consuming and exhausting, but they can pay off in terms of additional information gained, which may have a crucial bearing on your parent's future adjustment.

What Do Other People Have to Say?

Other people's opinions can be extremely helpful. Some families prefer to gather as much information pro or con on a specific home prior to a first visit, while others decide to visit cold and check out their impressions with informed people afterward. The families of residents already living in a home can tell you about their experiences, and the nursing home staff is usually willing to suggest names for you to contact. Community agencies, physicians, clergymen are all good sources of information and may even be willing to tell you why they prefer one institution over another. A final source can be the state agency which licenses the homes you are visiting.

It is safer to use more than one source of information. When talking to families of residents, always keep in mind that emotions run high when a relative is institutionalized. Sons and daughters may be ruled by strong personal feelings and prejudices not universally shared; so weigh all violent opinions carefully. If a friend says of an institution you are considering, "That snake pit! They killed my father there!" she may possibly be justified, but you would be wise to check further. Similarly, don't accept blindly a daughter's glowing report of Apple Tree Manor. Her views may be colored by her relief that someone else is finally taking care of her difficult, demanding, troublemaking mother.

If you are completely repelled by your visit to one nursing home, you may decide to reject it without further investigation. But if you are leaning toward another one, it would be safer to check it through several sources and see if your positive feelings are reinforced. No one person or agency is acquainted with, or even interested in, every aspect of good nursing care. All informants have their own personal or professional bias. A nursing home shopper acts like a computer —allowing all relevant information to be fed in and hoping that eventually a definitive answer to the original question, "What's the right nursing home for Mother?" will appear on the print-out.

What to Look for When You Visit

Prospective applicants and their families find a checklist helpful on nursing home visits. Because the tours have such emotional undertones, visitors often blank out on many questions they planned to ask and forget essential things they wanted to see. (A sample checklist is provided in Appendix C-1, pages 306–10, but you may want to develop your own to cover your specific requirements.) Some items on the list can be quickly settled by simple observation, others by talking to residents and members of the staff.

You probably will have checked out the home's overall licensing status prior to your visit, but if not, now is the time to review it and to find out whether specific staff members are licensed also. Licensing is crucially important, and if a home is unlicensed, try to avoid it, because you can be sure there is something seriously wrong with it. Some states also require that the administrators be licensed. Always check this qualification, too, because the administrator is the key figure—the one who sets the tone of the entire institution. Other personnel on staff should be licensed or certified whenever possible: physicians, registered nurses, occupational and physical therapists, dieticians, and social workers.

Once the routine items are taken care of, a visitor needs to be concerned with three broad areas in each institution: the quality of the medical, nursing, and other therapeutic services; the quality of the hotel or housekeeping services; and finally, the *climate* of the home—its social life and pyschological atmosphere.

Medical, Nursing, and Therapeutic Services

MEDICAL SERVICE

Every home should have a physician available in case of emergency—on staff or on call. Some good homes allow residents to be treated by their own private physicians as often as necessary. Other patients must depend on the home's physicians, and it is important to find out how often they visit. (In some states it is mandatory that all nursing home residents be visited by a physician once a month.) If a resident does not have a private physician and there is none on staff, be sure to find out how the home guarantees regular medical attention.

Other specialized medical consultants should be available—either on staff or within easy call—for psychiatric, dental, eye, and foot care. Those specialties are far from minor or incidental ones, and become more and more essential with age. Even the best nursing home cannot be expected to serve as a fully equipped hospital, but every institution should have an ongoing arrangement with a nearby hospital for acute illnesses. If there is no hospital nearby, it is important to find out how the home functions in emergency situations.

NURSING SERVICE

The competence and humanity of the nursing staff probably affects resident morale more than any other service. Nurses, aides, and orderlies have more continuing contact with residents than anyone else on staff, and their attitudes and behavior have great impact. In a skilled nursing facility, one or more R.N.s—depending on the size of the home—should be on duty at all times, giving medication and directly supervising the care of residents. Licensed practical nurses with at least one year of specialized geriatric training should be on duty round-the-clock on all shifts. In an intermediate care facility all nursing duties should be directed by a registered nurse.

SPECIALIZED THERAPEUTIC SERVICES

Highly competent medical and nursing staffs are essential, but they cannot be responsible for all aspects of nursing home care.

Other services, some of which may be required by state health codes, are also essential if an elderly resident's ability to function is to be restored or even merely maintained: occupational therapists, physiotherapists, dieticians, social workers with clinical training.

WHAT ABOUT THE MENTALLY IMPAIRED RESIDENT?

The care of the elderly with advanced chronic brain disorder is a fledgling art that has so far only developed limited therapeutic skills. But the backward approach to senility is a thing of the past —or it should be. You have a right to expect that any good nursing home will have a positive approach to the mentally impaired, shared by staff members in all services. The attitude involves tremendous patience, understanding, and warmth toward the residents formerly written off as hopeless or impossible to reach. No surefire therapeutic tools have been developed yet to deal successfully with the problems of mental impairment, but the search continues, and some measures are effective in offering some structure and meaning to the lives of the very disoriented.

Some homes are trying out programs of reality orientation, motivation, and attitude therapy—attempts to help patients recapture a little or some of their cognitive powers lost through disuse, the traumatic brain damage of a stroke, or the insidious physical damage to the brain as seen in arteriosclerosis.

In the past, older people with severe mental impairment were usually placed in state hospitals, but after the establishment of Medicaid most states have tended to transfer their elderly patients, except those considered dangerous, out of the hospitals and into nursing homes and domiciliaries. If your father is suffering any serious mental impairment, it is particularly important to make sure that the home he enters is equipped to deal with his condition. Psychiatrists and specially trained staff members should be available.

IS IT ALL SHADOW OR SUBSTANCE?

Many nursing homes boast a wide variety of special services. They offer in their brochures an impressive staff of professionals to prospective applicants and their families. But visitors are advised to ascertain by personal observation whether the boasted services are actually making an impact and whether the professionals are in evidence. Are the residents clean and properly dressed during the day? By what time? Are physical and occupational therapy rooms in use or empty, showing little sign of ongoing programs? Are residents involved in activities, or are they lined up in rows against the wall staring into space? Are they responsive to each other and to what is happening around them? Do you feel you've walked into Sleeping Beauty's palace and found a perfectly set scene with all the actors fast asleep? Poor nursing homes rely on sleep as a great problem-solver and often medicate residents heavily in order to avoid trouble. Even when there are high standards of professional staffing, efficiency, and cleanliness, steer clear of homes where residents spend much of their time in bed and asleep.

Hotel Services: How Good Is the Housekeeping?

Every institution must provide room and board for its residents, but the mere existence of basic requirements is not enough—they should also be provided in an attractive physical plant which includes comfortable rooms, a safe, clean environment, and furnishings appropriate and comfortable for residents with disabilities. An older person can adjust much more quickly to attractive, familiar surroundings than to a hospital atmosphere suggesting coldness, efficiency, and sterility. A home-like effect can be achieved when residents can furnish their own rooms with personal items. Pleasant living requires more than well-furnished bedrooms. There should also be comfortable public rooms and dining halls, recreation rooms, special-purpose rooms where residents can have some privacy, and ideally some opportunity for fresh air and sunshine outdoors. Even urban institutions can provide terraces and roof gardens.

The Climate: A Home-like or Sterile and Repressive Atmosphere?

Judging the climate and making an accurate prediction of the prevailing "weather patterns" can be one of the most challenging parts of any nursing home visit. This may be the major factor determining whether your parent will make a reasonably good adjustment to nursing home life or will slip further into emotional or physical deterioration. Accurate weather prediction is notoriously difficult. Professional facilities and services in one home may meet your highest hopes, but the fine quality may be neutralized by an atmosphere of coldness and repression. An unfortunate climate may not prevent you from selecting a particular home (if everything else seems to suit your needs), but it may be enough to warn you that there may be trouble ahead in the future.

A variety of indicators predict quite reliably the social and psychological atmosphere of any home. Some are subtle and difficult to pick up; others, built into the organization of the home. One group of indicators reveals the way in which residents interact with each other:

1. Are there socialization groups and opportunities for socialization? Recreational opportunities for everyone, or just for the alert and active residents?
2. Is there respect for privacy for individuals? For couples?
3. Is there a resident council where residents can join together in discussing *their home* and make recommendations for its improvement? Suggest innovations?
4. Is there consideration given to the selection of roommates? Of tablemates? A poor selection can result in misery all around.

Another group of indicators involves the interaction between the staff and the residents, and the relationships between the staff and the residents' families:

1. Does the staff and administration welcome criticism and suggestions from relatives? Do they consider this behavior as interference and troublemaking?
2. In addition to an active residents' council, is there a relatives' auxiliary with machinery for airing grievances, problems, and suggestions?
3. Are residents treated with dignity and respect? Beware of homes where the staff calls the residents by their first names. It is often a sign that residents are not regarded as full-fledged citizens—they may be disabled and dependent, but they are still all first class.
4. Does the staff deliver affectionate treatment along with competent care? Making a perfect bed, giving a bedpan comfortably, bathing a patient skillfully are all important parts of their job; so are kind words, sympathetic gestures, an understanding laugh, and a quick hug. Relatives sometimes resent such intimacies on the part of the staff, labeling them phony and insincere. But the human touch can work wonders and may be the only thing a sightless, paralyzed, or even disoriented resident responds to.

The ideal atmosphere combines friendliness, warmth, and concern. It permits residents to maintain a sense of personal dignity. It respects privacy, allows individuality, and has room for some degree of freedom. It is not easy to achieve, and even though it may appear spontaneous and undirected, it usually is just the opposite and results from explicit expectations percolating down from the top—from the Board of Directors and administration through the supervisors and professionals.

Personal Preferences May Dictate Choices

In addition to finding a home with high performance in all areas, some families have their own particular needs. Homes can be found which answer a variety of individualized demands. (In California there is even one institution which caters mainly to old, blind, non-English-speaking Japanese men and women.) Your own needs may not be so specific, but you may know that your mother will only be happy in an environment corresponding to her cultural, religious, or ethnic background. It may be crucial for her, if she is an orthodox Jew, that she live in a place where the dietary laws are strictly observed. If she is foreign-born and has difficulty with English, she may need someone around who understands her language. Equally crucial can be the location and setting of the home —whether it is in the country, the suburbs, or the city.

❖ THE FARMER FAMILY was delighted to find a top-flight home conveniently located in their own suburban town. There were beautiful grounds and a view of rolling hills from every window, and the family fully expected old Mrs. Farmer to make a good adjustment there. She had certainly seemed favorably impressed when she visited before her placement. To her children's great disappointment, however, she remained withdrawn and apathetic, while the nurses reported she slept badly and ate little. Eventually it was discovered that she hated the country and pined for city sights and sounds. Born under the Third Avenue El in New York City, she had lived all her life on a busy main thoroughfare. Fire engines, ambulances, and noisy traffic never disturbed her sleep, but crickets, bullfrogs, early-rising birds, and the wind rustling in the trees outside her window terrified her and kept her sleepless. Neither she nor her children had considered that possibility when they selected the home.

When everything else is equal, proximity can be the deciding factor in selection of one home over another. You may know already that your mother thrives on close contact with you or another of her children. Frequent visits will be crucial to her well-being. If so, it may be better for everyone if she selects a home nearby, even if it is imperfect, where you can visit easily without disrupting your life completely. A more distant place may offer a wider range of services, but those benefits will not serve instead of family visits. You know your own mother best!

When There Is No Choice

It is tragic that for many people in many places, there is no choice, or only a limited choice. When your mother begins to deteriorate, you may look into all the nursing homes within a wide radius of your community and find nothing available to meet your standards. Because of family finances, the state of your own health, or the absence of workable alternatives, you may be forced to settle for mediocrity or worse. If—after you have obtained a good assessment of your mother's condition, involved her in the search for a nursing home, and inspected them all—you are forced to settle for an institution that falls far below your hopes, you will receive in return for all your efforts the cold comfort that you are not to blame. You can rightfully blame society at large when you see at close range the narrow, limited, inadequate provisions made for the nation's elderly citizens.

Making the Final Decision

Eventually all the relevant data will have been collected, and you may find that several nursing homes emerge as worth considering. In all likelihood no single one will satisfy every one of your hopes, and there will probably be pros and cons in each. But despite the fact that there are several possibilities to choose from, most families find the period leading up to a final decision to be a time of anxiety, insecurity, and guilt.

A Time of Crisis for Everyone

Regardless of the degree of planning and the excellence of the institution selected, nursing home placement, although providing relief from some difficult problems, symbolizes for many people irrevocable changes in familiar and valued relationships.

This is the moment when families must accept the fact that someone else will be taking care of an ailing parent from now on. For many families it represents the end of a long struggle to maintain their parent in the community. They will have to deal with the guilt they feel when they admit that they are unwilling, incapable, or inadequate to continue providing care themselves. It may also be the time when a daughter who has considered the possibility of taking her father into her own home must realize that she has made her final decision and that she cannot (because of conflicting demands in her life) or will not (because of her conflicted feelings about her father) ever ask him to live with her.

At this time, when family unity is most desirable, family tensions often run high: between husbands and wives—"If you weren't so selfish you'd let my mother live with us"—or between brothers and sisters—"We'd love to take Father, but how can we when we travel so much? Why don't you take him?"

Difficult as this period prior to nursing home placement can be for the relatives, it can be even more painful, more terrifying, for the older person involved. Your father's nursing home placement can represent the ultimate in a series of losses he has suffered: the loss of his household and his role as a householder. All the roles which in combination made up his status in society are now gone. At an advanced age he faces an identity crisis: "Who am I?" and "What am I doing here?" He must now adapt to someone else's routines and regulations because, no matter how small, intimate, or family-like the nursing home, certain basic routines must be carried out. Even the best home requires the surrender of some independence, and that is a cruel loss for independent men and women who formerly prided themselves on their self-reliance and self-sufficiency.

The Family Conference

Because of the state of crisis, one family member may be tempted to take matters into his own hands, bring order out of chaos, and settle everything with a dictatorial edict: "It's all arranged—Mother is going to move into Fairmont Manor a week from Friday." It may seem at the moment like a shortcut to sanity, but dictatorial edicts often produce revolutions and mutinies among the lower ranks. Relatives may end up blaming each other, and the older person involved may make a poor adjustment to the institution he feels he has been forced to enter.

A family conference is the alternative to dictatorial rule, and provides the forum for open communication between all members, including the older person himself. Here is the opportunity to air all objections, discuss all disagreements, and consider all preferences. While it is easier if the interested parties can meet and talk face to face, it is important to involve the family members living far away. Even though your brother lives on the opposite coast, think twice before plunging ahead with your own plans the minute you hear his voice on the long-distance phone telling you, "Go ahead and do what you think best." Later on you may be accused of high-handed behavior, poor judgment, and ignoring his feelings. Even if he shows little interest at the time of the placement, he may appear months later at your mother's nursing home and tell her, "If I'd been around I'd never have let them put you in a place like this."

The family conference may not produce unanimity—some relatives may only give half-hearted approval of the plans made. Sparks may fly and old conflicts may be rekindled, but better now than later, when decisions have been made and are more difficult to reverse.

Honesty

Honesty is all-important during the family conference and during all the discussions and preparations prior to nursing home placement, yet that is the very time when everyone tends to resort to half truths. Brothers and sisters may not exactly lie to each other, but they may not tell the whole truth either. A son may not lie to his mother, but he may beat around the bush so much that she ends up totally bewildered about what is happening to her. Parents of young children quickly learn that half truths cause more damage than whole ones. Who would tell a little boy these days that going to the dentist is nearly as much fun as going to the zoo? What a surprise he'd be in for—and how he'd hate dentists ever after!

A daughter who has gone by the book in selecting a nursing home, consulting and involving her mother all along the way, may lose valuable ground with a few misguided half-truths at the time of admission: "This is only for a little while until you feel better," or "You only need stay here while we're on vacation," or "Let's see how it works out—if you don't like it I'll come and get you."

Half truths are not born out of maliciousness or cruelty. They arise from the mixed bag of feelings discussed earlier in this book, compounded by the shame and guilt connected to a nursing home placement. But the lack of a clear-cut message can reduce an already bewildered parent to helpless apathy, unable to find any gratifying compensations in the new environment. The absence of a positive adjustment within the home will produce continuing emotional upheavals for the relatives outside. Half truths will finally come home to roost.

❖ MARION CARPENTER HAD lived with her younger son since the death of her husband twenty-five years earlier. An older married son lived half an hour away with his wife and family. The younger son decided to keep his mother with him after his father's death, and although he had several women friends, he never married. Mrs. Carpenter became increasingly confused as she neared her ninetieth birthday—wandered out of her apartment, forgot to turn off the gas. In addition her son, now in his mid-fifties, had begun to face his own lonely life with neither a wife nor children. His desire for his own freedom, combined with his mother's confusion, led him to place her in an intermediate-care facility. Mrs. Carpenter accepted the placement willingly on the surface since she seemed aware of her condition and anxious about her own safety.

So far so good. BUT. . . . John Carpenter allowed his mother to believe that she could always return to live with him if she wanted to. His "promises" stemmed from his guilt and his long-standing conflicts about his mother. She, underneath it all, felt angry, believing that he had rejected her for another woman. They both kept their old neurotic tensions alive and burning. John remained free, but miserable and unable to enjoy his new life. He and his mother fought constantly with each other and with the staff and became a great burden to everyone.

Reliable nursing homes know all about the use of half truths and will not accept an application from family members alone but insist that the parent involved make the application himself, if he is mentally competent and knows exactly what is happening.

Becoming a Nursing Home Resident

When Moving Day Comes—Admission and Early Adjustment

The transition to nursing home life can be an orderly, carefully maneuvered undertaking, unless the move is made directly from a hospital to the home and a speedy, efficient transfer is necessary. But whether the transition is hectic or leisurely, it is well to remember that the admission itself is a traumatic process for prospective residents and their relatives as well. There must be room for a variety of feelings at that time: irritation, anger, recrimination, depression, and disappointment. Intermingled with all those painful feelings may also be a sense of relief for everyone, both the new resident and the family, that "the worst is over."

To a certain extent a sense of relief is warranted, because the long and often wearying period of uncertainty and indecision is past. But it is certainly too soon to sit back complacently—a long and sometimes equally wearying period of adjustment lies ahead. Now, as the nursing home staff enters into the picture, a relationship which was formerly two-sided—involving children and an elderly parent— becomes three-sided. A delicate balance must be found between a hands-off, no-interference approach and an overly involved one; the best way to achieve this balance is to aim for it from the beginning.

Doing Their Own Thing

Whenever possible, the older person should be in charge of his own move, taking the major responsibility even if it slows things up and inconveniences everyone a little. He should discuss the date of his admission and make the arrangements for the closing of his own home, the handling of his finances, and the choice of clothing and furniture he will take with him (assuming the home allows this). If he cannot manage those procedures physically, he should at least direct them and be consulted all along the way. He may want to distribute his belongings to special friends and relatives, a process that is more time-consuming and less efficient than calling someone, such as an auctioneer or the Salvation Army, capable of removing everything in a matter of hours. He may find it more reassuring to think of his treasured possessions remaining with friends rather than going to strangers. If he's indecisive, don't make decisions for him, but help him make a choice for himself. "Your blue coat is pretty shabby—do you want to take that, or your new brown one?" is a better ploy than "I'm packing your new brown coat; that old blue one's not worth taking." Don't be surprised, either, at the unlikely array of items he decides to bring. "Surely you're not taking that mothy old pillow—it's falling apart!" But that mothy old pillow may involve a lifetime of memories. It may be too precious to leave behind and may be just the thing that will add a familiar touch to a strange room in a stranger place.

The more deeply involved he is, the less he will be likely to feel that he has been coerced and treated like a child, and the deeper will be his commitment to his new home. He will be able, if permitted to do his own thing, to link his former life with his new one.

Doing their own thing, however, does not invariably guarantee the desired results, and even the most understanding approach may not succeed with someone who is consistently negative.

❖ THE GORDON FAMILY was keenly aware of the need to allow old Mrs. Gordon to do her own thing. While she was in traction in the hospital they discussed nursing home placement with her, visited various homes themselves, reported about each one in detail, and let her decide on the one she preferred. Instead of moving her directly to the home from the hospital, they made complicated arrangements to allow her to return to her own house for a week and direct the disposal of her possessions as well as her own packing. The family prided themselves that never once during the whole difficult period had they told her what to do. It came as quite a shock to them, therefore, to hear her frequently refer to that period as "the time you made me give up my house and sent me to this place."

Once They Are in Residence

Each home has its own approach to welcoming a new resident, and it is now that the new three-sided staff-family-resident relationship begins. Some homes treat the admission process with the greatest consideration, assigning trained staff members to help the newcomer, remaining close by his side, and helping to orient him to his new surroundings. This procedure is particularly helpful for the mildly confused or blind person.

Other homes, which are excellent in different ways, are perfunctory about the admission process and do little to introduce the new resident to the new surroundings. If your mother senses a laissez-faire attitude when she comes in, she may want you to be around with her as much as possible in the early days. Frequently the home itself will ask relatives to spend considerable time with a new resident even when the staff is available and ready to help. Other homes prefer relatives to stay in the background in the early days, until the new resident has settled in.

New residents must make some dramatic adaptations during their early days in the home. Already exhausted physically from the strains of moving and emotionally by the assortment of feelings aroused by the move, they must now become familiar with new patterns of living: new daily routines, new rules, and new roommates. A newcomer may wake up in the night and ask in bewilderment, "What's that strange person doing in my bedroom?" In the midst of all these new adjustments, they must continue to adapt to the physical disabilities which made nursing home placement necessary in the first place. It's not surprising that it is often a very rocky time.

There May Be Reversals

Many new residents suffer physical and mental reversals during this adjustment period. Although occasionally severe and devastating, these may only be temporary setbacks which improve significantly with time.

Your own parent may be in that fortunate group that adjusts quickly and shows rapid improvement in a few weeks. Speedy changes for the better are often seen in the malnourished elderly, whose overall condition improves remarkably with a balanced diet. Sociable people, who felt cruelly isolated in their own homes or apartments prior to placement, often flourish when they find companionship again, and those who have made the move independently without pressure or persuasion from relatives make the transition more easily.

Everyone Makes Mistakes

In their eagerness to speed up the adjustment or because of a continuing unresolved sense of guilt, families often make mistakes. It is impossible to catalogue the endless variety of human errors made by relatives whose intentions are good and whose judgment is poor, but two common ones should be avoided.

Beware of Early Visits Home

Weekends away, overnight visits, or even dinner invitations, instead of making the adjustment process less painful for new residents, usually do the opposite. Adapting to the strange atmosphere involves a slow, steady progression from one stage to the next. Each day that passes helps to erase strangeness. Shuttling back and forth between an old life and a new one is confusing and the physical travel adds stress at an already stressful time. It will be hard to refuse if your mother begs to visit or pines to have Sunday dinner with the family, but one Sunday dinner might set back her adjustment by several weeks. Residents themselves often sense the potentially harmful effects of visits outside and refuse all invitations.

❖ "Not yet, thank you," said one particularly sprightly old lady, repeatedly refusing her relatives' invitations to dinner. "Not while I'm in training."
"Training for what?" they asked.
"I'm training myself to stand the terrible cooking in this place," was the answer, and she waited four months before accepting an invitation.

Beware of Panic

Nursing home professionals report that it can take as much as six months for an old person to make a reasonable adjustment to institutional life. But the ups and downs of the period are hard to take, and too often families and staffs are quick to panic and to regret the admission or feel that the resident has been placed in an inappropriate part of the home. This may turn out to be true eventually, but it is too early to jump to conclusions. Patience and helpful support can go a long way in helping a resident return to his former self. Jumping the gun, taking drastic measures, insisting that another home would be better and moving him, will only put him under further stress and compound his problems.

What If They Don't Adjust?

The adjustment process can take as long as six months. Some residents adjust with a kind of passive acceptance, neither happy nor unhappy, abiding by the daily routines and participating in activities with little enthusiasm. Others are active participants obviously flourishing, deeply involved, ready to take responsibility, full of ideas for changes. But then, sadly, there will always be some who never adjust at all, remaining actively unhappy and finding no redeeming compensations in home life. They may sink irreversibly into mental or physical decline.

Families always hope for a positive adjustment, but it is hard to predict at the outset whether this will happen. Nursing home professionals who have seen hundreds of elderly people and screened dozens of applicants are unable to say who will do well in institutional life and who will not. Even if the outcome could be reliably predicted—even if someone devised a test to prove that Mr. Jenkins will never adjust to nursing home living—there may be no other workable alternative for Mr. Jenkins, and placement will have to be made anyhow.

The children of residents who never adjust have a particularly difficult burden to bear: they must watch their parents' unhappiness and pain, at the same time suffering feelings of guilt and shame for their involvement in the placement. But blaming themselves will not help, nor will it help to blame the staff or the institution. The difficulties of the elderly in our society often go far beyond their children's help and the help of any institution.

In the ideal situation, the staff, the family, and the resident will emerge after the adjustment period with a smoothly working relationship, a three-sided partnership in which each side assumes different responsibilities. The resident does something that no one else can do for him: adjusts and adapts. The staff offers something which the family cannot: twenty-four-hour-a-day skilled protective care. And the family offers something the staff cannot: intimate affection, links with the past, and contact with the community outside. While the ideal situation is hard to reach and all three sides are often in conflict with each other, some kind of workable relationship can usually be developed.

The Role of the Staff

Staff members are responsible for the ongoing functioning of every nursing home—they are the physicians, the nurses, the orderlies, the aides, the therapists, the cooks. But they are human beings, too, with human reactions, and they cannot perform miracles with severely sick or disabled old people. They appreciate praise and gratitude, bristle at unfair criticisms, resent uncalled-for interference with their work. On any institutional staff there may be individuals who are lazy, hostile, sloppy, inefficient, surly, or neurotic, and they deserve to be reported for their faults. But there may be many—one hopes more—individuals who are skillful, sensitive, thoughtful, conscientious, and genuinely devoted to the older people in their care. They deserve to be praised for their work, although that reward is usually forgotten.

Family and Staff Interaction

When mutual feelings of respect exist between staff and family, when neither feels second-class citizenship, the resident will reap the benefit. The staff will feel free to consult the family, and the family to consult the staff.

But even when free and easy communication is encouraged, families should not forget that every nursing home must run on a schedule and personnel may not always be available. It is wise to check ahead about the most convenient time to talk to a doctor, a nurse, or a social worker. Since most professionals are overworked and busy, it is also wiser to keep your consultations within reasonable limits, and your anxieties in check. When there is no emergency and you only have minor concerns, it would make sense if you took care of all of them in one meeting rather than separate ones—for example, "Doctor, I've noticed quite a few things that worried me about Mother's condition in my last few visits. Could I talk with you about them sometime this week?"

Staff members all the way down the line are likely to be more receptive to families who respect schedules and abide by rules. They have a right to be irritated by people who break rules arbitrarily or ask that unnecessary exceptions be made "just this once." Sneaking in food forbidden medically on a resident's diet, disregarding visiting hours, taking a resident out without notice—all those actions are frustrating to the staff and add extra problems.

Tipping and giving gifts (even on Christmas or special occasions) is frowned on in most reputable homes; in some states it is prohibited by the health code. But relatives and residents quite routinely ignore this prohibition. Families should think twice, however, because tipping staff members at any level is equivalent to treating them like servants, buying their favors, implying that they cannot be trusted to do their jobs without being bribed. It's only human to want to express your gratitude to someone who has been particularly attentive to your mother, but there are other ways to say thank you. Staff members are always appreciative when grateful families send notes praising their efforts to the administrator or the board of trustees. Translated into more concrete rewards, those notes can lead to promotions, but the appreciation is not always viewed in such crass terms. Nursing home personnel like to be thanked in person for their efforts and to know that the care they have given an elderly resident has been recognized and valued.

The Role of the Family

Although not involved in the health and physical well-being of the residents, the family plays an equally important role in nursing home life. It maintains the old bonds of affection, understands its own relative's idiosyncratic needs, and provides the link with the community outside. Frequent visits are very supportive for most old people, but close relationships can also be kept going long-distance. Regular communications—cards, letters, phone calls, photographs, newspaper clippings—can reassure elderly men and women that their close ties are still strong and that those they love are still constantly concerned about their welfare.

Nursing home residents, while they often thrive on family contact, can also manage to get along without it. Close friends can act as substitutes—other residents and sometimes even staff members step in to fill the gaps left by absent or disinterested relatives. Occasionally residents previously torn by longstanding destructive relationships use their nursing home placement as an opportunity to withdraw from family battles, turning to new relationships within the home.

The extent of your own involvement with your own resident-parent will depend on your old relationship, your own availability, and your parent's needs and receptivity.

MEETING THE NEED FOR AFFECTION

Although some residents do manage without their families and others withdraw from them, for most there is no substitute for a warm, concerned family. Your mother may be widowed, her sisters and brothers and close friends gone or ill. Who else is there besides you and her other children who really understands her, remembers her past, understands her cultural heritage, and appreciates her former talents and her triumphs? She can talk about her personal history to her new friends in the home, and she probably will, but you have lived through much of it with her and can add your memories to hers.

Reasonable residents do not demand unreasonable amounts of visiting; the quality of each visit rather than its frequency or length is its most important therapeutic variable. Forcing yourself to visit your mother every day—out of guilt or pity—will leave you feeling tired, put-upon, and irritable after a few months, and she will be quick to sense your mood. Knowing that she will have a good long talk with you every Sunday afternoon will mean more to her than if you dash in every day at odd hours, when she least expects you, and dash out again before she has collected her thoughts. A regular Sunday (or any other day) visit can be anticipated with pleasure through the days that precede it and enjoyed in retrospect in the days that follow it.

THE VISIT HOME

Nursing home residents, contrary to popular misconceptions, are not shut-ins. Unless seriously handicapped physically or mentally, they are often capable of leaving the home if someone volunteers to take them. A variety of outside activities can be enjoyed—meals in restaurants, movies, concerts, picnics, church services, lectures— as well as special events—Christmas, Thanksgiving, birthdays. You may want to bring your mother home to your house to stay for a few days, and many families schedule such visits at regular intervals.

All those outings should be planned well in advance, out of consideration for the home's staff, and also because the elderly usually find sudden changes in routine very disruptive. The benefits of outside visits are unlimited: they provide an invigorating change of scene, a stimulating series of forgotten experiences, and a chance to reinforce old personal and cultural ties. But those very benefits can be overstimulating and taxing for the frail elderly. Finally adjusted to the nursing home environment, they once again—even though for only a brief time—must adapt to different surroundings, foods, and people. Even if a visit at *your* home seemed to go well, it would be wise to check with your mother's nurses after she returns to *her* home to find out whether she seemed any worse for her outing. The nurses may also be able to advise you how long the visits home should be and how often they should occur.

The rules and regulations governing all visits should be checked before any resident is taken out. Many homes have their own particular concerns, and numerous restrictions have been imposed in recent years.

There are, of course, self-sufficient, somewhat withdrawn residents who require little emotional nurturing from anyone—family, friends, or staff. They may let it be known that they prefer to be alone, retired into a shell—a form of adaptation to institutional life that suits them best. Their relatives may be upset when invitations are refused or accepted reluctantly, but if visits home are not enjoyed by anyone, they are hardly worth the effort.

KEEPING THE ELDERLY IN TOUCH WITH THEIR COMMUNITIES

Nursing home residents, although they need twenty-four-hour-a-day care, can still be deeply interested in the world outside. Some residents become recluses, but most are eager to be informed about "what's going on out there," and their families are their best informants. They also usually want to be informed truthfully; just because they are disabled or ill, they do not deserve to be protected from all unpleasant realities. Bad news as well as good news should be shared, although many families try to hide the bad and are particularly reluctant to reveal the death of a close relative, a friend, or even a pet. "Don't let Mother know!" is often the first thought in everyone's mind when tragedy strikes, but Mother, even though she seems confused and disoriented, is usually quick to sense when something is wrong. She may then become more confused, wondering what that "something" is that no one will talk about. It is unrealistic to try to hide the death of a close friend or family member, and the attempt usually leads to more trouble. If Uncle Joe used to visit her regularly, how will she be able to understand why he doesn't come any more? It may be less painful for her to accept his death than to sit day after day thinking he has forgotten her.

The old can often accept tragedy much better than you think they can—possibly even better than you do. They may even be able to help you if you give them the chance. People living into their seventies or eighties have had plenty of time and opportunity to experience tragedy. If you deny them their right to hear painful news, then you also deny them an equally important right: to share in the pain of the people they love. No wonder that kind of treatment leaves them feeling excluded. Although no one should live on a constant diet of bad news, the chance to share in family problems may be the one thing that penetrates the self-involvement shown by so many nursing home residents—and old people in general.

❖ PEOPLE USED TO TURN to Mary Philips when they were in trouble. She was valued as a concerned mother and grandmother and a helpful friend until she became ill and entered a nursing home.

There she seemed to withdraw into herself and showed little interest in anyone else. Visitors were shocked at the change in her and tried to rouse her with reports of family and community activities—but only the pleasant ones. She showed little interest in those and quickly changed the subject back to her favorite one: herself. One day her son, overburdened by his own problems, let slip the news of her grandson's arrest on drug charges. Instead of having the adverse effects everyone might have feared, that was the news that finally roused her, and she responded to it with all her former concern and understanding. Afterward, her family was able to resume their old relationship with her, turning to her with their troubles and thereby reassuring her that she was still part of their lives.

Community ties involve more than just news bulletins of happy or sad events. Residents may be eager to know how their clubs and church groups are doing. If they are not physically able to be taken to meetings, club members are often willing to visit the home periodically at the invitation of residents and families. Well-equipped institutions provide a selection of books, papers, and magazines, but if your own mother has some special interest not met in her particular home, you may be able to bring in the kind of material she misses. If her sight is poor, you may be able to provide newspapers and books specially printed for the partially sighted in large type, although these are not available everywhere. You may be able to encourage local business people you know to become involved in "home life." Some are already doing this: stores in some towns stay open on occasional Sundays exclusively for nursing home shoppers, and one enterprising merchant in the East has a traveling department store which he takes from institution to institution. If the shoppers cannot come to his store, he takes his store to the shoppers.

MEETING IDIOSYNCRATIC NEEDS

You and your family, who know your mother best, also know her special needs and interests One of the dangers of institutional life is that those highly personal details can be overlooked by the staff which, because of lack of time, may tend to treat everyone in a uniform way. A loving daughter will know what kind of underwear her mother finds most comfortable, what kind of powder she likes after the bath, which flower is her favorite, and which fruit she enjoys the most. A son may be tuned in to his father's need for a night light and his intense aversion to the only newspaper circulated in the home. All those little needs may seem inconsequential, but when they are added up they can make the difference between happiness and unhappiness in the home.

Families also are aware of the particular talents of their relatives. Those talents often pass unnoticed in the confusion of the adjustment period, and if no one asks directly, "Can you play the piano,

Mr. Fisher?'' Mr. Fisher may never reveal that talent himself. Creative residents can enrich the entire nursing home environment, as well as their own lives, if they are allowed to put their talents to use.

The Demanding Resident

Some elderly residents make insatiable demands on their families: telephoning constantly, insisting on more visits than anyone can reasonably manage to make, complaining loudly about poor care, and accusing every relative of selfishness and lack of concern. That kind of demanding behavior is sometimes seen right after admission, and if it is out of character and dealt with calmly by the family, it may subside after the difficult period is over. It may also result because a nursing home resident, forced to give up control in so many areas of daily life, may need to assert himself in whatever way he can.

But if people have been demanding, selfish, and resentful prior to admission, they are likely to continue that way, and their families will have to learn how to deal with them. Easier said than done, such families will say; if they haven't learned to say no to a domineering mother in fifty years, it's hard to begin. But some of the fearsome power of a dominant mother may fade in the nursing home setting, and it is possible for her family—even at that late date—to tell her firmly, without becoming rejecting, just how much they can be expected to do for her. They may even learn to say no at last.

Demanding behavior, whatever its causes, is used by elderly residents as a way to trap their relatives. If you spend inordinate amounts of time with your father just because he insists—you are trapped. If you become guilty when your father complains about the "miserable conditions" in the home—you are trapped. Complaints should be considered and checked for validity, of course, but the worst trap of all is allowing yourself to become involved in a power struggle with the staff over your father's care. He'll never give up behavior that produces just the results he thinks he wants until you set limits on your time and energy and involvement. When he realizes that further demands are fruitless, he will gradually—it is hoped—begin to focus less on you and more on his involvement with other residents.

The Demanding Family

Families resort to demanding behavior just as frequently as their resident relatives. They may disguise their demands by being oversolicitous, by incessant visiting, and by constant complaints and interference with the staff, all of which may put an undue emotional strain on their own relatives. There are always reasons for such behavior. A son may be trying to curry his mother's favor, to stay in good with her. A daughter may be continuing a lifetime of sibling rivalry, still competing with her sisters and trying to prove that she's the best one after all. Children may be overly attentive to quiet their guilt or to protect their share of an expected inheritance. Excessive behavior from families is as destructive as excessive behavior by residents and becomes even more destructive if the staff gets drawn in.

❖ FRANCES WILSON, a rather simple person herself, had raised three successful professional children, all of whom were very dependent on her and very competitive with each other. When she was seventy-nine she became seriously disoriented and her children arranged for nursing home placement. They did not really accept her mental deterioration, which they aggravated by their demands. She deteriorated further after placement, partly in retribution for their action and partly to withdraw from further conflict.

Her oldest daughter took the leadership among her siblings, as she had always done, and constantly found fault with the staff. She blamed them for not rehabilitating her mother but at the same time interfered with their efforts to help. Most of her hostility she aimed at nonprofessional personnel—aides and orderlies—whom she snubbed. They reacted with understandable hostility, some of which rubbed off on the old lady. As the three-way battle continued, her condition regressed to the point where she became incontinent and noncomprehending, and deteriorated beyond help.

Help for the Troubled Family and Resident

Most competent homes have social service staffs capable of helping with troubled family relationships. Psychiatric consultation may also be available. The trouble may be recognized first by a staff member who, hearing that a family's behavior is too demanding on a resident or overly critical of personnel, suggests a consultation. Similarly, families who are being drained by a relative's demands, or are in serious conflict with the nurses, may ask for help themselves. When no services are available or additional ones are needed, help can be found outside the institution from social workers, social agencies, or private psychotherapists.

When Things Go Wrong

Things can go seriously wrong with nursing home care even in the best-run institutions. If you have selected your mother's home with

great care, you may find it hard to believe that any criticism you feel
(or any complaint she makes) could be valid, and you may wonder
at first if the trouble lies in your own unreasonable expectations or
in your mother's unreasonable demands. But when you are convinced that a complaint is justified, you have a duty to speak up
about it, or even to take drastic action.

A move to another institution, disruptive though it can be, may
be the only humane way to escape mistreatment. If you find your
mother's basic needs are constantly neglected—if she suffers from
bedsores (decubiti), is frightened and withdrawn, and the staff is
callous to her condition or pooh-poohs your concern—you may be
forced to move her. But you have a further responsibility beyond
her personal welfare: a responsibility to other residents and an
obligation to lodge a detailed complaint with the proper authorities.

THE FORCED TRANSFER

You may run into a situation which is particularly frightening to
you and your parents: a forced transfer to another home. Some bad
nursing homes, of course, are closed by the authorities, and a transfer in that case is welcome. But others decide that they no longer
want certain classifications of patients and, in order to receive more
reimbursement, discharge them to other institutions. The utilization
and review committee in your parent's institution may decide he no
longer needs the level of care he is receiving and must be moved.
Relocations of that sort can be very harmful, particularly to the
physically and mentally frail, and often they are carried out with
little warning and preparation. Since such relocations usually take
place with the approval of the Medicaid authorities, you can seek
a reprieve through the fair hearing process in your state department
of social services. Since the legal and civil rights of your parents are
being abused, you should also consult a lawyer or a community
legal service.

If you and your parent decide a move is necessary, or if you have
no choice because the home is being closed, it is absolutely essential
that time is provided for a smooth transition. Time is needed both
to find a new facility, and for your parent to prepare both emotionally and physically for the change in his life.

In general, however, the situation is less drastic or clear-cut. You
may find some conditions wanting and others good, neither bad
enough to warrant a move nor good enough to reassure you. When
things are going reasonably well, you may be tempted to adopt a
"Don't make waves" or "Don't rock the boat" philosophy. But a
series of minor incidents added up over time can produce major

setbacks. Poorly prepared meals, rudeness or callousness from a staff member, missing clothing, beds still unmade or residents still in night clothes at noon—all should be reported. In nursing homes, as in all institutions, there is a chain of command, and if you do not find satisfaction at the first level, take your complaint on up—from floor nurse to nursing supervisor or administrator. Complaints may be aired through resident councils by residents themselves or through relatives' auxiliaries by the families. Those groups can exert great pressure on the administration to improve general welfare, and therefore general morale, but they are not found in every institution; often they exist in name only.

When no such machinery exists, the proper authority can be alerted in a business-like way by letter or telephone. You have a right to expect an answer to any complaint. If no answer is received and the problem continues, repeat the process until you see action. If you run into a stone wall but are reluctant to transfer your parent, there are higher authorities for complaints outside the institution. Philanthropic institutions have boards of trustees or are supervised by umbrella philanthropic organizations. All nursing homes are accountable to the state department of health which licenses them, and there are legal channels through which families can take legal action. Such drastic steps should not be necessary in responsible homes where concerned administrators welcome consumer feedback, aware that a constant dialogue between staff, residents, and families produces the most constructive results.

DON'T BE AFRAID

Families often fear that their complaints will cause the staff to retaliate against their helpless relatives. Actually, experience—in well-run homes—shows that a resident who speaks up for his rights or has a vocal and alert family to speak up for him usually receives better care. Keeping quiet or being afraid allows a bad situation to get worse, and rather than retaliation, responsible consumer feedback usually produces improved services. Pity the timid residents who are afraid to complain and have no families to back them up, they are the more likely victims. There is growing public pressure at present for the appointment of nursing home advocates to protect the rights of such helpless residents.

A Reasonable Goal

This chapter has laid out basic steps to nursing home selection. It has reviewed procedures likely to make the transition to institutional life less painful, and supportive behavior to encourage a satisfying adjustment after placement. BUT steps and procedures, easy enough to describe on paper, are not so easy to follow exactly as directed. Imperfection is predictable at some stage.

Human behavior has its own built-in imperfections, too. When facing nursing home placement with their elderly parents, some children handle the process with total success, while others fail completely. But in general, well-intentioned children will ride a seesaw between success and failure. You may find it difficult to behave according to this book. Some recommendations will run counter to your personality. Patience, understanding, and empathy cannot be produced just because an emergency calls for those qualities, nor can they ever operate consistently. Rather, they are likely to fluctuate according to other pressures in your life. Your most realistic goal may be to help your mother or father in the direction of a *reasonably* satisfying adjustment and, in the process, to achieve a *reasonably* peaceful state of mind for yourself.

10.

Taking a Stand

❖ KITTY BRADEN dropped out of college before her first child was born and went back to finish after her youngest child reached junior high school. In her first semester her mother died and Kitty, unable to let her nearly blind father live alone, brought him to live with her. Kitty dropped out of college for the second time.

*

❖ JACK PHILIPS, a science teacher with three children—one in college already and the other two moving up through high school—learned last year that his mother, after a long struggle with cancer, had used up all her health insurance benefits and her money, and could no longer pay for the medical and nursing care she needed. Jack and his brothers now share those expenses. Jack moonlights on the evening shift at the Lomax Plant.

*

❖ MARY MURPHY, although sad and lonely in the early days after her father's death, was a little ashamed of the thoughts that kept running through her head: " . . . No more Medicare forms to fill out . . . no more frantic scrambling for homemakers and nurses . . . no more emergency calls in the middle of the night . . . no more visits to that terrible old neighborhood . . . no more canceling our plans because Dad has another attack. . . . Thank God, all that's over. . . ."

Those three families—and numbers like them—prove false the popular belief, "Children in modern society neglect their old parents." Such families know they do everything they can for their old parents under the circumstances. The only thing they do not do is try to change the circumstances.

If adequate, protected alternative living arrangements had been available for their fathers, Kitty and Mary would not have had to disrupt their own lives. If adequate insurance coverage for chronic illness had been available for his mother, Jack would not have had to moonlight. None of these children would have loved their parents less, but they would have had to sacrifice less of their personal lives. For a long time now society has been calling the younger generations to task for their shortcomings. The message has been, "You are not taking good enough care of your elderly relatives." Perhaps it is finally time for those generations to call society to task for its shortcomings, with the message, "*You* are not taking good enough care of your elderly citizens."

Although society has made much progress in this century, it too often fails the elderly who are frail, dependent, incapacitated. It also frequently fails the elderly who are independent and determined to stay that way. How long will independence continue for an old man who has an inadequate income, substandard housing, and little health protection? Those necessities can no longer be seen as "family matters" and left up to the families to provide.

Some try to deny society's failures by pointing to its progress. They say, "Look how far we've come in the forty years since Social Security. Look how far we've come in the last ten years, since the passage of the Older Americans Act. Look at Medicare. Look at Medicaid. Look at SSI. Look at the millions of old people who are getting *some* help!" Those statements are partially true. It can be legitimately argued that many federal programs do benefit the elderly: income benefits, financing of health care, protection of rights with laws preventing discrimination against older workers, programs of fundamental research on aging in the recently created National Institute of Aging, federal supports for state and local organizations providing services to the elderly. All these provisions back up the assertion that things are looking up for older Americans now.

But the fact that the elderly today have more support than they used to does not mean they have enough support. And the fact that in *some* places *some* services are being set up, improved, or expanded, does not help the elderly who do not live in those places but live one hundred, two hundred, or five hundred miles away. The overall needs of the elderly across the country are still inadequately and unevenly met.

Because of lack of services in your own community you may, like Kitty Braden, feel obligated to reorganize your life in order to take care of your widowed father. Or, if that is not possible, he may be forced to accept institutional placement. That initial placement may not be a final solution either, and you may have to move him to a

second institution if the first one is closed down or provides poor
care.

There is a general call out today for more support and additional
services, although a cynic might paraphrase Mark Twain's comment
about the weather—everybody's talking about the needs of the
elderly but nobody's doing much about them. At the present time
a greater danger comes, not from too little addition, but from too
much subtraction—from moving backward instead of moving forward. In the current economic pinch there is an ever-present threat
of cutbacks in existing benefits and services. Anyone living through
the financial crises of the cities is becoming used to nightly news
bulletins announcing drastic curtailments of services or the outright
closing down of hospitals, clinics, senior centers, and meal programs. Whenever there is a need to save money, the most obvious
place to look for cuts is frequently found in the funds for the
elderly.

The greatest opposition to cutbacks and the greatest pressure for
increments has come, until now, from the elderly themselves, who
are becoming more vocal and better organized to protect their own
well-being and state their own demands. Pressure has also come
from professionals, young and old, active in the field of aging. A
notable success in rousing public awareness came when the nursing
home scandals were uncovered after years of covert operations.

Little pressure has come yet, however, from a potentially powerful group: the families of the elderly, who have merely hovered
anxiously on the sidelines accepting their personal guilt, settling for
stopgap measures, complaining to themselves about their problems,
but rarely making their voices heard. Perhaps it has happened because private citizens have tended to think of elderly relatives as
family, rather than public, responsibilities. As individual sons and
daughters, they may have supported measures designed to improve
the general welfare of the elderly, but how much more powerful
they could be if they raised a collective voice. Perhaps they remain
silent out of ignorance, uncertain how to go about speaking collec-
tively. Perhaps they hesitate to speak out, fearing that by asking
society to help their parents they would be asking for charity and
forced to accept the stigma of welfare. Perhaps they feel guiltily
aware that they could be doing more themselves, and are not. Perhaps they fear that by demanding greater public support for their
parents, they would expose themselves as evading their responsibilities as sons and daughters.

Pressing for social action is another way for sons and daughters
to behave responsibly to their parents and, in the long run, a more

constructive way. Social action will not separate parents from children. Even if the day ever comes when the elderly are well supported, well fed, well housed, and well nursed, those with close relationships will continue to turn to their children for benefits only the intimate family can provide. Children and close family members are usually tuned in to the idiosyncratic needs of their elderly relatives and offer the special personal understanding and individual affection that is essential and no one else can provide. Impersonal, large-scale operations can lend basic support, but when public support comes in the door, private relationships will *not* fly out of the window. They will continue to yield their traditional benefits.

The children of the elderly, sandwiched in between an older and a younger generation, must give in two directions at the same time. They receive no compensation for that double burden, and they are usually the most heavily taxed. They have a right to stand up and shout, "We need help, too!" "Pay attention to us!" They also have a right to hope that someone listens.

Attention, Legislators, Insurance Underwriters, Employers!

Social Security, the dream of the thirties, is in danger of becoming the disillusion of the seventies. Unless those benefits and their related supplements keep up with rising living costs, many more elderly men and women now teetering at the poverty threshold will fall below it. It is small comfort to have a monthly check if the money it brings barely covers the barest monthly expenses. The inequalities of the system, particularly as they affect elderly women, need to be evened out so that becoming a widow does not also usually mean becoming poorer.

Regulations which prevent the elderly from working, or which penalize them for working, need modification. The rulings at present carry a double penalty: the elderly are denied the right to earn more than a minimal amount of monetary income, and they are simultaneously denied the right to earn the psychic income which comes from feeling useful and productive. Once these regulations are modified, other modifications are necessary, particularly in the attitudes of employers reluctant to take on elderly employees.

Adequate health insurance, not only against acute illness but against chronic illness as well, is long overdue. It should cover a variety of health services needed by the disabled and incapacitated at home, not only in the hospital. The children of the elderly, many of whom are willing and able to care for a disabled father or mother, have a right to financial assistance, in the form of either tax reduction or some type of government subsidy to help to defray their outlays of time and effort. Such small compensation would inevitably cost less in public funds than a nursing home bill covered in full by Medicaid. A subsidy or tax rebate might provide just the necessary balance to offset the tipping point that forces nursing home placement of many elderly people.

Attention, Planners, Builders, Architects!

Numbers of elderly men and women are trapped at present, because of low incomes, in substandard housing, in decaying neighborhoods, with landlords who have no interest in tenant welfare once the rent is paid. Other aging mothers and fathers, who would prefer independent arrangements, are trapped in stressful living situations in their children's homes for lack of financial resources to pay separate rents.

Government subsidies, presently lagging seriously behind, are essential to provide low-cost housing—or special units within larger complexes—to meet the variety of elderly needs. The layout of each individual structure should be geared to safety and comfort, with services built into the overall design, so that tenants have help readily available for meals, housekeeping, and medical attention. The need for housing for the elderly is estimated at 120,000 new housing units annually, but only 45,000 units have actually been built in the last eight years.

It is unlikely that the need for new special housing will be met in the near future, so only small numbers will benefit for many years. Those who continue, out of choice or out of necessity, as tenants in their previous living quarters could be offered rent reductions or rent subsidies instead, while tax rebates could be available to home-owners. There is a trend in this direction in some communities but so far no nationwide pattern.

The elderly at all income levels need housing—not only the low-income elderly—and there should be a variety of styles in a variety of locations. Because of the tremendous diversity among the elderly millions, it cannot be assumed that any one type of housing will suit all tastes. Some people may head south to warmer climates but others, as recent studies show, may head north to colder climates.

Retirement does not have to involve uprooting or moving. Many old people want to stay right where they are despite difficult climates. They see no reason, because of advancing age, to trade familiar winter snows for alien sunny beaches, but their own communities may not offer appropriate housing: small enough, cheap enough, manageable enough.

❖ WHY SHOULD ELLEN VORST—retired after thirty years of teaching in one small affluent community—be forced to move to another town when her house becomes too big for her to manage alone? She would like to stay where she is, but zoning in her own town forbids apartments, so she has no choice. Why should exile be the reward for years of dedicated community service?

Even when they decide voluntarily to move to a retirement community, all the elderly do not have the same requirements. They may all require living arrangements which provide a range of services, but those services can be provided in a variety of settings. The physical environment is important to one couple, while the psychological atmosphere is more important to another. There should be options open: country, urban, or suburban locations; large communities or small clusters; much communal interaction or freedom for independent living. Older people are sometimes only happy in age-segregated communities where their contacts are with their elderly contemporaries. Others dread such exclusive ghettos and look instead for age-integrated communities offering ongoing contacts with their own generation, and with children, teenagers, and young adults as well.

Attention, Physicians, Psychiatrists, Nurses, Social Workers!

Adequate health care, like adequate housing, is predicated on adequate funding, and many older Americans today are going without good health care because of the tremendous expense involved and the many gaps in insurance coverage.

Here again, money is not the only roadblock. The medical professions have had to focus on an awesome number of physiological and psychological ills which threaten human life, and the highest priorities have been assigned to understanding these ills, learning how to treat and cure them. Professionals have not been able to focus as intently on the special problems of the elderly or to give high priority to their care, treatment, and understanding. Perhaps, in addition, the healing professions have been less interested in the care of chronic conditions, which so often are the fate of the elderly and which defy healing. Or perhaps these professions have also incorporated the fears, the denial, and the avoidance of the subject of aging prevalent in the larger society.

The priority ratings are in the process of realignment, and there is growing recognition that the physical and emotional health of older men and women must be better understood. That recognition is being reflected in some medical schools—the training ground for future physicians—where programs are now being offered to provide experience in geriatric medicine. Public support is needed in order to assure a greater allocation of funds to underwrite the continuing development of these programs, not only in the medical professions, but in allied fields—nursing and social work—as well.

Join the Action

Appeals for help, for attention, can be sent out to legislators, planners, architects, physicians, psychiatrists—but who can be sure these appeals will be heard and answered?

A significant influence leading to the enactment of important new federal legislation and appropriations to benefit the elderly in the past decade has been the organized pressure and vocal demands of the elderly themselves in such groups as the Gray Panthers, the American Association of Retired Persons, the National Council of Senior Citizens, and the Association of Retired Federal Employees. Whatever success those growing organizations have achieved may have come from their do-it-yourself philosophy. Instead of remaining silent until someone else recognized their needs and passed legislation to benefit them, they pressured for legislation on their own behalf, using the same formula developed by other minority groups—blacks and Indians and by women. None of the vocal groups have gained as much as they asked for, but they have gained something more than they had before.

The hard-pressed generation in the middle can be thought of as a minority, too, with special problems of its own that have been ignored. No one talks about that minority and no one hears from it. It does not have the built-in qualities which make for an easily mobilized pressure group. It is uncohesive and dispersed—scattered geographically, fragmented socially and economically. Its one shared problem is its only common bond, but that may become a

unifying force when members of the minority learn that as individual protesters they will not gain what they want.

If they want tax relief in return for the support and services they
personally offer their elderly parents, they will have to organize and
demand it. If they suffer because their community is poor in services
for the elderly they are more likely to get those services—and respite from daily routines—if they work for them together.

Many families, however, although ready and eager to do something, have little experience in community action. They may never
have organized anything before and may have little idea of how to
get started. A good way for such novices to begin could be to take
a look at what other people have been doing in other places and to
examine programs which are already established and working successfully elsewhere. All across the country, in scattered locations,
small effective programs can be found which benefit only a limited
number of older people. Those programs can be used as models and
duplicated again and again, thereby benefiting an increasing number of older people. Some of those successful pilot projects are
described in "Designs for Action for Older Americans," a series of
pamphlets published by the Office of Human Development of the
Department of Health, Education, and Welfare. (See Appendix F.)

No one individual family can establish a program—original or
imitative—alone. But a number of families working in partnership
can demonstrate why a program is needed, how it can be put into
operation, and how many people it will benefit. Then they can
apply for funds from a public or private source for a small-scale
pilot project. If the pilot project is successful, it can be expanded
with continuing funds over subsequent years.

There is nothing new in such procedures. They have been used
often in the past by families of patients suffering from certain devastating diseases—cystic fibrosis, muscular dystrophy, cerebral
palsy. Parents of mentally retarded children met together to develop
shelters, workshops, and camps when these facilities were lacking
in their communities. Young mothers and fathers, unable to find
local nursery schools, joined together to begin their own, even if
they started out taking turns in each others' playrooms.

Meal services for the elderly, transportation services, sitting services, escort services, clubs, homemaker groups can all be started by
small groups in communities where there are few formal programs.
A preliminary informal organization can do more than provide
needed assistance; it can give families a chance to discuss their
mutual problems, to raise possible solutions, and to begin to discover perhaps for the first time that they are not alone and that the

clout of the group is stronger than the clout of the individual—that combined voices carry over greater distances than a single voice.

The same kind of informal family organization can make progress in the nursing home setting as well as in the outside community. Friends and relatives of the elderly are being organized in New York City, under a special grant from the Greater New York Fund, as "watchdog groups" to monitor nursing home operations and push for improved services. Similar family watchdog groups need to be organized for the protection of nursing home residents in every community across the country.

Family watchdog groups to monitor standards and prevent abuses are needed, not only in nursing homes, but in every service offering care for the elderly, because there is room for corruption and abuse in every one. Scandals have already rocked the nursing home "industry." Adult homes, boarding homes, and residences are being exposed every day for providing substandard living conditions. Medicare and Medicaid funds have been misused by doctors and health care providers. Similar abuses will creep into any new programs that are established for the elderly in the future unless there is careful monitoring by public agencies and alert family consumer groups. There is a move at present in the Department of Health, Education, and Welfare to make Medicare and Medicaid funds available to profit-making home care services. While such funds may stimulate a long-overdue increase in the home care services so essential to the well-being of the elderly, new opportunities for misuse of funds will be provided at the same time. Unless carefully supervised, the home care services may, before long, end up playing a new version of the nursing home scandals.

New Images for Old

Images are important in American society, and once a negative image has been projected it has a tendency to cling. Because the term *sixty-five-and-over* has developed a generally negative image, older people are too often brushed aside. Too many valuable resources have been and continue to be wasted, too many skills abandoned, too much knowledge unused, too many talents buried, too much initiative stifled. Many older people, flatly rejecting popular stereotypes, go right ahead and live just the kind of life they want to live or are able to live. Their own personal experience proves that contentment, creativity, understanding, self-reliance may be intensified rather than diminished in the later decades. They are proud, not ashamed, of their age, and want the world to know it: "What can I do for you today, young lady?" asked the salesman jovially. "First you can stop calling me 'young lady,' " replied his elderly customer, "because I'm an old woman. Then you can show me a nylon hairbrush."

Other aging people are less forthright. They move toward old age with dread. They spend their energies denying their years, afraid to identify themselves as old. Believing that the benefits of life can only be found in the younger years, they never allow themselves to discover the positive benefits of the older years. Still others, while identifying themselves as old, accept the stereotypes and allow themselves to feel useless, dependent, and finished long before it is necessary.

As the baby boom of the 1940s becomes the geriatric boom of the year 2000, the elderly sector of the population is expected to reach 29 million. At some point later in the twenty-first century, one quarter of the population may be "sixty-five-and-over." Society may have been able to believe that 10 percent of its members were outside the mainstream, but 25 percent will not be so easy to ignore.

Public and private attitudes have been changing, but they will need to change more dramatically. In recent years, as the elderly have become more visible, the focus on that group has been largely on their needs and their problems. To the other negative images of aging, therefore, another image has been added: that of the underdog, always a prime attention-getter. We tend to rally for the underdog. When we finally became aware of the inhuman conditions in certain nursing homes and the victims became real people on our TV screens, we reacted to the nursing home scandals with more public outrage. But as the miseries suffered by some elderly men and women were made so dramatically clear, they inevitably underscored and reinforced the longstanding negative images: To be old is to be helpless. To be old is to be dependent. To be old is to be useless. To be old is to be unhappy.

Just as organized pressure coming from the elderly themselves has influenced legislation, pressure from the same source is also working to modify negative images and stereotypes. The revised image being projected emphasizes diversity. It urges public concern for the old who are sick and helpless and dependent. It does not leave out the old who are cantankerous, difficult, rigid, repetitive, resentful, eccentric, or the old who are useful, creative, imaginative, optimistic, resourceful, involved, adventurous.

The generation in the middle can help to change the negative images if it is willing to take the time to notice how often the images are false. Once it becomes clear that there are endless possibilities available in the years "sixty-five-and-over," just as there are in the years "sixty-five-and-under," there may be less reason to dread the years ahead and less cause to turn away from those who have arrived at old age already. The new image may not take hold in time to help our parents, but it may take hold in time to help someone else's parents—or perhaps ourselves—or our children.

Appendix A

WHERE TO FIND HELP

1. STATE OFFICES ON THE AGING

The list that follows is excerpted from *The Directory of State Agencies Designated to Administer Title III and VII of Older Americans Act,* Administration on Aging, Office of Human Development, Office of the Secretary, Department of Health, Education, and Welfare.

Alabama

Commission on Aging
740 Madison Avenue
Montgomery 36104
(205) 832-6640
  Mr. Jesse T. Todd, Chairman
  Mr. Emmett Eaton, Executive
    Director

Alaska

Office on Aging
Department of Health and Social
  Services
Pouch H
Juneau 99811
(907) 586-6153
  Mr. M. D. Plotnick, Coordinator

Arizona

Bureau on Aging
Department of Economic Security
543 East McDowell, Room 217
Phoenix 85004
(602) 271-4446
  Mr. Lawrence W. Martin, Chief

Arkansas

Office on Aging and Adult Services
Department of Social and
  Rehabilitation Services
7 and Gaines
P.O. Box 2179
Little Rock 72202
(501) 371-2441
  Mr. Luther Miller, Chairman
  Mr. Elmer Zelsman, Acting Director

California

Office on Aging
Health and Welfare Agency
455 Capitol Mall, Suite 500
Sacramento 95814
(916) 322-3887
  Mr. Archer Kirkpatrick, Chairman
  Mrs. Janet J. Levy, Director

Colorado

Division of Services for the Aging
Department of Social Services
1575 Sherman Street
Denver 80203
(303) 892-2651/2586
  Mr. Robert B. Robinson, Director

Connecticut

Department on Aging
90 Washington Street, Room 312
Hartford 06115
(203) 566-2480
 Mr. Charles E. Odell, Commissioner

Delaware

Division of Aging
Department of Health and Social
 Services
2407 Lancaster Avenue
Wilmington 19805
(302) 571-3481/3482
 Ms. Eleanor L. Cain, Director

District of Columbia

Division of Services to the Aged
Department of Human Resources
1329 E Street, N.W.
Washington 20004
(202) 638-2406
 Mr. Curtiss E. Knighton, Chief

Florida

Division of Aging
Department of Health and
 Rehabilitation Services
1323 Winewood Boulevard
Tallahassee 32301
(904) 488-4797
 Mrs. Margaret Jacks, Director

Georgia

Office of Aging
Department of Human Resources
47 Trinity Avenue
Atlanta 30334
(404) 894-5333
 Ms. Mary Kay Jernigan, Director

Hawaii

Commission on Aging
1149 Bethel Street, Room 311
Honolulu 96813
(808) 548-2593
 Mrs. Shimeji Kanazawa, Chairman
 Mr. Renji Goto, Director

Idaho

Idaho Office on Aging
Statehouse
Boise 83720
(208) 964-3833
 Mr. John McCullen, Director
 Mr. David Mueller, Assistant
 Director

Illinois

Department on Aging
2401 West Jefferson Street
Springfield 62762
(217) 525-5773
 Mr. Kenneth W. Holland, Director

Indiana

Indiana Commission on Aging and
 Aged
Graphic Arts Building
215 North Senate Avenue
Indianapolis 46202
(317) 633-5948
 Mr. Sidney Levin, Chairman
 Mr. Maurice E. Endwright,
 Executive

Iowa

Commission on the Aging
415 West 10 Street
Jewett Building
Des Moines 50319
(515) 281-5187
 Dr. Woodrow Morris, Chairman
 Ms. Leona Peterson, Executive
 Director

Kansas

Department of Social and
 Rehabilitation Services
Division of Social Services
Services for the Aging Section
State Office Building
Topeka 66612
(913) 296-3465
 Dr. A. F. Bramble, Director

Kentucky

Aging Program Unit
Department for Human Resources
403 Wapping Street
Frankfort 40601
(502) 564-6930
  Mr. Harold Mann, Director

Louisiana

Bureau of Aging Services
Division of Human Resources
Health and Human Resources
  Administration
P.O. Box 44282, Capitol Station
Baton Rouge 70804
(504) 389-2171/6518
  Mrs. Priscillia R. Engolia, Director

Maine

Office of Maine's Elderly
Community Services Unit
Department of Health and Welfare
Augusta 04330
(207) 622-6171/ask for 289-2561
  Mr. Richard Michaud, Director

Maryland

Office on Aging
State Office Building
301 West Preston Street
Baltimore 21201
(301) 383-5064/2100
  Matthew Tayback, Sc.D., Director
  Mr. Harry F. Walker, Deputy
    Director

Massachusetts

Department of Elderly Affairs
120 Boylston Street
Boston 02116
(617) 727-7751/7752
  Ms. Rose Claffey, Secretary

Michigan

Office of Services to the Aging
3500 North Logan Street
Lansing 48913
(517) 373-5230
  Mr. Ron Kivi, Acting Director

Minnesota

Governor's Citizens Council on Aging
Suite 204
Metro Square Building
7 and Robert Street
St. Paul 55101
(612) 296-2770
  Mr. Cy Carpenter, Chairman
  Mr. Gerald A. Bloedow, Executive
    Secretary

Mississippi

Council on Aging
P.O. Box 5136
Fondren Station
510 George Street
Jackson 39216
(601) 354-6590
  Mr. Horace L. Kerr, Executive
    Director

Missouri

Office of Aging
Division of Special Services
Department of Social Services
Broadway State Office Building
P.O. Box 570
Jefferson City 65101
(314) 751-2075
  Mr. Jacques O. Lebel, Director

Montana

Aging Services Bureau
Department of Social and
  Rehabilitation Services
P.O. Box 1723
Helena 59601
(406) 449-3124
  Mr. Daniel P. Kelly, Chief

Nebraska

Commission on Aging
State House Station 94784
300 South 17 Street
Lincoln 68509
(402) 471-2307
  Mr. Donald Russell, Chairman
  Mr. Glen J. Soukup, Executive
    Director

Nevada

Division of Aging
Department of Human Resources
201 S. Fall Street, Room 300
Nye Building.
Carson City 89701
(702) 885-4210
　Mr. John B. McSweeney,
　　Administrator

New Hampshire

Council on Aging
P.O. Box 786
14 Depot Street
Concord 03301
(603) 271-2751
　Mr. Philip Robertson, Chairman
　Mr. Paul Hendrick, Director

New Jersey

Division on Aging
Department of Community Affairs
P.O. Box 2768
363 West State Street
Trenton 08625
(609) 292-3765
　Mr. James J. Pennestri, Director

New Mexico

Commission on Aging
408 Galisteo, Villagra Building
Santa Fe 87503
(505) 827-5258
　Mr. Clifford Whiting, Chairman
　Mr. Roberto Mondragon, Director

New York

Office for the Aging
New York State Executive
　Department
855 Central Avenue
Albany 12206
(518) 457-7321
　Mr. Garson Meyer, Chairman
　Mr. Warren G. Billings, Deputy
　　Director

New York State Office for the Aging
2 World Trade Center, Room 5036
New York 10047
(212) 488-6405
　Mr. Harold Scher, Senior Field
　　Representative

North Carolina

Governor's Coordinating Council on
　Aging
Department of Human Resources
Administration Building
213 Hillsborough Street
Raleigh 27603
(919) 829-3983
　Mr. Robert Q. Beard, Executive
　　Director

North Dakota

Aging Services
Social Services Board of North
　Dakota
State Capitol Building
Bismarck 58505
(701) 224-2577
　Mr. Gerald D. Shaw, Supervisor

Ohio

Commission on Aging
34 North High Street
Columbus 43215
(614) 466-5500/5501
　Mr. Sidney Specter, Chairman
　Mr. Martin A. Janis, Commissioner

Oklahoma

Special Unit on Aging
Department of Institutions
Social and Rehabilitative Services
P.O. Box 25352, Capitol Station
Oklahoma City 73125
(405) 521-2281
　Mr. Roy R. Keene, Supervisor

Oregon

Program on Aging
Human Resources Department
772 Commercial Street, S.E.
Salem 97310
(503) 378-4728
　Mrs. Edward L. Hughes,
　　Coordinator

Pennsylvania

Office for the Aging
Department of Public Welfare
Capitol Associates Building
7 and Forster Street
Harrisburg 17120
(717) 787-5300
  Mr. Robert C. Benedict,
    Commissioner

Puerto Rico

Gericulture Commission
Department of Social Services
P.O. Box 11697
Santurce 00908
(809) 722-2429
  Mrs. Maria Isabel Vazquez,
    Executive Director

Rhode Island

Division on Aging
Department of Community Affairs
150 Washington
  Providence 02903
(401) 277-2858
  Mrs. Eleanor F. Slater, Chief

South Carolina

Commission on Aging
915 Main Street
Columbia 29201
(803) 758-2576
  Mr. John Lumpkin, Jr., Chairman
  Mr. Harry Bryan, Executive
    Director

South Dakota

Office on Aging
Department of Social Services
St. Charles Hotel
Pierre 57501
(605) 224-3656
  Mr. James V. Anderson,
    Administrator

Tennessee

Commission on Aging
Room 102 S and P Building
306 Gay Street
Nashville 37201
(615) 741-2056
  Dr. William E. Cole, Chairman
  Mr. Paul Duncan, Acting Director

Texas

Governor's Committee on Aging
8th Floor Southwest Tower
211 East 7 Street
P.O. Box 12786, Capitol Station
Austin 78711
(512) 475-2717
  Dr. Alton O. Bowen, Chairman
  Mr. Vernon McDaniel, Executive
    Director

Utah

Division of Aging
Department of Social Services
345 South 6 East
Salt Lake City 84102
(801) 328-5422
  Mr. Iver C. Moore, Director

Vermont

Office on Aging
Agency of Human Services
81 River Street (Heritage 1)
Montpelier 05602
(802) 770-7894
  Mrs. Pearl Somani, Director

Virginia

Office on Aging
830 East Main Street
Suite 950
Richmond 23219
(804) 770-7894
  Mr. Edwin Wood, Director

Virgin Islands

Commission on Aging
P.O. Box 539
Charlotte Amalie
St. Thomas 00801
(809) 774-5884
  Mrs. Gloria M. King, Executive
    Secretary

Washington

Office on Aging
Department of Social and Health
  Services
P.O. Box 1788, M.S. 45-2
Olympia 98504
(206) 753-2502
  Dr. Roy Schiendelheim, Acting
  Director

West Virginia

Commission on Aging
State Capitol
Charleston 25305
(304) 348-3317
  Mr. Clement R. Bassett, Chairman
  Dr. Louise B. Gerrard, Executive
  Director

Wisconsin

Division on Aging
Department of Health and Social
  Services
1 West Wilson Street, Room 686
Madison 53702
(608) 266-2536
  Mr. Duane Willadsen,
  Administrator

Wyoming

Aging Services
Department of Health and Social
  Services
Division of Public Assistance and
  Social Services
New State Office Building West,
  Room 288
Cheyenne 82002
(307) 777-7561
  Mr. James Hammer, Director

2. INFORMATION AND REFERRAL SERVICES

The following selected list of information and referral services is reprinted with the permission of the Community Council of Greater New York, Inc. It is excerpted from the Council's *1975–1976 Directory of Social and Health Agencies of New York City.*

United States

Arizona

Community Council Serving
  Maricopa County
1515 East Osborn Road
Phoenix 85014
(602) 263-8853
County-Wide Information and
  Referral Service
(602) 263-8856
Mrs. Corazon Doyle, Director
  Area Served: Maricopa County

Information and Referral Service, Inc.
3833 East Second Street Room 7
Tucson 85716
(602) 881-1794
Judith Wagner, Director
  Area Served: Metropolitan Tucson
  and Pima County, but no
  restrictions

California

Information and Referral Service of
  Los Angeles County, Inc.
621 South Virgil Avenue
Los Angeles 90005
Administration, (213) 380-1450
Service, (213) 380-2913
Information and Referral Service
Mrs. Barbara H. Thies, Executive
  Director
  Area Served: Los Angeles County

San Fernando Valley Branch
6851 Lennox Avenue
Van Nuys 91405
(213) 785-8861
Mrs. Eleanor K. D. Grossman,
  Director
  Area Served: Los Angeles County

Emergency Assistance and Referral
  Agency
2319½ J Street
Sacramento 95816
(916) 454-5071
Emergency Financial Assistance
  Information and Referral Services
  for Health and Welfare Services
Dorene Lynch, Executive Director
  Area Served: Sacramento and East
  Yolo counties

Guideline
P.O. Box 2671
San Diego 92112
(714) 238-1111
Information and Referral Service
David Cuney, Director

United Bay Area Crusade
2015 Steiner Street
San Francisco 94115
(415) 563-1220
Information and Referral Service
Mary M. Raftis, Director
  Area Served: Alameda, Contra
  Costa, Marin, San Francisco, and
  San Mateo counties

Colorado

Department of Community Services,
  Mile High United Way
1375 Delaware Street
Denver 80204
(303) 573-6666
Information and Referral Service
Mrs. Amelia B. Barnard, Director
  Area Served: Metropolitan Denver

Connecticut

Darien United Fund and Community
  Council, Inc., The
34 Old Kings Highway
South Darien 06820
(203) 655-8775
Mary R. Seagrave, Executive Director
Information Service (203) 655-1234
  Area Served: Darien

Community Answers
101 West Putnam Avenue
Greenwich 06830
(203) 661-6004
Barbara B. Gregorich, Executive
  Director
Information and Referral Service
  Area Served: Greenwich

Information and Referral
1 State Street
New Haven 06510
(203) 624-3136
Answering service after office hours
Information and Referral Services
  Area Served: Greater New Haven
    area, including East Haven,
    Hamden, Milford, New Haven,
    North Haven, Orange, West
    Haven, and Woodbridge

Greater Norwalk Community Council
182 Wolfpit Avenue
Norwalk 06851
(203) 847-4576
James M. Gersitz, Executive Director
Information and Referral Service for
  the Elderly ("Senior Service")
(203) 846-9700
Robert Carter, Director
  Area Served: Norwalk and Wilton

State Department of Health,
  Southeast Regional Office
401 West Thames Street
Norwich 06360
(203) 889-8341
Information and Referral Service
Mrs. Margaret Poffenberger, Director

United Way of Stamford
62 Palmer Hill Road
Stamford 06901
(203) 348-7711
Information Service
John V. Cunningham, Executive
  Director
Francis Donnon, Planning Director
  Area Served: Stamford

Information and Referral Service
P.O. Box 2688
Waterbury 06720
(203) 757-9855
James E. Burke, Coordinator

Community Council of the Capitol
  Region
68 South Main Street
West Hartford 06107
(203) 521-8822
Information and Referral Service
Mrs. Helen B. Fisher, Coordinator
(203) 521-7150
  Area Served: Greater Hartford,
    including twenty-nine suburban
    towns

Commission for the Elderly of the
  Town of Westport
YMCA Building
59 East State Street
Westport 06880
(203) 227-4131
Information and Referral Service
Joyce Roessler, Executive Coordinator

District of Columbia

United Way of the National Capital
  Area
95 M Street, Southwest
Washington 20024
(202) 488-2110
Mrs. Elizabeth G. Sarpy, Associate
  Executive Director
  Area Served: Alexandria, Arlington,
    Fairfax, Falls Church, Prince
    William County, Virginia;
    District of Columbia;
    Montgomery and Prince Georges
    counties, Maryland

Florida

Community Service Council of
  Broward County
1300 South Andrews Avenue, P.O.
  Box 22877
Fort Lauderdale 33315
(305) 525-4361
Mrs. Lois Howell, Chief of Social
  Services
Information and Referral Service

Community Planning Council
1045 Riverside Avenue
Jacksonville 32204
(904) 358-1919
Information and Referral Service
Mrs. Pansy Mattair, Coordinator
  Area Served: Duval County

United Way of Dade County
955 Southwest Second Avenue
P.O. Box 010790
Miami 33130
(305) 854-8311

Citizens' Information and Referral
  Service
902 Southwest Second Avenue
Miami 33130
(305) 856-0606
Dino Caros, De Wayne Little,
  Co-directors

Volunteer Action Center
902 Southwest Second Avenue
Miami 33130
(305) 854-8311
Helene Rand, Director
  Area Served: Dade County
    (Twenty-eight municipalities)

Human Service Center
625 Twiggs Street
Tampa 33602
Mrs. Rhoda F. Reid, Program Director
Information and Referral Service

Georgia

Information and Referral Service
167 Walton Street, Northwest
Atlanta 30301
(404) 522-7370
Mrs. Doris Bradley, Director

United Community Services
428 Bull Street
Savannah 31402
(912) 234-6136
Information and Referral Department
Paul E. Parks, Executive Director
  Area Served: Chatham County

Hawaii

Volunteer Information and Referral
  Service
200 North Vineyard Boulevard, Room
  603
Honolulu 96817
(808) 521-4566
  Area Served: City and county of
    Honolulu
Suicide and Crisis Center
(808) 521-4555
  Area Served: City and county of
    Honolulu

Illinois

Council for Community Services in
  Metropolitan Chicago
61 East Jackson Boulevard
Chicago 60604
(312) 427-9151
Community Referral Service
(312) 427-9623
Virginia Carpentette, Director
  Area Served: Metropolitan Chicago,
    Including Cook, Du Page, and
    Lake Counties

Indiana

Community Service Council of
  Metropolitan Indianapolis
English Foundation Building
615 North Alabama Street, Room 410
Indianapolis 46204
(317) 634-4311
Information and Referral Service
Helen Daniels, Director Central
  Services
  Area Served: Metropolitan
    Indianapolis

Iowa

Greater Des Moines United Way
700 Sixth Avenue
Des Moines 50309
(515) 244-8646
24 hours—7 days a week;
(515) 244-1181
Information and Referral Services
Mrs. Jeanne Pointer, Information and
  Referral Specialist
  Area Served: Greater Des Moines
    and Polk County

Kansas

Community Information and Referral
  Service, Community Planning
  Council
420 Insurance Building
Wichita 67202
(316) 267-4327
Ann Dorsey, Information and Referral
  Coordinator
  Area Served: Greater Wichita area
  Johnson County. See Missouri:
    Kansas City
  Wyandotte County. See Missouri:
    Kansas City

Kentucky

Crisis and Information Center
Preston and Chestnut Streets
Louisville 40202
(502) 598-4313
Linda L. Hays, Director
Information and Referral Service
  Area Served: Louisville and the
    following counties: Jefferson,
    Oldham, Henry, Trimble,
    Spencer, Bullitt, and Shelby
  Boone County. See Ohio:
    Cincinnati
  Campbell County. See Ohio:
    Cincinnati
  Kenton County. See Ohio:
    Cincinnati

Louisiana

Volunteer and Information Agency,
  Inc.
211 Camp Street, Room 709
New Orleans 70130
(504) 525-7131
Mrs. Katherine Jubin, Associate
  Director
Information and Referral Service
  Area Served: Metropolitan New
    Orleans (Orleans, Jefferson, St.
    Tammany, and St. Bernard
    parishes)

Maryland

Health and Welfare Council of
  Central Maryland, Inc.
901 Court Square Building
200 East Lexington Street
Baltimore 21202
(301) 752-4146
Information and Referral Service
(301) 685-0525
Mrs. Rosemary Chappelle, Director
  Area Served: Metropolitan
    Baltimore area, comprising
    Baltimore City, Anne Arundel,
    Baltimore, Carroll, Hartford, and
    Howard counties
Information and Referral Service for
  the Aging
901 Court Square Building
200 East Lexington Street
Baltimore 21202
(301) 685-0525
Mrs. Rosemary Chappelle, Director
  Area Served: Baltimore City
    Montgomery County. See District
      of Columbia: Washington
    Prince Georges County. See District
      of Columbia: Washington

Massachusetts

United Community Planning
  Corporation (UCPC)
14 Somerset Street
Boston 02108
(617) 742-2000
Information, Referral, and Voluntary
  Action Center
Arthur L. Davis, Director
  Area Served: Sixty-two cities and
    towns in the metropolitan Boston
    area

Michigan

United Community Services of
  Metropolitan Detroit
51 West Warren Avenue
Detroit 48201
(313) 833-3430
Toll-free line for residents in
  Tri-County area outside Detroit:
  1(800) 522-1183
Evelyn M. Fraser, Associate Director,
  Central Services
Community Information Service
  Area Served: Detroit; Macomb,
    Oakland, and Wayne counties

United Fund of Genesee and Lapeer
  Counties
202 East Boulevard Drive
Flint 48503
(313) 232-8131
Information and Referral Center
Nola J. Olinger, Supervisor
  Area Served: Flint and Genesee
    County; inquiries from
    Shiawassee and Lapeer counties

Voluntary Action Center
415 Commerce Building
Grand Rapids 49502
(616) 459-4537
Community Information and Referral
  Center
(616) 459-4537
Barb Garver, Director
  Area Served: Kent County and
    surrounding counties

Minnesota

Community Health and Welfare
  Council of Hennepin County, Inc.
404 South Eighth Street
Minneapolis 55404
(612) 333-6193
Community Information and Referral
  Service
Marjorie J. Carpenter, Director
  Area Served: No limitations

Information and Referral Center
333 Sibley Street
St. Paul 55101
(612) 291-1431
Emery Barrette, Director

Missouri

Voluntary Action Center
Union Station, Room 120
Kansas City 64108
(816) 421-4980
Metropolitan Information and
  Referral Center
Mrs. Ann Jacobson, Director
  Area Served: Metropolitan Kansas
    City, including Jackson, Clay,
    Platte, Cass, and Ray counties in
    Missouri, and Johnson,
    Wyandotte, and Leavenworth
    counties in Kansas

Health and Welfare Council of
  Metropolitan St. Louis
915 Olive Street
St. Louis 63101
(314) 241-9240
Information and Referral Service
Community Resource Information
  System
Mrs. Jane D. Leopold, Director
  Area Served: St. Louis City and
    County, Franklin, Jefferson, and
    St. Charles counties

New Jersey

Help Line of North Essex
388 Pompton Avenue
Cedar Grove 07009
(201) 857-0300
Geoffrey Kennedy, Project Director

Health and Welfare Council of
  Bergen County, Inc.
389 Main Street
Hackensack 07601
(201) 343-4900
Sylvia Berg, Executive Director
Information and Referral Service
  Area Served: Bergen County

Hudson County Council of Social
  Agencies
857 Bergen Avenue
Jersey City 07306
(201) 434-2628
Maureen F. Doneian, Executive
  Director

United Way of Essex and West
   Hudson
303–309 Washington Street
Newark 07102
(201) 624-8300
Information and Referral Service
Ms. Yolanda Arencibia, Director
   Area Served: Newark, Irvington,
      Belleville, Nutley, The Oranges,
      Maplewood, and West Hudson

Princeton Area Council of
   Community Services
221 Witherspoon Street
Box 201
Princeton 08540
(609) 924-5865
Mrs. Janet Pearson, Director

Community Services Council for
   Monmouth County, Inc.
16 Spring Street
Red Bank 07701
(201) 842-5627
Albert Meyers, Executive Director
Information and Referral Service
   Area Served: Monmouth County

Greater Mercer Comprehensive
   Planning Council
602 Greenwood Avenue
P.O. Box 2103
Trenton 08607
(609) 396-1583
Samuel A. Kahn, Executive Director
Information and Referral, Social and
   Health Planning, Child Care (4C)
   Planning
   Area Served: Mercer County

New Mexico

Community Council of Albuquerque,
   Inc.
307 Fourth Street S.W.
P.O. Box 1775
Albuquerque 87103
(505) 842-0180
Information and Referral Service
Mrs. Nancy Barfield, Director
   Area Served: Bernalillo County

New York

Council of Community Services of
   the Albany Area, Inc.
P.O. Box 8653
877 Madison Avenue
Albany 12208
(518) 489-4791
James P. Heron, Executive Director
Information and Referral Service
   Area Served: Albany area

Central Services
742 Delaware Avenue
Buffalo 14209
(716) 881-1000
Curt Johnson, Director

Research and Planning Council for
   Community Services
350 Genesee Building
Genesee Street
Buffalo 14202
(716) 852-8750
John F. Hickey, Secretary and
   Executive Director
Information and Referral Service
   Area Served: Erie County

Voluntary Action Center of Ontario
   County
108 South Main Street
Canandaigua 14424
(315) 394-7650
Mrs. Marilyn Herrgesell, Director

Nassau County Department of Senior
   Citizen Affairs
Old County Road
Carle Place 11514
(516) 535-4414
Information and Referral Service
(Telephone Reassurance Service)
Mrs. Adelaide Attard, Director
   Area Served: Nassau County

Health and Welfare Council of
   Nassau County, Inc.
384 Clinton Street
Hempstead 11550
(516) 538-3200

Information and Referral Service on
   the Aging
(516) 535-4414

Information and Referral Service on
   Health, Nassau County Department
   of Health
County Office Building
Mineola 11501
(516) 535-3410

Mental Health Information Service,
   Mental Health Association
186 Clinton Street
Hempstead 11550
(516) IV 9-2322
   Area Served: Nassau County

Nassau County Department of Health
240 Old County Road
Mineola 11501
(516) 535-3410
Information and Referral Service
Jean M. Jones, Director of Public
   Health Social Work
   Area Served: Nassau County

Community Council of Greater New
   York
225 Park Avenue South
New York 10003
(212) 777-5000
Information Services Department
Jerry A. Shroder, Director
Information Bureau
Sylvia Norwalk, Chief
   Area Served: The five boroughs of
      New York City

Greater New York Fund
99 Park Avenue
New York 10016
(212) 986-8100
Mrs. Beulah C. Watson, Adviser for
   Welfare and Health Services
Information and Referral Service

Voluntary Action Center
826 Pine Avenue
Niagara Falls 14092
(716) 285-8461
Mrs. Mary Murray, Director

Rockland County Health Department
Sanatorium Road
Pomona 10970
(914) 354-0200

Community Health Information and
   Referral Service
Mrs. Eve Lodge, Director, Social
   Service Division
   Area Served: Rockland County

United Community Chest of Greater
   Rochester, Inc.
70 Bragdon Place
Rochester 14604
(716) 454-2770
Ted L. Moore, Executive Director
Information Service Department
Virginia Voll, Director
   Area Served: Monroe County

Suffolk Community Council
1173 Route 25A
P.O. Drawer 840
Stony Brook 11790
(516) 751-8666
Helen J. Gould, Executive Director
Information and Referral Service
   Area Served: Suffolk County

Volunteer Center
103 East Water Street
Syracuse 13202
(315) 474-7011
Community Information and Referral
   Service
Ruby Leachtenauer, Director

Call for Action
WTLB Kellogg Road
Washington Mills 13479
(315) 797-0120
Mrs. Etta Peabody, Director

Westchester Community Service
   Council, Inc.
713 County Office Building
White Plains 10601
(914) WH 9-0370
Information Bureau
Mrs. Mary E. Hotte, Director
Information Services
   Area Served: Westchester County

North Carolina

Voluntary Action Center
690 Coliseum Drive
Winston-Salem 27106
(919) 724-7474
Mrs. Patricia Vaughn, Director

Ohio

Community Chest and Council
2400 Reading Road
Cincinnati 45202
(513) 621-5000
Community Chest United Appeal
Information Center
Area Served: Five-county area—
Boone, Campbell, and Kenton
counties, Kentucky; Clermont
and Hamilton counties, Ohio

Community Information Service
1001 Huron Road
Cleveland 44115
(216) 696-4262
Fred Isaacs, Director

Ohio Citizens Council for Health and
Welfare
8 East Long Street Room 200
Columbus 43215
(614) 224-8416
Thane Griffin, Executive Director
Information and Referral Service
Judith M. Tieman, Information
Specialist
Area Served: Ohio

Health and Welfare Planning Council
of the Dayton Area
184 Salem Avenue
Dayton 45406
(513) 461-5810 (8:30 A.M.–5 P.M.)
(513) 226-0202 (24 hours)
Information and Referral Service
Mrs. Rosanna T. Scherer, Director
Area Served: Montgomery, Greene,
and Preble counties

United Central Services
1 Stranahan Square
Toledo 43604
(419) 244-3728
Information, Counseling, and Referral
Center
Carolyn Jo Davis, Director
Area Served: Greater Toledo

Oklahoma

Community Council of Central
Oklahoma, Inc.
312 Park Avenue
P.O. Box 1474
Oklahoma City 73101
(405) CE 6-8441
Information and Referral Service
Loretta Ore, Director
Area Served: Canadian, Cleveland,
and Oklahoma counties

Community Service Council of
Greater Tulsa
1430 South Boulder
Tulsa 74119
(918) 585-5551
Pat Hein, Secretary
Information and Referral Service
Area Served: Greater Tulsa

Oregon

Tri-County Community Council
718 West Burnside
Portland 97209
(503) 228-9131
Information and Referral Service
Mrs. Jackie Dehner, Director
Area Served: Clackamas,
Multnomah, and Washington
counties

Pennsylvania

Health and Welfare Council, Inc.
7 Benjamin Franklin Parkway
Philadelphia 19103
(215) LO 8-2474
Community Information and Referral
Service
Mrs. Carmen J. Moore, Director
Area Served: Delaware,
Montgomery, and Philadelphia
counties

Information and Volunteer Services of
Allegheny County
200 Ross Street
Pittsburgh 15219
(412) 261-6010
Aaron Sacks, Executive Director
Information and Referral Services and
Volunteer Action Center
Area Served: Allegheny County

Rhode Island

Council for Community Services
229 Waterman Street
Providence 02906
(401) 351-6500
Information and Referral Service
Frank H. Cavallaro, Director
  Area Served: State of Rhode Island
    and surrounding communities

South Carolina

United Way of Richland and
  Lexington Counties
1845 Assembly Street
P.O. Box 152
Columbia 29202
(803) 765-2375
Information and Referral Service
Mrs. Ann Gilbert, Director
  Area Served: Lexington, Richland,
    Fairfield, and Newberry counties

Tennessee

United Way of Greater Memphis
3485 Poplar, Suite 1
Memphis 38111
(901) 323-8381
Information and Referral Service
Mrs. Vicki Chaney, Director
  Area Served: Memphis
    metropolitan area

Texas

Community Council of Greater Dallas
1720 Life Building
311 South Akard Street
Dallas 75202
(214) RI 1-5851
Information and Referral Service
(214) 742-4385
Mrs. Orvilline White, Director
  Area Served: Dallas County

Community Welfare Planning
  Association
215 Main Street
Houston 77002
(713) 224-1701
Information and Referral Service
24-hour coverage
Ms. Forrest F. Kelley, Director
  Area Served: Houston and Harris
    county

Information and Referral
406 West Market
San Antonio 78205
(512) 224-2371
Margaret Smith, Director

Utah

Community Services Council, Salt
  Lake Area
2033 South State
Salt Lake City 84115
(801) 486-2136
Community Information Service
Lowell L. Bennion, Executive Director
  Area Served: Salt Lake County

Virginia

Voluntary Action Center
12420 Warwick Boulevard, Suite A
Newport News 23606
(804) 595-2201
Information and Referral Service
Mrs. Elsie W. Meehan, Director
  Area Served: Hampton, James City
    County, Newport News,
    Williamsburg, and York County

Health-Welfare-Recreation Planning
  Council
500 East Plume Street
Norfolk 23510
(703) 625-4543
Information Center of Hampton
  Roads
Frances B. Gilbert, Director
  Area Served: Cities of Chesapeake,
    Franklin, Hampton, Nansemond,
    Newport News, Norfolk,
    Portsmouth, Suffolk, and Virginia
    Beach; counties of Accomack, Isle
    of Wight, Northampton,
    Southampton, and York

Information and Referral Services
2501 Monument Avenue
Richmond 23220
(804) 353-1201
Jeanne Diana, Director
  Alexandria. See District of
    Columbia: Washington
  Arlington. See District of Columbia:
    Washington
  Fairfax. See District of Columbia:
    Washington
  Falls Church. See District of
    Columbia: Washington
  Prince William County. See District
    of Columbia: Washington

Washington

Information and Referral Service
  (Crisis Clinic), Inc.
1701–17 Avenue
Seattle 98122
(206) 323-2100
Business, (206) 321-1882
Resource Information Service
Jeanne Roth, Program Director
  Area Served: Seattle and King
    County

West Virginia

United Community Services, Inc.
P.O. Box 2416
Huntington 25725
(304) 522-0349
Information and Referral Service
  Area Served: Cabell and Wayne
    counties

Wisconsin

United Community Services of
  Greater Milwaukee, Inc.
606 East Wisconsin Avenue
Milwaukee 53202
(414) 271-0738
Information and Referral Service
Mrs. Clarice Green, Director
  Area Served: Greater Milwaukee
    Area, including Milwaukee
    County and part of Ozaukee,
    Washington, and Waukesha
    counties

Canada

British Columbia

United Way of Greater Vancouver
1625 West Eighth Avenue
Vancouver V6J IT9
(604) 731-7781
   Area Served: Vancouver City,
     North and West Vancouver,
     Burnaby, Richmond, and
     University Endowment Lands

Manitoba

Social Planning Council of Winnipeg
177 Lombard Avenue, Suite 501
Winnipeg R3B OW6
(204) 943-2561
F. Lloyd Lenton, Executive Director
Henry L. Chapin, Research Associate
Information Service
   Area Served: No limitations

Ontario

Canadian Council on Social
  Development
55 Parkdale Avenue
Box 3505, Station C
Ottawa, KIY 4G1
(613) 728-1865
Publications and Information Bureau
Norman Dahl, Director
   Area Served: All Canada

Community Information Center
377 Rideau Street
Ottawa K1N 5Y6
(613) 238-2101
Community Information Service
Mrs. Huguette Petruk, Director
   Area Served: Ottawa and district

Community Information Centre of
  Metropolitan Toronto
110 Adelaide Street E., 4th floor
Toronto M5C 1L1
(416) 863-0505
Mollie E. Christie, Executive Director
Information Service
   Area Served: Metropolitan Toronto

Quebec

Centre de Référence du Grand
  Montréal—Information and Referral
  Centre of Greater Montreal
759 Victoria Square, Suite 54
Montreal H2Y 2J7 (514) 842-9751
Jeannine Boyer, Executive Director
Claire C. Warkentin, Associate
  Director
Information and Referral Service
   Area Served: Greater Montreal

Appendix B

SELECTED SERVICES AND
PROGRAMS FOR THE ELDERLY
AND THEIR FAMILIES

1. HOMEMAKER–HOME HEALTH AIDE SERVICES

There are over 1,700 homemaker–home health aide programs in the country, about half of which are in agencies certified for Medicare. Some of these are licensed or certified by the state. Others have received approval from various professional organizations such as the National League for Nursing. The following list is adapted from the *1976 Directory of Homemaker–Home Health Aide Services* approved by the National Council for Homemaker–Home Health Aide Services, Inc. It is reprinted here with their permission. This list consists only of those agencies (as of April 1976) that are members of the National Council.

Alaska

Alaska Home Health Aide Service,
   Inc.
Anchorage Regional Office
519 West Eighth Avenue, Suite 204
Anchorage 99501

Alaska Home Health Aide Service,
   Inc.
Fairbanks Regional Office
510 Second Avenue, Room 315
Fairbanks 99701

Alaska Home Health Aide Service,
   Inc.
Juneau Regional Office (central office)
325 Gold Street
Juneau 99801

California

Homemaker Division
Family Service of Long Beach
1041 Pine Avenue
Long Beach 90813

Visiting Nursing Association of
   Pomona–West End, Inc.
Homemaker–Home Health Aide
   Service
5156 Holt Boulevard
Montclair 91763

Homemaker Service of San Diego
8123 Engineer Road
San Diego 92111

Health Conservation, Inc.
Homemaker–Home Health Aide
   Service
278 Post Street, #402
San Francisco 94108

San Francisco Home Health Service
2940–16th Street, Suite 301
San Francisco 94103

Homemaker Service of Santa Clara
   County, Inc.
2908 Scott Boulevard
Santa Clara 95050

Colorado
Community Homemaker Service, Inc.
1375 Delaware Street
Denver 80204

Connecticut
Homemaker–Home Health Aide
   Service of the Branford Area, Inc.
40 Kirkham Street
Branford 06405

Homemaker Service, Inc.
41 Church Road
Clinton 06413

Homemaker–Home Health Aide
   Services
Family and Children's Aid, Inc.
75 West Street
Danbury 06810
   Branch Office:
   156 East Avenue
   Norwalk 06851

Homemaker Service
Department of Social Services
Town of Greenwich
P.O. Box 929
Greenwich 06830

Homemaker–Home Health Aide
   Service of Guilford, Inc.
55 Park Street
Guilford 06437

Homemaker–Home Health Aide
   Service
Family Service Society
36 Trumbull Street
Hartford 06103

Greater Middletown Homemaker
   Service, Inc.
27 Washington Street
Middletown 06457

Homemaker Services Bureau of
   Greater New Haven
1 State Street
New Haven 06511

Homemaker–Home Health Aide
   Service
The Family Service Association of
   Southern New London County
11 Granite Street
New London 06320

The United Workers of Norwich, Inc.
Homemaker–Home Health Aide
   Service
34 East Town Street
Norwich 06360

Homemaker–Home Health Aide
   Service
Quinebaug Valley Health and
   Welfare Council, Inc.
80 Main Street
Putnam 06260

Homemaker–Home Health Aide
   Service of the District Nursing
   Service of Ridgefield
13 Catoonah Street
Ridgefield 06877

Valley Homemaker Service, Inc.
8 Old Mill Lane
Simsbury 06070

Homemaker–Home Health Aide
   Service of Stamford-Darien, Inc.
1845 Summer Street
Stamford 06905

The Housatonic Homemaker–Health
   Aide Service, Inc.
P.O. Box 951
West Cornwall 06796

Regional Health Services, Inc.
384 Main Street, Box 764
Winsted 06098

District Of Columbia
Homemaker Health Aide Service of
   the National Capital Area, Inc.
1825 Connecticut Avenue, N.W.,
   Room 100
Washington 20009

Florida

Visiting Homemaker–Home Health
  Aide Services, Inc.
1860 N.W. Second Avenue
P.O. Drawer 'E'
Boca Raton 33432

Family Counseling Center
Homemaker–Home Health Aide
  Service
118 North Meteor
Clearwater 33515

Georgia

Athens Community Council on
  Aging, Inc.
230 South Hull Street
Athens 30601

Illinois

Child and Family Services
Homemaker Service Division
234 South Wabash Avenue
Chicago 60604

The Salvation Army
Family Service Division
Homemaker Service Unit
10 East Pearson
Chicago 60611

The Visiting Nurse Association of St.
  Clair County
Homemaker–Home Health Aide
  Service
1269 North 89th Street
East St. Louis 62203

Indiana

Lake County Department of Public
  Welfare—Homemaker Service
800 Massachusetts Street
Gary 46402

Iowa

Family Service Agency
Homemaker Service
400 Third Avene, S.E.
Cedar Rapids 52401

Homemaker Service of Scott County,
  Inc.
416 West Fourth Street
Davenport 52801

Home Care–Home Service of Des
  Moines, Polk County
602 East First Street
Des Moines 50309

Hardin County Homemaker–Home
  Health Aide Service, Inc.
County Office Building
Eldora 60527

Maine

Home Health Services Agency of the
  Counseling Center
41 Illinois Avenue
Bangor 04401

Diocesan Human Relations Services,
  Inc.
District VI—Services Center
York County Homemaker Service
41 Birch Street
Biddeford 04005

Diocesan Human Relations Services,
  Inc.
District V—Services Center
Aroostook County Homemaker
  Service
15 Vaughn Street
Caribou 04736

Diocesan Human Relations Services,
  Inc.
District IV—Washington County
Homemaker–Home Health Aide
  Service
99 Main Street
Orono 04473

Diocesan Human Relations Services,
  Inc.
District I—Services Center
Holy Innocents' Home Care Center
P.O. Box 4184, Station A
Portland 04101

Diocesan Human Relations Services,
Inc.
District III—Services Center
Kennebec/Somerset Home Aide
Service
44 Main Street
Waterville 04901

Massachusetts

Homemaker Service
Family Service Association of Greater
Boston
34½ Beacon Street
Boston 02108

Homemaker–Home Health Aide
Service of Greater Fall River, Inc.
101 Rock Street, Room 22
Fall River 02720

Holyoke Visiting Nurse Association,
Inc.
Homemaker–Home Health Aide
Service
359 Dwight Street
P.O. Box 246
Holyoke 01040

Intercommunity Homemaker Service,
Inc.
1150 Walnut Street
Newton Highlands 02161

Homemaker–Home Health Aide
Service
Catholic Charities
Diocesan of Worcester, Inc.
26 Vernon Street
Worcester 01610

Michigan

Visiting Nurse Association of
Metropolitan Detroit
4421 Woodward Avenue
Detroit 48201

Minnesota

Ebenezer Society
Home Service Program
2523 Portland Avenue
Minneapolis 55404

Home Services Association, Inc.
1954 University Avenue
St. Paul 55104

Nebraska

Madonna Homemakers, Inc.
5407 South Street
Lincoln 68506

New Jersey

Visiting Homemaker Service of
Warren County, Inc.
Court House Annex
P.O. Box 237
Belvidere 07823

Visiting Homemaker Service of
Bergen County, Inc.
10 Grand Street
Englewood 07631

Visiting Homemaker Service of
Hudson County, Inc.
857 Bergen Avenue
Jersey City 07306

Chr-I11 Service, Inc.
60 South Fullerton Avenue
Montclair 08742

Visiting Homemaker Service of
Morris County
62 Elm Street
Morristown 07960

Visiting Homemaker Service of Ocean
County, Inc.
57 East Water Street
Toms River 08753

Visiting Homemaker Service of
Greater Trenton—Mercer Street
Friends Center
151 Mercer Street
Trenton 08611

Visiting Homemaker Service of
Central Union County, Inc.
525 North Avenue East
Westfield 07090

New York

Visiting Homemaker Service of
  Suffolk County, Inc.
50 Elm Street
Huntington 11743

Homemaker–Home Health Aide
  Service
Family and Children's Society of
  Broome County, Inc.
676 Main Street
P.O. Box 150
Johnson City 13790

The Children's Aid Society
Homemaker Service
150 East 45 Street
New York 10017

Home Health–Homemaker Services—
  G.H.I.
326 West 42nd Street
New York 10036

Home Aides of Central New York,
  Inc.
224 West Onondaga Street
Syracuse 13202

Family Service Society of Yonkers
Homemaker Service
219 Palisade Avenue
Yonkers 10703

North Carolina

Mecklenburg County Department of
  Social Services—Homemaker
  Service
301 Billingsley Road
Charlotte 28211

Ohio

Home Aide Service
2400 Reading Road
Cincinnati 45202

Center for Human Services
Homemaker–Home Health Aide
  Service
1001 Huron Road
Cleveland 44115

Family Service Agency of Springfield
  and Clark County, Inc.
Homemaker Service
1007 Tecumseh Building
Springfield 45502

Oklahoma

Mary Mahoney Memorial Health
  Center
Community Health Project
12716 N.E. 36th Street
P.O. Box 307
Spencer 73804

Oregon

Metropolitan Family Service
Homemaker Service
2281 North West Everett Street
Portland 97210

Salem Area Family Counseling Service
Homemaker Service
990 Commercial Street, S.E.
Salem 97302

Pennsylvania

Centre County Home Health Service
315 West High street
Bellefonte 16823

Homemaker–Home Health Aide
  Service, Inc.
520 East Broad Street
Bethlehem 18018

Montgomery County
  Homemaker–Home Health Aide
  Service, Inc.
650 Blue Bell West Skippack Pike
Blue Bell 19422

Homemaker Service of Erie County,
  Inc.
110 West Tenth Street
Erie 16501

Homemaker–Home Health Aide
  Service of Chester County, Inc.
222 North Pottstown Pike, Box 7
Exton 19341

Homemaker–Home Health Aide
  Service, Inc.
2001 North Front Street
Harrisburg 17102

Home Nursing Agency of Blair
  County
Homemaker–Home Health Aide
  Service
509 Walnut Street
Hollidaysburg 16648

Lebanon County Homemaker–Home
  Health Aide Service, Inc.
365 North Ninth Street
Lebanon 17042

Homemaker Service of Delaware
  County, Inc.
10 South Monroe Street
Media 19063

Homemaker Service of the
  Metropolitan Area, Inc.
1015 Chestnut Street, Suite 1100
Philadelphia 19107

Homemaker Service
Jewish Family Service of Philadelphia
1610 Spruce Street
Philadelphia 19103

Visiting Nurse Association of
  Allegheny County, Inc.
Homemaker–Home Health Aide
  Service
815 Union Place
Pittsburgh 15212

Berks County Home Service
241 South Fifth Street
Reading 19602

Homemaker–Home Health Aide
  Services
Lutheran Social Services, South
  Region
750 Kelly Drive
York 17404

Rhode Island

Homemaker–Home Health Aide
  Services of Rhode Island
265 Melrose Street
Providence 02907

South Carolina

Homemaker Service Division
Charleston County Department of
  Social Services
The Center, Room 409
Charleston 29403

Texas

Home Management Service, A Unit of
  the Visiting Nurse Association
4606 Greenville Avenue
Dallas 75206

Family Service Association of San
  Antonio, Inc.
Homemaker–Home Health Aide
  Service
230 Pereida Street
San Antonio 78210

Wisconsin

Visiting Homemaker–Home Health
  Aide Service
Manitowoc Family Service
  Association
701 Buffalo Street
Manitowoc 54220

Family Service of Milwaukee
Homemaker Service
P.O. Box 08517
Milwaukee 53208

Family Service of Racine, Inc.
Homemaker–Home Health Aide
  Service
820 Sixth Street
Racine 53403

Canada

Family Service Association of
  Edmonton
Homemaker Service
9919 106th Street
Edmonton, Alberta T5K 1E2

Visiting Homemaker Association of
  Ottawa, Inc.
485 Bank Street
Ottawa, Ontario K2P 1Z2

2. FAMILY SERVICE AGENCIES

Counseling and psychotherapeutic services to older persons and their families, while not widespread, are provided by some psychiatrists, psychologists, and clinical social workers privately and in a variety of settings: family agencies, outpatient psychiatric clinics, hospitals, and nursing homes. The following list of accredited and provisional member agencies of the Family Service Association of America is excerpted from its 1976 *Directory of Member Agencies,* and is used here with its permission. While each of these agencies meets FSAA professional standards, it should be noted that not all are prepared to provide ongoing services to the elderly and their families. Any agency that is not will attempt to provide the elderly person and his family with appropriate referrals to available services. Many of these agencies have additional local offices not listed here.

Member Agencies United States

Alabama

Family Counseling Association of
  Jefferson County
3600 Eighth Avenue South
Birmingham 35222
(205) 324-3411
Miss Lorene Putsch, Executive
  Director
  Area Served: Jefferson, Shelby, and
    Walker counties (persons who
    live or work there)

Counseling and Growth Center
12 Traylor Island
Huntsville 35801
(205) 539-2666, 534-0186
Clinton Clay, Executive Director
  Area Served: Madison County

Family Counseling Center
450 Government Street
Mobile 36602
(205) 433-6556
Robert A. Fox, Executive Director
  Area Served: Mobile County
    (persons who live or work there)

Family Guidance Center
925 Forest Avenue
Montgomery 36106
(205) 262-6669
Roy E. Swader, Executive Director
  Area Served: Autauga, Elmore, and
    Montgomery counties (persons
    who live or work there)

Arizona

Family Service of Phoenix
1530 East Flower
Phoenix 85014
(602) 264-9891
William A. Baker, Executive Director
  Area Served: Phoenix, plus
    Chandler, Glendale, Scottsdale,
    and Sun City

Jewish Family and Children's Service
  of Phoenix
2033 North 7 Street
Phoenix 85006
(602) 257-1904
Mrs. Lois Tuchler, Executive Director
  Area Served: Maricopa County

Family Counseling Agency
151 South Tucson Boulevard #262
Tucson 85716
(602) 327-4583
Leonard Banes, Executive Director
  Area Served: Tucson metropolitan
    area

Arkansas

Family Service Agency
North Little Rock Community Center
  Building
P.O. Box 500
North Little Rock 72115
(501) 758-1516
Jack R. Seward, Executive Director
  Area Served: Lonoke, Prairie, and
    Pulaski counties

California

Alameda Family Service Agency
746 Eagle Avenue
Alameda 94501
(415) 521-4151
Arthur H. Michel, Executive Director
  Area Served: Alameda (persons
    who live or work there), plus
    limited service to surrounding
    area

Family Service of Berkeley
2015 6 Street
Berkeley 94710
(415) 845-1929
Carolyn Moore, Executive Director
  Area Served: Berkeley, plus Albany
    and Kensington

Family Service Agency of San Mateo
  County
1870 El Camino Real
Burlingame 94010
(415) 692-0555
J. Donald Cameron, Executive
  Director
  Area Served: San Mateo County

Glendale Family Service Association
3443 Ocean View Boulevard
Glendale 91208
(213) 248-2286
Mrs. Eileen Vargish, Executive
  Director
  Area Served: Glendale; other
    residents of Los Angeles County
    if time and staff permit

Family Service of Los Angeles
1521 Wilshire Boulevard
Los Angeles 90017
(213) 484-2944
Miss Mary Bischoff, Executive
  Director
  Area Served: Metropolitan Los
    Angeles area served by
    Metropolitan office. Additional
    offices serve northern, western,
    and southeastern communities of
    the county

Jewish Family Service
6505 Wilshire Boulevard
Los Angeles 90048
(213) 852-1234
Arnold R. Saltzman, Executive
  Director
  Area Served: Los Angeles County,
    except Santa Monica and Long
    Beach

Family Service of the East Bay
445 30 Street
Oakland 94609
(415) 834-5433
James A. Graham, Executive Director
  Area Served: Alameda County,
    except cities of Alameda and
    Berkeley

Family Counseling Service of Palm
  Springs
3120 Civic Drive
Palm Springs 92262
(714) 327-3701
Arnold Lieberman, Executive Director
  Area Served: Palm Springs, plus
    Cathedral City, Desert Hot
    Springs, Rancho Mirage, and
    Thousand Palms; families from
    neighboring communities without
    services will be seen when staff
    time is available

Family Service Association of the
  Mid-Peninsula
375 Cambridge Avenue
Palo Alto 94306
(415) 326-6576
Chester F. Villalba, Executive Director
  Area Served: Mid-Peninsula
    Region, including Atherton, East
    Palo Alto, Los Altos, Los Altos
    Hills, Menlo Park, Palo Alto,
    Portola Valley, Stanford, and
    Woodside

Foothill Family Service
118 South Oak Knoll Avenue
Pasadena 91101
(213) 792-5141
Michael E. Miller, Executive Director
  Area Served: Pasadena, plus
    Altadena, Arcadia, Bradbury,
    Duarte, La Canada-Flintridge, San
    Marino, Sierra Madre, South
    Pasadena, and Temple City
    (persons who live or work there);
    other residents of Los Angeles
    County served if staff time is
    available

Family Service of Pomona Valley
  (Provisional Member Agency)
2055 North Garey Avenue
Pomona 91767
(714) 593-7408
Percy Bernstein, Executive Director
  Area Served: Claremont, Diamond
    Bar, La Verne, Pomona, San
    Dimas, and Walnut; also, anyone
    who lives or works in the United
    Way area

Family Service Association of
  Riverside
3903 Brockton Avenue
Riverside 92501
(714) 686-3706
Marshall Jung, Executive Director
  Area Served: Riverside, plus
    Arlanza, Arlington, Corona,
    Coronita, Edgemont, El Cerrito,
    Glen Avon, Highgrove, Home
    Gardens, La Sierra, March Air
    Force Base, Mira Loma, Norco,
    Pedley, Rubidoux, and
    Sunnymead

Family Service Agency of the Greater
  Sacramento Area
709 21 Street
Sacramento 95814
(916) 448-8284
Thomas W. Wolfanger, Executive
  Director
  Area Served: Sacramento County,
    plus Broderick, Bryte, West
    Sacramento, and Placer County

Family Service Agency
1669 North E Street
San Bernardino 92405
(714) 886-6737
Edward L. Freemon, Executive
  Director
  Area Served: San Bernardino, plus
    Big Bear Lake, Bloomington,
    Colton, Crest Forest, Del Rosa,
    Grand Terrace, Highland, Lake
    Arrowhead, Loma Linda, Muscoy,
    and Rialto. Outpatient mental
    health clinic services available to
    anyone residing in San
    Bernardino County

Family Service Association of San
  Diego County
7645 Family Circle
San Diego 92111
(714) 279-0400
  Area Served: San Diego and San
    Diego County. Metropolitan area
    served by central office and
    Southeast office; additional offices
    serve northern, southern, and
    eastern communities

Family Service Agency of San
  Francisco
1010 Gough Street
San Francisco 94109
(415) 474-7310
Clarence E. Richardson, Executive
  Director
  Area Served: City and County of
    San Francisco

Family Service Agency of Santa
  Barbara
800 Santa Barbara Street
Santa Barbara 93101
(805) 965-1001
Edwin H. Aspinwall, Executive
  Director
  Area Served: Santa Barbara County

Jewish Family Service of Santa
  Monica
1424 4 Street
Santa Monica 90401
(213) 393-0732
Meyer Lightman, Executive Director
  Area Served: Santa Monica, plus
    Ocean Park

Family Service Association of Orange
  County
17421 Irvine Boulevard
Tustin 92680
(714) 838-7377
John P. Turner, Executive Director
  Area Served: Orange County,
    including Anaheim, Fullerton,
    Garden Grove, Huntington
    Beach, Newport Beach, San Juan
    Capistrano, and Santa Ana

Colorado

Human Services
1555 Xavier Street
Denver 80204
(303) 825-3283
Harry J. Walter, III, Executive
  Director

Jewish Family and Children's Service
  of Colorado
Allied Jewish Federation Building
300 South Dahlia Street, Suite 101
Denver 80222
(303) 321-3115
Jerry Grossfeld, J. D., Executive
  Director
  Area Served: State of Colorado

Connecticut

Family Services—Woodfield
800 Clinton Avenue
Bridgeport 06604
(203) 368-4291
Richard Lewis, Jr., Executive Director
  Area Served: Bridgeport, plus
    Easton, Fairfield, Monroe,
    Stratford, and Trumbull

Catholic Family Services—
  Archdiocese of Hartford
244 Main Street
Hartford 06106
(203) 522-8241
Edward J. Power, Executive Director
James F. Watt, Assistant Executive
  Director, In Charge of Hartford
  Office
  Area Served: Hartford, plus Avon,
    Bloomfield, Burlington, Canton,
    East Granby, East Hartford,
    Farmington, Glastonbury,
    Granby, Hartland, Manchester,
    Newington, Rocky Hill,
    Simsbury, South Windsor, West
    Hartford, Wethersfield, and
    Windsor

Child and Family Services of
  Connecticut
1680 Albany Avenue
Hartford 06105
(203) 236-4511
Robert I. Beers, Executive Director
  Area Served: Hartford District
    Office serves the Capitol Region
    Planning Area. Northeast Office
    serves Tolland and Windham
    counties, plus the towns in
    Hartford County east of the
    Connecticut River, except East
    Hartford

Family Service Society
36 Trumbull Street
Hartford 06103
(203) 278-9374
Mrs. Anne Wolf, Executive Director
  Area Served: Hartford, plus
    Bloomfield, East Hartford,
    Farmington, Glastonbury,
    Manchester, Newington, Rocky
    Hill, South Windsor, West
    Hartford, Wethersfield, and
    Windsor

Family Service Association of
Middlesex County
27 Washington Street
Middletown 06457
(203) 347-3346
Frank M. Ehlers, Executive Director
Area Served: Middlesex County

Family Counseling and Children's
Services of Central Connecticut
92 Vine Street
New Britain 06052
(203) 223-9291
Manuel W. Strauss, Executive
Director
Area Served: New Britain, plus
Berlin, Bristol, East Berlin,
Forestville, Kensington, and
Plainville

Family Counseling of Greater New
Haven
1 State Street
New Haven 06511
(203) 865-1125
William F. Mecca, Executive Director
Area Served: New Haven, plus
Branford, East Haven, Guilford,
Hamden, Madison, North Haven,
Orange, West Haven, and
Woodbridge

Jewish Family Service of New Haven
152 Temple Street
New Haven 06510
(203) 777-6641
Ms. Evelyn Weber Brownstein,
Executive Director
Area Served: Greater New Haven,
plus Ansonia, Branford, Derby,
East Haven, Guilford, Hamden,
Milford, North Haven, Orange,
Seymour, Shelton, Waterbury,
West Haven, and Woodbridge.

Family Service Association of
Southern New London County
11 Granite Street
New London 06320
(203) 442-4319
Allan R. Cutting, Executive Director
Area Served: Southern half of New
London County, including
Montville at upper limit

Family and Children's Services
60 Palmer's Hill Road
Stamford 06902
(203) 324-3167
Miss Margaret V. Murta, Director
Area Served: Stamford, Darien, and
New Canaan

Jewish Family Service of Greater
Hartford
333 Bloomfield Avenue
West Hartford 06117
(203) 522-8265
Mrs. Marion Macarof, Executive
Director
Area Served: Hartford, East
Hartford, West Hartford, plus
Avon, Bloomfield, Farmington,
Glastonbury, Manchester,
Newington, Rocky Hill,
Simsbury, South Windsor,
Wethersfield, and Windsor

Delaware

Family Service of Northern Delaware
809 Washington Street
Wilmington 19801
(302) 654-5304
Robert M. Weaver, Executive Director
Area Served: New Castle County

District of Columbia

Family and Child Services of
Washington
929 L Street, Northwest
Washington 20001
(202) 232-6510
John G. Theban, Executive Director
Area Served: District of Columbia

Florida

Family Counseling Center
118 North Meteor
Clearwater 33515
(813) 441-4582
Wesley W. Jenkins, Executive
Director
Area Served: Pinellas County

Family Service Agency
1300 South Andrews Avenue
P.O. Box 22877
Fort Lauderdale 33316
(305) 524-8286
Ethel Lawrence, Executive Director
  Area Served: Broward County

Family Consultation Service of
  Jacksonville and Duval County
1639 Atlantic Boulevard
Jacksonville 32207
(904) 396-4846
Miss Hazel M. Young, Executive
  Director
    Area Served: Duval County and
    Orange Park

United Family and Children's Services
2190 Northwest 7 Street
Miami 33125
(305) 643-5700
Paul K. Reed, Jr., Executive Director
  Area Served: Dade County

Jewish Family and Children's Service
1790 Southwest 27 Avenue
Miami 33145
(305) 445-0555
Leon D. Fisher, Executive Director
  Area Served: Dade County

Family Service Bureau of Brevard
  County
1770 South Cedar Street
P.O. Box 63
Rockledge 32955
(305) 632-5792
J. Moulton Thomas, Jr., Executive
  Director
  Area Served: Brevard County

Family Counseling Center of Sarasota
  County
3205 South Gate Circle
Sarasota 33579
(813) 955-7017
Emil Codol, Executive Director
  Area Served: Sarasota County

Family Counseling—Travelers Aid of
  Palm Beach County (Provisional
  Member Agency)
208 Clematis Street
West Palm Beach 33401
(305) 655-4483
Thomas Esslinger, Executive Director
  Area Served: Palm Beach County

Georgia

Child Service and Family Counseling
  Center
1105 West Peachtree Street, Northeast
Atlanta 30309
(404) 873-6916
Miss Mary Margaret Carr, Executive
  Director
    Area Served: Clayton, Cobb,
    DeKalb, Douglas, Fulton,
    Gwinnett, and Rockdale counties

Family Counseling Center
654 First Avenue, Box 1825
Columbus 31902
(404) 327-3238
Romolo A. Cannamela, Director
  Area Served: Columbus, plus
    commuting distance area of
    fifty-mile radius

Family Counseling Center of Macon
  and Bibb County
309 Robert E. Lee Building, 830
  Mulberry Street
Macon 31201
(912) 745-2811
W. Homer Reddick, Executive
  Director
    Area Served: Bibb County; also
    active military personnel of
    Warner Robbins Air Force Base
    in Houston County and persons
    eligible under CHAMPUS

Family Counseling Center of
  Savannah
428 Bull Street
Savannah 31401
(912) 233-5729
  Area Served: Chatham County
    (persons who live or work there)

Hawaii

Child and Family Service
200 North Vineyard Boulevard,
   Building B
Honolulu 96817
(808) 521-2377
Myron R. Chevlin, Executive Director
   Area Served: Island of Oahu

Illinois

Family Service and Visiting Nurse
   Association of the Alton-Wood
   River Region
211 East Broadway
Alton 62002
(618) 465-2539
Kathleen Rogers, Executive Director
   Area Served: Alton and Wood
      River, plus Bethalto, Brighton,
      Cottage Hills, East Alton,
      Fosterburg, Godfrey, Hartford,
      Moro, Roxana, and South Roxana

Family Service of McLean County
418 Eddy Building, 427 North Main
   Street
Bloomington 61701
(309) 828-4343
Jo Stephen Major, Executive Director
   Area Served: McLean County

Family Service of Champaign County
303 South Wright Street
Champaign-Urbana 61820
(217) 356-2547, 356-1846
Brian M. Turner, Executive Director
   Area Served: Champaign County

Jewish Family and Community
   Service
1 South Franklin Street
Chicago 60606
(312) FI 6-6700
Sidney J. Berkowitz, Executive
   Director
   Area Served: Cook County; also
      Jewish families living in
      communities outside county with
      no other organized resource to
      meet their needs; also, by
      contractual arrangement with
      Jewish Federation of Northwest
      Indiana, family counseling service
      to persons living in East Chicago,
      Gary, Hammond, and
      neighboring communities

United Charities of Chicago Family
   Service Bureau
64 East Jackson Boulevard
Chicago 60604
(312) 939-5930
A. Gerald Erickson, Executive
   Director
Mrs. Alice Q. Ayres, Director, Family
   Service Bureau
   Area Served: City of Chicago and
      metropolitan area not covered by
      other family service agencies

Family Service Agency of DeKalb
   County
3131 Sycamore Road, P.O. Box 831
DeKalb 60115
(815) 758-8616
Floyd Flowers, Executive Director
   Area Served: DeKalb County

Family Counseling Center
36 Loisel Village Shopping Center
East St. Louis 62203
(618) 397-2542
Anthony J. Naves, Executive Director
   Area Served: East St. Louis, plus
      Belleville, Collinsville,
      Edwardsville, Fairview
      Heights-Caseyville Township,
      Granite City, Madison, Venice,
      and adjacent smaller towns and
      villages

Family Service Association of Greater
Elgin Area (Provisional Member
Agency)
164 Division Street, Room 808
Elgin 60120
(312) 695-3680
Don Taylor, Executive Director
    Area Served: Elgin, plus Bartlett,
    Hanover Township portion of
    Hanover Park, St. Charles, South
    Elgin, Streamwood, Valley View
    and Wasco

Family Service Association of DuPage
County
999 North Main Street
Glen Ellyn 60137
(312) 469-2340
Lawrence Berson, Executive Director
    Area Served: DuPage County

Family Service of South Lake County
777 Central Avenue
Highland Park 60035
(312) ID 2-4981
Mrs. Ann C. Quisenberry, Executive
Director
    Area Served: Highland Park, plus
    Barrington, Deerfield, Highwood,
    Lake Bluff, Lake Forest,
    Libertyville, Long Grove, and
    Mundelein
    Barrington Office serves Barrington
    and Long Grove
    Mundelein Office serves Mundelein
    area

Family Service and Mental Health
Center of Oak Park and River
Forest
101 North Marion Street
Oak Park 60301
(312) 383-0900
David Rochlis, Executive Director
    Area Served: Oak Park and River
    Forest

Counseling and Family Service
2142 North Knoxville Avenue
Peoria 61603
(309) 685-5287
Henry Suozzi, Executive Director
    Area Served: Peoria, plus Fulton,
    Tazewell, and Woodford
    counties. Counseling/social
    service to the elderly also
    available at various locations in
    Marshall and Stark Counties

Family Service Agency of Adams
County
400 North Twelfth Street
Quincy 62301
(217) 222-8254
James F. Eckert, Executive Director
    Area Served: Adams County; also
    peripheral counties

Family Service Center of Sangamon
County
1308 South 7 Street
Springfield 62703
(217) 528-8406
Larry L. Lee, Executive Director
    Area Served: Sangamon County

Indiana

Family Counseling Service of Elkhart
County
329 West Franklin Street
Elkhart 46514
(219) 523-4402
Kenneth L. Kruger, Executive Director
    Area Served: Elkhart County
        (persons who live or work there);
        also areas outside county,
        depending on available time

Family and Children's Service
217 Southeast Eighth Street
Evansville 47713
(812) 425-5181
Edward F. Ebert, Executive Director
    Area Served: Vanderburgh County,
        plus Posey and Warrick counties
        (persons who live or work there);
        outside areas as staff loads permit

Family and Children's Services
2424 Fairfield Avenue
Fort Wayne 46807
(219) 744-4326
Frank L. Sieh, Executive Director
  Area Served: Allen County (persons
    who live or work there) and
    others on a full-fee basis

Family Service Association
615 North Alabama Street
Indianapolis 46204
(317) 634-6341
James N. Miller, Executive Director
  Area Served: City of Indianapolis,
    plus Boone, Hamilton, Hancock,
    Hendricks, Marion, and Morgan
    counties

Jewish Family and Children's Services
1475 West 86 Street., Suite E
Indianapolis 46260
(317) 255-6641
Julius Markfield, Executive Director
  Area Served: Marion County

Family Service Agency of Tippecanoe
  County
515 Columbia Street
Lafayette 47901
(317) 742-2584, 742-7492
Ms. Lillian Kaplan, Executive Director
  Area Served: Tippecanoe county
    (persons who live or work there)

Family and Children's Center
1411 Lincoln Way West
Mishawaka 46544
(219) 259-5666
Robert E. Pollitt, Executive Director
  Area Served: State of Indiana

Family Counseling Service
615 East Washington Street
Muncie 47305
(317) 284-7789
Fred Hefter, Executive Director
  Area Served: Delaware County
    (persons who live or work there);
    also areas outside county,
    especially Henry, Jay, and
    Randolph counties

Family Service Association of Wayne
  County
42 South 9 Street
Richmond 47374
(317) 962-6343, 966-0774
C. William Taylor, Jr., Executive
  Director
  Area Served: Wayne County
    (persons who live or work there)

Family Service Association in Terre
  Haute
620 Eighth Avenue
Terre Haute 47804
(812) 232-4349
Robert Conaty, Executive Secretary
  Area Served: Clay, Greene, Parke,
    Sullivan, Vermillion, and Vigo
    counties; other areas as time
    permits

Iowa

Family Service Agency
400 Third Avenue., S.E.
Cedar Rapids 52401
(319) 398-3574
Alice Eicher, Agency Manager
  Area Served: Linn County; also
    clients from outside the county
    on a full cost-of-service fee basis

Family and Children's Service of
  Davenport
115 West Sixth Street
Davenport 52803
(319) 323-1853
Kenneth C. Boyd, Executive Director
  Area Served: Scott County, plus
    Muscatine

Family Service–Travelers Aid
700 Sixth Avenue
Des Moines 50309
(515) 244-1181, Ext. 51
Eugene P. Krauss, Executive Director
  Area Served: Polk County, plus
    Norwalk (persons who live or
    work there)

Family Service Center
Boys and Girls Home and Family
  Service
2601 Douglas Street
Sioux City 51104
(712) 277-4031
Thomas Martin, Executive Director
  Area Served: Sioux City, plus South
  Sioux City, Nebraska (persons
  who live or work there); also area
  within sixty-mile radius of city
  on fee basis if time permits

Family Service League
505 Cedar Street
P.O. Box 538
Waterloo 50704
(319) 235-6271
Clarence E. Coleman, Executive
  Director
  Area Served: Black Hawk County

Kansas

Family and Children's Service
5424 State Avenue
Kansas City 66102
(913) 287-1300
Bernard R. O'Brien, Executive
  Director
  Area Served: Wyandotte County
  (persons who live or work there);
  also outside areas at full fee as
  time permits. Any military family
  eligible

Family Service and Guidance Center
2055 Clay Street
Topeka 66604
(913) 234-5663
Allan H. Marquardt, Administrative
  Director
Arthur W. Hoyt, M.D., Medical
  Director
  Area Served: Shawnee County

Kentucky

Family Counseling Service
620 Euclid Avenue
Lexington 40502
(606) 266-0425
Hank Galbraith, Executive Director
  Area Served: Bourbon, Clark,
  Fayette, Franklin, Harrison,
  Jessamine, Madison, Scott, and
  Woodford counties

Family and Children's Agency
1115 Garvin Place
Louisville 40203
(502) 583-1741
Harold Schaars, Executive Director
  Area Served: Jefferson and Shelby
  counties, Kentucky, and Floyd
  County, Indiana; also beyond
  these areas as resources permit

Louisiana

Family Counseling Service of East
  Baton Rouge Parish
544 Colonial Drive
Baton Rouge 70806
(504) 924-6244
Donald E. Perrin, Executive Director
  Area Served: Ascension, East Baton
  Rouge, Iberville, Livingston, St.
  James, and West Baton Rouge
  parishes

Family Service Society
535 Gravier Street
New Orleans 70130
(504) 524-7471
Albert L. Harriett, Executive Director
  Area Served: Jefferson, Orleans, St.
  Bernard, and St. Tammany
  parishes

Family Counseling and Children's
  Services
864 Olive Street
Shreveport 71104
(318) 222-0759
Richard I. Day, Executive Director
  Area Served: Bossier and Caddo
  parishes

Maine

Community Counseling Center
187 Middle Street
Portland 04111
(207) 774-5727
Donald M. Demuth, Executive
 Director
  Area Served: Portland, plus Cape
    Elizabeth, Cumberland, Falmouth,
    Freeport, Gorham, North
    Yarmouth, Raymond, Scarboro,
    South Portland, Westbrook,
    Windham, and Yarmouth

Maryland

Family and Children's Society
204 West Lanvale Street
Baltimore 21217
(301) 669-9000
Ernest H. Smith, Executive Director

Jewish Family and Children's Service
5750 Park Heights Avenue
Baltimore 21215
(301) 466-9200
Milton Goldman, Executive Director
  Area Served: Metropolitan
    Baltimore

Family Service Agency of Washington
 County
5 Antietam Professional Center
138 East Antietam Street
Hagerstown 21740
(301) 733-5858
Mrs. Alice B. Sencindiver, Executive
 Director
  Area Served: Washington County
    (persons who live, work, or
    attend school there)

Family Service of Prince George's
 County, Inc.
Lanhan Building, 7580 Annapolis
 Road
Lanham 20801
(301) 459-2121
Nathan S. Nackman, Executive
 Director
  Area Served: Prince George's
    County (persons who live, work,
    or attend school there)

Family Service of Montgomery
 County
1 W. Deer Park Road, Suite 201
Gaithersburg 20760
(301) 840-2000
Charles P. Brambilla, Executive
 Director
  Area Served: Montgomery County

Maryland Children's Aid and Family
 Service Society
303 West Chesapeake Avenue
Towson 21204
(301) 825-3700
Toll-Free Number from Maryland
 Communities:
(800) 492-4704
Philip C. Vail, Executive Director
  Area Served: Allegany, Baltimore,
    Caroline, Carroll, Cecil,
    Dorchester, Harford, Howard,
    Kent, Queen Anne, and Talbot
    counties in Maryland and
    Mineral County in West Virginia

Massachusetts

Family Service Association of Greater
 Boston
34½ Beacon Street
Boston 02108
(617) 523-6400
Patrick V. Riley, Executive Director
  Area Served: Boston office serves
    Boston; plus Chelsea, Revere, and
    Winthrop
  Northeast Family Service Center,
    (617) 324-8181, serves Malden,
    plus Burlington, Everett,
    Medford, Melrose, North
    Reading, Reading, Stoneham,
    Wakefield, Winchester, and
    Woburn
  Northwest Family Service Center,
    (617) 625-5638, serves Somerville,
    plus Arlington, Bedford, Belmont,
    Lexington, and Watertown
  South Shore Family Service Center,
    (617) 471-0630, serves Quincy
    plus Braintree, Hingham,
    Holbrook, Hull, Milton, Norwell,
    Randolph, Scituate, and
    Weymouth
  Southwest Family Service Center,
    (617) 444-9303, serves Needham,
    plus Canton, Dover, Medfield,
    Millis, Sharon, and Westwood

Jewish Family and Children's Service
31 New Chardon Street
Boston 02114
(617) 226-6641
Simon Krakow, Executive Director
  Area Served: Boston and the
    metropolitan area

Cambridge Family and Children's
  Service
99 Bishop Richard Allen Drive
  (formerly Austin Street)
Cambridge 02139
(617) 876-4210
Albert T. Calello, Jr., Executive
  Director
  Area Served: Cambridge (persons
    who live, work, or study there)

Concord Family Service Society
Community Agencies Building
Concord 01742
(617) 369-4909
Mrs. Rita S. Williams, Executive
  Director
  Area Served: Concord, plus Acton,
    Bedford, Boxboro, Carlisle,
    Harvard, Lincoln, Littleton,
    Maynard, and Stow

Family Service of Dedham
  (Provisional Member Agency)
18 Norfolk Street
Dedham 02026
(617) 326-0400
Mrs. Barbara P. Kovar, Executive
  Director
  Area Served: Dedham, Foxboro,
    Franklin, Norwood, and
    Westwood

Family Service Association
101 Rock Street
Fall River 02720
(617) 678-7541
Donald J. Emond, Executive Director
  Area Served: Fall River, plus
    Assonet, Somerset, Swansea, and
    Westport; also, under some
    circumstances, Tiverton (Rhode
    Island)

Children's Aid and Family Service
47 Holt Street
Fitchburg 01420
(617) 345-4147
Mrs. Timothy J. Shea, Executive
  Director
  Area Served: Fitchburg, plus
    Ashburnham, Ashby, Leominster,
    Lunenburg, Townsend, and
    Westminster

Holyoke Family Service Society
328 Maple Street
Holyoke 01040
(413) 532-7324
Alfred Millette, Executive Director
  Area Served: Granby, Holyoke, and
    South Hadley

Family Service Association of Greater
  Lawrence
430 North Canal Street
Lawrence 01840
(617) 683-9505
Brian J. Langdon, Executive Director
  Area Served: Lawrence, plus
    Andover, Methuen, and North
    Andover

Family Service of Greater Lowell
201 Thorndike Street
P.O. Box 1091
Lowell 01853
(617) 459-9326
Miss M. Louise Collins, Executive
  Director
  Area Served: Lowell, plus Billerica,
    Chelmsford, Dracut, Dunstable,
    Tewksbury, Tyngsboro, and
    Westford (Massachusetts);
    Pelham (New Hampshire)

New Bedford Child and Family
  Service
141 Page Street
New Bedford 02740
(617) 996-8572
John E. McManus, Executive Director
  Area Served: New Bedford, plus
    Acushnet, Dartmouth, East
    Freetown, Fairhaven, Marion,
    Mattapoisett, and Rochester

Family Counseling Service (Region West)
74 Walnut Park
Newton 02158
(617) 969-6550
Robert B. Hill, Executive Director
 Area Served: Newton, plus
  Brookline, Waltham, and
  Wellesley. Natick Office also
  serves Sherborn; Suburban Office
  serves Sudbury, Wayland, and
  Weston

Berkshire Center for Families and Children
472 West Street
Pittsfield 01201
(413) 448-8281
 Area Served: Berkshire County

Child and Family Service of Springfield
367 Pine Street
Springfield 01105
(413) 737-1426
Francis X. Morrissey, Executive Director
 Area Served: Hampden County,
  except Holyoke

Family Service Organization of Worcester
31 Harvard Street
Worcester 01608
(617) 756-4646
Walter A. Olson, Executive Director
 Area Served: Worcester, plus
  Auburn, Boylston, Grafton,
  Holden Leicester, Millbury, North
  Grafton, Oxford, Paxton,
  Shrewsbury, Sterling, West
  Boylston, and towns beyond in
  the Central Massachusetts Region

Jewish Family Service of Worcester
646 Salisbury Street
Worcester 01609
(617) 755-3101
 Area Served: Worcester, plus
  Auburn, Boylston, Grafton,
  Holden, Leicester, Millbury,
  North Grafton, Paxton,
  Shrewsbury, and West Boylston.
  Families outside this area but in
  Worcester County may be served,
  provided full cost of service is
  paid

Michigan

Child and Family Service of Washtenaw County
2301 Platt Road
Ann Arbor 48104
(313) 971-6520
James W. Brogdon, Executive Director
 Area Served: Washtenaw County;
  Plymouth Office serves Plymouth
  and Plymouth Township

Catholic Social Services of Wayne County
9851 Hamilton Avenue
Detroit 48202
(313) 883-2100
Timothy F. Ryan, Director
 Area Served: Wayne County

Family Service of Detroit and Wayne County
51 West Warren Avenue
Detroit 48201
(313) 833-3733
Francis M. Moynihan, Executive Director
 Area Served: Detroit and Wayne
  County except Plymouth
  Township

Family Service Agency of Genesee County
Room 310, 202 East Boulevard Drive
Flint 48503
(313) 234-2627
Eugene Talsma, Executive Director
 Area Served: Genesee County

Family Service Association of Kent
   County
1122 Leonard N.E.
Grand Rapids 49503
(616) 774-0633
Charles A. Burkholder, Executive
   Director
   Area Served: Areawide, primarily
      Kent County

Family Service and Children's Aid of
   Jackson County
729 W. Michigan Avenue
Jackson 49201
(517) 782-8191
Kenneth V. McGuagh, Executive
   Director
   Area Served: Jackson County; also
      adoption service and service to
      unmarried parents in Hillsdale
      and Branch counties

Children's Aid and Family Service of
   Macomb County
57 Church Street
Mount Clemens 48043
(313) 468-2656
Donald R. Gruber, Executive Director
   Area Served: Macomb County

Family and Children Services of
   Oakland
50 Wayne Street
Pontiac 48058
(313) 332-8352
Robert J. Janes, Executive Director
   Area Served: Pontiac office serves
      the townships of Addison, Avon,
      Brandon, Independence, Oakland,
      Orion, Oxford, Pontiac, and
      Waterford, plus Troy north of
      Square Lake Road
   South Oakland Office serves the
      townships of Bloomfield,
      Farmington, Southfield, Troy,
      West Bloomfield, plus the cities
      of Berkley, Birmingham,
      Bloomfield, Ferndale, Hazel Park,
      Madison Heights, Oak Park,
      Royal Oak and Southfield
   West County Office serves the
      townships of Commerce
      Groveland, Highland, Holly,
      Lyon, Novi, Oxford, Rose,
      Springfield, and White Lake

Catholic Social Services of Oakland
   County
1424 East Eleven Mile Road
Royal Oak 48067
(313) LI 8-4044
Leonard R. Jagels, Director
   Area Served: Oakland County

Jewish Family Service
24123 Greenfield
Southfield 48075
(313) 559-1500
Samuel Lerner, Director
   Area Served: Macomb, Oakland,
      and Wayne counties

Minnesota

Family Service Society
200 New Garrick Building, 128 West
   First Street
Duluth 55802
(218) 722-7766
Gene C. Bard, Executive Director
   Area Served: Duluth, plus Canosia,
      Fredenberg, Gnesen, Grand Lake,
      Hermantown, Homecroft,
      Lakewood, Midway, Normanna,
      Pike Lake, Proctor, Rice Lake,
      Solway, and U.S. Airbase;
      selected services to Carlton,
      Cook, Lake, and other portions of
      St. Louis County

Family and Children's Service
414 S. Eighth Street
Minneapolis 55404
(612) 340-7444
Earl J. Beatt, Executive Director
   Area Served: Hennepin County,
      plus Anoka, Blaine Village,
      Columbia Heights, Hilltop,
      Fridley, and Spring Lake Park in
      Anoka County and rural area in
      northern Carver County

Jewish Family and Children's Service
811 La Salle Court
Minneapolis 55402
(612) 338-8771
Irving G. Nudell, Executive Director
   Area Served: Greater Minneapolis
      area

Family Service of St. Paul
104 Wilder Building, 355 Washington
  Street
St. Paul 55102
(612) 222-0311
Ronald G. Reed, Executive Secretary
  Area Served: Ramsey County, plus
    Dakota and Washington counties
  South Suburban Office serves
    northern Dakota County and
    southern Washington County,
    including Cottage Grove, Inver
    Grove Heights, Mendota Heights,
    Newport, St. Paul Park, and
    South St. Paul
  Stillwater office serves eastern
    Washington County

Mississippi

Family Service Association of Greater
  Jackson
P.O. Box 5161, 1510 North State
  Street, Suite 201
Jackson 39216
(601) 353-3891
Roy E. Povall, Executive Director
  Area Served: Jackson Metropolitan
    area: fifteen-mile radius including
    Brandon, Clinton, Flowood, Pearl,
    and Raymond (persons who live,
    work, or attend school there)

Missouri

Family and Children Services of
  Kansas City
3515 Broadway, Suite 300
Kansas City 64111
(816) 753-5280
Mr. J. R. Majors, Executive Director
  Area Served: Kansas City, plus
    Blue Springs, Buckner,
    Grandview, Independence, Lake
    Lotawana, Lee's Summit, Oak
    Grove, Raytown, and Sugar
    Creek
  Clay-Platte Counties Office, (816)
    254-4343, serves Claycomo,
    Gladstone, Kansas City North,
    Liberty, North Kansas City,
    Parkville, Platte City, Pleasant
    Valley, and Riverside

Johnson County, Kansas, Office,
  (913) 642-4300, serves Overland
  Park, plus Fairway, Leawood,
  Lenexa, Merriam, Mission,
  Mission Hills, Prairie Village,
  Roeland Park, Shawnee, South
  Park, and Westwood

Jewish Family and Children Services
1115 East 65 Street
Kansas City 64131
(816) 333-1172
Lee M. Kalik, Executive Director
  Area Served: Kansas City
    metropolitan area, comprising
    Cass, Clay, Jackson, and Platte
    counties (Missouri) and Johnson
    and Wyandotte counties (Kansas)

Family Guidance Center
200 Corby Building, Fifth and Felix
St. Joseph 64501
(816) 364-1501
Norman Tolo, Executive Director
  Area Served: St. Joseph; also
    outlying counties in northwest
    Missouri, depending on need and
    staff time available

Catholic Family Service
4140 Lindell Boulevard
St. Louis 63108
(314) 371-4980
Thomas J. O'Donnell, Executive
  Director
  Area Served: St. Louis City, plus
    St. Louis and St. Charles counties

Family and Children's Service of
  Greater St. Louis
2650 Olive Street
St. Louis 63103
(314) 371-6500
Anthony DeMarinis, Executive
  Director
  Area Served: St. Louis City and St.
    Louis County. St. Charles Office
    serves Jefferson and St. Charles
    counties

Jewish Family and Children's Service
9385 Olive Boulevard
St. Louis 63132
(314) 993-1000
Harry Rubinstein, Executive Director
  Area Served: St. Louis City, plus
    St. Louis and St. Charles
    counties; also area served by
    Jewish Federation of Southern
    Illinois, especially Madison and
    St. Clair counties (Illinois)

Lutheran Family and Children's
  Services
333 Missouri Building, 634 North
  Grand Avenue
St. Louis 63101
(314) FR 1-3333
Arnold H. Bringewatt, Executive
  Director
  Area Served: Family counseling,
    family life education, and day
    care. Greater St. Louis area; social
    advocacy services, statewide

Nebraska

Family Service Association of Lincoln
1133 H Street
Lincoln 68508
(402) 432-3327
John B. Vogt, Executive Director
  Area Served: Lancaster County

Family Service of Omaha–Council
  Bluffs
2240 Landon Court
Omaha 68102
(402) 345-9118
Mr. Leslie W. Nummela, Executive
  Director
  Area Served: Radius of sixty miles

Nevada

Family Counseling Service
318 South Maryland Parkway
Las Vegas 89101
(702) 382-2924
Frank A. Brown, Executive Director
  Area Served: Southern Nevada

New Jersey

Family Counseling Service of
  Somerset County
339 West Second Street
Bound Brook 08805
(201) 356-1082
Anthony Provenzano, Executive
  Director
  Area Served: Somerset County and
    Borough of Middlesex

Family Counseling Service
217 South Sixth Street
Camden 08103
(609) 964-1990
William Doerr, Executive Director
  Area Served: Camden County
    (including persons, and their
    families, employed by any
    Camden industry); also families
    referred by Episcopal clergymen
    in South Jersey area, and migrant
    agricultural families in Gloucester
    County

Family Service of West Essex
388 Pompton Avenue
Cedar Grove 07009
(201) 857-0050
Linda Reynolds, Acting Executive
  Director
  Area Served: Caldwell, plus Cedar
    Grove, Essex Fells, Fairfield,
    Livingston, North Caldwell,
    Roseland, Verona, and West
    Caldwell

Jewish Family Service of Southern
  New Jersey
2393 West Marlton Pike
Cherry Hill 08034
(609) 662-8611
Seymour Siegel, D.S.W., Executive
  Director
  Area Served: Camden and
    Burlington counties

Family Counseling Service
10 Banta Place
Hackensack 07601
(201) 342-9200
Gloria B. Warshaw, Executive
  Director
  Area Served: Alpine, Bogota,
    Cliffside Park, Edgewater,
    Englewood, Fairview, Fort Lee,
    Hackensack, Leonia, Palisades
    Park, Ridgefield, Ridgefield Park,
    Teaneck and Tenafly; also
    employees of industry
    participating in United Fund of
    Bergen County. Service to other
    residents of Bergen County in
    programs for Aging and Family
    Development Workshops, and as
    professional time permits

Jewish Family Service of the Jewish
  Federation of Community Services
  of Bergen County, New Jersey
170 State Street
Hackensack 07601
(201) 488-8340
Beatrice H. Okun, Director
  Area Served: All of Bergen County,
    except East Paterson, Fair Lawn,
    Rochelle Park, and Saddle Brook

Family Service Association of
  Middlesex County
901 Raritan Avenue
Highland Park 08904
(201) 572-0300
Vincent Cancilla, Executive Director
  Area Served: Highland Park, plus
    Carteret, East Brunswick, Edison
    Township, Helmetta, Jamesburg,
    Madison Township, Metuchen,
    Milltown, Monroe Township,
    New Brunswick, North
    Brunswick, Perth Amboy,
    Piscataway Township, Sayreville,
    South Amboy, South Brunswick,
    South River, Spotswood, and
    Woodbridge Township

Family Service of Morris County
62 Elm Street
Morristown 07960
(201) 538-5260
Irma M. Fritschman, Executive
  Director
  Area Served: Morris County

Family Service Bureau of Newark
15 Fulton Street
Newark 07102
(201) 624-0913
Edward V. Kilduff, Executive Director
  Area Served: Newark, plus
    Arlington, Belleville, Harrison,
    Irvington, Kearny, and North
    Arlington

Family Counseling Center of Sussex
  County (Provisional Member
  Agency)
46 Trinity Street
Newton 07860
(201) 383-9492
Robert W. Young, Acting Director
  Area Served: Sussex County

Nutley Family Service Bureau
155 Chestnut Street
Nutley 07110
(201) 667-1884
Miss Elizabeth A. O'Malley,
  Executive Director
  Area Served: Nutley (persons who
    live or work there)

Jewish Family Service of North Jersey
1 Pike Drive
Wayne 07470
(201) 595-0111
Abraham D. Davis, Executive Director
  Area Served: Paterson and vicinity,
    plus Allendale, East Paterson, Fair
    Lawn, Franklin Lakes, Lincoln
    Park, Midland Park, Pequannock
    Township, Pompton Lakes,
    Riverdale, Saddle Brook-Rochelle
    Park, Waldwick, Wayne, and
    Wyckoff

Family Counseling Service of Paterson
and Vicinity
49 Colfax Avenue
Pompton Lakes 07442
(201) 839-2234
Miss Jean Baxter, Executive Director
Area Served: Passaic County

Family Service Agency of Princeton
120 John Street
Princeton 08540
(609) 924-2098
Paul Kurland, Executive Director
Area Served: Princeton, plus
Centerville (north of Pennington
Borough), Cranbury, East
Windsor, Hightstown, Kingston,
Lawrenceville (south of Cold Soil
Road), Mount Rose (east of
Hopewell), Plainsboro, Rocky
Hill, lower South Brunswick
Township, and West Windsor

Family Counseling Service of
Ridgewood and Vicinity
2–4 Garber Square
Ridgewood 07450
(201) 445-7015
George P. Tierney, Executive Director
Area Served: Glen Rock,
Ho-Ho-Kus, Midland Park,
Ridgewood, Waldwick, and
employees of industry in
northwest Bergen County
participating in Bergen County
United Fund

Family Service Association of Summit
43 Franklin Place
Summit 07901
(201) 273-1414
Mrs. Mary E. Nightingale, Executive
Director
Area Served: Summit, plus New
Providence, and Springfield
(persons who live or work there)

Family Service Association
M-5 Broad Street Bank Building, 143
East State Street
Trenton 08608
(609) 393-1626
Miss Elizabeth Northcutt, Director
Area Served: Trenton, plus Ewing,
Hamilton, Hopewell, and
Lawrence townships; also,
Hopewell Borough, Pennington,
Robbinsville, and Yardville

Jewish Family Service of Trenton
51 Walter Street
Trenton 08628
(609) 882-9317
Byron L. Pinsky, Executive Director
Area Served: Trenton, plus
Bordentown, Chesterfield
Township, Ewing, Fieldsboro,
Hamilton, Hopewell, Lawrence
Township, Pennington, and
Roebling (New Jersey);
Morrisville and Yardley
(Pennsylvania)

Family Service Association of Atlantic
County
4000 Black Horse Pike
West Atlantic City 08232
(609) 645-2942
Oliver Gerland, Jr., Executive Director
Area Served: Atlantic County

New Mexico

Family Counseling Service
4011–13 Silver Avenue, S.E.
Albuquerque 87108
(505) 265-8596
Carl P. Doeing, Executive Director
Area Served: Bernalillo, Sandoval,
Torrence, and Valencia counties

New York

Family and Children's Service of
Albany
12 South Lake Avenue
Albany 12203
(518) 462-6531
Robert D. Neely, Executive Director
Area Served: Albany County, plus
East Greenbush, Nassau, city of
Rensselaer, and Schodack

Child and Family Services
330 Delaware Avenue
Buffalo 14202
(716) 849-1515
Richard F. Mastronarde, Executive
  Director
  Area Served: Erie County and
    North Tonawanda

Jewish Family Service of Erie County
615 Sidway Building, 775 Main Street
Buffalo 14203
(716) 853-9956
Albert E. Deemer, Executive Director
  Area Served: Erie County and
    surrounding area

Family Service Society of the Corning
  Area
85 Denison Parkway, East
Corning 14830
(607) 962-3148
Irvin D. Weaver, Executive Director
  Area Served: Greater Corning area

Family Services of Chemung County
709 John Street
Elmira 14901
(607) 733-5696
Henry C. Smallback, Director
  Area Served: Chemung County

Family Counseling Service of the
  Finger Lakes (Provisional Member
  Agency)
182 North Street
Geneva 14456
(315) 789-2613
David G. Lamb, Executive Director
  Area Served: Ontario, Seneca,
    Wayne, and Yates counties

Family Service League of Suffolk
  County
642 New York Avenue
Huntington 11743
(516) HA 7-1768
Mr. Jesse Nemtzow, Executive
  Director
  Area Served: Suffolk County

Family Service of Jamestown
308 East Fifth Street
Jamestown 14701
(716) 488-1971
Dagne D. Strothers, Executive
  Director
  Area Served: Jamestown, plus
    Chautauqua and Cattaraugus
    counties (as funding permits)

Family and Children's Society of
  Broome County
676 Main Street
P.O. Box 150
Johnson City 13790
(607) 729-6206
Rosemary Wilson, Executive Director
  Area Served: Broome County and
    contiguous areas both in New
    York State and in northern
    Pennsylvania

Jewish Family Service
33 West 60 Street
New York 10023
(212) JU 6-2900
Sanford N. Sherman, Executive
  Director
  Area Served: Manhattan, Bronx,
    Brooklyn, and Staten Island

Family and Children's Service of
  Niagara Falls, New York
826 Chilton Avenue
Niagara Falls 14301
(716) 285-6984
Mrs. Anne M. Schaefer, Executive
  Director
  Area Served: Niagara Falls, plus
    Bergholtz, Colonial Village,
    Dickersonville, Fort Niagara,
    Lewiston, Martinsville, Model
    City, Pekin, Ransomville, St.
    Johnsburg, Sanborn, Tuscarora
    Reservation, Walmore, Wurlitzer,
    and Youngstown
  Lockport Office serves Cambria,
    Hartland, city and town of
    Lockport, Newfane, Pendleton,
    Royalton, Summerset, and
    Wilson

Family Counseling Service of
  Dutchess County
50 North Hamilton Street
Poughkeepsie 12601
(914) 452-1110
John T. Ericksen, Executive Director
  Area Served: Dutchess County

Family Service of Rochester
31 Gibbs Street
Rochester 14604
(716) 232-1840
Paul L. Yutzy, Executive Director
  Area Served: Monroe, Ontario, and
    Wayne counties

Family and Child Service of
  Schenectady
246 Union Street
Schenectady 12305
(518) 393-1369
Ronald J. Bigley, Executive Director
  Area Served: Schenectady County

Staten Island Family Service
25 Victory Boulevard
Staten Island 10301
(212) 447-6364
Sidney Herling, Executive Director
  Area Served: Staten Island

Child and Family Service
678 West Onondaga Street
Syracuse 13204
(315) 474-4291
Relda Jean Johnson, Ph.D., Executive
  Director
  Area Served: Onondaga County

Family Services of Greater Utica
167 Genesee Street
Utica 13501
(315) RE 5-5269
Robert E. Stone, Executive Director
  Area Served: Utica, plus Barneveld,
    Chadwicks, Clark Mills,
    Clayville, Clinton, Frankfort,
    Herkimer, Holland Patent, Ilion,
    Kirkland, New Hartford, New
    York Mills, Mohawk, Prospect,
    Remsen, Sauquoit, Washington
    Mills, Whitesboro, and Yorkville

North Carolina

Family Counseling Service
Allen Center, 331 College Street
Asheville 28801
(704) 253-9314
Bob Henderson, Executive Director
  Area Served: Buncombe County

Family and Children's Service
301 South Brevard Street
Charlotte 28202
(704) 372-7170
Edward Nadelman, Executive Director
  Area Served: Mecklenburg and
    Union counties

Family Counseling Service of Durham
809 West Chapel Hill Street
Durham 27701
(919) 688-7387
Robyn G. Wall, Executive Director
  Area Served: Durham County

Family Service—Travelers Aid
  Association of Greensboro
1301 New Elm Street
Greensboro 27401
(919) 273-3691
Harold F. Needle, Executive Director
  Area Served: Greensboro, plus
    Brown's Summit, Climax, Colfax,
    Gibsonville, Guiford College,
    Julian, McLeansville, Monticello,
    Oak Ridge, Pleasant Garden,
    Sedalia, Sedgefield, Stokesdale,
    Summerfield, and Whitsett

Family Guidance Center (A division
  of Family Mental Health Services)
346 Third Avenue, N.W.
Hickory 28601
(704) 328-5361
Paul E. Blackstone, Executive Director
  Area Served: Catawba County

Family Service Bureau
113 Gatewood Avenue
High Point 27260
(919) 883-1709, 883-2119
Lester F. Hamilton, Executive Director
  Area Served: High Point and
    Thomasville United Fund area,
    including Archdale, Jamestown,
    Randleman, and Trinity (persons
    who live or work there)

Family Service—Travelers Aid
  Association of Wake County
518 West Jones Street
Raleigh 27603
(919) 834-6264
Armand Occhetti, Executive Director
  Area Served: Wake County
    (persons who live or work there)

Family Service—Travelers Aid
208 First Union National Bank
  Building
P.O. Box 944
Wilmington 28401
(919) 763-5189
S. P. Bradsher, Executive Director
  Area Served: Brunswick, New
    Hanover, and Pender counties,
    plus Reigelwood

Family Services
610 Coliseum Drive
Winston-Salem 27106
(919) 722-8173
R. Winfred Tyndall, Executive
  Director
  Area Served: Forsyth County
    (persons who live or work there)

North Dakota

Children's Village—Family Service
1721 South University Drive
P.O. Box 528
Fargo 58102
(701) 235-6433
Harry S. Myers, Executive Director
  Area Served: State of North Dakota
    plus Dilworth and Moorhead,
    Minnesota

Ohio

Catholic Service League
640 North Main Street
Akron 44310
(216) 762-7481
  Miss Rita M. Silvestro, Executive
  Director
  Area Served: Summit County,
    except Barberton

Family and Children's Service Society
  of Summit County
90 North Prospect Street
Akron 44304
(216) 762-7601
William A. Baker, Executive Director
  Area Served: Summit County,
    except area served by Family
    Service of Cuyahoga Falls

Jewish Family Service
750 White Pond Drive
Akron 44320
(216) 867-3388
Nathan Pinsky, Executive Director
  Area Served: Akron, plus Cuyahoga
    Falls, Hudson, Kent, Medina,
    Ravenna, Silver Lake, Stow, and
    Wadsworth

Family Counseling Services
618 Second Street, N.W.
Canton 44703
(216) 454-7066
Paul Klassen, Executive Director
  Area Served: Canton United Way
    area, which includes eastern
    three-quarters of Stark County,
    except city of Alliance

Family Service of the Cincinnati Area
2343 Auburn Avenue
Cincinnati 45219
(513) 381-6300
John D. Minor, Executive Director
  Area Served: Clermont and
    Hamilton counties (Ohio) and
    Boone, Campbell, and Kenton
    counties (Kentucky)

Jewish Family Service
1710 Section Road
Cincinnati 45237
(513) 351-3680
Morton R. Startz, Executive Director
  Area Served: Jewish residents of
    United Appeal five-county area:
    Butler and Hamilton counties
    (Ohio) and Boone, Campbell, and
    Kenton counties (Kentucky)

Catholic Counseling Center
1001 Huron Road
Cleveland 44115
(216) 696-6650
Anthony DeBaggis, Jr., Executive
  Director
  Area Served: Diocese of Cleveland,
    primarily Cuyahoga, Geauga, and
    Lake counties

Center for Human Services
1001 Huron Road
Cleveland 44115
(216) 241-5861
  Martin E. Langer, Executive
    Director.
  Area Served: Cuyahoga, Geauga,
    Lake, and Northern Medina
    counties

Jewish Family Service Association of
  Cleveland, Ohio
2060 South Taylor Road
Cleveland 44118
(216) 371-2600
Burton S. Rubin, Executive Director
  Area Served: Cuyahoga County

Family Counseling and Crittenton
  Services
248 South High Street
Columbus 43215
(614) 221-7608
William L. White, Executive Director
  Area Served: Franklin County

Jewish Family Service
1175 College Avenue
Columbus 43209
(614) 237-7686
Peter M. Glick, Executive Director
  Area Served: Franklin County

Family Service of Cuyahoga Falls
507 Portage Trail
Cuyahoga Falls 44221
(216) 928-1159
Ray A. Carter, Executive Director
  Area Served: Cuyahoga Falls, plus
    Hudson, Munroe Falls, Silver
    Lake, Stow, and neighboring
    townships upon request

Family Service Association
184 Salem Avenue
Dayton 45406
(513) 222-9481
Joseph McDonald, Executive Director
  Area Served: Montgomery, Greene,
    and Preble counties; also
    residents of Clinton, Darke,
    Fayette, Miami, and Shelby
    counties as time permits
  Xenia and Fairborn offices serve
    Greene County

Family Service of Butler County
111 Buckeye Street
Hamilton 45011
(513) 868-3245
Mrs. Irma Sandage, Executive Director
  Area Served: Butler County

Child and Family Service
616 South Collett Street
Lima 45805
(419) 225-1040
Rosalie Stluka, Executive Director
  Area Served: Allen County (persons
    who live or work there or
    contribute to the Lima area
    United Way)

Family Service Association of Lorain
  County
4370 Oberlin Avenue
Lorain 44053
(216) 282-4273
Richard J. Lung, Executive Director
  Area Served: Greater Lorain County
    United Fund area, including
    Vermilion and Florence
    townships in Erie County

Family Counseling Services of
  Western Stark County
612 First National Building
Massillon 44646
(216) 832-5043
Mrs. Ethel Fridline, Executive Director
  Area Served: Massillon, plus
    western Stark County

Family Service of Erie County
(Provisional Member Agency)
412 Jackson Street
Sandusky 44870
(419) 627-0712
George C. Williston, Executive
Director
Area Served: Erie County United
Fund area (i.e., Erie County
except for Vermilion and Florence
townships)

Family Service Agency of Springfield
and Clark County
1007 Tecumseh Building., 34 West
High Street
Springfield 45502
(513) 325-5564
Alfred Liming, Executive Director
Area Served: Clark County

Family Service Association
224 North Fifth Street
Steubenville 43952
(614) 282-3221
Gordon M. Garrison, Executive
Director
Area Served: Jefferson County
(Ohio) and Follansbee, Weirton,
and Wellsburg (West Virginia)

Family Services of Greater Toledo
1 Stranahan Square
Toledo 43604
(419) 248-6643
Seymour Plawsky, Executive Director
Area Served: Lucas, Ottawa, and
Wood counties

Family Service Association
455 Elm Road., N.E.
Warren 44483
(216) 392-3671
Robert W. McLean, Executive
Director
Area Served: All of Trumbull
County

Children's and Family Service
Oak Hill Professional Building., 420
Oak Hill Avenue
Youngstown 44502
(216) 743-3196
James R. Bennett, Executive Director
Area Served: Mahoning County and
Columbiana, East Liverpool, East
Palestine, Girard, Hubbard,
Lisbon, Niles, and Salem

Oklahoma

Sunbeam Family Services
616 North West 21 Street
Oklahoma City 73103
(405) 528-7721
Larry L. Brown, Executive Director
Area Served: Oklahoma County
and immediately adjacent areas

Family and Children's Service
650 South Peoria Avenue
Tulsa 74120
(918) 587-9471
Richard I. Borden, Executive Director
Area Served: Tulsa County

Oregon

Metropolitan Family Service
2281 North West Everett Street
Portland 97210
(503) 228-7238
Ronald Yoder, Executive Director.
Area Served: Clackamas,
Multonomah, and Washington
counties

Pennsylvania

Family and Children's Service of
Lehigh County
411 Walnut Street
Allentown 18102
(215) 435-9651
John F. Von Glahn, Executive
Director
Area Served: Lehigh County, except
area solicited by Bethlehem
United Fund

Children's Aid and Family Service of
Beaver County
1445 Market Street (W.B.)
Beaver 15009
(412) 775-8390
Miss Mildred J. Smolkovich,
Executive Director
Area Served: Beaver County

Family Counseling Service of
Northampton County
520 East Broad Street
Bethlehem 18018
(215) 867-3946
John L. Diamond, Executive Director
Area Served: Bethlehem, Easton,
and Northampton (Pennsylvania),
plus Phillipsburg (New Jersey)
and surrounding area solicited by
the Bethlehem United Fund, the
Forks of the Delaware United
Fund, and the Northampton
Community Chest

Family Service Association of Bucks
County
20 West Oakland Avenue
Doylestown 18901
(215) 345-0550
Donald I. Ovrebo, Executive Director
Area Served: Bucks County;
Doylestown office serves central
and upper county area, and
Langhorne Office serves lower
county area

Family and Children's Service
121 Locust Street
Harrisburg 17101
(717) 238-8118
Glen Winter, Executive Director
Area Served: Dauphin and Perry
counties, plus Camp Hill, Enola,
Grantham, Lemoyne,
Mechanicsburg, New
Cumberland, Overview,
Shiremanstown, Summerdale,
West Fairview, and
Wormleysburg

Family and Children's Service of
Lancaster County
630 Janet Avenue
Lancaster 17601
(717) 397-5241
Allen R. Smith, Executive Director
Area Served: Lancaster County

Family and Community Service of
Delaware County
100 West Front Street
Media 19063
(215) LO 6-7540
Mrs. Maria E. Shelmire, Executive
Director
Area Served: Delaware County

Family Service & Children's Aid
Society of Venango County
202 West First Street
Oil City 16301
(814) 646-1283
Robert A. Carone, Executive Director
Area Served: Venango County; also
outlying counties as needed

Children and Family Service of
Episcopal Community Services
225 South Third Street
Philadelphia 19106
(215) WA 5-8110
Samuel J. Yerkes, Jr., Acting Executive
Director, Episcopal Community
Services
Paul M. Gezon, Director, Children
and Family Service
Area Served: Philadelphia, plus
Bucks, Chester, Delaware, and
Montgomery counties

Family Service of Philadelphia
311 South Juniper Street
Philadelphia 19107
(215) PE 5-7900
Richard W. Inglis, Executive Director
Area Served: Philadelphia

Jewish Family Service of Philadelphia
1610 Spruce Street
Philadelphia 19103
(215) KI 5-3290
Benjamin R. Sprafkin, Executive
  Director
    Area Served: Philadelphia, plus
      Abington, Ambler, Ardmore,
      Bala-Cynwyd, Broomall, Bryn
      Mawr, Devon Berwyn, Drexel
      Hill, Elkins Park, Flourtown,
      Gladwyne, Glenside, Havertown,
      Jenkintown, Manoa, Melrose
      Park, Merion, Narbeth,
      Overbrook Park, Paoli, Penn
      Valley, Penn Wynne, Plymouth
      Meeting, Radnor, Roslyn,
      Springfield, Upper Darby,
      Wyncote, and Wynnewood

Jewish Family and Children's Service
234 McKee Place
Pittsburgh 15213
(412) 683-4900
Nathaniel Goodman, Executive
  Director
    Area Served: Allegheny County

Family Service of Montgomery
  County
One Plymouth Meeting, Room 600
Plymouth Meeting 19462
(215) 825-1520
Marvin Poyourow, Executive Director
    Area Served: Plymouth Meeting
      office serves central Montgomery
      area, including the boroughs of
      Bridgeport, Conshohocken,
      Norristown, and West
      Conshohocken, plus the
      townships of East and West
      Norrition, Plymouth, Worcester,
      and part of Upper Merion
    Eastern Montgomery Branch, (215)
      886-3636, serves the boroughs of
      Ambler, Bryn Athyn, Hatboro,
      Jenkintown, and Rockledge, plus
      the townships of Abington,
      Cheltenham, Horsham, Lower
      Gwynedd, Lower Moreland,
      Plymouth, Springfield, Upper
      Dublin, Upper Moreland,
      Whitemarsh, and Whitpain

    Main Line Branch, (215) MI2-5354,
      serves Ardmore, plus
      Bala-Cynwyd, Bryn Mawr,
      Devon, Gladwyne, Haverford,
      Havertown, Merion, Narberth,
      Newton Square, Penn Valley,
      Penn Wynne, Rosemont, St.
      Davis, Villanova, Wayne, and
      Waynnewood
    North Penn Branch, (215) 368-8195,
      serves the boroughs of Hatfield,
      Lansdale, and North Wales, plus
      the townships of Franconia,
      Hatfield, Lower Salford,
      Montgomery, Salford, Skippack,
      Towamencin, Upper Gwynedd,
      and Upper Salford
    Pottstown Branch, (215) 326-1610,
      serves the borough of Pottstown,
      plus the townships of Limerick,
      Lower Frederick, Lower
      Pottsgrove, New Hanover, North
      Coventry, Perkiomen, Pottsgrove,
      Schwenksville, Upper Frederick
      Upper Pottsgrove, West
      Pottsgrove, and part of Douglas
    Upper Perkiomen Branch, (215)
      679-6949, serves the boroughs of
      Collegeville, Green Lane,
      Schwenksville, and Trappe, plus
      the townships of East Greenville,
      Green Lane, part of Hereford,
      Lower Frederick, part of Lower
      Providence, Marlborough,
      Pennsburg, Perkiomen, Red Hill,
      Skippack, part of Upper
      Frederick, and part of Upper
      Hanover

Family Service of Lackawanna County
615 Jefferson Avenue
Scranton 18510
(717) 342-3149
Miss Helen M. Moffat, Executive
  Director
    Area Served: Lackawanna County

Family Service of Warren County
8 Pennsylvania Avenue, West
Warren 16365
(814) 723-1330
James W. Krider, Jr., Executive
  Director
    Area Served: Warren County (other
      appropriate referrals accepted)

Family Service—Mental Health
  Centers of Chester County
310 North Matlack Street
West Chester 19380
(215) 696-4900
Curtis L. Clapham, Executive Director
  Area Served: Chester County

Family Service Association of
  Wyoming Valley
73 West Union Street
Wilkes-Barre 18702
(717) 823-5144
Mrs. Anne Vernon, Executive Director
  Area Served: Luzerne County,
    except Hazelton and vicinity

Family and Children's Service of
  Lycoming County
221 West Fourth Street
Williamsport 17701
(717) 326-5125
  Area Served: Lycoming County

Rhode Island

Child and Family Services of Newport
  County
24 School Street
Newport 02840
(401) 849-2300
Charles H. Nickrenz, Executive
  Director
  Area Served: Newport County

Family Service Society of Pawtucket
  and Vicinity
33 Summer Street
Pawtucket 02860
(401) 723-2124
John Carr, Executive Director
  Area Served: Pawtucket, plus
    Central Falls, Cumberland, and
    Lincoln

Family Service
75 Charlesfield Street
Providence 02906
(401) 331-1350
Mrs. B. Jae Clanton, Executive
  Director
  Area Served: Providence, plus
    Barrington, Bristol, Charleston,
    Coventry, Cranston, East
    Greenwich, East Providence,
    Exeter, Foster, Gloucester,
    Hopkinton, Johnston,
    Narragansett, North Kingston,
    North Providence, Richmond,
    Scituate, Smithfield, South
    Kingston, Warren, Warwick,
    West Greenwich, West Warwick,
    and Westerly; southern
    Massachusetts, Attleboro,
    Rehoboth, and Seekonk

Jewish Family and Children's Service
229 Waterman Street
Providence 02906
(401) 331-1244
Paul L. Segal, Executive Director
  Area Served: State of Rhode Island

South Carolina

Charleston County Department of
  Social Services
409 County Center
Charleston 29403
(803) 723-5541
William J. Knowles, Director
  Area Served: Charleston County

Family Service of Charleston County
Community Services Building
30 Lockwood Boulevard
Charleston 29401
(803) 723-4566
Mr. H. B. Free, Executive Director
  Area Served: Berkely, Charleston,
    and Lower Dorchester counties

Family Service Center
1813 Main Street
Columbia 29201
(803) 779-3250
J. B. Brannen, Executive Director
  Area Served: Lexington and
    Richland counties

Family Counseling Service-Travelers
  Aid for Greenville County
Ninth Floor, Insurance Building
Box 10306, Federal Station
Greenville 29603
(803) 232-2434
Mrs. Amelia K. Croft, Executive
  Director
    Area Served: Greenville County

South Dakota

Family Service
1728 South Cliff Avenue
Sioux Falls 57105
(605) 336-1974
William E. Lowe, Executive Director
    Area Served: Sioux Falls, plus
      Beresford and Dell Rapids United
      Fund areas on sliding-scale fee
      basis; other surrounding areas on
      full-cost basis

Tennessee

Community Services of Greater
  Chattanooga
323 High Street
Chattanooga 37403
(615) 267-2138
Tommy R. Perkins, Executive Director
    Area Served: Hamilton County
      (Tennessee) and Chattanooga
      metropolitan area extending into
      Catoosa, Dade, and Walker
      counties (Georgia)

Child and Family Services of Knox
  County
114 Dameron Avenue
Knoxville 37917
(615) 524-7483
Charles E. Gentry, Executive Director
    Area Served: Knox County; also
      surrounding areas on a full-cost
      basis

Family Service of Memphis
161 Jefferson Avenue
Memphis 38103
(901) 525-1681

Mrs. Ruth G. Joyner, Executive
  Director
    Area Served: Shelby County and
      surrounding communities in
      Tennessee, Arkansas, and
      Mississippi

Family and Children's Service
201 23 Avenue N
Nashville 37203
(615) 327-0833
G. Martin Amacher, Executive
  Director
    Area Served: Metropolitan
      Nashville area

Texas

Family Service of Amarillo
900 South Lincoln
Amarillo 79101
(806) 372-3202
Fred Gene Hill, Executive Director
    Area Served: Texas Panhandle

Child and Family Service
419 West Sixth Street
Austin 78701
(512) 478-1648
    Area Served: Travis County

Family and Children's Services
650 Main Street
Beaumont 77701
(713) 833-2668
Donald O. Robertson, Executive
  Director
    Area Served: Beaumont and North
      Jefferson County

Family Counseling Service
507 South Water Street
Corpus Christi 78401
(512) 882-2546
Gerald D. Kizerian, Executive Director
    Area Served: Corpus Christi, plus
      Alice, Aransas County, Beeville,
      Bishop, Kingsville, Portland, and
      Robstown. Exceptions made
      when necessary and possible

Family Guidance Center
2200 Main Street
Dallas 75201
(214) 747-8331
Paul Cromidas, Executive Director
  Area Served: Dallas County

Family Service of El Paso
2930 North Stanton Street
El Paso 79902
(915) 533-2491
Robert J. Kemp, Executive Director
  Area Served: El Paso County

Family Service—Travelers Aid
  Association of Tarrant County
Hunter Plaza, 212 Burnet Street
Fort Worth 76102
(817) 335-2401
After 5: 924-4231
Crisis Intervention Service:
  Caller Service (24 hours) (817)
    336-3355
  Business (817) 336-5921
Glen Good, Executive Director
  Area Served: Tarrant County

Family Service Center of Galveston
  County
509 Texas Building
Galveston 77550
(713) 762-8636
John F. Willis, Executive Director
  Area Served: Galveston and
    portions of Galveston County

Family Service Center of Houston and
  Harris County
3635 West Dallas
Houston 77019
(713) 524-3881
E. F. Christman, Jr., Executive
  Director
  Area Served: Harris and Brazoria
    counties
  Bay Area Office serves southern
    Harris County, plus mainland
    part of Galveston County

Jewish Family Service
4131 South Braeswood Boulevard
Houston 77025
(713) 667-9336
Mrs. Ruth Hutton Fred, Executive
  Director
  Area Served: Harris County; also,
    occasionally, nearby communities

Family Service Association
2206 Broadway
Lubbock 79401
(806) 747-3488
Margaret Elbow, Executive Director
  Area Served: Lubbock County

Family Services of Midland, Texas
9 Rivercrest Building, 2101 West Wall
Midland 79701
(915) 683-4241
Linda H. George, Executive Director
  Area Served: Midland County

Family Service Center
Brown Center, 2353 9 Avenue
Port Arthur 77640
(713) 985-2514
Walter R. Pattison, Jr., Executive
  Director
  Area Served: South Jefferson
    County, plus mid-Jefferson
    County

Family Services Association of San
  Antonio
230 Preida Street
San Antonio 78210
(512) 226-3391
James R. Gamble, Jr., Executive
  Director
  Area Served: Bexar County

Family Counseling and Children's
  Services
213 Community Services Building
201 West Waco Drive, P.O. Box 464
Waco 76703
(817) 753-1509
Miss Patt Laidler, Executive Director
  Area Served: McLennan County

Virginia

Social Service Bureau (Public)
110 Municipal Building, P.O. Box
  3300
Danville 24541
(804) 799-6543, Ext. 242
Franklin R. Joseph, Superintendent
  Area Served: Danville

Northern Virginia Family Service
803 West Broad Street
Falls Church 22046
(703) 533-9727
Sidney A. Berman, Executive Director
  Area Served: Falls Church and
    Alexandria, plus Arlington,
    Fairfax, Loudoun, and Prince
    William counties

Peninsula Family Service and
  Travelers Aid
1520 Aberdeen Road, P.O. Box 7315
Hampton 23666
(804) 838-1960
Edwin C. Cotten, Executive Director
  Area Served: Newport News, plus
    Hampton and York County

Family Service of Central Virginia
1010 Miller Park Square
Lynchburg 24501
(804) 845-5944
William H. Aiken, Executive Director
  Area Served: Lynchburg and
    Bedford, plus Amherst,
    Appomattox, Bedford, and
    Campbell counties

Family Service/Travelers Aid
222 19 Street West
Norfolk 23517
(804) 622-7017
Earl D. Morris, Executive Director
  Area Served: Cities of Norfolk,
    Chesapeake, and Virginia Beach

Jewish Family Service of Tidewater
7300 Newport Avenue, P.O. Box 9503
Norfolk 23505
(804) 489-3111
Irv Loev, Executive Director
  Area Served: Norfolk, Portsmouth,
    Virginia Beach, and eastern part
    of Chesapeake

Child and Family Service—Travelers
  Aid
355 Crawford Street
Portsmouth 23704
(804) 397-2121, 397-3311
Mrs. Dorothy P. Evans, Executive
  Director
  Area Served: Portsmouth City, plus
    the Deep Creek and Western
    Branch boroughs of Chesapeake

Family and Children's Service of
  Richmond
1518 Willow Lawn Drive
Richmond 23230
(804) 282-4255
Larry G. Betts, Executive Director
  Area Served: Richmond, plus
    Chesterfield, Hanover, and
    Henrico counties

Jewish Family Services
4206 Fitzhugh Avenue
Richmond 23230
(804) 358-2359
Mrs. Anne P. Lane, Executive
  Director
  Area Served: Richmond, plus
    Chesterfield and Henrico counties
    and any localities within a
    fifty-mile radius of the city of
    Richmond

Family Service of Roanoke Valley
518 Carlton Terrace Building, 920
  South Jefferson Street
Roanoke 24016
(703) 344-3253
Max W. Davis, Executive Director
  Area Served: Cities of Roanoke and
    Salem plus Botetourt, Craig, and
    Roanoke counties (persons who
    live or work there)

Washington

Family and Child Service of
  Metropolitan Seattle
500 Lowman Building, 107 Cherry
  Street
Seattle 98104
(206) 447-3883
Joseph H. Kahle, Executive Director
  Area Served: King County

Family Counseling Service
820 Paulsen Building
Spokane 99201
(509) 838-4128
Mrs. Grace W. McWilliams, Executive
  Director
  Area Served: Spokane County

Family Counseling Service
1008 South Yakima Avenue
Tacoma 98405
(206) 627-6105
Miss Catherine Anzovino, Executive
  Director
  Area Served: Pierce County
    (persons who live or work there)

West Virginia

Family Service of Kanawha Valley
414 Professional Building, 1036
  Quarrier Street
Charleston 25301
(304) 342-7176
Jim L. Frampton, Executive Director
  Area Served: Kanawha and Putnam
    counties

Family Service of Marion and
  Harrison Counties
201 Virginia Avenue, P.O. Box 1265
Fairmont 26554
(304) 366-4750
Mrs. Patricia Kronjaeger, Executive
  Director
  Area Served: Marion and Harrison
    counties

Children and Family Service
  Association
Multi Service Center
109 North Main Street
Wheeling 26003
(304) 233-2350, 233-6300
Manuel J. Viola, Executive Director
  Area Served: Brooke, Marshall, and
    Ohio counties (West Virginia),
    and Belmont, Jefferson, and
    Monroe counties (Ohio)

Wisconsin

Family Service Association of the Fox
  Valley (Provisional Member
  Agency)
1000 West College Avenue
Appleton 54911
(414) 739-4226
Robert C. Gellert, Executive Director
  Area Served: Appleton, Combined
    Locks, Grand Chute, Kaukauna,
    Kimberly, and Little Chute
  Neenah office serves Neenah and
    Menasha

Family Service Association of Beloit
423 Bluff Street
Beloit 53511
(608) 365-1244
Miss Borghild Boe, Director
  Area Served: Beloit and Clinton
    (Wisconsin), plus South Beloit,
    Rockton, and Roscoe (Illinois)
    areas

Family Service Association of Brown
  County
1546 Dousman Street
Green Bay 54303
(414) 499-8768, 499-8769
Terrence J. Steeno, Executive Director
  Area Served: Brown County; also
    residents of neighboring counties
    as time permits

Family Service Association
1707 Main Street
LaCrosse 54601
(608) 782-5480
Glenn Austad, Executive Director
  Area Served: LaCrosse (Wisconsin)
    and La Crescent (Minnesota);
    services to surrounding area,
    provided staff time is available

Family Service
2059 Atwood Avenue
Madison 53704
(608) 249-8521
Ray Redding, Executive Director
    Area Served: Dane County

Family Service of Milwaukee
2819 West Highland Boulevard, P.O.
    Box 08517
Milwaukee 53208
(414) 342-4558
David L. Hoffman, Executive Director
    Area Served: Greater Milwaukee
    area

Jewish Family and Children's Service
1360 North Prospect Avenue
Milwaukee 53202
(414) 273-6515
Ralph Sherman, Executive Director
    Area Served: Greater Milwaukee
    County

Family Service of Racine
420 Seventh Street
Racine 53403
(414) 634-2391
Alan R. Exner, Executive Director
    Area Served: Racine County

Member Agencies, Canada

Alberta

Family Service Association of
  Edmonton
Family Service Building, 9919 106 St.
Edmonton T5K 1E2
(403) 424-4161
Donald W. Storch, Executive Director
  Area Served: Metropolitan
  Edmonton

British Columbia

Family Services of Greater Vancouver
1616 W. Seventh Avenue
Vancouver V6J 1S5
(604) 731-4951
C. E. R. Thompson, Executive
  Director
  Area Served: Vancouver and
  University area, plus
  municipalities of Burnaby, North
  Vancouver, Richmond, and West
  Vancouver

Manitoba

Family Services of Winnipeg
264 Edmonton Street
Winnipeg R3C 1R9
(204) 947-1401
Winnie Fung, Executive Director
  Area Served: Greater Winnipeg

Ontario

Family Services of
  Hamilton–Wentworth
22 Tisdale Street, S.
Hamilton L8N 2V9
(416) 528-1494
John A. Vedell, Executive Director
  Area Served: Hamilton–Wentworth
  region and city of Burlington

Family Service Centre of Ottawa
119 Ross Avenue
Ottawa K1Y 0N6
(613) 725-7201
Miss Evelyn McCorkell, Executive
  Director
  Area Served: Regional municipality
  of Ottawa–Carleton

Family Service Association of
  Metropolitan Toronto
22 Wellesley Street, E.
Toronto M4Y 1G3
(416) 922-3126
Robert Couchman, Executive Director
  Area Served: Metropolitan Toronto

Family Service Bureau of Windsor
Carnegie Tower
450 Victoria Avenue
Windsor N8X 3L9
(519) 256-1831
Edwin C. Clarke, Executive Director
  Area Served: Greater Windsor
  United Community Services area
  and environs

Quebec

Family Service Association of
  Montreal
Division of Ville Marie Social Service
  Centre
4515 St. Catherine Street, W.
Montreal H3Z 1R9
(514) 934-0721
William E. Duncan, Executive
  Director
  Area Served: Montreal and included
  municipalities

Saskatchewan

Family Service Bureau
20–39 22 Street E.
Saskatoon S7K 0G7
(306) 244-0127
E. S. Cardwell, Executive Director
  Area Served: City of Saskatoon

3. WORK AND VOLUNTEER OPPORTUNITIES FOR THE ELDERLY

The following information is excerpted from *Older Americans Are Our National Resource,* Department of Health, Education, and Welfare Pamphlet No. 74–20810.

PAID EMPLOYMENT

The U.S. Department of Labor, through its Older American Community Service Program, provides opportunities for paid employment for the elderly in the following government programs.

Green Thumb

Sponsored by the National Farmers Union in 24 states. Provides part-time work in conservation, beautification, and community improvement in rural areas or in existing community service agencies. Applicants should have a rural or farming background and must take a physical examination. Write: Green Thumb, Inc., 1012 14th Street, N.W., Washington, D.C. 20005.

Operation Mainstream Program

Administered by the Forest Service of the U.S. Department of Agriculture in about 20 states under an agreement with the U.S. Department of Labor. Offers employment to older persons on an average of three days a week in conservation and beautification projects. Write: USDA Forest Service, Room 3243, South Agriculture Building, 12th and Independence Avenue, S.W., Washington, D.C. 20250.

Senior Aides

Administered by the National Council of Senior Citizens in 33 urban and rural areas. Offers part-time work in community service agencies in a variety of activities from child care and adult education to home health and homemaker services. Write: National Council of Senior Citizens, 1511 K Street, N.W., Washington, D.C. 20005.

Senior Community Aides

Sponsored by the National Retired Teachers Association and the American Association of Retired Persons in 31 cities. Recruits, trains, and finds part-time work for aides in public or private service programs, assisting in child care centers, vocational education classes, or clerical positions and building security. Write: NRTA/AARP, 1909 K Street, N.W., Washington, D.C. 20036.

Senior Community Service Aides

Sponsored by the National Council on the Aging in 18 urban and rural areas. Provides part-time work in Social Security and state employment service offices, public housing, libraries, hospitals, schools, food and nutrition programs. Aides also help provide escort services, homemaker and home repair services, and outreach for information and referral. Write: National Council on the Aging, 1828 L Street, N.W., Washington, D.C. 20036.

VOLUNTEER SERVICE
ACTION
806 Connecticut Avenue, N.W.
Washington, D.C. 20525

Toll-free number: (800) 424-8580

ACTION is an independent government agency which provides centralized coordination and administration of domestic and international volunteer activities sponsored by the federal government. The following ACTION programs provide opportunities for volunteer service for elderly persons.

Foster Grandparent Program
Men and women sixty years old or older, with low incomes, may volunteer to work with children on a one-to-one basis four hours a day, five days a week. Foster grandparents receive a small stipend for their services. There are Foster Grandparent Programs all across the country. For information about individual locations, call or write: ACTION (see above).

Peace Corps
Older Americans have been serving in the Peace Corps, along with younger volunteers, since it started in 1961. Peace Corps volunteers are assigned to serve in developing countries for two years. They receive a monthly living allowance and, at the end of their service, a cumulative readjustment allowance. For information, call or write: ACTION.

Retired Senior Volunteer Program (RSVP)
RSVP volunteers, sixty and over, are placed in community activities which suit their interests. They work with children and the handicapped, help other older people, or serve in a variety of community programs. Volunteers may be reimbursed for out-of-pocket expenses. There are 600 RSVP programs across the country. For information about individual areas, write: your state office on the aging, or ACTION.

Senior Companion Program
Started in 1974, this program was modeled after the Foster Grandparent Program. Senior companions serve adults with special needs, including the elderly, in their own homes, in nursing homes, or in other institutions. Volunteers receive small stipends for their services. For information, call or write: ACTION.

Service Corps of Retired Executives (SCORE)
As SCORE volunteers, retired business people help owners of small businesses or community organizations who are having problems with management. Since 1965 SCORE volunteers have helped more than 175,000 enterprises succeed. Volunteers may be reimbursed for out-of-pocket expenses. For information, call or write: any Small Business Administration regional or district office, or ACTION.

Volunteers in Service to America (VISTA)
A national corps of volunteers working in urban ghettoes, small towns, rural areas, Indian reservations, or wherever there is poverty in America. VISTA volunteers serve for one year and may reenroll if they so request. While serving, they receive a monthly living allowance and are paid a cumulative monthly stipend when they complete their service. For information, call or write: ACTION.

Appendix C

CHECKLISTS FOR EVALUATING SERVICES

NURSING HOMES

I. **Where to start**

   A. Get a list of nursing homes in your area from

      1. Hospital Social Service Departments
      2. Local Department of Health and Department of Social Services
      3. State Department of Health and Department of Social Services
      4. County Medical Society
      5. Social Security District Office
      6. State and Local Office of the Aging
      7. Your physician, clergyman, relatives, friends

   B. Visit several before making a decision.

II. **What to notice about the general atmosphere**

   A. Are visitors welcome?

      1. Are you encouraged to tour freely?
      2. Do staff members answer questions willingly?

   B. Is the home clean and odor-free?

   C. Is the staff pleasant, friendly, cheerful, affectionate?

   D. Are lounges available for socializing?

III. **Is attention paid to the patients' morale?**

   A. Are they called patronizingly by their first names or addressed with dignity as "Mr.," "Mrs.," "Miss"_____?

   B. Are they dressed in nightclothes or street clothes?

   C. Do many of them appear oversedated?

   D. Are they allowed to have some of their own possessions?

   E. Are they given sufficient privacy?

      1. Are married couples kept together?
      2. Are "sweethearts" given a place to visit with each other in complete privacy?

F. Is good grooming encouraged?

    1. Beautician and barber available?

G. Is tipping necessary to obtain services?

IV. **What licensing to look for**

A. State Nursing Home License

B. Nursing Home Administrator License

C. Joint Committee on Accreditation of Hospital Certificate

D. American Association of Homes for the Aging

E. American Nursing Home Association

V. **Location**

A. Is it convenient for visiting?

B. Is the neighborhood safe for ambulatory residents?

C. Is there an outdoor garden with benches?

VI. **Safety considerations**

A. Does the home meet federal and state fire codes?

    1. Ask to see the latest inspection report.
    2. Are regular fire drills scheduled?

B. Is the home accident-proof?

    1. Good lighting?
    2. Hand rails and grab bars in halls and bathrooms?
    3. No obstructions in corridors?
    4. No scatter rugs or easily tipped chairs?
    5. Stairway doors kept closed?

VII. **Living arrangements**

A. Are the bedrooms comfortable and spacious?

B. Is the furniture appropriate?

    1. Enough drawer and closet space?
    2. Doors and drawers easy to open?
    3. Can residents furnish their rooms with personal items?

C. Can closets and drawers be locked?

D. Is there enough space between beds, through doorways, and in corridors for wheelchairs?

E. Are there enough elevators for the number of patients?

    1. Are elevators large enough for wheelchairs?

VIII. **Food services**

A. Is there a qualified dietician in charge?

    1. Are special therapeutic diets followed?
    2. Are individual food preferences considered?

B. Are you welcome to inspect the kitchen?

C. Are menus posted?

    1. Do the menus reflect what is actually served?

D. Are dining rooms cheerful?

   1. Are patients encouraged to eat in the dining room rather that at the bedside?

   2. Is there room between the tables for the passage of wheelchairs?

E. Are bedridden patients fed when necessary?

   1. Is food left uneaten on trays?

F. Are snacks available between meals and at bedtime?

   1. Are snacks scheduled too close to meals in order to accommodate staff shifts?

   2. Is there too long a period between supper and breakfast the next morning?

IX. Medical services

A. Is there a medical director qualified in geriatric medicine?

B. Are patients allowed to have private doctors?

C. If there are staff physicians, what are their qualifications?

   1. Is a doctor available twenty-four hours a day?

   2. How often is each patient seen by a doctor?

D. Does each patient get a complete physical examination before or upon admission?

E. Does the home have a hospital affiliation or a transfer agreement with a hospital?

F. Does each patient have an individual treatment plan?

G. Is a psychiatrist available?

H. Is provision made for dental, eye, and foot care as well as other specialized services?

I. Are there adequate medical records?

X. Nursing services

A. Is the nursing director fully qualified?

B. Is there a registered nurse on duty at all times?

C. Are licensed practical nurses graduates of approved schools?

D. Is there adequate nursing staff for the number of patients?

E. Is there an in-service training program for nurse's aides and orderlies?

XI. Rehabilitation services

A. Is there a registered physiotherapist on staff?

   1. Good equipment?

   2. How often are patients scheduled?

B. Is there a registered occupational therapist on staff?

   1. Is functional therapy prescribed in addition to diversionary activities?

C. Is a speech therapist available for poststroke patients?

D. Is the staff trained in reality orientation, remotivation, and bladder training for the mentally impaired?

XII. Group activities

    A. Is the activities director professionally trained?

    B. Are a variety of programs offered?

        1. Ask to see a calendar of activities.

    C. Are there trips to theaters, concerts, museums for those who can go out?

    D. Are wheelchair patients transported to group activities?

    E. Is there a library for patients?

    F. Is there an opportunity to take adult education courses or participate in discussion groups?

XIII. Social services

    A. Is a professional social worker involved in admission procedures?

        1. Are both the applicant and family interviewed?

        2. Are alternatives to institutionalization explored?

    B. Is a professional trained social worker available to discuss personal problems and help with adjustment of patient and family?

    C. Are social and psychological needs of patients included in treatment plans?

    D. Is a professional trained social worker available for consultation to the staff?

        1. On social and psychological problems of patients?

        2. On roommate choices and tablemates?

XIV. Religious observances

    A. Is there a chapel on the grounds?

    B. Are religious services held regularly for those who wish to attend?

    C. If the home is run under sectarian auspices, are clergy of other faiths permitted to see patients when requested?

XV. Citizen participation

    A. Is the Patient Bill of Rights prominently displayed and understood?

    B. Is there a resident council?

        1. How often does it meet?

        2. Does it have access to the administrator and department heads?

    C. Is there a family organization?

        1. How often does it meet?

        2. Does it have access to the administrator and department heads?

    D. Do the patients vote in local, state, and federal elections?

        1. Are they taken to the polls?

        2. Do they apply for absentee ballots?

XVI. Financial questions

    A. What are the basic costs?

        1. Are itemized bills available?

        2. Are there any extra charges?

    B. Is the home eligible for Medicare and Medicaid reimbursement?

        1. Is a staff member available to assist in making application for these funds?

   2. Is assistance available for questions about veterans' pensions? Union benefits?
   C. What provision is made for patients' spending money?

HOMEMAKER–HOME HEALTH AIDE SERVICES

Adapted from the "Basic National Standards for Homemaker-Home Health Aide Services" established by the National Council for Homemaker–Home Health Aide Services, Inc.

   1. Does the agency from which you are seeking services have legal authorization to operate? Is it licensed or certified?

   2. Is the agency accountable to a regulatory body (government agency, national council, or board of directors) that monitors the quality of the services?

   3. Does the agency have written personnel policies, job descriptions, and a wage scale established for each job category?

   4. Does the agency provide you with both the services of a homemaker–home health aide and a supervisor who makes periodic visits to check on the care given?

   5. Is a professional person (registered nurse or trained social worker) responsible for a plan of care?

   6. Does the agency provide in-service training for the homemaker–home health aide?

   7. Is this training provided by qualified professionals?

   8. Is the agency eligible for Medicare and Medicaid reimbursement?

   9. Does the agency make regular reports to the community and to certifying bodies?

Appendix D

DIRECTORIES
TO CONSULT

Directory of Agencies Serving the Blind

American Foundation for the Blind
15 West 16th Street
New York, N.Y. 10011
$6.00

Directory of Diocesan Agencies of Catholic Charities

National Conference of Catholic Charities
1346 Connecticut Avenue
Washington, D.C. 20036
$2.00

Directory of Homemaker–Home Health Aide Services

National Council for Homemaker–Home Health Aide Services
67 Irving Place
New York, N.Y. 10003
$3.00

Directory of Information and Referral Services

United Way of America
National Agencies Division
801 North Fairfax Street
Alexandria, Virginia 22314

Directory of Jewish Federations, Funds, and Councils

Council of Jewish Federation and Welfare Funds
315 Park Avenue South
New York, N.Y. 10010
$3.50

Directory of Legal Aid and Defender Services

National Legal Aid and Defender Association
1155 East 60th Street
Chicago, Illinois 60637
$3.50

Directory of Medicare Providers and Suppliers of Services

U.S. Department of Health, Education, and Welfare
Social Security Administration
Government Printing Office
Superintendent of Documents
Washington, D.C. 20402
$2.70

.Lists by state all Medicare-approved hospitals, skilled nursing facilities, home health agencies (including visiting nurse associations), outpatient physical therapy facilities, independent laboratories, portable X-ray units, renal disease treatment centers.

Directory of Non-Profit Homes for the Aging

American Association of Homes for the Aging
374 National Press Building
Washington, D.C. 20004
$2.00

A Directory of Senior Centers in the U.S.

U.S. Department of Health, Education, and Welfare
Social and Rehabilitation Service
Administration on Aging
Government Printing Office
Superintendent of Documents
Washington, D.C. 20402
$2.00

Lists 1,200 centers by state and city with definition of program types, services, and activities (for example: meals, transportation, recreation activities, counseling, and community services).

Directory of Senior Opportunities and Services Programs

Older Persons Programs
Office of Economic Opportunity
Washington, D.C. 20506

Directory of United Funds and Councils

United Way of America
801 North Fairfax Street
Alexandria, Virginia 22314
$8.00

Family Service Association Directory

Family Service Association of America
44 East 23rd Street
New York, N.Y. 10010
$5.00

Health Insurance Plans Other Than Blue Cross or Blue Shield Plans or Insurance Companies—1970 Survey

Research Report No. 35 of Office of Research and Statistics
U.S. Department of Health, Education, and Welfare
Social Security Administration
U.S. Government Printing Office
Superintendent of Documents
Washington, D.C. 20402
$1.30

See appendix of this report for alternative health insurance plans.

Lutheran Health and Welfare Directory

Division of Welfare Services
Lutheran Council in the U.S.A.
315 Park Avenue South
New York, N.Y. 10010
$1.50

Mental Health Directory

National Clearing House for Mental Health Information
U.S. Department of Health, Education, and Welfare
5600 Fishers Lane
Rockville, Maryland 20852
$3.75

National Associations with Programs in the Field of Aging

National Council on the Aging
1828 L Street, N.W.
Washington, D.C. 20036
$1.00

A National Directory of Housing for Older People

Revised edition, 1969.
362 pages, paperback. Order number: 6910
$5.50
National Council on the Aging
1828 L Street, N.W.
Washington, D.C. 20036

Lists approximately 400 housing facilities designed or adapted to meet the needs of older people who are able to live independently. Entries include apartment houses, retirement communities, residence clubs and hotels, and mobile home parks.

A significant feature is the "Guide for Selection," which discusses in detail the pros and cons of moving to a new community or into homes of relatives; what to look for and look out for in retirement housing; and the advantages, disadvantages, and costs of various types of living arrangements.

Listings are arranged geographically, by state and community. Each entry includes information on sponsorship, location, size, and type of facility; costs; services available on the premises and in the community; eligibility requirements; admission procedures.

1974 Directory of Senior Centers and Clubs: A National Resource

Compiled by the National Institute of Senior Centers.
558 pages, softbound. Order number: 7413
National Council on the Aging
1828 L Street, N.W.
Washington, D.C. 20036
$10.00

Lists approximately 4,900 programs, supplying data on auspices; year established; number of full-time professionals, part-time volunteer and student staff; number of members or participants and average daily attendance; eligibility requirements; fees, schedule, days open; cost of meals served on premises and home-delivered; services, including transportation, recreation, education, information and referral, counseling, outreach, employment, health, volunteer opportunities. Notes social action programs and accommodation for wheelchairs. A useful resource for social service agencies, information and referral centers, family counselors, area agencies on aging, and all who seek activities and services for older people in communities throughout the United States.

Public Welfare Directory

American Public Welfare Association
1155 16 Street, N.W.
Washington, D.C. 20036
$15.00

Lists all government agencies with names, addresses, phone numbers, HEW regional offices, state offices (aging, health, social services), county offices.

Your Medicare Handbook

U.S. Department of Health, Education, and Welfare
Social Security Administration
U.S. Government Printing Office
Superintendent of Documents
Washington, D.C. 20402

Lists insurance carriers who handle Medicare claims and also sell supplemental coverage. May be obtained from any Social Security office as well as from the Government Printing Office.

Appendix E

Common Diseases and
Symptoms of the Elderly

1. DISEASES

Some diseases, although they may also occur earlier in life, are much more likely to appear in the later years. Listed below are a number of common diseases that afflict the elderly and some ways in which they may be treated. *All patients should, of course, consult their medical doctors for diagnosis and treatment of their own individual conditions.*

Arteriosclerosis

This is a general term for a number of diseases of the blood vessels associated with the thickening and hardening of the arteries. Arteriosclerosis involves the narrowing and closing of a blood vessel due to accumulation of fats, complex carbohydrates, blood and blood products, fibers, tissues, and calcium deposits in its inner wall.

Arteriosclerosis is also related to hypertension, or high blood pressure, in that it is more severe where hypertension is present. The extent of arterial involvement increases with age and can affect all the arteries of the body, including those of the brain. When the blood supply to the brain is reduced by narrowing of the arteries supplying the brain, disturbances in behavior and cognition may result.

Arteriosclerosis in the aged is treated primarily by reducing the blood fats by diet where they are significantly elevated. Drugs to reduce blood fats at this age are not of proven value and must be used with caution to avoid side effects. Definitely, elevated blood pressure should be reduced with a low-salt diet and the milder antihypertensive drugs. Cigarette smoking should be discontinued, and a program of supervised physical activity is helpful, as is the control of obesity. Surgical procedures for obstruction of blood vessels in the chest, neck, heart, and extremities may be of value after careful work-up and evaluation of the benefits and risks involved.

Arthritis

Arthritis is a general term referring to any degeneration or inflammation of the joints. It is classified according to its acuteness or its duration and according to the specific joints involved, along with other considerations. Many older Americans suffer from arthritis, some to a mild degree and others severely.

The most common form, called *osteoarthritis,* is due to the wear and tear process involving the joints that accompanies aging. Osteoporosis, or thinning of the bones with aging, especially in women, contributes to the sum total of arthritis. Inflammatory involvement in the joints, *rheumatoid arthritis,* is less common in the aged. *Gout,* a metabolic disease of the joints accompanied by severe pain and signs of inflammation, is also seen in the aged.

Treatment of arthritis varies with the cause and includes physiotherapy, use of cortisone products and aspirin, orthopedic devices, and increased dietary vitamins and calcium-containing foods. There are specific drugs for treating gout. The use of female sex hormones for treating osteoporosis is controversial.

Bronchitis

Bronchitis is an inflammation of the cells that line the bronchial air tubes. It may be caused by infection, or by chronic irritation following the inhalation of some harmful substance. Infectious bronchitis is treated with antibiotics. In the case of chronic bronchitis, cessation of cigarette smoking is, of course, imperative. If untreated, chronic bronchitis will progress gradually into pulmonary emphysema.

Pulmonary emphysema, which results when the air sacs in the lungs are damaged, is often found in heavy smokers. The patient suffers from recurrent episodes of shortness of breath and a persistent hacking cough. Treatment centers around relief of chronic bronchial obstruction and inflammation and the provision of oxygen to the remaining air sacs. Devices have been developed to aid the emphysema patient in breathing, and a variety of drugs and exercises are of value.

Cancer

Cancer, or malignant tumor, involves the growth of new tissues that can spread from one part of the body to another. Cancer can occur in the throat, larynx, mouth, gastrointestinal tract, skin, bones, thyroid, bladder, kidney, and so forth. As cancer symptoms in the aged may be atypical, or may be ignored by the aged patient afflicted with other symptoms and often with a poor memory, comprehensive annual examinations are vital to early detection and treatment.

Prompt detection and therapy are crucial to treatment of cancer by surgery, X-ray, or chemical means. As life expectancy in the aged is limited and the growth of many of the cancers that afflict them is slow, there should be careful consideration of the value and potential side effects of potent methods of therapy before they are undertaken.

Congestive Heart Failure

Congestive heart failure is a condition wherein the heart muscle has been so weakened that its pumping performance is impaired and it cannot provide sufficient circulation for body tissues. This condition may be produced by other heart problems, such as hypertensive heart disease, coronary heart attacks, and rheumatic heart disease. It may also be produced by conditions such as chronic lung disease, anemia, infection, and emotional stress.

Treatment for congestive heart failure is directed at improving the heart's pumping efficiency, eliminating excess fluids, and reducing the overload on the heart. Digitalis is often used to strengthen the heart muscle, and diuretics to remove excess fluid from the body. Treatment of the precipitating disease, such as hypertension, overactivity of the thyroid gland, or anemia, is also necessary.

Coronary Heart Disease

This disease, which is present in almost all individuals over the age of seventy in the United States, involves deterioration of or damage to the vessels that supply blood to the heart. In older persons it is superimposed on a heart where there is a general decrease in muscle-cell size and efficiency, and where there is a progressive lack of ability to deal with stress.

One serious condition that can result from coronary heart disease is *acute myocardial infarction,* wherein the blood supply to the heart is cut off. In the elderly it is not unusual for there to be no apparent symptoms accompanying an infarction, in contrast to the crushing pain experienced by younger persons. Substitution symptoms are also common in the elderly. For example, when the elderly heart fails under the stress of acute myocardial injury, blood may back up behind the left side of the heart into the blood vessels of the lungs, causing shortness of breath instead of chest pain. Or the blood may back up behind the right side of the heart and cause congestion of the abdominal blood vessels; in this case abdominal distress will be substituted for chest pain. In still other cases, the flow of blood from the weakened heart into the brain is diminished, with resultant dizziness and faintness rather than chest pain.

Modern treatment of the complications of acute myocardial infarction (which include irregular heartbeat and heart failure) with newer drugs, oxygen, and electrical equipment is saving many lives and enabling the period of bed rest to be shortened. Favorable cases now get up out of bed and into a chair much earlier than before, and cardiac rehabilitation is begun early with good results. Cardiac shock, however, remains a difficult problem with a high mortality rate.

A common episode in individuals with less severe coronary heart disease is *angina pectoris.* This condition results from a temporary inadequacy in the blood supply to the heart. It is characterized by severe but brief radiating pain over the mid-chest and is treated commonly and safely with nitroglycerin.

Diabetes

The most common form of diabetes is *diabetes mellitus,* a chronic inherited disease in which a deficiency of insulin or a disturbance in the action of insulin interferes with the body's ability to metabolize carbohydrates. The elderly diabetic may present few or no clinical symptoms. In fact, complications arising from diabetes may be the first signs of this disease in the elderly. Cataracts, neuritis, heart attacks, and glaucoma, for example, are more frequent in the diabetic. There is a relatively high incidence of diabetes in the aged, with severe complications involving the larger blood vessels.

Most elderly diabetics require only control of their diet. Loss of weight and avoidance of obesity are also helpful. Insulin injections are needed by only a small number. An occasional severe case requires very careful treatment by all available means. The foot care of elderly diabetics should be managed by a podiatrist, since their poor circulation and their lowered resistance to infection make them prone to infection, which may be followed by the dread complication of gangrene.

Diseases of the Ear

The ear consists of the external, the middle, and the inner ears. Problems in any of them can affect hearing. Any condition that prevents sound from reaching the eardrum can cause a hearing loss. Common problems affecting the external ear include impacted ear wax and swelling of the tissues lining the canal caused by inflammation. Problems that frequently affect the middle ear include fluid accumulation and infection within the inner ear cavity. Hearing losses caused by conditions of the external or middle ear are known as *conductive* losses, since they affect the pathway by which sound is conducted to the inner ear.

Conductive hearing losses are frequently treatable by a physician. Hearing problems involving the middle ear in the aged are similar to those occurring earlier in life. The most common cause is infection. In the elderly, however, infection may indicate a more serious disease, such as diabetes. Hearing loss in the middle ear that is not due to infection can often be corrected by surgery. Lesions of the inner ear, if not too extensive, can be helped by the proper use of hearing aids.

Another type of hearing loss results from damage to the inner ear. That is *sensorineural* hearing loss, often called *nerve deafness.* The inner ear houses the nerve structures that receive the sound waves and begin to transmit them to the brain. In most instances, sensorineural losses are irreversible.

Diseases of the Eye

Cataracts are opaque spots that form in the lens of the eye and interfere with the passage of light rays. Often the first indication is a blurring and dimming of vision. If the retina is essentially normal, as it often is, the removal of the clouded lens can lead to restoration of a gratifying amount of vision. Surgical advances have made the removal of cataracts comparatively easy, even for the aged and infirm. Cataract removal can be performed under local anesthesia. Many surgeons now allow patients out of bed the day after the operation. Since the lens is needed for focusing, special glasses are required after it has been removed.

Glaucoma, a major cause of blindness, is characterized by increased pressure in the eyeball because fluid is unable to drain properly. The disease develops slowly and painlessly but can be arrested if detected early enough. Thorough evaluation by an ophthalmologist is needed to determine who will benefit from surgery and who requires appropriate therapy with eyedrops and drugs. Routine determinations of the pressure in the eyes of aged individuals are essential for the detection of glaucoma before symptoms, and at times irreversible damage, develop. Such determinations, as part of annual comprehensive examinations or in large-scale screening drives for glaucoma alone, are of great value.

Macular disease is a degeneration of the area of the retina that permits perception of fine details, such as print. When macular disease results from inflammation, it may respond to cortisone drugs that have anti-inflammatory effects. When it has considerably progressed, older persons with poor sight can be helped with low-vision aids such as magnifying devices.

Hypertension

Hypertension, otherwise known as high blood pressure, over long periods of time can lead to arterial disease and eventually to heart failure, cerebral thrombosis (blood clot) or hemorrhage, or kidney failure. In the elderly, high blood pressure is unlikely to be of recent origin, and much of the damage to the arterial system has already been done. Hypertension in the aged may lead to a stroke, or the rupture of a blood vessel in the brain. Most strokes in elderly persons, however, are caused by thrombosis, or blockage by a blood clot in the cerebral vessel, already narrowed by hardening of the arteries or extreme diminution of the blood supply through such a narrowed vessel.

Hypertension in the aged should be treated by restricting salt in the diet and by drugs. Only the milder drugs should be used in the aged, since the more powerful ones can cause sudden, severe falls in blood pressure, which in themselves can cause strokes or heart attacks.

Lung Diseases

Chronic, obstructive lung disease affects the passages that carry air to the lung areas where oxygen from inhaled air is exchanged for carbon dioxide from the blood—a process essential for life. Chronic bronchitis and emphysema are two important lung diseases affecting the elderly. The aged are also unusually susceptible to pneumonia, particularly those who are bedbound, inactive, or afflicted with a difficulty in swallowing that results in the aspiration of liquids or food into the lungs.

Neuritis

Neuritis is a disease of the peripheral and cranial nerves characterized by inflammation and degeneration of the nerve fibers. It can lead to loss of conduction of nerve impulses and consequently to varying degrees of paralysis, loss of feeling, and loss of reflexes. Although the term *neuritis* implies inflammation, this is not invariably present. Neuritis may affect a single nerve or involve several nerve trunks.

Diagnostic work-up by a neurologist is indicated. Treatment with cortisone products and vitamins may be helpful, as well as treatment of specific causes, such as diabetes, pernicious anemia, or alcoholism.

2. SYMPTOMS AND COMPLAINTS

The following are some of the more common symptoms and complaints of the elderly. Wrongly regarded by many older patients as being the natural consequences of aging and therefore not worth mentioning to a busy doctor, these symptoms—and indeed, all others—should be reported to a physician by the older person or his family.

Breathlessness

Breathlessness, known as *dyspnea,* is common in the aged and may reflect heart failure, disease of the lungs, anemia, or weakness. It is exaggerated in the presence of obesity.

Difficulty in Swallowing

Dysphagia, or difficulty in swallowing, is a common complaint of elderly persons which cannot be ignored. Its onset in old age calls for examination to rule out a malignancy of the esophagus. Dysphagia may indicate the need for a change in diet to soft, minced, or liquid foods. Bedridden or wheelchair-bound aged persons with marked dysphagia should be fed only by properly trained personnel, to avoid possible aspiration of food into the lungs, which may cause a secondary severe pneumonia or even death by suffocation.

Fainting

Fainting, or *syncope,* may result from a variety of neurological and surgical causes in the aged, as well as from anemia. A careful neurological work-up is indicated.

Transitory disturbances of the circulation to the brain may be overlooked unless special testing is done. Major injury may result from falls accompanying fainting spells in the aged.

Fatigue

Fatigue is sometimes a symptom of boredom. If it is coupled with marked inactivity and negativism, it may strongly suggest depression. However, fatigue may also be a symptom of organic disease. It is a particularly prominent symptom of heart disease, anemia, and malnutrition. Persistent fatigue should therefore be checked into by a physician.

Giddiness or Dizziness

Dizziness, or *vertigo,* may occur even in old people who are well, but there are innumerable possible causes, and this condition should always be looked into. Even when it is not a symptom of illness, vertigo is a common cause of falls, with consequent injuries such as the too-frequent, disabling fracture of the hip.

Headaches

Headaches seem to be less common in later life, and it follows that when severe headaches do occur in an older person, they are not to be ignored. They may be due to muscle strain resulting from poor posture, or to infection of the sinuses. More severe headaches may be caused by lesions within the skull or by inflammation of the walls of blood vessels in the head.

Impaired Hearing

Impaired hearing is not inevitable in old age, although some degree of hearing loss is common, especially for high-pitched sounds. Every effort should be made to determine the cause of hearing loss in the aged. Careful examination by an ear specialist should be followed, if necessary, by audiometry and the painstaking process of being fitted for a hearing aid. Loss of hearing may lead to physical danger —for instance, from an unnoticed approaching car. Hearing loss may also lead to isolation and even to paranoid behavior, as those who are not able to understand others will feel cut off from them and may even mistake what they are saying as being of a hostile nature.

Inability to Sleep

The inability to sleep, or *insomnia,* may be a consequence of various discomforts, or else it may be evidence of a psychiatric upset. Persons suffering from anxiety often experience some difficulty in falling asleep, and those who are depressed tend to wake early and toss and turn. Both anxiety and depression are common in the elderly. Some older people are convinced that they must, above all things, have a great deal of extra repose. Others, because of loneliness or boredom, tend to go to bed early at night after having slept during the afternoon as well, and cannot understand why they wake early and cannot get back to sleep. They do not appreciate the lessened need for sleep that accompanies aging.

Lack of Appetite

While there are wide variations in older persons' eating habits, just as in those of the young, a sudden change in appetite should be considered a symptom to be reported. Lack of appetite, or *anorexia,* is a symptom of physical or mental difficulty. A thorough medical work-up is needed, followed by a psychiatric evaluation.

Loss of Vision

Aside from the condition of *presbyopia*—loss of elasticity in the lens, or farsightedness—poor vision is not so inevitable as many old people expect. It may be a symptom of a number of underlying conditions which, if treated properly and promptly, are amenable to medical intervention. Therefore, any impairment of vision in an older person warrants examination by an ophthalmologist.

Seizures

Seizures, or convulsions, may involve the entire body, or only a part. Whatever the extent, there are involuntary twitchings of the muscles and usually unconsciousness. They may have their onset in old age. Since they may be a symptom of some underlying disease or abnormal condition, they call for a careful examination by a neurologist. Seizures are often successfully treated with appropriate medication.

Appendix F

SUGGESTED READINGS

COMPREHENSIVE REFERENCE WORKS

Binstock, R. H., and Shanas, Ethel, eds. *Handbook of Aging and the Social Sciences.* New York: Van Nostrand Reinhold, 1976 (in press).

Birren, James, and Schaie, K. W., eds. *Handbook of Aging and the Individual.* New York: Van Nostrand Reinhold, 1976 (in press).

Butler, Robert, M.D. *Why Survive? Being Old in America.* New York: Harper & Row, 1975.

Palmore, Erdman, ed. *Normal Aging: Reports from the Duke Longitudinal Study, 1955–1969.* Durham, N.C.: Duke University Press, 1970.

Riley, Matilda White, *et al.* eds. *Aging and Society,* Vol. 1, *An Inventory of Research Findings;* Vol. 2, *Aging and the Professions;* Vol. 3: *A Sociology of Age Stratification.* Washington, D.C.: Russell Sage Foundation (distributed through Basic Books), 1968–1969.

Rossman, Isidore, Ph.D., M.D. *Clinical Geriatrics.* Philadelphia: J. B. Lippincott Co., 1971.

Shanas, Ethel, and Streib, Gordon, eds. *Social Structures and the Family: Generational Relations.* Englewood Cliffs, N.J.: Prentice-Hall, 1965.

Tibbitts, Clark, ed. *Handbook of Social Gerontology: Societal Aspects of Aging.* Chicago: University of Chicago Press, 1960.

Woodruff, Diana, and Birren, James, eds. *Aging: Scientific Perspectives and Social Issues.* New York: Van Nostrand Reinhold, 1975.

REFERENCES TO SELECTED PROBLEMS

Brody, Elaine M. "The Etiquette of Filial Behavior." *Aging and Human Development* 1 (1970).

Butler, Robert, M.D., and Lewis, Myrna. *Aging and Mental Health: Positive Psychosocial Approaches.* St. Louis, Mo.: C. V. Mosby Co., 1973.

————. *Sex over 60.* New York: Harper & Row, 1976.

Kübler-Ross, Elizabeth. *On Death and Dying.* New York: Macmillan Co., 1969.

————. *Questions and Answers on Death and Dying.* New York: Macmillan Co., 1974.

Litwak, Eugene, and Szelenyi, Ivan. "Primary Group Structures and Their Functions: Kin, Neighbors, and Friends." *American Sociological Review* 34, no. 4 (August 1969): 465–81.

Lopata, Helen. *Widowhood in An American City.* Cambridge, Mass.: Schenkman Publishing Co., 1972.

Mathiason, Geneva, ed. *Criteria for Retirement.* New York: G. P. Putnam's Sons, 1953.

Neugarten, Bernice L., and Weinstein, Karol K. "The Changing American Grandparent." *Journal of Marriage and the Family* 12, no. 2 (May 1964): 199–204.

Rodstein, Manuel, M.D. "The Aging Process and Disease." *Nursing Outlook,* 12 (November 1964): 43–46.

Simos, Bertha G. "Adult Children and Their Aging Parents." *Social Work* 18, no. 3 (May 1973): 78–85.

Sussman, Marvin B., and Burchinal, L. G. "Kin Family Network: Unheralded Structure in Current Conceptualizations of Family Functioning." *Marriage and Family Living* 24 (August 1962): 231–40.

Weissman, Adrian D., and Kastenbaum, Robert. *The Psychological Autopsy: A Study of the Terminal Phase of Life,* Community Mental Health Journal Monograph no. 4. New York: Behavioral Publications, 1968.

SOURCES ON SERVICES TO THE ELDERLY AND THEIR FAMILIES

American Cancer Society's Statewide Conference on "Home Care of the Cancer Patient." *Proceedings.* Syracuse, N.Y., May 10, 1973.

American Red Cross. *Home Nursing Textbook.* New York: Doubleday & Co., 1963.

Blenkner, Margaret; Bloom, M.; Wasser, Edna; and Neilson, Margaret. "Protective Services for Old People: Findings from the Benjamin Rose Institute Study." *Social Casework,* (1971): 483–522.

Freed, Anna O. "The Family Agency and the Kinship System of the Elderly." *Social Casework* 56 (December 1975): 579–86.

Galton, Lawrence. *Don't Give Up on an Aging Parent.* New York: Crown Publishers, 1975.

Himber, Louis L. *Dollars and Sense After 60.* Federation of Protestant Welfare Agencies, Inc., 281 Park Avenue South, New York, N.Y. 10010.

House Ways and Means Committee. Testimony of the National Council on Homemaker—Home Health Aid Services. Washington, D.C.: Government Printing Office, 1975.

Kamerman, Sheila B., and Kahn, Alfred J. *Social Services in the United States: Policies and Programs.* Philadelphia: Temple University Press, 1976.

Kastenbaum, Robert, and Kandy, Sandra E. "The 4% Fallacy: A Methodological and Empirical Critique in Extended Care Facility Population Statistics." *International Journal of Aging and Human Development* 4 (1973): 15–21.

Kinoy, Susan K. "Home Health Services for the Elderly." *Nursing Outlook* 17 (September 1969): 59–62.

Percy, Charles H. *Growing Old in the Country of the Young—with a Practical Resource Guide for the Aged and Their Families.* New York: McGraw-Hill Book Co., 1974.

Shinn, Eugene B., and Robinson, Nancy Day. "Trends in Homemaker–Home Health Aid Services." *Abstracts for Social Workers* 10, no. 3 (fall 1974).

Stohl, Dora J. "Preserving Home Life for the Disabled." *American Journal of Nursing* 72, no. 9 (September 1972): 1645–50.

U.S. Senate Special Committee on Aging. *Home Health Services in the United States,* by Brahna Trager, Home Health Consultant. Washington, D.C.: Government Printing Office, 1972.

————. Testimony of National Council for Homemaker–Home Health Aide Services, Inc., to the Senate, October 1975.

The White House Conference on Aging, 1971. *Toward a National Policy on Aging.* Final report. Vols. 1 and 2, 1973.

HELPFUL BOOKLETS

American Cancer Society. *Guidelines for Development of a Community Home Care Program,* by Gerard Diesfeld, M.D.

> Available from American Cancer Society, New York State Division, 6725 Lyons Street, P.O. Box 7, East Syracuse, N.Y. 13057.

Citizens for Better Care. *How to Choose a Nursing Home: A Shopping and Rating Guide.*

> Available from Citizens for Better Care, 960 East Jefferson Avenue, Detroit, Mich. 48207.

League of Women Voters in New York State. *The Citizen Lobbyist: A Guide to Action in Albany.*

> Available from League of Women Voters, 817 Broadway, New York, N.Y. 10003.

National Council on Aging.

Age, Physical Ability, and Work Potential, by Leon F. Coyle, M.D., and Pamella Marsters Hanson.

Furniture Requirements for Older People. Order number 6303.

Housing and Living Arrangements for Older People. Order number 7214.

Retirement Income. Order number 7217.

> Available from the National Council on Aging, 1828 L Street, Northwest, Washington, D.C. 20036.

Information Canada. *Senior Citizens.* Order number IC24-3/1.

> Available from Information Canada Mail Order Service, 171 Slater Street, Ottawa, Ont. K1A OS9.

U.S. Department of Agriculture Home and Garden Bulletins.

Your Money's Worth in Foods.

A Guide to Budgeting for the Retired Couple.

> Available from U.S. Government Printing Office, Superintendent of Documents, Washington, D.C. 20402.

U.S. Department of Health, Education, and Welfare, Office of Human Development Administration on Aging. *Publications of the Administration on Aging.*

This booklet lists 43 publications concerning, but not limited to, retirement planning, consumer guides, employment opportunities, information and referral services, home-delivered meals, transportation, and legal matters. One publication—*To Find the Way to Services in Your Community*—is printed in Spanish.

This booklet also lists pamphlets in the series "Designs for Action for Older Americans," including:

A Centralized Comprehensive Program. A project report on a comprehensive senior-center-based program in Nashville, Tenn. Order number DHEW (SRS) 72-20906.

Countrywide Information and Referral. A project report on services of the Council of Social Agencies in Westchester, N.Y. Order number DHEW (SRS) 72-20907.

Employment Referral. A project report on how older citizens in Norwalk, Conn., created an organization to help other elderly people get jobs. Order number DHEW (SRS) 72-20904.

Group Volunteer Service. A report on SERVE, a project using older volunteers in Staten Island, N.Y. Order Number DHEW (SRS) 72-20905.

Interfaith Opportunity Center of Hartford, Conn. A report on a center established by eight churches in Hartford, which multiplied resources far beyond efforts of individual churches. Order number DHEW (SRS) 72-20903.

Psychiatric Care. A report on the Cambridge, Mass., program to meet special needs of older people with mental health problems. Order number DHEW (SRS) 72-20901.

Statewide Community Organization. Tells how a North Dakota statewide community organization has initiated activity programs through clubs and centers in 73 communities in the state. Order number DHEW (SRS) 72-20908.

What Churches Can Do. A report on the Satellite Housing Program of Churches in Oakland, California. Order number DHEW (SRS) 72-20900.

Available from U.S. Government Printing Office, Superintendent of Documents, Washington, D.C. 20402, or from the Administration on Aging, 330 Independence Avenue Southwest, Washington, D.C. 20201.

U.S. Department of Health, Education, and Welfare, Social Security Administration.

Your Medicare Handbook.

Your Social Security.

Applying for a Social Security Number.

Medicaid-Medicare—Which Is Which?

How Medicare Helps During a Hospital Stay.

Medicare Coverage in a Skilled Nursing Facility.

Estimating Your Social Security Retirement Check.

Increase in the Social Security Earnings Base.

Higher Social Security Payments.

If You Work After You Retire.

Introducing Supplemental Security Income.

Supplemental Security Income for the Aged, Blind, and Disabled.

Important Information About Your Supplemental Security Income Payments.

Questioning the Decision on Supplemental Security Income Claims.

> Available from U.S. Government Printing Office, Superintendent of Documents, Washington, D.C. 20402, or from your local Social Security Office.

U.S. Senate Special Committee on Aging. *Protecting Older Americans Against Overpayment of Income Taxes.*

> Available from U.S. Government Printing Office, Superintendent of Documents, Washington, D.C. 20402.

OTHER READINGS

De Beauvoir, Simone. *The Coming of Age.* New York: Warner Paperback Library, 1970.

———. *A Very Easy Death?* New York: Warner Paperback Library, 1973.

Harris, Louis, and associates. *The Myth and Reality of Aging in America.* Washington, D.C.: National Council on the Aging, 1975.

Simmons, Leo. *The Role of the Aged in Primitive Society.* New Haven, Conn.: Yale University Press, 1945.

INDEX

accidents, 74, 169, 170. *See also* safety measures
ACTION, 304–5
Adams, John, 130
adolescence, 37–8, 66, 141, 143
adult children, 4, 8–10, 11, 36–7; absent, 51, 196–7, 220; anxieties of, 3–4, 11, 148–9; burdens on, 28–9, 237–8; as caretakers, 45–52, 53, 237; contact with parents, 8–9; emotionally based behavior of, 33–8; evaluating importance of, 185–6; feelings of, 15–28, 104; female, 45–6; financial contributions of, 166–7; games of, 167–8; guilt feelings of, 29–33, 143, 144, 185–6, 219–20, 222; living with parents, 152–4; loyalty conflicts of, 40, 41, 42–3, 54–8; needs of, 240, 241; parental death and, 52–3, 109–11, 121–3; parental demands on, 144–5; parental remarriage and, 113–14; parental sexuality and, 119–20; as parents' financial managers, 197–8; planning role of, 145–7, 168; political and social action of, 239–40; reactions to aging, 24–9; rejection of help of, 199–200; response to parental lifestyle, 115, 140–1. *See also* families; feelings; sibling relationships
ageism, 65
aging. *See* aging parents; aging process; elderly people; old age
aging parents: ability to function, 174; assessment of, 171–8; contact with children, 8–9; death of, 52–3, 109–11, 121–3; factors in helping, 101, 137–8; family roles of, 42; feelings toward, 15–39; financial assessment of, 175–6;

financial contributions to, 54, 83, 166–7; as grandparents, 56–8; honest communication with, 10, 61, 123–8, 148–51, 230–1; independent and capable, 139–41; lifestyles of, 115, 140–1; living with, 152–4; normal emotions of, 87–8; as pawns in sibling battles, 50–1; physical assessment of, 172–3; professional assessment of, 175, 176–8; pseudo-helpless, 141–5; psychological assessment of, 173–4; unreasonable demands of, 143–5. *See also* aging process; care of the elderly; elderly people; families; old age
aging process, 64–96; adaptive behavior patterns, 85–92; dependency scale, 138–9; emotional responses to, 24–8; ignorance about, 142; increased interest in, 7–8; individual variations, 6–7, 69, 71, 74–5; misconceptions about, 65–7; nutrition and, 148, 175; physical, 69–75; physical compensations for, 72–3, 81; psychological effects, 85–96; research on, 71, 73; sex and, 115–20; treatable problems, 73–4. *See also* deterioration; old age
Alabama, 159, 208
alcohol and alcoholism, 86, 148
Alice's Adventures in Wonderland (Carroll), 139–40
American Association of Homes for the Aging, 207
American Association of Retired Persons (AARP), 8, 150, 164, 243, 304
American Cancer Society, 187
American Red Cross, 181

American society, 5–8; emphasis on youth, 68, 84; failure of, 32, 176, 237–40; financial support for the elderly in, 155–67; health-care reform, 242–3; housing for the elderly, 196, 240–1; increase in elderly population, 7; old age in, 7–8, 27, 32–3, 60, 65–6, 78–82, 84–5, 219; parent-child living arrangements in, 152; sexual attitudes, 23; substandard nursing homes in, 204–5
Anderson, Robert, 39
anger, 21–2, 35, 114, 222; extreme, 92–3, 94; at loss, 88, 100; at parents, 17, 24–5, 26, 29, 37, 45, 144
anxiety, 86, 88, 92, 144, 173, 187; and cardiovascular difficulties, 95. See also fear
appetite, 93, 320–1
Arizona, 159
Arkansas, 159
arteriosclerosis, 73, 215, 315
arthritis, 7, 67, 72, 74, 75, 76, 119, 150, 170, 180, 315–16
Association of Retired Federal Employees, 243
avoidance of change, 77–8, 79, 90–1, 199–200

baby boom, 246
behavior patterns, 18–19, 88–92; adult children's, 33–8; attempts to modify, 141; demanding, 232; denial, 89–90; guilt-invoking, 143; living in the past, 88–9; mistrustful, 90; overdoing it, 92; preparatory mourning, 89; pseudo-helpless, 141–3; ritualistic, 92; stubbornness and avoidance of change, 90–1; worship of independence, 91. See also mental disorders
blind, the, 72, 158, 170, 180; American treatment of, 84; community services for, 194–5; directory of agencies serving, 311. See also eyes and vision
blood pressure, 72, 148
bones, 70; diseases of, 70, 71, 316
brain, aging process and, 69, 70, 72, 215
brain syndromes: organic, 86, 93, 94–5; research on, 95; reversible, 72, 95, 172; symptoms, 72, 86
breathlessness (dyspnea), 319
British Medical Journal, 130
bronchitis, 316, 319
Brooks, Mel, 34
Butler, Robert, 46–7, 132, 172

California, 160, 218
cancer, 72, 74, 129, 148, 170, 316
Cardozo, Benjamin, 80
care of the elderly: at home, 164, 181–4, 187–92; communication about, 184–5; custodial, 163; emergency, 165, 186; long-term intensive, 180–2, 209; out of home, 192–5; protective/supportive, 179–80; refusal of, 199–200; temporary and occasional, 178–9. See also community services
caretaker, 45–52, 181, 184; communicating with, 62; daughter as, 45–6; faultfinding with, 35; grandchild as, 57; as martyr, 49–50; motives of, 48, 49; outside help for, 187; parents' choice of, 46–8; pseudo, 48–9; sibling relationships of, 47–8, 49–53; volunteer, 48–9. See also homemaker–home health aide services; nursing homes
Carroll, Lewis, 139–40
cataracts, 73, 317, 318
Catholic Charities: directory of diocesan agencies, 311
childhood, 27, 66, 104; attitudes toward, 27; emotional education in, 18–19; unhappy, 93; role establishment, 36–37, 43–5
children: fears, 20; sexual feelings, 22–3, 26
children of the elderly. See adult children
chronic illness, 66; insurance for, 240–1; medical expenses, 162, 164; nursing care, 188, 189; treatment, 73–4
Chukchees, 131
Churchill, Jennie, 113
Churchill, Winston, 113
clergymen, 76, 101, 187, 207, 212
clinic services, 165, 194
communes, 115
communication, 10, 61, 184–5; about aging process, 148–50; of bad news, 230–1; about death, 123–8; on nursing home placement, 220–2; outside help with, 175; on physical incapacity, 148–51; sibling, 61–3
Community Council of Greater New York: Directory of Social and Health Agencies of New York City, 254–64
community services for the elderly, 10, 171, 200–1; action for, 243–5; arranging, from a distance, 196–7; day care, 194–5; employment agencies, 166; escort, 191; food, 163, 190, 193, 244; homemaker–home health aide, 188–90; household management, 188–90, 191; ideal, 186; information and referral, 187, 207; legal, 195, 312; locating, 186–7; medical directories, 173; for mentally impaired, 199; overall assessment, 176–8; protective, 199; psychiatric, 173–4; senior centers, 193; sitters, 192; standards and quality of, 188, 189–90; telephone reassurance programs, 190–1; transportation, 191, 193–4; visiting nurses, 188; visitors, 192. See also care of the elderly
Congress of Senior Citizens, 8, 84, 150
Connecticut, 190
Consumer Reports, 164

convulsions, 321
Cousins, Norman, 133
crime, 78, 170, 191
crises, 169–70; family response to, 41–3,
    60–1, 178–9; warning signals, 170

day care, 194–5
deaf, the, 84, 94. *See also* ears and hearing
death and dying, 10, 39, 66, 92, 121–34;
    attitude of elderly, 125–6, 128, 132–3;
    of close family members, 77; communi-
    cating about, 123–30; emotional stages
    of, 127; environment for, 126–7, 133–4;
    family's feelings on, 26, 121–2, 128;
    favorite parent's, 110; fear of, 88, 125,
    128; postponement of, 130; preparation
    for, 88–9, 94; professionals' attitude to,
    126; right-to-die controversy, 130–3; of
    spouse, 93, 103, 170; study of, 127. *See
    also* euthanasia; mourning; widowhood
death dip, 130
death wish, 31
deathbed promises, 149–50
De Beauvoir, Simone, 121
denial: of parents' aging, 35–6; of physical
    symptoms, 59, 141, 149; as reaction to
    aging, 89–90
Denmark, 84
dentists and dental care, 163, 164, 165,
    186, 214
dependency, 82–5, 114, 170; financial, 83;
    in institutions, 83; in marriage, 107;
    premature, 144–5; response to, 90; scale
    of, 138–9; widowhood and, 111–13
depression, 86, 88, 92, 100, 173, 187, 222;
    as mental disorder, 93
"Designs for Action for Older Americans,"
    244
deterioration, 69–73, 94–5, 100, 120, 149;
    denial of, 36; discussion about, 149–50;
    emotional aspects, 60, 173; family
    response to, 61; mental, 180. *See also*
    aging process; old age
diabetes, 74, 148, 170, 317
Dial-a-Bus, 194
Dial-a-Car, 194
dieticians, 213, 215
diets, 148, 175, 182; religious, 218. *See also*
    nutrition
disability and the disabled, 83, 153, 158,
    169–201; assessing, 171–8; care, 178–97;
    chronic, 179; kinds and causes, 169–70;
    planning for, 149; special housing for,
    195–6; recuperation factors, 170, 171. *See
    also* care of the elderly; dependency
disease and illness, 73, 148, 149, 170;
    chronic, 66, 73–4, 162, 164, 188, 189,
    240–1; common, 315–21; crisis stage,
    170; diagnosis of, 172; emotional impact
    of, 173; lowered resistance to, 71;
    premature, 100

divorce, 105, 153; financial reasons for, 208
doctors. *See* physicians
Donahue, Thomas R., 158
drugs, 72, 148, 163, 164, 165, 182
Durant, Ariel, 97
Durant, Will, 97

ears and hearing, 70, 71, 73, 74, 94;
    diseases and impairment of, 150, 317–18,
    320
elderly people: adaptive capacity, 74–5, 79,
    138–9, 141; behavior patterns, 58–60,
    88–94; death attitudes, 125–6, 128,
    132–3; financial problems and resources,
    79–82, 83, 85, 154–67; health statistics
    on, 65–6, 74; individuality of, 138–9,
    242; information needs, 148; leading
    causes of disability in, 74; legal rights
    of, 200; as percent of population, 7;
    political clout of, 8, 83–4, 243, 246;
    resistance to change, 77–8, 79, 90–1,
    199–200; role changes, 26, 78–9, 100;
    self-image of, 66, 245–6; sexual
    misconceptions of, 118–19; social
    isolation of, 75–8, 85, 151; suicide rate,
    93; telling the truth to, 123–30, 230–1;
    voting patterns, 8; works and volunteer
    opportunities for, 304–5. *See also* aging
    parents; aging process; old age
emergency care, 165, 186
emotions. *See* feelings
emphysema, 316, 319
Employee Retirement Income Security Act
    of 1974, 158
employment for the elderly, 304–5; second
    careers, 8, 166
Empty Nest Syndrome, 98
escort services, 191, 244
Eskimos, 79; euthanasia, 131
estates. *See* inheritance
Europe, 84, 196
euthanasia, 130–3; "active" and "passive,"
    132
Euthanasia Educational Council, 132
extramarital housekeeping, 157
eyeglasses, 148, 163, 165
eyes and vision, 7, 69–70, 71, 73, 74, 88,
    150, 164, 214, 321; diseases of, 73, 170,
    317, 318. *See also* blind, the

fainting (syncope), 319–20
families, 8–9, 40–63, 177; adult children's,
    40, 41, 42–3, 54–8, 220; aging parent's
    role, 42; caretaker role, 45–52, 53, 180;
    crisis and, 41–3, 60–1, 178–9; effect of
    conflict in, 60–1; extended, 32; favorite
    child's, 44–5, 48, 55–6; grandparent-
    grandchild relationship, 56–8; home
    nursing by, 181–4; improving
    communication in, 61–3, 175, 220–2;
    in-laws, 42–3, 55–6; loss of unity in,
    52–5; money quarrels, 53–5, 154–5; in

mourning and widowhood, 109–13; nuclear, 8–9, 32; of nursing-home residents, 219–22, 225, 226, 227–9, 230–1, 232–3; parental manipulation of, 58–62; role changes, 26, 43–4, 78–9; role-playing, 36–7; sibling relationships, 41, 42, 43–5, 50–1, 52–4, 220–1; social action of, 239–40, 243–5; two- and three-generation, 153–4. *See also* adult children; aging parents; sibling relationships

family service agencies, 174, 187; listed by state, 271–303

Family Service Association of America, 187; directory of member agencies, 271–303, 313

fatigue, 93, 320

favorite child, 44–5, 48, 55–6; spouse of, 55–6

fear, 26, 191; adult child's, 20–1, 26, 144; of death, 88, 125, 128; due to ignorance, 142; of loss, 34–5; of parents, 20–1; role-playing and, 36–7; of travel, 91. *See also* anxiety

federal programs, for the aging, 7–8, 10, 158, 161, 190, 193, 196, 238, 304; elderly people's view of, 32. *See also* United States government

Federal Retirement System, 158

feelings, 10, 15–39, 104; changes in, 19, 24; adult child's, for parent, 15–24, 104, 144; behavior based on, 15–16, 33–8; childhood formation of, 17–19, 20–1, 22–3; contradictory, 16–18, 24–5; death wish, 31; guilt, 29–33, 34, 35, 48, 93, 143, 144, 185, 219; importance of acknowledging, 15–16, 38–9; interrelatedness of, 29–30; lack of, 19–20; negative, 21–4; normal elderly, 87–92; about old age, 26–8; prolonged adolescent, 37–8; psychoanalytic view, 17; in response to aging process, 24–8; results of unresolved, 33–8. *See also* families; names of feelings

financial hardship, 79–82, 83, 85; of widows, 106

financial management: legal steps for, 197–8

financial resources of the elderly, 101–2, 153, 154–67; children's contributions, 166–7; effect of remarriage on, 115; indirect noncash supplements, 160–1; medical insurance, 161–6; pensions, 81, 102, 157–8, 208; planning ahead, 167–8; recovery process and, 176; Social Security, 155–7; statistics on, 80, 155; Supplemental Security Income (SSI), 158–60

Florida, 159, 163

food services, 163, 190, 193, 244

food stamps, 161

foot care, 163, 214, 317

Foster Grandparent Program, 305

Freud, Sigmund, 22, 111, 123

Frost, Robert, 69

gangrene, 317

Georgia, 159, 196

geriatric medicine, 71, 72, 84, 172–3, 214. *See also* disease and illness; physicians

glaucoma, 170, 317, 318

gout, 316

government. *See* federal programs for the elderly; United States government

Gramp (Jury), 184

grandparents, 56–8

Gray Panthers, 8, 84, 150, 243

Greater New York Fund, 245

Green Thumb, 304

guilt feelings, 29–33, 34, 35, 48, 93, 143, 144, 185, 219; personal, 30–1; shared communal, 31–3

handicapped, the. *See* blind, the; deaf, the; disability and the disabled

Harris, Louis, 5, 85

Harris Poll, 5

headaches, 320

health, 101–2; assessing, 171–4, 176–8; statistics on, 65–6, 74

health aides, 183

health care: inadequacy of, 242–3; planning, 147–50. *See also* medical care for the elderly

health education, 148

Health and Happiness of Your Old Dog, The (Whitney), 7

health insurance plans, 81, 163–4, 189; directory of, 313; inadequacy of, 240–1. *See also* Medicare and Medicaid

Health Research Group, 173

hearing. *See* ears and hearing

hearing aids, 73, 148

heart attacks, 72, 88, 148, 180, 317

heart conditions, 119, 179–80; aging process and, 70; angina pectoris, 317; congestive heart failure, 72, 316; coronary heart disease, 74, 317

Heller, Joseph, 35–6

high blood pressure, 72, 148

home health care, 164, 245

home nursing, 181–4; of the mentally impaired, 182–3; rewards of, 183, 184; things to consider, 183–4. *See also* care of the elderly

homemaker–home health aide services, 188–90; checklist for, 310; directory of, 265, 311; listing by state, 265–71

homosexuality, 115

honesty, 221–2

hospitals, 133, 146, 174, 186, 194; assessment services of, 176–7; day care, 194–5; death in, 126–7; diets in, 148; emergency services, 165; homemaker–

home health aide services, 189; intensive care procedures, 127; medical-school affiliations, 173; Medicare review boards, 163; nursing home arrangements with, 214

household management, 188; outside help, 35, 188–90, 191

housing for the elderly, 85; federal programs, 196; inadequacy of, 241–2; planning for, 151–2; special-care, 195–6; statistics on, 196, 241

hypertension, 315, 318–19

hypertensive vascular disease, 74

hypochondriasis, 86, 93–4

I Knock at the Door (O'Casey), 123

I Never Sang for My Father (Anderson), 39

illness. *See* disease and illness

impotence, 116, 119

incest taboo, 23

income. *See* financial resources of the elderly

incompetency proceedings, 198–9

incontinence, 95

independence, 67; loss of, 79–82; worship of, 91. *See also* dependency

Indiana, 159, 190

indifference, 19–20

infirmities: denial of, 59; exaggeration of, 59–60

inflation, 80–1, 155

information and referral services, 187, 207; directory of, 311; list of, 254–64; nursing home, 207

inheritance, 49, 155; sibling quarrels about, 53–5; and second marriages, 113

in-laws of aging parents, 55–6

insomnia, 93, 320

institutionalization, 10–11, 83, 181, 202–36; advance planning for, 205–6, 210; consulting parents on, 205–6; deciding on, 203–4; family's reaction to, 219–21; financial considerations, 207–9; parent's reaction to, 220. *See also* nursing homes; nursing home residents

insurance. *See* health insurance

intensive care facilities, 209

intermediate care facilities, 32, 209, 210, 211

International Ladies Garment Workers Union, 192

intervivos trust, 197, 198

Iowa, 159

Iroquois, 80, 184

isolation, 75–8, 85, 151, 187, 193

Israel, 196

Japan: old age in, 33

Jefferson, Thomas, 130

Jewish federations, funds, and councils: directory of, 311

Jews, 130, 218

Job (biblical), 80

Johnson, Virginia E., 117

joint tenancy, 197, 198

Jury, Dan, 184

Jury, Mark, 184

Kansas, 160

Kennedy, John Fitzgerald, 69

Kentucky, 159

Kinsey, Alfred, 117

Kipling, Rudyard, 109

Kübler-Ross, Elisabeth, 127, 128, 129, 133

legal services, 132, 195; directory of, 312; for financial management, 197–8; incompentency proceedings, 198–9

legislation to benefit the elderly, 7–8, 243–5; Older Americans Act, 8, 161, 166–7, 191, 238, 248–53; pension reform, 158; Social Security Act, 80, 81. *See also* federal programs for the elderly

life expectancy, 106; increases in, 7; of older people, 167

life-sustaining procedures, 131

living will, 132

Loneliness, 108, 151, 187

Loneliness (Moustakas), 122

Lopata, Helen, 108

loss, 67–96; reaction to, 74–5, 79, 85–96. *See also* deterioration; old age

Louisiana, 159

lung capacity, 70–1

lung diseases, 74, 319

Lutheran Health and Welfare Directory, 313

macular disease, 318

Maine, 159

major medical protection, 164

malnutrition, 72, 175, 190

marriage counselors, 101

marriage and marital relationships, 10, 41, 42–3, 55–6, 97–106; caretaker's, 46; discord in, 103–5; durable, 97–8; divorce, 105, 153, 208; favorite child's, 55–6; finances and, 101–2, 157; group, 115; in middle age, 98, 104; old age adjustments in, 97–106; second, 98, 113–15, 118, 120; statistics on, 97–98

Maryland, 159

Masters, William H., 117

masturbation, 117

maturity, 37, 66

meals and meal services, 163, 190, 193, 244

Medicaid. *See* Medicare and Medicaid

medical care for the elderly: geriatric, 71, 72, 84, 85, 172–3, 214; locating, 172–3; psychiatric, 173–4. *See also* health care; nursing homes; physicians

medical expenses, 81, 102, 161–6; average yearly, 162; for chronic illness, 162, 164, 240–1; health maintenance organizations,

164; Medicare and Medicaid coverage, 162–3, 165–6; private insurance programs, 163–4
Medicare and Medicaid, 81, 162–3, 164, 165–6, 173, 187, 188, 189, 234, 238, 245; applying for, 162; compared, 165–6; coverage provided by, 162–3, 165; day-care funding, 194; form filing, 163; nursing home coverage, 207, 208, 209
Medicare providers and suppliers of services, directory of, 163, 312
medication, 148, 182. See also drugs
memory loss, 72, 86, 170, 182
men: remarriage of, 113; sexual failure of, 119
menopause, 98, 116, 118
mental disorders, 68, 72, 85–96, 165, 170, 182–4, 188; depression, 93; effect on family, 85–6; frequency, 86; home care for, 182–3; hypochondriasis, 93–4; illness and disability related to, 173–4; incompetency, 198–9; nursing home care for, 215; physiologically based, 86; psychosis, 94. See also brain and brain syndromes
Mental Health Directory, 313
Metropolitan Life Insurance Company, 146
middle age, 66, 68; marriage relations in, 98, 104; physical ailments, 74
middle generation. See adult children
Miller, Arthur, 53
ministers. See clergymen
Mississippi, 159
Missouri, 159
mistrustful behavior, 90
money, 82; as control, 60; family dissension over, 53–54. See also financial resources, of the elderly
Montana, 159
More, Thomas, 131
mourning, 87, 92, 93, 123; emotional and physical reactions, 106–7; generational differences, 109–11; preparatory, 89; prolonged, 109; stages of, 111
Moustakas, Clark E., 122
moving, 151–2
Myth and Reality of Aging in America, The (Harris), 66, 85

national associations with programs in the field of aging, 313
National Council on Aging, 5, 193, 304
National Council of Homemaker–Home Health Aide Services, Inc., 189, 265
National Council of Senior Citizens, 243, 304
National Directory of Housing for Older People, 313
National Institute of Aging, 238
National League for Nursing, 265
National Retired Teachers Association, 304
needs of the elderly: basic, 32; criteria for,

137–8; health care, 242–3; meeting, 237–47; sexual, 23, 115; transportation, 84. See also care of the elderly
neighborhoods, 77–8, 79, 151
neighbors, 76, 140, 179
Nebraska, 196
Neugarten, Bernice, 56
neuritis, 74, 317, 319
neurosis, 30, 86
New Deal, 80
New Mexico, 159
New York City, 245
New York State: conservatorship law, 198; nursing home costs, 208
New York Times, 78, 97, 119
non-profit homes for the aging, directory of, 312
North Carolina, 159
North Dakota, 159
nostalgia, 88–9
nuclear family, 8–9, 32
nurses and nursing service, 76, 133, 165, 189, 207, 243; practical, 188, 214; registered, 174, 188, 213, 214; visiting, 176, 183, 188, 189
nursing homes, 32, 35, 61, 103, 105, 149, 171, 176, 186, 194, 202–36; application to, 222; checklists for, 306–10; complaints, 233–4, 235; costs, 207–9; hospital arrangements of, 214; initial visit to, 210, 211; intermediate care facilities, 32, 209, 210, 211; licensing of, 212, 213; limitations of, 202–3; limited choice of, 218–19; locating, 206–7; medical services, 214; negative images of, 202, 203, 204; nursing services, 214; physical plant, 216; public ignorance of, 210–11; psychiatric care, 214, 215; scandals, 196, 204–5, 207, 211; selection of, 210–19; sexual rules in, 119; skilled care facilities, 209, 210, 211; social and psychological atmosphere, 216–17; specialized therapy in, 214–15; staff, 212, 213, 214, 215, 217, 222, 224, 226–8, 232–3; state health codes on, 215; statistics on, 66, 205; substandard, 146; types of care in, 209–10; types of sponsorship, 206; "watchdog groups," 245. See also institutionalization; nursing home residents
nursing home residents, 10–11, 210–11, 212, 222–35; admission and adjustment of, 222–6, 227–8; communicating bad news to, 230–1; community contact for, 231; condition of, 210–11, 215–16; dying, 127; emotional needs, 223, 228–9, 230–1; family of, 51, 52, 219–22, 225, 226, 227–9, 230–1, 232–3; interaction of, 217; individual needs, 218, 231–2; physical and mental reversals of, 224–5; possessions of, 223; relocation of, 233–5; role loss of, 79; visits home, 225,

229–30; voluntary, 203. *See also* institutionalization; nursing homes
nutrition, 72, 85, 148, 175, 182, 190
Nutrition Program for the Elderly, 193

O'Casey, Sean, 123
occupational therapists, 174, 213, 215
Ohio, 159, 196
Oklahoma, 160
old age: adjustment to, 74–5, 76, 79, 81, 86–7; advance planning for, 5–6, 145–67; American, 7–8, 27, 32–3, 60, 65–6, 78–82, 84–5, 219; beliefs vs. reality of, 4–5; changing images of, 245–7; dependency in, 82–5, 138, 141–5; facts of, 65–7; financial insecurity in, 79–82; folklore about, 27–8; Japanese, 33; losses of, 67–96; marital relations in, 97–106; mental stability in, 85–96; older generation's view of, 66, 71; physical improvements, 72; physical losses of, 69–75; possibilities of, 96; research on, 238; role loss in, 78–9, 100; sexual activity in, 115–20; social losses of, 75–8. *See also* aging parents; aging process; elderly people
Older American Community Service Program, 304
Older Americans Act, 8, 238; Community Service Employment Program, 166–7; state agencies of, 248–53; Title VII, 161, 193
Older Americans Are Our National Resource, 304
Olivier, Laurence, 119
Olsen, Tillie, 104
On Death and Dying (Kübler-Ross), 127
Operation Mainstream Program, 304
orgasm, 119
osteoporosis, 70, 71, 316
overexertion, 92
overinvolvement, 38
oversolicitousness, 34

paralysis, 180
parent-child bond, 20–1. *See also* adult children; aging parents; families; feelings
Peace Corps, 305
pensions, 81, 102, 157–8, 208; inflation and, 156
Peterson, Merrill, 130
physical incapacity. *See* disability and the disabled
physical therapy, 165, 213, 215
physicians, 70, 101, 119, 127, 129, 132, 133, 172–3, 186, 187, 198, 199, 207, 212; concerns of, 174; geriatric training of, 172–3; nursing home, 213, 214
planning, for old age, 5–7, 145–68, 171; by the elderly, 150; financial, 154–67; health care, 147–50; housing, 151–2; importance

of, 145–6, 149–50; resistance to, 146–7; value of, 168
pneumonia, 319
poverty, 79, 190, 208; effect on marriage, 101–2; threshold of, 156–7, 240. *See also* financial resources of the elderly
power of attorney, 197, 198
practical nurses, 188, 214
presbyopia, 321
Price, The (Miller), 53
prostate surgery, 119
prosthetic devices, 73, 165, 175
psychiatric problems, 92–4
psychiatrists, 127, 132, 173, 186, 198, 214
psychoanalysis, 17, 30
psychological problems. *See* mental disorders
psychosis, 86, 94
psychosomatic ailments, 86, 93
public assistance, 81
public health nurses, 188
Public Welfare Directory, 314

Questions and Answers on Death and Dying (Kübler-Ross), 133

recreation and entertainment, 150, 182, 194
recuperation: financial factors, 175–6; individual factors, 170, 171
registered nurses, 174, 188, 213, 214
relatives. *See* families
religion, 110, 131
remarriage, 98, 113–15, 120; age differences and, 118; children's reactions to, 113–14; reason for, 115; Social Security and, 157; statistics on, 113
research: age and sex, 118; brain syndrome, 95
Retired Seniors Volunteer Program (RSVP), 150, 305
retirement, 76, 242; mandatory, 80; marital adjustment in, 98–105; second careers, 8, 166; Swedish system, 99. *See also* pensions
retirement communities, 151, 185, 242
ritualistic behavior, 92, 110
right to die. 130–3
Role of the Aged in Primitive Society, The (Simmons), 131
roles: changes in, 26, 43–4, 78–9; childhood, 36–7, 43, 44–5; favorite-child, 44–5; loss of, 78–9, 100; traditional women's, 46
Roosevelt, Franklin D., 80

safety measures, 148, 151
Saturday Review, 133
savings, 80, 81
scapegoating, 38
Seagull, The (Travers), 119
second careers, 8, 166
seizures, 321

self-belittlement, 60
self-pity, 142–3
senility, 70, 72, 95, 172, 215
Senior Aides, 304
senior centers and clubs, 193; directory of, 312, 314
Senior Community Service Aides, 304
Senior Companion Program, 305
senior opportunities and services programs; directory of, 312
Service Corps of Retired Executives (SCORE), 305
sexuality of the aged, 10, 23, 115–20; barriers to, 118; denial of, 36; education on, 148; facts about, 117
Shakespeare, William, 26, 31, 68, 116
shame, 23–4, 30, 93, 144
sibling relationships, 35, 37, 41, 42, 43–5, 233; caretaker's, 47–8, 49–52; favorite child's, 44–5, 55–6; money quarrels, 53–5; splits, 52–3. See also families
Simmons, Leo, 131
sitting services, 192, 244
social action, 240–5
social isolation, 75–8, 85, 151, 193
Social Security, 102, 115, 155–7, 162, 163, 165, 187, 195, 207, 208, 238, 304; amount of benefits, 156; Bureau of Hearings and Appeals, 160, 163, 167; compared with SSI, 160; for dependent spouse, 156, 157; inadequacy of, 156, 240. See also Medicare and Medicaid
Social Security Act, 80, 81
social service agencies, 186, 207
social workers, 76, 127, 132, 174, 175, 187, 189, 213, 215, 243
society. See American society
Something Happened (Heller), 35–6
South Dakota, 196
South Carolina, 159
spouse: nursing home cost responsibility, 208–9. See also marriage; remarriage; widowhood
state health codes, 227
state offices on the aging, 161, 248–53
state programs for the elderly, 165
statistics: on durable marriages, 97–8; finances of the elderly, 80, 155; health, 65–6, 74; housing, 196, 241; nursing home, 66, 205; pension, 158; SSI, 159–60
strokes, 73, 74, 76, 103, 129, 131, 149, 169, 180, 215
stubbornness, 90–1
suicide, 93, 109, 132–3
Supplemental Security Income (SSI), 158–60, 165, 166, 208, 238; compared with Social Security, 160; eligibility requirements, 158–9; special housing arrangements, 196; statistics, 159–60
Sweden, 84, 99
symptoms and complaints, 319–21

tax laws, 161, 244
Teachers Annuity and Insurance Association, 158
telephone reassurance programs, 190–1
Tennessee, 159
Texas, 159
thanatology, 127
therapeutic services, 165, 174, 213, 214–15
Thomas, Dylan, 126, 128
Thomas Jefferson and the New Nation (Peterson), 130
tobacco, 148
transportation services, 84–5, 191, 193–4, 244
Travers, Ben, 119
tuberculosis, 165
Twain, Mark, 239

understanding, 138
united funds and councils: directory of, 312
United States. See American society
United States government: Agriculture Department, 161; Bureau of Labor Statistics, 81; Congress, 193; Health, Education, and Welfare Department, 8, 157, 160, 193, 245; Labor Department, 304; Senate Special Committee on Aging, 8, 186; Treasury Department, 160. See also federal programs for the elderly
University of Chicago: grandparenting study, 56–7
urban elderly, 82
Utah, 159
Utopia (More), 131

Van Dusen, Henry P., 133
vertigo, 320
Very Easy Death, A (De Beauvoir), 121
veterans' pensions, 158
Victoria (queen of England), 109
vision. See eyes and vision
visiting nurses, 176, 183, 188, 189
visitor services, 192
Volunteers in Service to America (VISTA), 305

Washington Post, 158
Weinstein, Karol, 56
welfare services, 165, 166, 187, 207
West Virginia, 159
White House Conference on Aging (1961), 7
Whitman, Walt, 26–7
Whitney, George, 7
Why Survive? Being Old in America (Butler), 66–7
widowhood, 10, 67, 76, 106–9, 153; adjustment to, 108; dependency and, 111–13; freedom of, 107; life disruption in, 107–9; parent's, effect of,

109–11; preparatory, 106; radical moves in, 111–12; Social Security benefits, 157

Widowhood in an American City (Lopata), 108

Wilde, Oscar, 22

wills, 125; living, 132

wives, 103; in postretirement years, 98–99, 100. *See also* marriage; widowhood

women, 117; life expectancy, 106; remarriage, 113

Wyoming, 159

"Your Medicare Handbook," 163, 314

youth, 88, 141; cultural emphasis on, 68, 84; physical problems, 74; view of old age, 4–5, 66

About the Authors

Dr. Barbara Silverstone is Chief of Social Services at the Jewish Home and Hospital for Aged in New York City. She received her doctoral degree in social welfare from Columbia University and is adjunct assistant professor of Social Work at Columbia University. She is a member of the National Association of Social Workers Task Force on Social Services to the Aging. Her professional experience has encompassed a wide variety of settings from private practice to psychiatric clinics and has included individual and group psychotherapy with children, young adults, and the elderly and their families. She has served as a consultant to the Division on Aging, Federation of Protestant Welfare Agencies. Dr. Silverstone is the author of *Establishing Resident Councils* and "The Effects of Introducing a Heterosexual Living Space," and most recently contributed a chapter, "Beyond the One-to-One Treatment Relationship," to the *Handbook of Geriatric Psychiatry: For Psychiatrists and Primary Care Physicians.*

Helen Kandel Hyman graduated from Barnard College in 1942 and was a staff writer for CBS for eight years before becoming a free-lance writer and an author and translator of children's books. She has written extensively on mental health, medical, and family subjects, including over a hundred radio scripts, documentaries, and pamphlets for CBS, NBC, UNICEF, Family Service Society, American Hospital Association, and the Equitable Life Assurance Public Health Department. From sharing households both here and abroad with elderly relations from parents to great-aunts, she has garnered a rich experience that has helped to shape this book.